Debt and Housing Eme

DUNCAN FORBES is a solicitor in South Wales specialising in housing, welfare rights and debt. He combines legal practice with teaching, writing and consultancy and is a long-standing member of Legal Action Group's management committee. He is the author of *Action on Racial Harassment* (LAG) and co-author of *Voluntary but not Amateur* (London Voluntary Services Council).

NIC MADGE is a solicitor and partner with Bindman & Partners. He specialises in housing law. He has worked in a law centre and contributes regularly to *Legal Action*. He is co-author of *Defending Possession Proceedings* (Legal Action Group) and *Tribunal Practice and Procedure* (Law Society).

Debt and Housing Emergency Procedures

A practitioner's guide

Duncan Forbes, SOLICITOR

and

Nic Madge, SOLICITOR

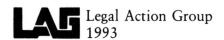 Legal Action Group
1993

This edition published in Great Britain 1993
by LAG Education and Service Trust Limited
242 Pentonville Road, London N1 9UN

British Library Cataloguing in Publication Data
A CIP catalogue record for this book is available from the British
Library.

ISBN 0-905099-42-7

Phototypeset by Kerrypress Ltd, Luton
Printed in Great Britain by BPCC-Wheatons Ltd, Exeter.

Preface

This book is for use in emergencies. The problems selected are those most likely to affect people in their own homes, although other debts (such as those arising from business transactions or business rates) may on occasion demand emergency legal action. Some topics (such as disputed gas and electricity bills) have been dealt with in greater detail because the law is uncertain or because the relevant information is difficult to find elsewhere. We have had to be selective and we hope that our selection reflects the day-to-day problems practitioners and advisers are likely to encounter.

Rent and mortgage arrears are not covered in Part I but in Part II on housing, in chapters 11 and 12 respectively.

Emergencies are disruptive and demanding, but in this type of work knowledge and experience are essential tools. Clients seeking emergency remedies will be feeling worried and powerless and this feeling will be exacerbated if an inappropriate remedy is chosen or delay is caused by lack of familiarity with the procedures. There are ways of interviewing and advising clients which may lessen the client's feeling of alienation. Distressed people are not always coherent in identifying what they want and solutions should not be imposed on them. It is essential to explain to clients as clearly as possible, both verbally and in writing, the nature and consequences of the proceedings, the procedural steps involved and the significance of any orders.

It may be that self-help in a particular situation will be more appropriate and more effective, and the client should be helped with practical information about benefits and rights to housing and referred to other agencies where necessary.

The emergencies described in this book can be divided into those where one needs to react to legal proceedings taken by other agencies or individuals and those where such proceedings need to be initiated. In the former case the client has no choice but to operate within the legal process, but in both types of proceedings lawyers may need to go beyond their normal role and may find themselves, for example, mediating between a local authority housing department and a tenant.

The law is stated at 31 March 1993 but we have indicated the likely effect of certain provisions coming into force later.

D.F.   N.M.

Acknowledgements

Duncan Forbes would like to thank Janet Ayles for all the hard work she did on the original script and amendments; Mike Wolfe for his advice; Birmingham Settlement and the Money Advice Association for allowing their personal budget sheet to be used as a basis for the budgeting sheet shown in chapter 2; the partners of Gabb & Co, Solicitors in Abergavenny for allowing free access to their excellent law library; the editorial staff of Legal Action Group; and his acupuncturist Flow Farmer for curing his repetitive strain injury – without which this book might never have reached production. Last but not least he would like to thank Clara Shirtcliff for her endless patience and support.

Contents

PART III PRECEDENTS

Debt emergencies

Housing emergencies

APPENDICES

Table of cases

Table of statutes

Table of statutory instruments

Part I

Debt emergencies

CHAPTER 1

Management of debt emergencies

Introduction

Part I of this book deals with the most common debt problems and the emergency legal remedies available to clients to avoid the methods of recovery at the disposal of different types of creditor. Many clients do not seek legal advice until the last minute. This means that recovery methods which should, in theory, not require emergency action will often, in practice, need to be dealt with as emergencies.

A legal remedy will not always be available and in many cases will not be necessary because a negotiated settlement can be achieved. Nevertheless, the fact that a legal remedy exists as a last resort places the debtor's negotiator in a much stronger position with the creditor.

It is beyond the scope of this book to provide a detailed strategy for managing multiple debt. However, there are two cardinal rules of common sense: first, clients should always be advised to give priority to paying off those debts where there are no legal remedies available to protect them, where those remedies are weak, or where the consequences of non-payment are most serious; second, except as a last resort where no legal remedy exists or as part of a carefully structured debt management package, a client should avoid borrowing in order to repay a debt.

Single debt emergencies

There are eight main stages for managing a single debt crisis. Only the final one involves the use of legal remedies, and all but the final one can often be completed at the first interview with the client.

Stage 1. Obtain accurate information about the debt and the creditor's intentions

At the initial interview, the client will often not have brought the necessary paperwork and may not be able to give sufficiently clear

3

instructions to enable an accurate assessment to be made of the extent and urgency of the problem. After brief details about the client and the nature of the problem have been obtained, accurate information on the following questions should be gathered.

a) How much money does the creditor think is owed?
b) What is the money for?
c) What payments have been made by the client, how long has the debt been outstanding and what agreements have been reached in the past for repayment?
d) What steps is the creditor planning to take, or have been taken already, to recover the debt?
e) When is the next step in the recovery process going to be taken, ie, how much time is there?
f) Will the creditor suspend recovery procedures while the client obtains advice and assistance?
g) What will the creditor accept as a negotiated settlement to avoid recovery procedures?
h) If the debt carries interest, will the creditor waive future interest?

Most of the common debts covered in this book involve creditors which are large institutions with computerised information systems and departments dealing specifically with debt recovery. The creditor will usually be able to answer all these key questions quickly, and most will do so over the telephone within minutes. The information can thus be obtained during the first interview with the client. It is usually possible to speak directly to recovery staff who have authority to negotiate and can stop or suspend recovery procedures. Generally, they will be able to trace the client's account from his or her name and address even if s/he has not brought any paperwork containing the account or reference number.

Stage 2. Obtain details of the client's income and expenditure and the availability of cash to pay outstanding debts and take full instructions on the manner in which the debt arose

A checklist for recording details of the client's income and expenditure is given on page 8 together with notes on its use.

It may seem odd that taking full instructions from the client is the second step rather than the first. This is primarily because so few clients have a record of how much is owed, what has been paid and so on, and if they do, they rarely bring the paperwork to the first interview. The details provided by the client of the manner in which the debt arose and the payments made may be vague. It may therefore be necessary to refer back to the creditor for more information on this aspect of the case before proceeding to the third step.

Stage 3. Decide whether the client is liable for the debt

Although it is beyond the scope of this book to deal with legal liability for all the debts in detail, the various chapters which follow consider some possible defences.

Stage 4. Ascertain any possible methods of increasing the client's income

It is essential to maximise the income of the client wherever possible. The following are examples of points that should be considered for maximising a client's income.

Benefits.   Check whether:

- the client, or partner, is entitled to the new lower rate of disability living allowance;
- the client, or partner, is being disqualified from unemployment benefit and whether there are grounds for appeal;
- the client, or partner, is receiving the correct premiums for income support and housing benefit including disability premiums;
- housing benefit deductions for non-dependants are correct;
- there is entitlement to family credit for those who are working and on low income;
- there is entitlement to housing benefit for two homes, eg, where a person has fled her or his previous home because of domestic violence;
- the income support being paid for interest on a secured loan is correct and in particular, if there has been a relationship breakdown, whether income support is being paid for interest on all secured loans whatever the reason they were taken out;
- a single parent is receiving the higher rate of child benefit.

Tax allowances   Check whether:

- a single parent is receiving a married person's tax allowance.

Maintenance.

- Consider the possibility of applying to the court to increase the rate of maintenance for a parent or child;
- Check whether a client might benefit from the provisions of the Child Support Act 1991.

Stage 5. Attempt to negotiate settlement or deferment of recovery

Negotiations should be started after details of the client's income and expenditure have been obtained, the feasibility of raising cash to pay off all or part of the debt has been assessed, and the client's liability for the debt has been determined. This first attempt at negotiations may also often be done over the telephone during the first interview with the client, by contacting the creditor's recovery section.

Settlement may involve asking the creditor to agree that a lesser sum is due, or occasionally that the client is not liable at all. More often, it will involve an agreement about the terms of repayment by the client on a weekly or monthly basis, perhaps after some immediate down-payment. Where the debt carries interest, it is advisable to try to get an agreement that future interest will be waived. Even if a settlement cannot be achieved over the telephone, many creditors may agree at this stage to defer recovery procedures for a fixed period, eg, 14 days, to allow time for more information to be obtained and written representations to be made. Where it is agreed that money is due to the creditor, details of the client's financial circumstances can be provided to show the level of repayments that s/he can afford.

No agreement should be made where there is little or no realistic possibility of the client meeting its conditions because instalments are too large or because s/he has no prospect of raising an agreed down-payment. It is also important to avoid creating further debt problems by allowing or forcing the client to borrow money in order to discharge some or all of the present debt. The reasonableness of an agreement will depend very largely on the availability of alternative legal remedies to the client if the creditor insists on an excessive level of repayment and on the importance to the client of avoiding the recovery method proposed by the creditor.

Stage 6. Assess the availability of legal remedies

If negotiations fail on the first occasion, legal remedies should be considered. These are dealt with in the following chapters, according to the type of debt.

Stage 7. Attempt again to negotiate settlement or deferment of
recovery using the threat of legal remedies as a bargaining factor

Very few debtors resist debt recovery procedures. Major creditors are, therefore, used to getting their own way and often demand wholly unreasonable terms of payment. If legal remedies are available, they are a strong bargaining counter and may make the creditor reconsider its position. The creditor should be contacted again and advised of the intention to use those remedies. In some cases, this attempt can be repeated if legal aid has been obtained to take legal action.

Stage 8. If all attempts at negotiation fail, the client will have no alternative but to agree the terms offered by the creditor, allow recovery methods or use the available emergency legal remedies to avoid recovery

Multiple debt emergencies

Where there are multiple debts, a methodical approach is essential ensuring that debts are appropriately prioritised and that a package of repayment terms is established, wherever possible, which is manageable within the limited resources available to the client.

In respect of each individual debt, the eight-point strategy listed above should be followed. Wherever possible the negotiation of any settlement should be delayed until the overall position has been reviewed after the stages suggested below have been completed. An assessment of the overall position may take some time, particularly if further information is required. In most cases, creditors should be requested to defer recovery procedures to allow for this process. Where creditors are not prepared to allow any time for the overall position to be assessed and for a sensible package of proposals to be made to all creditors, serious consideration may have to be given to making use of legal remedies, if only to buy time.

Should any application to the court be required, a carefully worked-out package of repayments based on a proper assessment of income and expenditure of the client will be more likely to persuade the court that the levels of repayment proposed are appropriate.

Serious consideration should be given in the case of multiple debt to whether an application should be made for an administration order if this is possible or whether the client should apply to become bankrupt or make a voluntary arrangement with his or her creditors. These are dealt with in detail in chapter 2.

Rescheduling debts

This section is designed to show advisers who have little experience of dealing with multiple debt the basic way in which the problem should be approached. It is based on a personal budget sheet which is original copyright material produced by National Debtline (a joint project of the

Birmingham Settlement and the Money Advice Association) and reproduced with permission.

Basic information
Date
Name of client
Address
Age
Other members of the household and their ages

Stage 1. Calculate weekly income (see note 1)

£

Wages or salary (see note 2)
Wages or salary (partner) (see note 2)
Unemployment benefit
Income support
Family credit
Retirement pension or works pension
Child benefit
Invalidity or sickness benefit
Maintenance
Non-dependant's contribution
Disability benefits
Other   ____
Total weekly income   ____

Notes

1 The checklist is shown using calculations on a weekly basis. It is possible to do the calculations on some other basis, usually monthly, provided that the figures at other stages are also calculated on a monthly basis, namely the outgoings and the offers of repayment of debts to creditors. When adjusting weekly figures to monthly, it is important to bear in mind that there are more than four weeks in a month. To translate from weekly to monthly payments the figures should be multiplied by 52 and divided by 12.

2 If wages or salary vary, an average figure should be entered here and it should be made clear that it is an average figure. It is suggested that the minimum and maximum figures are also indicated to show the range of variation from week to week. Wages or salary should be the net figure and this should be stated. Both the gross and net figures should be entered where possible although the net figure is the most important.

Stage 2. Calculate outgoings on a weekly basis

£

Mortgage
Mortgage endowment policy
Second mortgage
Rent
Council tax (see note 1)
Water rates
Ground rent or service charge
Buildings and contents insurance
Home repair and maintenance (see note 2)
Board and lodging costs
Life insurance and/or pension
Gas (see note 3)
Electricity (see note 3)
Other fuel (see note 4)
Housekeeping (see note 5)
Television and or video rental and licence fee*
Magistrates' court fines
Maintenance payments
Travelling expenses* (see note 6)
School meals and/or meals at work
Clothing and shoes (see note 7)
Furniture and bedding (see note 8)
Laundry*
Telephone*
Prescriptions and other health costs (see note 9)
Child-minding*
Car or motorbike expenses* (see note 10)
Hire purchase or conditional sale* (see note 11)
Pets*
Other*
    1
    2
    3
    4   £___
Total weekly outgoings   £___

Notes

*   Experience shows that both creditors and courts are unsympathetic to clients who spend money on items which creditors and courts regard as luxuries and that they may therefore regard the weekly expenditure on

these items as available to pay any debt. Where the client's circumstances mean that such items can be justified as an essential, eg, a telephone for a chronically sick client, this justification should be included on any statement of finances sent to creditors or produced for the courts.

Where it is suspected that it will be difficult to convince the court or a creditor that the outgoing is essential, it may be necessary to produce an edited version of the checklist for submission to creditors. Since many clients have expenditure which exceeds their income in any event, for negotiation purposes inclusion of those outgoings may not be necessary.

1 Where council tax is payable by instalments, there will be 10 instalments over a whole year. The weekly amount must therefore be calculated by multiplying the monthly instalment by 10 and dividing by 52.

2 Both tenants and owners have home repair and maintenance costs. Tenants will need an allowance for decorations and repairs to fixtures and fittings, eg, cupboard doors, tap washers, door handles, etc. Owner-occupiers may need a substantial amount depending on the condition of their property. An estimate should be made of the likely expenditure over a year and this should be divided by 52.

3 When calculating gas and electricity charges, it is important to average those for the warmer and colder parts of the year. Electricity companies will often be prepared to provide advisers with the number of units consumed in the past four quarters over the telephone though they will usually charge for written copies of the bill.

4 Other fuel includes expenses like coal, paraffin and bottled gas, and the expenses will need to be adjusted to take account of the fact that they will usually only be used during the winter months.

5 This will include food, household items and toiletries. The food costs should include both expenses on shopping trips that may be done weekly, eg, at the supermarket, as well as expenses that may occur on a daily basis, eg, purchasing milk, bread, etc. Allowance must be made for any special diets where necessary. Depending on the age, the cost of this item per member of the household could be between £12 and £25.

6 For example, fares or petrol getting to work, getting the children to school, getting to hospital for treatment and job-hunting.

7 The cost for every year will have to be estimated and divided by 52. It is important to ensure that allowance is made for children who

outgrow their clothes rapidly as well as school uniform. The sum could be between £3 and £7 per person.

8 For example this might be £1 per person.

9 Other health costs would include, for example, the cost of dentists and opticians.

10 Expenses would include the cost of insurance, tax, repairs and maintenance.

11 Items obtained on hire-purchase or conditional sale and other outgoings should be listed and an explanation included of why they are needed.

Stage 3. Calculate the weekly amount available for priority creditors

£

Total income
Deduct total outgoings
Weekly amount available for priority creditors

Stage 4. Calculate possible offers of repayment to priority creditors

	Balance owed £	Weekly offer of repayment £
Mortgage arrears		
Second mortgage arrears		
Rent arrears		
Community charge arrears		
Council tax arrears		
Water rates arrears		
Ground rent or service charge arrears		
Fuel debts:		
Gas		
Electricity		
Other		
Magistrates' courts arrears (including fines)		

Maintenance arrears

Other:

    1

    2

    3

    4

Total weekly priority debts repayment

Notes

This checklist includes the generally accepted priority debts which are dealt with in the remainder of this part of this book.

    The client is not going to be able to offer more in repayment than the sum available after the calculation at stage 3. If there is insufficient available after the calculation at stage 3 to make any offers of repayment to all the priority creditors, there are three alternatives:

– Where possible, the client may be able to reduce some expenditure.

– Where possible the client may be able to increase income.

– More likely, the client will not be able to do either of these things and even some of the priority creditors will not receive repayments to reduce the outstanding debt.

The debts which must take the greatest priority will depend upon individual circumstances. However, as a rule of thumb, fuel debts should have priority because the electricity and gas suppliers have wide powers to disconnect; fines should have priority because magistrates' courts are almost certain to imprison for non-payment and mortgage payments on mortgages that are not regulated agreements under the Consumer Credit Act 1974 should have priority because the court's powers to protect clients who are unable to repay the arrears are limited. In contrast, the courts have wide powers to protect those who are in arrears of water charges and rent, and the magistrates' court is more likely to remit arrears of maintenance, community charge and council tax.

Stage 5. Calculate any weekly sum remaining to pay non-priority debts

                                                    £

Money available to pay priority creditors
(from stage 3)

Deduct amount offered to priority creditors
(from stage 4)

Money available for repayment of non-priority
creditors

Stage 6. Calculate amounts of repayments to be offered to non-priority creditors

Creditor	Balance owed	Weekly offer of repayment
	£	£
1		
2		
3		
4		
5		
6		
	——	
Total owed	——	——
Total weekly payment		——

Notes

It is possible that no money is available to pay non-priority creditors. In practice, these are creditors who have to enforce their debts through the county court and High Court which have reasonably wide powers to protect debtors. However, it should be noted that if any creditor obtains a charging order, which could lead to the loss of a person's home, that creditor's debt should be treated as if it were a mortgage and becomes a high priority.

If the total debts are less than £5,000 and an administration order would be advantageous, a strategic decision not to pay non-priority debts may be taken in the hope that at least one creditor will take proceedings and obtain a judgment triggering the court's jurisdiction to make an administration order (see chapter 2).

CHAPTER 2

Administration orders, bankruptcy and voluntary arrangements

Introduction

There are three legal remedies available to a debtor for dealing with multiple debt, whereby he or she can seek to have the whole debt problem dealt with as one comprehensive package rather than dealing with each creditor and their various enforcement powers separately. These are administration orders, bankruptcy proceedings and voluntary arrangements under the Insolvency Act 1986. A table summarising their effect is on pages 31–4.

Administration orders

Section 13 of the Courts and Legal Services Act 1990 contains amendments to the County Courts Act 1984 which will enable administration orders to be used in a far wider range of cases. At present, an administration order is only available where a civil court judgment has been obtained against the client and his or her total debts are less than £5,000. Both these requirements will be changed when s13 of the 1990 Act is brought into force. The government has stated that this will take place at the end of 1994 following the introduction of computerisation into the county courts. Computerisation is necessary because of the substantial number of extra claims for administration orders that are anticipated.

An administration order is an order allowing an officer of the court to administer the estate of the debtor. Under it all the debts are dealt with together, and the money recovered from the client is divided between the various creditors in proportion to the amount of their debts.

Advantages

Distress, imprisonment, eviction, charging orders and bankruptcy may be prevented or impeded

Once an administration order has been made, no creditor whose debt was notified to the court by the debtor before the administration order was made or whose debt has subsequently been scheduled to the administration order can use any remedy 'against the person or property of the debtor' in respect of that debt except with the court's permission. The court can impose conditions if it decides to grant permission.[1] If proceedings in the county court have already begun to recover a debt, they will be automatically stayed once an administration order is made. However, there is no specific power for proceedings in other courts, eg, the High Court or magistrates' court, to be stayed; this is not the case in bankruptcy proceedings (see p23). There are a few exceptions to this general rule which are dealt with below.

The effect of an administration order can therefore be to prevent:

- local authorities levying distress for community charge or council tax;
- a magistrates' court instructing bailiffs to levy distress to collect fines, magistrates' courts orders or civil debts;[2]
- a creditor enforcing a county court judgment or High Court judgment by levying execution;
- tax collectors using distress as a method of collecting income tax, national insurance contributions, VAT etc.;[3]

---

1 County Courts Act 1984 s114(1).
2 An administration order prevents a 'creditor' from having any remedy against the personal property of the debtor. There are no reported cases in which a court has considered whether an administration order can be used to prevent enforcement of a fine or other sum payable under a magistrates' court order made in criminal proceedings. Such sums are payable to the magistrates' court so for an administration order to prevent enforcement the meaning of the word 'creditor' in the County Courts Act 1984 will have to include the magistrates' court itself. In principle there is no reason why that interpretation could not be placed on the Act but there is a risk that the courts would be reluctant to accept that an administration order was that far-reaching. In respect of money due under orders made by magistrates' in civil proceedings and maintenance orders, there will be no difficulty because the 'creditor' will be the other party to the proceedings. Note that in bankruptcy proceedings a debt includes sums due to Ministers of the Crown or Government departments (Insolvency Rules 1986 SI 1925 r6.96(4)) and the Courts have decided that the word 'debt' includes a fine (*Re Pascoe* [1944] 1 All ER 593). It would be perverse if the words 'creditor' and 'debt' were interpreted differently in bankruptcy from their meaning in administration order proceedings.
3 Outside the scope of this book.

- a local authority applying to a magistrates' court for imprisonment of the client for non-payment of the community charge or council tax;
- a magistrates' court imprisoning the client for non-payment of fines, magistrates' courts orders or civil debts;[4]
- a landlord enforcing a possession order through a warrant of possession;
- a building society, bank, or other lender enforcing a possession order for arrears of a loan secured on the person's home by enforcing a warrant of possession;[5]
- a creditor enforcing a county court judgment or High Court judgment by obtaining a charging order.

The effect of an administration order can be to impede:

- a creditor who wants to apply for the client's bankruptcy, which cannot be done without permission from the court unless the application is made within 28 days of the receipt by the creditor of the notification of an application for an administration order and the debt exceeds £1,500;[6]
- a landlord (including a local authority or housing association) trying to recover rent arrears by the use of distress, which cannot be done without the court's permission for sums in excess of six months' rent due prior to the date of the administration order; the landlord can still use distress for up to six months' arrears but the balance must be sought as one of the debts under the administration order.[7]

County court debt recovery proceedings will be stayed

When an administration order is made, the court that makes the administration order must serve a copy of it on every other court of which it is aware in which judgment has been obtained or proceedings are pending in respect of any debt which is scheduled to the administration order.[8] When it receives a notification of the administration order, any other county court must stay the proceedings, although it may allow costs already incurred by a creditor to be added to the debt.[9]

---

4   See note 2 above.
5   At present an administration order is only available if the total debts owed by the client are less than £5,000, so it is unlikely that someone with a mortgage will be able to use an administration order. But see p14 above.
6   County Courts Act 1984 s112(4).
7   County Courts Act 1984 s116.
8   County Court Rules 1981 Ord 39 r9.
9   County Courts Act 1984 s114(2).

The client may only have to pay part of the debts

The court making an administration order may reduce the amount payable to all the creditors (see p19 below).

Reduction of stress and cost

When an administration order is made the court assumes responsibility for distributing the money to creditors whose debts are scheduled to the order. This may remove a considerable source of stress for the client. However, the client will still need to deal with the remedies available to some creditors that are not impeded by the order or whose debts are not scheduled.

No fee is payable when applying for an administration order.

Disadvantages and limitations

Problems in obtaining future credit

Where a client has failed to make any payment which he or she is required to make by virtue of an administration order, the court can revoke the order and make an order applying s429 of the Insolvency Act 1986 to the client for up to two years. When applied, s429 makes it a criminal offence to obtain credit above a prescribed limit (currently £250) or enter into any transaction for the purposes of any business in which the debtor is engaged unless the debtor notifies the other party that s429 applies.

In addition, where an administration order is made, the notice of the administration order will be posted in the office of the court on public view. Credit reference agencies are likely to obtain information that an administration order has been made. This may make it difficult, if not impossible, for the client to obtain future credit.[10] However, the agencies will also have access to the register of county court judgments which will already have an entry for the judgment that gave rise to the administration order. An administration order may therefore not make it any more difficult to obtain credit than it would be anyway.

Creditors whose debts arise after an administration order is made

An administration order does not apply to any debt that is not scheduled to it (ie, listed in it). It therefore will not apply to creditors whose debts arise after it is made. However, such creditors do have the option to apply to be listed in the schedule to the administration order. If they apply and are listed, their rights to take action against the person or property of the

10   County Court Act 1984 s113(a).

debtor is the same as that of other creditors whose debts are listed.[11] It may also be possible for the debtor to have subsequent debts added to the schedule by seeking a review of the order.[12]

Enforcement by the court or any creditor[13]

All the remedies normally available to a creditor in the county court can be exercised by the court itself enforcing an administration order. This includes a garnishee order, a charging order and levying execution against goods, although the normal exemptions from execution in the Courts and Legal Services Act 1990 will apply (see p46).[14] In particular, the court can make an attachment of earnings order to secure any instalments due under an administration order either straightaway or if the client defaults.[15] If an attachment or earnings order is already in force, the court making an administration order can direct that in future it will secure payments under the administration order.[16]

Applications by creditors to enforce their debts

Creditors have a general right to apply for permission to enforce their debts even when an administration order has been made.[17] In principle, such permission should be refused since to allow individual creditors to enforce their debts would defeat the entire purpose of an administration order. However, creditors may be more likely to obtain permission if the payments they are receiving are inadequate to maintain the debt at its existing level or to begin reducing it. This would occur where interest was accruing at a significant rate. Court practices vary widely. Some will routinely give permission for priority creditors to enforce debts, a practice that should be challenged. Others will deal with the arguments properly on individual merits.

The court's powers

Jurisdiction

There are two essential criteria that must be satisfied for the court to have power to make an administration order:

11   County Court Rules 1981 Ord 39 r11(1).
12   County Court Rules 1981 Ord 39 r13(3).
13   County Court Rules 1981 Ord 39 r13(2).
14   County Courts Act 1984 s115 and s89 as amended by the Courts and Legal Services Act 1990 s15.
15   Attachment of Earnings Act 1971 s5.
16   Attachment of Earnings Act 1971 s6(3).
17   County Courts Act 1984 s114(1).

- there must be a court judgment against the client in a county court or in the High Court;
- the total debts of the client must not be more than £5,000.[18]

These may make the remedy unavailable in some important circumstances.

If it subsequently appears that the total debts are over £5,000 though they were believed to have been below £5,000, this does not invalidate an administration order that has already been made but the court may decide to set aside the order.[19]

Types of order

The court can make an administration order:

- providing for payment of debts by instalments;
- providing for payment of debts in full or only to such extent 'as appears practical to the court under the circumstances of the case';
- which is subject to conditions as to future earnings or income;
- which is to be reviewed after a specific length of time or at such intervals as the court may specify;[20]

The court can also:

- secure any amounts to be paid by an attachment of earnings order;
- levy execution against goods to enforce the administration order;
- take other steps to enforce the administration order, eg, by garnishee order.

Emergency applications

An administration order will effectively prevent creditors from using any enforcement methods. To avoid this, some creditors may use the period between an application for an administration order and the hearing to try to recover their debts. Emergency action may therefore be required to prevent this occurring.

Creditors seeking to enforce civil court judgments

Where a creditor is trying to enforce a judgment that has been obtained in a county court or in the High Court, an application can be made within those proceedings for enforcement to be stayed or suspended pending the determination of the administration order application. Attachment of earnings orders, garnishee orders and charging orders all require a hearing

18   County Courts Act 1984 s112. But see p14.
19   County Courts Act 1984 s112(5).
20   County Courts Act 1984 s112(6) and County Court Rules 1981 Ord 39 r8.

at which the court can decide to postpone the remedy. The court has general power to suspend or stay a warrant of execution.

Other creditors

Where a magistrates' court is taking action to recover a debt, the court may be prepared to suspend recovery procedures whilst an application for an administration order is pending.

The court has a general power to make injunctions which are ancillary to the main remedy sought.[21] There seems no reason in principle why such an injunction cannot be made in proceedings for an administration order to prevent a creditor from exercising any remedy against the person or property of the debtor once an application for an administration order has been made but before it has been heard. The Court has to be satisfied that there is a serious question to be tried as to whether an administration order should be made and then to go on to consider the balance of convenience. In most cases, the balance of convenience will clearly be in favour of restraining any particular creditor from enforcing their debt against the person or property of the debtor since this will prejudice other creditors. The whole purpose of an administration order is to provide equality between creditors rather than allowing one to gain advantage.

Alternatively, the client can ask the county court to which s/he has applied to expedite the hearing of the application for the administration order.

Procedure for obtaining an administration order

An application for an administration order is made on county court form N92. It is a simple form which must be verified by the client on oath.[22] The oath can be taken by an officer of the court at the time the application is lodged. The form requires the client to list all debts and also to include basic information on income and liabilities. The client should ensure that all debts of which he or she is aware are included in the application because it is only if a debt is included and accepted by the court that the remedies available to the creditor are affected.

The application is made to the county court for the district in which the client resides or carries on business[23] and does not have to be made in the court in which any judgment was obtained.

As well as the application form, the client must provide a copy of any

---

21   County Courts Act 1984 s38.
22   County Court Rules 1981 Ord 39 r3.
23   County Court Rules 1981 Ord 39 r2(1).

judgments, summonses or orders made in courts relating to any other debts.

When it receives the application, the court will send notification of it both to the debtor and to any creditor listed in the application together with a copy of the application itself. Any hearing must take place not less than 14 days after the application unless the time-limit is shortened using the court's general powers to abridge time.[24]

Any creditor who objects to a debt being scheduled must object in writing not less than seven days before the hearing.[25] Every debt that is listed is taken to have been proved unless it is objected to by a creditor and then disallowed or is required to be supplemented by evidence in which case the creditor must prove the debt.[26] If any particular debt is not proved, the court can either adjourn the whole application or make an administration order with that debt not being included in the schedule. The debt can then be included at a later stage.

Any creditor can produce evidence to show that an administration order should not be made or to argue about the precise terms of it.

Review of orders

The court may have made an administration order for a fixed period of time or stated that it should be subject to review at periodic intervals or after a certain length of time. In those circumstances, a review will take place automatically and the court will decide whether or not to continue the order.

However, in addition, the client can apply to the court to review the order. A creditor can also do so with the court's permission. In addition, the chief clerk or other officer of the clerk who is responsible for administering the order has a duty to bring to the attention of the court any matter which may make it desirable to review the order.[27] At least seven days' notice must be given of a hearing at which a review of the order will take place.

Powers on review

On a review the court can:
a) if satisfied that the debtor is unable from any cause to pay any instalment due under the order, suspend the operation of the order for such time and on such terms as it thinks fit;

24   County Court Rules 1981 Ord 39 r5 and Ord 13 r4.
25   County Court Rules 1981 Ord 39 r6.
26   County Court Rules 1981 Ord 39 r7.
27   County Court Rules 1981 Ord 39 r13.

b) if satisfied there has been a material change in any circumstances since the order was made, vary any provisions of the order;
c) if satisfied that the client has failed without reasonable cause to comply with any provision of the order or that it is otherwise just and expedient to do so, revoke the order either forthwith or on failure to comply with any conditions specified by the court; or
d) make an attachment of earnings order to secure the payments required by the administration order or vary or discharge any such attachment of earnings order already made.[28]

Payments to creditors and discharge of the order

Money paid into court under an administration order goes first towards the cost of the administration (which must not exceed 10p in the pound on the total amount of the debts) and secondly to pay off the debts in accordance with the order.

Debts are paid from time to time, ranking equally in proportion to the amount of the debt. An administration order is superseded and the debtor is discharged from her or his debt to the scheduled creditors where the amount that has been received by the court is sufficient:

- to pay each creditor scheduled to the order to the extent provided by the order;
- to pay the costs of the plaintiff in the action in respect of which the order was made;
- to pay the cost of the administration.[29]

This means that if the administration order originally stated that only a percentage of the debt should be paid, eg, 25 per cent of all debts, and the debtor has paid sufficient in to the court to cover this amount plus the costs of administration and the costs of the judgment creditor whose judgment was the basis for the order, then those debts are treated as being discharged. In that example, the remaining 75 per cent of each of the debts is no longer payable.

Bankruptcy

A bankruptcy order is an order placing the client's property and income under the control of the Official Receiver or Trustee. The receiver or trustee must sell any significant items of value and use the money raised and any excess income of the client (after deductions of living expenses for

28   County Court Rules 1981 Ord 39 r14(1).
29   County Courts Act 1984 s117(2).

the client and his or her family) to pay as much as possible towards the debts that the client owes. Most debts left unpaid after a fixed period cease to be payable.

Advantages

The bankruptcy court can stay any action, execution or other legal process against the property or person of the debtor at any time.[30] In addition, any court in which proceedings are pending may stay the proceedings or allow them to proceed subject to conditions.[31] Proceedings by secured creditors to enforce their security are exempt from these restrictions.[32] Once a bankruptcy order is made, no creditor will have any remedy against the property or person of the client or be able to inititiate any proceedings against the client except with the permission of the bankruptcy court.[33]

The rules are therefore different to those for administration orders (see above p15). In bankruptcy proceedings, other court action can be stayed immediately the petition is presented, even before the bankruptcy order is made. But, unlike with administration orders, no court proceedings are automatically stayed; an application must be made either to the bankruptcy court or to the court in which proceedings are pending. As for administration orders, creditors are automatically prevented from taking action against the property or person of the client. Under administration orders, creditors can be given permission by the court to take action against the person or property of the client; but no such power exists when a bankruptcy order is made. Under the bankruptcy rules, secured creditors are exempt from this restriction on their ability to enforce their security; no such exemption applies when an administration order is made, and secured creditors must seek leave to enforce their security just like other creditors. In practice, the kinds of enforcement that will be prevented or impeded will therefore be the same as for administration order (see page 15).[34] However, there is specific power for the court to stay any 'other legal process'. This should more clearly enable the court to stay proceedings for the recovery of fines through the magistrates' court.

During the bankruptcy, the receiver or trustee will make every effort to pay off as much as possible of the debts that are due. However, in most cases, the client will be discharged after 2–3 years and at that stage the

30   Insolvency Act 1986 s285(1).
31   Insolvency Act 1986 s285(2).
32   Insolvency Act 1986 s285(4).
33   Insolvency Act 1986 s285(3).
34   Insolvency Act 1986 s285.

creditors will not be able to recover the remainder of the sums owed unless their debt is secured.[35]

Receiver/trustee deals with all creditors

The receiver or trustee will take over the handling of all outstanding debts. For many clients this will substantially reduce the pressure and stress under which they have been living.

Basic domestic needs can still be met

The receiver or trustee will allow the client enough income and capital to meet his or her 'basic domestic needs' and those of his or her family.[36] What needs are basic will be subject to negotiation with the receiver or trustee, who in many cases will be the Official Receiver. The receiver or trustee may allow the client to keep items such as a television set that would have been removed by bailiffs levying distress or levying execution.

A certificate for summary administration may be made

A certificate for summary administration is a substantially simpler, quicker and less onerous form of bankruptcy (see below).

Disadvantages

Court fee and deposit payable

The client must pay a court fee (currently £20) and a deposit (currently £135). In London, the client will have to pay to verify the statement of affairs on oath. The court fee can be waived by making written application to the court explaining the circumstances but the deposit is always payable. A client who has not got that amount and cannot raise it is prevented from applying for a bankruptcy order. However, the deposit is to cover the costs of the trustee. If there will be sufficient assets to cover those costs, it may be possible to raise a loan from friends or relatives. This should be documented so that the money can be reclaimed as one of the costs of the bankruptcy which are the first call on any assets.

Client is likely to lose his or her home if it is owned

If the client owns his or her home, either solely or jointly with some other person, it is extremely likely that it will have to be sold to raise finance to pay debts. Sale by the receiver or trustee may be avoided if it is possible to show that the value of the home is less than the outstanding mortgage, but the lender may still seek possession for existing arrears or those that are

---

35   Insolvency Act 1986 s281.
36   Insolvency Act 1986 s310.

likely to arise. If the home is jointly owned, the receiver or trustee is likely to invite the other joint owner to purchase the client's share. If the joint owner is unwilling or unable to purchase it, the receiver or trustee will apply to the court for a sale to take place.

During the first year after making the bankruptcy order, the court must weigh up a number of factors when deciding whether the sale of a matrimonial home (whether owned jointly or just by the bankrupt spouse) should take place:

- the interests of the creditors
- the conduct of the non-bankrupt spouse in relation to his or her contribution to the bankruptcy
- the needs and financial resources of the non-bankrupt spouse
- the needs of any children.[37]

However, one year after the bankruptcy order, the interests of the creditors are assumed to outweigh all other considerations unless there are 'exceptional circumstances.'[38] The fact that a spouse and children will become homeless upon sale is not considered exceptional, so a sale after one year is almost inevitable.[39] A lender with a mortgage on the home can force a sale for mortgage arrears within that first year and the normal rules for mortgage possession actions apply (see chapter 12). There is no special protection.

Bank accounts will be frozen and then closed

The receiver or trustee may allow the client to open a bank account at a later stage, but for some time accounts will be frozen. The client will need sufficient cash for living expenses before applying for bankruptcy.

It is a criminal offence not to co-operate

Various offences exist, including a failure to disclose any relevant information,[40] concealing papers or property,[41] making false statements[42] and leaving the country with more than £500.[43]

All property and income belongs to the receiver/trustee

The life of the client and any dependants is entirely in the hands of the receiver or trustee, who has discretion whether to allow the client to

37   Insolvency Act 1986 s336(4).
38   Insolvency Act 1986 s336(5).
39   *In Re Citro* [1990] 3 WLR 880, CA.
40   Insolvency Act 1985 s353.
41   Insolvency Act 1985 ss354 and 355.
42   Insolvency Act 1986 s356.
43   Insolvency Act 1986 s358.

continue trading (if he or she is running a small business which is earning money), what domestic needs will be allowed for, what bank and building society accounts (if any) the client may have, whether the client should have a car etc. S/he can even redirect the client's mail.

Disqualification from some jobs and offices

A bankrupt client is disqualified from some jobs, eg, accountant or solicitor, and from some offices, eg, company director, MP, councillor or school governor.

Power to reopen old transactions

The receiver or trustee can investigate transactions that have already taken place. He or she can seek to set aside any gift or transaction made at an undervalue up to five years before the bankruptcy order.[44] A transaction is at an undervalue where the amount paid to the bankrupt person is less than the true value of the property sold. Whereas the transfer of property to a family member may effectively avoid a charging order to prevent a bailiff executing a warrant against goods, the receiver or trustee may recover the property or its value.

Any capital acquired during the bankruptcy will be used by the receiver/trustee

Any award of damages or any inheritance will become the property of the receiver or trustee if received during the bankruptcy and will be used to discharge debts.

Credit is restricted

A bankrupt client cannot obtain more than £250 credit without informing the lender of his or her bankruptcy.[45] To do so is a criminal offence. Obtaining any credit is likely to be a problem, as bankruptcy is a public matter and all credit reference agencies will be able to obtain the information that the client has been made bankrupt. Problems with obtaining credit may continue long after the bankruptcy has been discharged. Telephone, electricity and gas suppliers may refuse to supply without a guarantor, a large deposit or some kind of prepayment meter.

Stigma and adverse publicity

The stigma of bankruptcy is much less than it used to be but still exists for many clients. Bankruptcy orders are publicised in local newspapers

---

44   Insolvency Act 1986 s339.
45   Insolvency Act 1986 s360 and Insolvency Proceedings (Monetary Limits) Order 1986 SI 1996 art 3 Sch Part II.

outside London and may be publicised in such newspapers inside London. The client may be questioned about his or her financial dealings in open court if the Official Receiver decides to apply to the court for a public examination. The Official Receiver must apply for an examination if at least one half by value of the creditors make such a request.

Offences

Apart from offences that can be committed during the bankruptcy (see above), once a client is made bankrupt, the receiver or trustee may investigate whether anything has been done before the bankruptcy which as a result constitutes a criminal offence.

There are two serious offences. The first is committed where the client has given property away within the previous five years or made a transaction at an undervalue and cannot prove he or she did so without intent to defraud creditors.[46] The second is a failure to keep, preserve and (if requested) produce proper books of account relating to any business operated within the two years before the bankruptcy. There is a defence if the client can show that the failure was honest and excusable.[47]

Initial procedure

An application for a bankruptcy order is made by a petition. In London, the client takes the petition to the High Court; outside London, application is made to a county court having bankruptcy jurisdiction.[48] Courts having that jurisdiction are listed in the *County Court Practice*.

Apart from the fee and deposit, the client will need a standard form of petition and statement of affairs. Both forms are available from court offices. The statement of affairs must be verified on oath.

The client will need to show that:

- he or she is domiciled in England or Wales;
- he or she is personally present in England or Wales on the day the order is made;
- he or she has been ordinarily resident in England or Wales or carried on business there within the last 3 years;[49] and
- he or she is unable to pay his or her debts.[50]

When the documents are lodged, court practices vary. Some deal with

46 Insolvency Act 1986 s357.
47 Insolvency Act 1986 s361.
48 Insolvency Act 1986 s373.
49 Insolvency Act 1986 s265.
50 Insolvency Act 1986 s272.

the matter immediately; others fix a hearing date. It is in the client's interests for the application and the order to be made as quickly as possible. It is particularly important to begin proceedings quickly if particular creditors are threatening to take action or enforce a debt. Such proceedings can then be stayed or enforcement prevented.

The court may:

- dismiss the petition;
- stay proceedings (pending more information);
- refer the matter for consideration as to whether an voluntary arrangement should be made; or
- make a bankruptcy order.[51]

The jurisdiction to consider whether a voluntary arrangement can be made arises if the assets exceed £2,000, the unsecured debts are less than £20,000 and the client has had no previous undischarged bankruptcy or voluntary arrangement within the past five years.[52]

Certificate for summary administration

If the total debts are less than £20,000 and the client has not been an undischarged bankrupt or entered into a voluntary arrangement within the past five years, the court may make a certificate for summary administration (CSA).[53]

This has significant benefits over the usual bankruptcy order:

- The Official Receiver will act as trustee rather than a trustee appointed by the creditors (who would be an insolvency practitioner).[54]
- The Official Receiver's fee will be limited to the amount paid on commencement (unlike an insolvency practitioner's).
- There will be no creditors' meeting. (If there is no CSA, a creditors' meeting will be held. In practice, the largest creditors, usually banks, will appoint their own nominee as trustee.)
- There will usually be no investigation of the client's affairs over the past few years unless the Official Receiver decides in his or her discretion to carry out investigations.[55] (Where there is no CSA, the Official Receiver must report to the court that he has carried out an investigation, so the chances of any misdemeanours such as

---

51   Insolvency Act 1986 s278.
52   Insolvency Act 1986 s273 and the Insolvency Proceedings (Monetary Limits) Order 1986 SI 1996 Art 3 Sch Part II.
53   Insolvency Act 1986 s275 and Insolvency Proceedings (Monetary Limits) Order 1985 SI 1996 Art 3 Sch Part II.
54   Insolvency Act 1986 s297(2).
55   Insolvency Act 1986 s289.

transactions at an undervalue being discovered are substantially higher.)
- The client is automatically discharged from bankruptcy after two years unless he or she fails to co-operate or was bankrupt before within the past 15 years.[56]

Management of the client's assets and income

The Official Receiver (in a CSA case) or the trustee in bankruptcy will have the power to decide what happens to the client's assets and how much he or she should be allowed for domestic needs from any income that is available. All assets that will raise capital and any income above that required for domestic needs will be used to contribute to the paying of debts.

Discharge of bankruptcy order

Where a CSA has been made, the client is automatically discharged after two years unless he or she had previously been bankrupt within the 15 years before this bankruptcy order.[57] In non-CSA cases where there has been no other bankruptcy within 15 years, automatic discharge occurs after three years.[58] If the client is unco-operative, the Official Receiver can ask the court to delay discharge.[59] Clients who have been bankrupt before within the past 15 years have to apply to the court to be discharged.[60] The court can annul the bankruptcy if it turns out that the client had sufficient assets to pay his or her debts, or if those debts are paid off during the bankruptcy.[61]

Voluntary arrangements

A voluntary arrangement is a scheme whereby the creditors agree the level and timing of payments they will receive and once that agreement has been reached, most individual creditors are restrained from enforcing their debt.

---

56   Insolvency Act 1986 s279(2).
57   Insolvency Act 1986 s279(2)(a).
58   Insolvency Act 1986 s279(2)(b).
59   Insolvency Act 1986 s279(3).
60   Insolvency Act 1986 s282.
61   Insolvency Act 1986 s282.

Advantages over bankruptcy

- The client may be more likely to be allowed to carry on running a business provided some income is being generated.
- No stigma arises as the matter is private.
- Certain assets may be protected if creditors agree, eg, the debtor's home.
- The scheme may limit the interest that creditors receive.
- The scheme can be more carefully tailored to suit the situation of the client.
- An immediate interim order can be obtained from the court which prevents court action, execution or any other legal process from being begun or continued and prevents an application being made for bankruptcy.[62] The court has power to stay any proceedings.[63]

Disadvantages over bankruptcy

- The application for an interim order must identify an insolvency practitioner who will manage the scheme. He or she will not agree to act unless s/he is reasonably certain that his fees will be met.
- The client may end up paying more to creditors than if he or she obtained a bankruptcy order.
- Secured creditors are not bound by the scheme unless they individually agree[64] and so they can effectively prevent a scheme being adopted.
- The scheme requires the consent of at least 50% of unsecured creditors by value as well as of all secured creditors.

Which remedy may be useful?

The table below gives a summary of the effect on the various debts dealt with in this work of:
(1) an administration order;
(2) bankruptcy proceedings or a bankruptcy order;
(3) an interim order pending a voluntary arrangement or an agreed voluntary arrangement.

---

62   Insolvency Act 1986 s252.
63   Insolvency Act 1985 s254.
64   Insolvency Act 1986 s258(4).

(1) Administration order[65]

Kind of debt	Effect on debt
Mortgage arrears	Unlikely to be relevant, since total debts must be less than £5,000 before an administration order can be made, but an order means that mortgagee needs court's permission to enforce security and proceedings to recover possession are stayed pending the court's permission being obtained
Rent arrears	Landlord needs permission from the court making the administration order to enforce order for possession or to continue proceedings seeking a possession order
Civil debts	Creditor cannot enforce judgment without leave, eg, by warrant of execution, garnishee order or charging order, and any pending proceedings in the county court are stayed unless permission obtained to proceed
Fuel debts	If a composition order is made reducing the amount of debts payable, this becomes the amount due. However, the power to disconnect is unaffected if the sum due has not been paid
Water rates	As a county court judgment is required before the power to disconnect arises, proceedings to recover water rates will be stayed if an administration order is made and the court will include payments towards water rates in the order. The debt may be reduced by a composition order. The administration order should mean that the client is no longer in breach of any judgment, so the power to disconnect should no longer arise unless the client fails to pay under the terms of the administration order

65   Note that at present at least one county court judgment must exist to give jurisdiction to make an order (see p14).

Kind of debt	Effect on debt
Community charge and council tax	There is no power to stay proceedings in the magistrates' court but the local authority cannot take steps to enforce any liability order without permission from the county court that made the administration order
Magistrates' court orders, civil and matrimonial orders	There is no power to stay proceedings but the other party to the proceedings cannot take any steps to enforce any order without permission from the county court that made the administration order
Fines and orders in criminal proceedings	Position unclear but arguable that the court cannot take steps to enforce the fine by issuing a distress warrant or by committal to prison without permission from the county court that made the administration order

(2) **Bankruptcy application and bankruptcy order**
(3) **Interim order or agreed voluntary arrangement**

Kind of debt	Effect on debt
Mortgage arrears	Secured creditors still able to enforce their debt despite a bankruptcy order. A secured creditor cannot be obliged to consent to a voluntary arrangement, but if consent is given and includes provisions retricting the secured creditor's ability to enforce its security, that creditor is bound by those provisions
Rent arrears	Bankruptcy court, court to which an application for an interim order has been made pending a voluntary arrangement or the court dealing with possession proceedings may stay any such proceedings with or without conditions. When a bankruptcy order is made, the landlord needs leave of the court to commence possession proceedings and the landlord cannot levy distress except for the last six months' rent. Outstanding rent arrears cease to be payable once a bankruptcy order is

Kind of debt	Effect on debt
	discharged. It would appear that a landlord cannot enforce a possession order when a bankruptcy order has been made since a warrant of possession amounts to a remedy against the property of the debtor. Under a voluntary arrangment, rent arrears are recoverable if the terms of the agreement allow
Civil debts	The creditor cannot enforce any judgment if a bankruptcy order has been made. Proceedings to enforce a debt before any court can be stayed by that court, by the bankruptcy court or by the court which makes an interim order pending a voluntary arrangement. The creditor needs permission to begin proceedings to recover any debt whilst a bankruptcy order is in force. The outstanding debt ceases to be payable once the bankruptcy order is discharged. A voluntary arrangement may have restrictions on the amounts of debts that are to be paid and the remedies available.
Fuel debts	The power to disconnect is unaffected by a bankruptcy order or by an interim order but once a bankruptcy order is discharged, any outstanding fuel debts cease to be payable. A voluntary arrangement can include the terms under which fuel debts are payable
Water rates	The court considering a petition for bankruptcy or making an interim order pending a voluntary arrangement or the court in which proceedings have been issued to recover water rates arrears may stay the proceedings. Once a bankruptcy order has been made, permission is required to begin proceedings to recover water rates. If a judgment is obtained, the power to disconnect is unaffected by the existence of a bankruptcy order or interim order. However, when a bankruptcy order is discharged any outstanding water rates cease to be payable

Kind of debt	*Effect on debt*
Community charge and council tax	The bankruptcy court, the court making an interim order or the magistrates' court itself has power to stay proceedings in the magistrates' court. In addition, once a bankruptcy order is made the local authority cannot begin proceedings for a liability order without permission and cannot take steps to enforce any liability order.
Magistrates' court, civil and matrimonial orders	The bankruptcy court, the court making an interim order or the magistrates' court itself has power to stay proceedings in the magistrates' court. In addition, once a bankruptcy order is made the other party cannot begin proceedings for an order against the client without permission and cannot take steps to enforce any order
Fines and orders in criminal proceedings	The bankruptcy court, the court making an interim order or the magistrates' court can stay proceedings for recovery of a fine. It appears that the court cannot take steps to enforce the fine by issuing a distress warrant or by committal to prison during the bankruptcy

CHAPTER 3

Civil and consumer credit debts

Introduction

The following is a list of typical problems requiring emergency action:

- where the owner of goods which have been hired or provided on hire-purchase tries to recover them without taking court action;
- where a debtor is being harassed;
- where county court bailiffs or High Court sheriff's officers are expected to call to levy execution;
- where county court bailiffs or High Court sheriff's officers have already levied execution and sale of goods is imminent;
- where a garnishee order *nisi* has been obtained;
- where a charging order *nisi* has been obtained.

Apart from the debts covered in chapters 4 to 8, this chapter covers the majority of debts for which clients will be liable and which can be recovered through the county courts and the High Court. The jurisdiction of the county court is now unlimited in cases of action for contract and tort.[1] In addition, any actions in respect of regulated agreements under the Consumer Credit Act 1974 must be dealt with in the county courts.[2] It is primarily the county court procedure that is dealt with in this chapter because it is in the county court that most debts will be dealt with. Parallel procedures apply in the High Court.

This chapter therefore covers a wide range of debts including:

- sums due under court judgments for damages, eg, for personal injury in a car accident;
- sums due under a court judgment following the non-payment of a debt, eg, for the supply of goods or for building work etc.;
- sums due under a judgment for non-payment of a loan, eg, by a bank or

---

1 County Courts Act 1984 s15 as amended by the Courts and Legal Services Act 1990.
2 Consumer Credit Act 1974 s141.

other lender (for the enforcement of a mortgage securing a debt see chapter 12);
- sums due under hire-purchase and conditional sale agreements;
- sums recoverable by the Benefits Agency because of an overpayment of benefits.[3]

Consumer Credit Act 1974

Since many debts covered by this chapter will be affected by the Consumer Credit Act 1974, the important features of the Act are discussed below.

Definitions

'Regulated consumer credit agreement'
An agreement to provide credit is regulated if:
- the recipient is an individual or a partnership;
- the credit does not exceed £15,000; and
- it is not an 'exempt agreement'.[4]

The provider of the credit can be any person or organisation from a multinational public company to a close relative.
'Credit' includes:
- providing a loan;
- allowing a period of grace before payment is required, eg, where a shop allows payment to be made at the end of the month but provides the goods immediately;
- allowing the use of a credit card;
- providing goods on hire-purchase.[5]

Where the creditor has merely granted the debtor facilities to borrow (eg, credit card or bank overdraft) without fixing the amount, the agreement is regulated if the credit limit is less than £15,000. If there is no credit limit or it exceeds £15,000, the agreement for its use is regulated if the debtor cannot draw more than £15,000 at any one time, or if it is probable when the agreement is made that it will not exceed £15,000 or if charges increase when an amount less than £15,000 is reached.[6] Thus most agreements for the use of credit cards are regulated agreements. Agreements for bank overdrafts are usually also regulated.

3   Social Security Administration Act 1992 s71(10).
4   Consumer Credit Act 1974, s8.
5   Consumer Credit Act 1974, s9.
6   Consumer Credit Act 1974, s10.

'Regulated consumer hire agreement'

A hire agreement is regulated if it:

- is not a hire-purchase agreement;
- is capable of lasting more than three months;
- does not require the hirer to make payments exceeding £15,000; and
- is not an 'exempt agreement'.[7]

'Exempt agreement'

A consumer credit agreement may be exempt depending on the status of the credit and the type of transaction.

Exempt agreements secured by legal charges or mortgages. Local authorities, building societies, banks, some insurance companies, some national friendly societies and a few large church charities can create exempt agreements which are mortgages.[8] To be exempt the agreements must be for mortgages of land entered into either to enable the purchase of the land, the building of dwellings or business premises on the land, or the alteration, enlargement, repair or improvement of a dwelling or business premises on the land. There is a further requirement where the loan is to enable alteration, enlargement, etc., that the same creditor already has a mortgage to allow purchasing or building.[9]

The exemption is extended to cover mortgages arranged as refinancing of previous mortgages acquired to purchase, build, enlarge etc.[10]

First mortgages created by some lenders to enable people to buy their homes will be exempt. However, even first mortgages created by finance companies will not be exempt, though they will not be regulated if the amount of credit exceeds £15,000. A second mortgage will be exempt only if granted by the same lender as the first mortgage and only if granted for the purpose of works on the dwelling. Therefore, business loans secured on a home will not be exempt but will not be regulated if above the £15,000 limit; nor will second mortgages by banks be exempt where a different lender (eg, a building society) granted the first loan.

Where a home-owner transfers the mortgage to another lender as a method of refinancing, this further mortgage will be exempt provided that the new lender falls within the category of organisations listed above. On mortgages generally, see chapter 12.

---

7   Consumer Credit Act 1974 s15.
8   Consumer Credit Act 1974 s16 and Consumer Credit (Exempt Agreements) (No. 2) Order 1985.
9   Consumer Credit (Exempt Agreements) (No. 2) Order 1985 art 2.
10   Consumer Credit (Exempt Agreements) (No. 2) Order 1985 art 2(2)(c).

Other exempt agreements. The following types of transaction are exempt:

- where the number of payments required to repay a loan for goods involving a supplier, customer and credit, does not exceed four;
- where the credit arranged is not of a fixed amount but the account must be cleared at regular intervals by one payment, eg, some credit cards such as American Express, or a charge account with a shop;
- where the total charge for credit is less than whichever is the higher of 13 per cent or 1 per cent above the highest bank base rate 28 days before the agreement was made;[11]
- agreements for the hire of meters by electricity, gas and water suppliers;[12]
- ancillary agreements between a building society and a borrower whereby the borrower is able to defer payment of endowment premiums or building insurance instalments.[13]

'Small agreement'

A small agreement is a regulated consumer credit or consumer hire agreement involving less than £50. Where the amount of credit is not fixed (eg, credit card or overdraft), the agreement is a small agreement if the credit limit is £50 or less.[14] Hire purchase and conditional sale agreements are never small agreements, nor are loans secured on land.[15] Where several small agreements are entered into, they are covered by anti-avoidance provisions.[16]

Default notices under the Consumer Credit Act 1974

A creditor under a regulated agreement must serve a default notice before s/he can terminate an agreement because of a breach by the debtor, or demand repayment earlier than the agreement originally provided for or recover possession of any goods or land or take court action against the debtor.[17]

The regulations set out the information which must be contained in

---

11 Consumer Credit (Exempt Agreements) (No. 2) Order 1985 art 4.
12 Consumer Credit (Exempt Agreements) (No. 2) Order 1985 art 6.
13 Consumer Credit (Exempt Agreements) (No. 2) Order 1985 art 3.
14 Consumer Credit Act 1974 s17.
15 Consumer Credit Act 1974 s17(1)(a).
16 Consumer Credit Act 1974 s10(3) and (4).
17 Consumer Credit Act 1974 s87. There is an exception where the agreement is non-commercial, ie, where the lender is not seeking to make a profit, such as an agreement between friends (see Consumer Credit (Enforcement, Default and Termination Notices) Regulations 1983 SI No 1561 reg 2(9)).

the default notice, prescribe information on debtors' rights to apply for a time order and require the notice to recommend that the debtor consults a solicitor or a Citizens Advice Bureau.

The default notice must set out the breach complained of and what action the debtor must take to remedy the breach and allow at least seven days for the debtor to take such action.[18]

Cancellation of consumer credit agreements

A regulated agreement can be cancelled if there were oral negotiations with the debtor or hirer and the agreement was not signed at the business premises of the creditor or negotiator.

There is no right to cancel the following agreements:

- agreements for a mortgage to purchase land or for a bridging loan;[19]
- non-commercial agreements;
- most small agreements;
- agreements allowing a debtor to overdraw on a current account.[20]

The provision for cancellation is intended to cover agreements made by door-to-door salespersons or canvassers.

Where an agreement is cancellable, the debtor must be given notice of the right of cancellation. This must be sent by post to the debtor within seven days following the making of the agreement and must be contained either in a copy of the agreement or in a separate notice.[21] The notice must state the names and addresses of all the persons to whom notice of cancellation can be given. Certain creditors can obtain exemption from the requirement to give notice of the right of cancellation for some types of regulated agreement.[22]

The right to cancel begins at the moment the debtor signs the agreement and ends at the end of the fifth day following the day on which s/he received the posted copy notice of cancellation. If no notice of cancellation has been given, there is still a right to cancel, and the adviser should consider immediately whether this is desirable.

Notice of cancellation can be given in writing to the creditor, any negotiator (eg, a credit broker), a supplier of goods when goods are provided on credit and to anyone who acted for the debtor in any negotiations in the course of that person's business.

18   Consumer Credit Act 1974 s88.
19   Consumer Credit Act 1974 s67.
20   Consumer Credit Act 1974 s74.
21   Consumer Credit Act 1974 ss63 and 64.
22   Consumer Credit Act 1974 s64(4) and see the Consumer Credit (Notice of Cancellation Rights) (Exemptions) Regulations 1983 SI No. 1558.

Where an agreement is cancelled, sums already paid under the agreement become repayable to the debtor with the exception of £3 commission to a credit broker (if any).[23] If goods were supplied, these must be made available for collection but can be sent or returned by the debtor to any person on whom notice of cancellation could have been served except a person who acted for the debtor.[24] The debtor must take reasonable care of the goods until collected.[25] Where money has been paid by the creditor, this should be repaid to anyone on whom notice of cancellation could have been served (except a person who acted for the debtor) within one month or before the first instalment is due, in which case no interest arises.[26]

Termination of consumer credit agreements

Debtors under regulated hire, hire-purchase and conditional sale agreements have the right to terminate the agreement in certain circumstances.

Hire-purchase and conditional sale agreements

The debtor can terminate this kind of agreement at any time.[27] However, if s/he has paid less than one-half of the total price, s/he must make the payments up to one-half unless the agreement is more generous than this, for example, where the agreement allows termination when only one-third of the payments have been made.[28]

Certain assumptions are made in the calculations of one-half of the total price. First, special rules apply where there are installation charges.[29] For example, where the total price is £500 but £100 is for installation, half the total price for termination purposes is arrived at by deducting the installation price, calculating half of the remainder (ie, £200) and adding back the installation charge. Thus half the total price is £300. Second, if the debtor has contravened an obligation to take reasonable care of land or goods, the amount required to be paid by the debtor is increased by the amount required to compensate the creditor for that contravention.[30]

If the creditor takes court action, or the debtor applies for a

---

23   Consumer Credit Act 1974 s70.
24   Consumer Credit Act 1974 s72(5).
25   Consumer Credit Act 1974 s72(3).
26   Consumer Credit Act 1974 s71.
27   Consumer Credit Act 1974 s99.
28   Consumer Credit Act 1974 s100.
29   Consumer Credit Act 1974 s100(2).
30   Consumer Credit Act 1974 s100(4).

declaration, the court can hold that a smaller amount than half the total price is payable if the creditor's loss is less than half the total price.[31]

If the debtor terminates the agreement but fails go give back the goods the court must order their return rather than allow the debtor to pay their value, unless it considers it unjust to do so.[32]

Hire agreements

The debtor can terminate a hire agreement but only if the notice of termination expires at least 18 months after the agreement began.[33] Three months' notice or a rental period must be given, whichever is less.[34] Thus, an agreement with monthly payments can be terminated by one month's notice given after 17 months.

The right to terminate does not arise if the debtor hired the goods for business use.[35] Payments already due under the agreement remain due but future instalments cease to be payable. Notice can be given to any person authorised to receive rentals under the agreement.

Defences to claims by creditors under Consumer Credit Act 1974

Misrepresentation or breach of contract by the supplier

Where the supplier of goods or services is in breach of contract or there has been a misrepresentation, this may be raised as a defence by way of set-off or as a counterclaim in an action for money due to the supplier.[36] In addition, the creditor is liable for any breach of contract or misrepresentation by the supplier so the supplier's conduct can be raised as a defence to a claim by the creditor. The most common breach of contract by a supplier is a breach of one of the terms implied by the Sale of Goods Act 1979, the Supply of Goods (Implied Terms) Act 1973, or the Supply of Goods and Services Act 1982. For example, if defective goods are brought with a credit card, the fact that the goods are defective is a defence to a claim by the credit card company for payment.

No valid notice of default

In most cases, a notice of default must have been served and have expired

---

31   Consumer Credit Act 1974 s100(3).
32   Consumer Credit Act 1974 s100(5).
33   Consumer Credit Act 1974 s101(3).
34   Consumer Credit Act 1974 s101(4).
35   Consumer Credit Act 1974 s101(7).
36   Consumer Credit Act 1974 s75.

before any proceedings can be taken to enforce an agreement.[37] The form of default notice is prescribed and must state the nature of the alleged breach of the agreement and if the breach is capable of remedy, what action is required to remedy it and the date before which that action is to be taken.[38]

Creditor not licensed

In addition to committing a criminal offence a creditor cannot enforce any regulated agreement (other than a non-commercial agreement) if unlicensed at the time the agreement was made, unless the Director General of Fair Trading makes an order allowing it to become enforceable.[39] If the Director has not already made such an order, it is a complete defence to proceedings for enforcement of a regulated agreement that the creditor does not have a licence. Among other factors, the Director must consider the degree to which the debtor has been prejudiced by the creditor's conduct. Consideration should be given to making representations to the Director to persuade him or her to refuse to allow enforcement.

Agreement improperly executed

If an agreement is improperly executed, it can be enforced only with leave of the court.[40] The court can make an enforcement order if and only if it considers it just to do so, having regard to the prejudice to any person resulting from any contravention, the culpability for it and to its other powers.[41] These other powers include the power to reduce or discharge any sum payable by the debtor under the agreement;[42] to suspend operation of any order or impose conditions;[43] and to vary the agreement where this is just.[44]

The court is prohibited from allowing enforcement of an improperly executed agreement in the following circumstances:

a) where the agreement was not properly signed unless the debtor or hirer has signed some document which contains all the necessary prescribed details even though that document was not in the right format and the

---

37   Consumer Credit Act 1974 s87.
38   Consumer Credit Act 1974 s88 and Consumer Credit (Enforcement, Default and Termination Notice) Regulations 1983 SI No. 1561 as amended.
39   Consumer Credit Act 1974 s40.
40   Consumer Credit Act 1974 s65.
41   Consumer Credit Act 1974 s127(1).
42   Consumer Credit Act 1974 s127(2).
43   Consumer Credit Act 1974 s135.
44   Consumer Credit Act 1974 s136.

signature was not acquired in the right manner. There must therefore be some kind of agreement that was signed by the debtor or hirer containing the essential information.

b) where the agreement was cancellable and a proper notice of the right to cancel was not given to the debtor or a copy of the agreement was not supplied before the proceedings were started.[45]

An agreement is to be considered improperly executed in the following circumstances:

– where the agreement is cancellable and proper notices have not been given.[46]
– where copies of the agreement have not been given as required;[47]
– where the document is not in the form required by regulations;[48]
– where the document has not been signed in the manner required by regulations;[49]
– where the document is not legible;[50]
– where the document does not contain all the terms prescribed.[51]

In order to raise a defence of improper execution, it will be necessary to prove what prejudice has arisen to the debtor by reason of the default, including, where possible, what steps the debtor would probably have taken if the agreement had been properly executed, eg, not entering into the agreement.

Recovery methods

Only the recovery methods which give rise to emergency situations are covered below. In addition, the court has power to make an attachment of earnings order and appoint a receiver.

Recovery of goods hired or on hire-purchase by the owner without court action

A creditor can recover goods only if s/he still owns them, ie, under a hire

45   Consumer Credit Act 1974 s127(3) and (4).
46   Consumer Credit Act 1974 s64 and see page 39.
47   Consumer Credit Act 1974 ss62 and 63.
48   Consumer Credit Act 1974 s60 and Consumer Credit (Agreements) Regulations 1983 SI No. 1553.
49   Consumer Credit Act 1974 s62 and Consumer Credit (Agreements) Regulations 1983.
50   Consumer Credit Act 1974 s61.
51   Consumer Credit Act 1974 ss60 and 61 and Consumer Credit (Agreements) Regulations 1983.

agreement, hire-purchase agreement or conditional sale agreement. The terms of the agreement will make clear that ownership of the goods remains with the creditor. Under a hire-purchase agreement, the hirer has an option to purchase at the end of the term, unsually for a very small final payment. Under a conditional sale agreement, the debtor must pay the final payment and thus become the owner at the end of the agreement. In both cases, until the final payment is made, the creditor remains the owner.

If a regulated agreement other than a non-commercial one requires the debtor to keep the goods in his or her possession or control, it is an offence to fail to inform the creditor of the whereabouts of the goods within seven days of a written request.[52] This provision applies to hire, hire-purchase and conditional sale agreements.

Unless the debtor agrees to return goods voluntarily, no action, either through the courts or by physical recovery, can be taken unless a default notice has been served and has expired.[53]

If a valid default notice has been served and has expired, the creditor can recover goods without court action except in two circumstances where a court order is required:

- where access to private premises is required;
- where goods are statutorily protected.

Where access to private premises is required[54]

Any clause in the written agreement giving the creditor right of access in contravention of this provision is void.[55] However, if the creditor enters premises with permission given at the time of entry then a court order is unnecessary, although it is not clear whether the occupier or the debtor has to give permission.[56] If the creditor enters premises without permission, action can be taken for breach of statutory duty.[57] Household goods which are hired or on hire-purchase, eg, video, cooker, furniture, etc, cannot, therefore, be recovered without a court order unless the debtor allows the creditor to enter the home. A car on hire-purchase cannot lawfully be retaken if it is parked in a private drive but can if it is left in the road.

---

52   Consumer Credit Act 1974 s80.
53   Consumer Credit Act 1974 s87.
54   Consumer Credit Act 1974 s92(1).
55   Consumer Credit Act 1974 s173(1).
56   Consumer Credit Act 1974 s173(3).
57   Consumer Credit Act 1974 s92(3).

Where goods are statutorily protected

Goods subject to a regulated hire-purchase or conditional sale agreement cannot be recovered by the creditor without a court order if at least one-third of the total price has been paid.[58] Any term of the agreement purporting to give the creditor a right to recover goods after one-third of the total price has been paid is void.[59] 'Total price' means all sums payable under the agreement but special rules apply when there are installation charges.[60]

If the creditor retakes the goods in breach of this provision the agreement terminates, the debtor is automatically released from all future liability and the debtor can reclaim all the money s/he has already paid.[61] If the debtor agrees to the creditor retaking the goods this provision gives no protection.

Recovery of a debt under a warrant of execution against goods

A warrant of execution is an authority to the county court bailiff to seize, remove and sell the goods of a debtor.[62] In the High Court, a writ of *fieri facias (fi fa)* is an authority for the High Court sheriff and his or her officers to seize, remove and sell the goods of a debtor. Where the court has ordered payment under a judgment to be made by instalments, a warrant can be issued only where there has been a default in payment of at least one instalment.[63] However, once one instalment has been missed, a warrant of execution can then be issued for the full amount due under the judgment.[64] A client can therefore avoid a warrant of execution being issued by keeping to the terms of any order for payment by instalments. As we shall see, if there has been a breach of any instalment arrangement, the client can also make an application to the court for the issue of a warrant of execution to be suspended on different terms as to future instalments.

Under a warrant of execution issued by the county court or a writ of *fi fa* issued by the High Court, the bailiff or sheriff's officer can only remove the goods that belong to the debtor personally though this will include goods that are jointly owned with some other person. They can also seize

---

58   Consumer Credit Act 1974 s90(1).
59   Consumer Credit Act 1974 s173(1).
60   Consumer Credit Act 1974 ss189(1) and 90(2) and see page 40.
61   Consumer Credit Act 1974 s91.
62   County Courts Act 1974 s85.
63   County Courts Act 1974 s86.
64   County Court Rules 1981 Ord 26 r1.

any money, cheques, bonds, etc.[65] The following items are exempt from seizure:

- tools, books, vehicles and other items of equipment which are necessary for the client for use personally in his or her employment, business or vocation;
- such clothing, bedding, furniture, household equipment or provisions as are necessary for satisfying the basic domestic needs of the client and his or her family.[66]

The bailiff or sheriff cannot break into the home unless he or she has already gained access on a previous occasion and a walking possession agreement has been signed. See page 60 for the meaning of a 'walking possession agreement'.

Recovery of a debt by obtaining a garnishee order

A garnishee order is an order to a person who owes the debtor money requiring that the money should be paid direct to the creditor rather than to the debtor. For example, where a debtor has a bank account, a garnishee order can be obtained against the bank requiring that the bank pay whatever is due to the creditor direct or as much as there is in the bank account.

Where a creditor applies for such an order, the application is made without notice to the debtor. Without giving the debtor any opportunity to respond, the court will make an order to show cause[67] known as a 'garnishee order *nisi*'. This is an order requiring the garnishee, ie, the bank or other person or organisation which is alleged to owe the debtor money, to attend court and explain why a garnishee order should not be made. This order has the immediate effect of attaching the money that is due from the garnishee to the debtor or as much of that debt as is sufficient to pay off the debt and costs until the matter is further considered by the court. This order can, for example, freeze a bank account pending the hearing. The application for a garnishee order need not specify the account number or a particular branch of a bank. The creditor must give as much information as possible relating to the branch and the account number and must give the name and last known address of the debtor and state

---

65   Supreme Court Act 1981 s138 and County Courts Act 1984 s89 as amended by Courts and Legal Services Act 1990 s15.
66   Supreme Court Act 1981 s138 and County Courts Act 1984 s89(1) as amended by Courts and Legal Services Act 1990 s15.
67   County Court Rules 1981 Ord 30 r1.

that to the best of the creditor's information or belief the bank has money belonging to the debtor.[68]

The order 'to show cause' must be served on the judgment debtor at least seven days after a copy of it has been served on the garnishee and it must be served on the garnishee at least 15 days before the hearing.[69] This means that the debtor will not be told about the garnishee order *nisi* until at least seven days after the order is made and in practice it is likely to be longer. The idea is to give the garnishee, eg, a bank, time to freeze the accounts before the debtor has warning of the application and can start withdrawing money. However, it can mean that a debtor is unable to draw money and has had his or her bank account frozen without knowing the reason why and being unable to take any action to do anything about it.

Recovery of a debt by application for a charging order

A charging order charges an asset of the debtor with the payment of sums due or to become due under a court judgment.[70] In practice, the most significant type of charging order is one charging a person's home and it is this kind of order that will be dealt with in this chapter. Enforcement of a charging order is either by an order for sale or the appointment of a receiver.[71] A creditor can seek a charging order even where the debtor has kept to an order for payment by instalments.

A charging order can be made against a home that is jointly owned and, despite the interest of the other parties who own the house and any children that may live there, an order for sale can still be made.

Where a creditor applies for a charging order, the court will first consider whether there is enough evidence to suggest that a charging order should be made. If the court is satisfied, it will make a charging order *nisi* which charges the debtor's home immediately and will also fix a hearing at which it will be decided whether to make a charging order absolute.[72]

Reducing future liabilities

Where the debtor has a continuing liability, eg, where interest is accruing on a debt such as a loan from a bank or where there is a hire-purchase or hire agreement where instalments are continuing to be payable, the client

68   County Court Rules 1981 Ord 30 r2.
69   County Court Rules 1981 Ord 30 r3.
70   Charging Orders Act 1979 s1.
71   Charging Orders Act 1979 s3(4).
72   County Court Rules 1981 Ord 31 rr1(4) and 2(1).

should be advised about the possible methods of reducing any future liability.

In all cases, where interest is arising, a request should be made to the creditor to waive future interest. Such a request will need to be accompanied by a detailed income and expenditure statement showing that the client is unable to make the payments required. Experience shows that many creditors are prepared to waive interest if they can be convinced that the client has little realistic prospect of paying both the sum outstanding and future interest on that sum.

Cancellation of the agreement

Consideration should also be given to whether the client has a right to cancel the agreement if the client wishes to do so. The rules on cancellation are discussed on page 39. It should be noted, in particular, that the right to cancel continues until seven days after the debtor has received notice of the right of cancellation by post. If such notice of cancellation has never been given then the right to cancel is still in existence even though the agreement itself may have been made a very considerable time ago. The consequences of cancellation are explained on page 40.

Termination of the agreement

Even if the client has not got the right to cancel the agreement, if it is a hire agreement or a hire-purchase or conditional sale agreement, the client may have a right to terminate it, thus ensuring that some or all of the future instalments are not payable. An explanation of the circumstances in which a client may terminate an agreement is given on page 40.

Preventing recovery of goods without a court order

Making removal physically impossible

The most effective strategy for preventing removal of goods without a court order is to make it physically impossible. There are a number of ways of doing so:

- hide the item concerned;
- remove the item concerned from the home to an alternative site;
- ensure that the item concerned remains within locked premises;
- in the case of a car, ensure that it is parked within a locked garage;
- refuse access when requested to allow it.

Note that although the client may remove the item concerned from his or her home to an alternative site, it is a criminal offence to fail to give the owner of the goods information about the whereabouts of the item within seven days of a written request.[73] This does not prevent the client from moving the item once again the day after written notification has been given to the creditor of its whereabouts.

Many people, when asked by a credit company to allow access for goods to be removed, allow them in. They do not realise that the creditor has no right of access and needs a court order to recover the goods if they are within private premises. If it is agreed with the client he or she is going to make it physically impossible for the creditor to remove the goods without obtaining a court order, it is important to advise the client that s/he has no obligation whatsoever to allow access unless there is a court order in force. S/he is entitled to refuse to answer the door and to obstruct the door to prevent access.

Making removal unlawful

As explained on page 44, a creditor has the legal right to remove goods only in certain circumstances if the goods are provided under an agreement which is a regulated agreement under the Consumer Credit Act 1974. If the agreement is not regulated and the contract provides that the creditor has a right of access to the premises at which the goods are kept, this provision will apply and the creditor will have a right of access to recover the goods. However, in practice most agreements are regulated.

Request a copy of the agreement and information
By making a written request and paying 50p, a debtor under a regulated agreement is entitled to receive a copy of the agreement and to receive certain information about the account.[74]

Precedent 1 in part III shows a letter requesting such information. Under a fixed-sum credit agreement, the client is entitled to details of the total sum he or she has paid, the sums which have become payable and are unpaid, the dates when each of those sums became due and the sums which are to become payable under the agreement.[75] Under a running-account credit agreement, the client is entitled to details of the state of the account, the amount payable under the agreement and the amounts and dates of

---

73   Consumer Credit Act 1974 s80.
74   Consumer Credit Act 1974 ss77 to 79.
75   Consumer Credit Act 1974 s77 and see the notes to precedent 1 in Part III for an explanation of the meaning of the term fixed-sum credit agreement.

future payments that will become due.[76] Under a hire agreement, the client is entitled to details of the sum which has become payable under the agreement but remains unpaid and the date when each instalment became due.[77] In each case, the details provided must be in a statement signed by or on behalf of the creditor. The provisions do not apply to a non-commercial agreement. The creditor must supply the information within 12 working days excluding the date of the request.[78] It is a criminal offence to fail to give the information within one month of the request.[79]

More importantly, if a request has been made but the creditor has failed to provide the information within the 12 days, the creditor cannot take any steps to enforce the agreement until the information is provided. It is only once the 12-day period has expired that the creditor is prevented from taking any steps. It seems likely that the creditor cannot even issue a default notice during the period of non-compliance.

Information and a copy of the agreement should always be requested, not only to check the form and content of the agreement, but also to buy time to consider other steps. Requests for information can be repeated at monthly intervals and, in each case, if the creditor fails to provide the information within the 12 days, the creditor is prevented from taking further steps to enforce the agreement. If the creditor is inefficient, significant amounts of time can be bought for the client in this way.

Keep the goods on private premises

If the goods are kept on private premises and the agreement is a regulated agreement, the creditor has no right of access to those premisees without the permission of the owner or occupier. Parking a car on a driveway should be sufficient to prevent repossession. However, it is far more secure to park the car in a garage which is locked because some creditors are not as scrupulous as they should be.

Bring the payments up to one-third of the total price

As explained on page 45, goods provided under a regulated agreement cannot be recovered by the creditor without a court order if at least one-third of the total price has been paid. If the amount paid by the client is less than this sum, and the client has the available resources, he or she can bring the payments up to one-third of the total price in order to obtain

---

76   Consumer Credit Act 1974 s78 and see the notes to precedent 1 in Part III for the meaning of the term running-account credit agreement.
77   Consumer Credit Act 1974 s79.
78   Consumer Credit (Prescribed Periods for Giving Information) Regulations 1983 reg 2 SI No 1569.
79   Consumer Credit Act 1974 ss77(4), 78(6) and 79(3).

protection of the goods and require the creditor to obtain a court order before recovering them.

If the creditor retakes the goods without a court order when one-third of the total price has been paid, the agreement automatically terminates and not only is the client released from all future liability under the agreement but is entitled to recover from the creditor all sums that have already been paid.[80]

Obtain a 'time order' from the court

A time order is an order made by the county court:

- for the payment by the client of any 'sums owed' under a regulated agreement by instalments that the court fixes having regard to the means of the client; and
- for the remedying by the client of any breach of the agreement.[81]

In addition to changing the instalments, the court has general power to include in the order 'such provision as it considers just for amending any agreement in consequence of a term of the order'.[82]

The definition of 'sums owed'

There are conflicting decisions in the county courts about the meaning of the words 'sums owed'. One interpretation was that the meaning of the words 'sums owed' included both arrears outstanding and the capital originally lent under the agreement if the agreement required all the capital to be repaid when there was a default (as most agreements do).[83] The alternative interpretation was that a time order could only be made in respect of the arrears.[84] More recently, the Court of Appeal has confirmed that in its view the meaning of the words 'sums owed' is that all sums that have become payable under the agreement are included.[85] This means that if the loan agreement specifies that the full sum becomes repayable where there is default, the county court has power to make a time order in respect of capital, interest and arrears. One county court has gone further and decided that 'sums owed' includes all capital and interest payable under

---

80   Consumer Credit Act 1974 s91.

81   Consumer Credit Act 1974 s129.

82   Consumer Credit Act 1974 s136.

83   *Cedar Holdings Ltd v Jenkins* October 1987 *Legal Action* 19; *National Guardian Mortgage Corporation v Wilkes* (1991) 22 July, Luton County Court, see October 1991 *Legal Action* 16; *Cedar Holdings Ltd v Thompson* (1991) 20 September, Croydon County Court, see *Adviser* No 32 p25; *Cedar Holdings Ltd v Aguiraldo* (1992) 25 March, Bow County Court, see *Adviser* No 32 p24.

84   *Ashbroom Facilities Ltd v Bodley* (1988) 10 November, Birmingham County Court, referred to in *County Court Practice* 1991 ed. p1131.

85   *First National Bank plc v Syed* [1991] 2 All ER 250, CA *per* Dillon LJ.

the agreement, even if the whole loan does not become repayable on default.[86]

In hire-purchase and conditional sale agreements, the court is specifically given power to make a time order that deals with future payments that will become due under the agreement.[87]

The client can apply for a time order in proceedings taken by the creditor to enforce the debt. However, the client does not have to wait for the creditor to take steps to enforce an agreement through the courts before applying for a time order. S/he can apply for a time order as soon as a default notice or some other notice terminating the agreement has been served.[88]

Legal aid is available if the client applies for a time order without waiting for the creditor to take proceedings. Although the application relates to the time and mode of payment, the debtor is the applicant and not the defendant so the restriction on legal aid for defending debt cases does not apply.[89]

Powers of the court

The court can alter for example:

- the period of repayment, eg, from weekly to monthly;
- the rate of payment, eg, from instalments of £100 per month to £20 per month;
- the length of the loan, eg, from three years to 10 years;
- the agreement in any other way necessary to give effect to the above.[90]

The general power to amend the agreement 'as it considers just' arguably allows the court to alter the rate of interest charged under the agreement to bring the rate of interest into line with the revised instalments that the court has ordered. This has certainly been the way in which the courts have interpreted the legislation in a number of cases.[91]

Once a time order is made, the creditor cannot take any action to enforce the agreement as long as the debtor complies with the time order. The creditor can apply to vary or revoke the time order at any time and the court has a general discretionary power to do so.[92]

---

86   *Wimbledon and South-West Finance plc v Winning* (1992) 19 June, Oxford County Court, see *Adviser* No 35 p25.
87   Consumer Credit Act 1974 s130(2).
88   Consumer Credit Act 1974 s129(1)(b).
89   Legal Aid Act 1988 Sch 2 Pt II para 5.
90   Consumer Credit Act 1974 ss129 and 136.
91   For example, see *Cedar Holdings Ltd v Thompson* Croydon County Court 20 September 1991 see *Adviser* No 32 p25.
92   Consumer Credit Act 1974 s130.

Because of the time it may take to obtain a time order, where the creditor is threatening to come and remove goods and there is no way in which the goods can be physically or legally protected, eg, a car on which less than one-third of the hire-purchase price has been paid and which the client cannot park on private premises, steps will have to be taken to get the court to expedite the hearing of the time order application. The court has a general discretion to shorten any time periods required under the court rules and can fix a hearing at short notice.[93] In some courts, when the application for a time order is filed, it will be sufficient to make a written request to the court to expedite the hearing provided an affidavit is filed setting out the reason why the matter is urgent. The district judge in these courts will be prepared to deal with the matter on the basis of the affidavit evidence and make a decision that expedition of the hearing is necessary. In other courts, an application will have to be made in person to the district judge for the notice periods required by the court rules to be shortened and for an early hearing. The practice of the local district judge should be ascertained.

An application for a time order is given in precedent 2 in part III. An affidavit in support requesting an expedited hearing in respect of an application to set aside judgment for water charges is shown in precedent 13 and can be amended for these purposes as well. A letter to the court requesting an expedited hearing is shown in precedent 8.

Debt unenforceable

If the creditor is not licensed or the agreement has been improperly executed, it cannot be enforced without an order of a court. See page 42.

Reopen the agreement on the grounds that it is an extortionate credit bargain

A court has power to reopen a credit bargain if it finds it to be 'extortionate'.[94] This power applies to all forms of credit bargain, not just ones which are regulated agreements under the Consumer Credit Act 1974.

A credit bargain is extortionate if it requires the debtor or a relative of the debtor to make payments (whether unconditionally or on certain contingencies) which are grossly exorbitant, or if it otherwise grossly contravenes ordinary principles of fair dealing.[95]

In deciding this issue, the court must have regard to the evidence on the following issues:

93   County Court Rules 1981 Ord 13 r4.
94   Consumer Credit Act 1974 s137.
95   Consumer Credit Act 1974 s138.

- interest rates at the time the agreement was made;
- the age, experience, business capacity and state of health of the debtor;
- the degree to which the debtor was under financial pressure at the time of the agreement and the nature of that pressure;
- the degree of risk accepted by the creditor having regard to the value of any security provided;
- the creditor's relationship with the debtor (if any); and
- whether or not a colourable cash price (ie, a deliberately inflated cash price) was quoted for any goods or services included in the credit bargain.

If the court decides that the credit bargain was extortionate, it can set aside the whole or part of any obligation imposed upon the client, require the creditor to repay all or part of the sums paid and alter the terms of the credit agreement for the purpose of relieving the client from payment of any sums in excess of that 'fairly due and reasonable'.[96]

Because of the urgency of the matter, if an application for the reopening of an agreement on the grounds that it is extortionate is made to the court, steps will have to be taken to expedite the hearing unless the creditor is prepared to withhold enforcement until the court has had an opportunity to consider the matter. The procedure for obtaining an expedited hearing is the same as when making an application for a time order (see page 53).

Legal action to prevent removal

Most creditors will comply with the law. Once the client has made it physically impossible or unlawful for the creditor to seize the goods without a court order, the creditor will take steps to go to court rather than break the law. Nevertheless, there will be some creditors who will still make attempts to remove goods without going through the expense and trouble of court proceedings. In such circumstances, the client has the following options to prevent the goods being removed.

Trespass

A creditor or debt collector has no right to enter private premises without permission. For example, a creditor only has the same implied right as anyone else to enter a front garden and walk up to a front door and a client can withdraw that implied right merely by informing the creditor. The creditor will then be trespassing on setting foot inside the garden.

Many agreements for the hire, hire-purchase or conditional sale of

---

96   Consumer Credit Act 1974 s139.

goods state in them that the creditor has a right of entry to the client's home to recover the goods if there has been a breach of the agreement. If the agreement is not covered by the Consumer Credit Act 1974, this will give the creditor a right of entry. However, if the agreement is covered by the Consumer Credit Act 1974 and is a regulated agreement, the Act specifically states that the creditor has no right of entry except under an order of the court.[97] The statute will override any term of the agreement.

If a creditor does trespass or threatens to trespass on private premises to recover goods, any future trespass that is expected can be restrained by an injunction in an action in the county court. The procedure is discussed further below.

Nuisance

A creditor who has been kept off the premises and who still remains outside and pesters, shouts, etc from the street or landing may be committing a common law nuisance. A nuisance is not easily defined, but it is behaviour which is causing a nuisance in practice and which is unreasonable. A nuisance can also be restrained by an injunction. Again, an application for an injunction can be made in the county court and the procedure is discussed below.

Breach of the Consumer Credit Act 1974

If a client has been told that the creditor is coming back to collect the goods at a later time and it is expected that an attempt will be made to enter private premises to collect goods, an injunction can be obtained in advance to prevent such action because it will be a breach of statutory duty.

Precedent 4 in part III shows model particulars of claim seeking an injunction to restrain a creditor from entering private premises to recover goods and from causing a nuisance. Precedent 5 shows a supporting affidavit and explains the procedure.

Dealing with harassment of debtors

It is a criminal offence, with the object of coercing a debtor to pay money claimed under a contract:
- to harass the debtor with demands for payment 'which in respect of their frequency or the manner or occasion of making any such demand, or of any threat or publicity by which any demand is accompanied, are

97 Consumer Credit Act 1974 s92.

calculated to subject him or members of his family or household to
alarm, distress or humiliation';
- to falsely represent that a failure to pay can lead to criminal
  proceedings;
- to falsely represent that the collector is authorised in some
  official capacity to claim or enforce payments; or
- to give out any document falsely representing it to be of some official
  character or which falsely represents itself as having some official
  character when the collector knows it does not.[98]

The penalty is a fine of up to £5,000. This provision does not prevent a
collector taking reasonable steps or using the court process.[99]

Some of the tactics used by finance companies border on criminal
behaviour. In the authors' view, it is arguable that the following activities
amount to a criminal offence:

- contacting the debtor at work on any occasion unless the debtor has his
  or her telephone extension where s/he can talk privately or has agreed
  to be contacted at work;
- contacting the employer asking for details of pay (the creditor might
  argue this is reasonable but the employer should not disclose this
  information so the contact has no valid purpose);
- contacting neighbours to obtain information about the debtor where
  the reason for the request for information is disclosed to the
  neighbours;
- calling at the home very frequently at odd hours;
- making home visits in such a manner that the purpose of the visit is
  deliberately made obvious to neighbours.

Prosecution will either be by the police, the Crown Prosecution Service
or by the local authority trading standards department. Complaints
should initially be made to the trading standards department since in
practice the police and Crown Prosecution Service are unlikely to be
particularly interested.

A particular problem of protecting debtors from harassment arises in
the case of loan sharks. These are people who are generally not registered
under the Consumer Credit Act 1974 but take advantge of the needs of
those on low income for immediate cash to meet other debts and lend
money at extortionate rates of interest, without documentation and in
circumstances where violence is often threatened or potentially likely to
happen if debts are not repaid. In some circumstances, loan sharks can also

98   Administration of Justice Act 1970 s40.
99   Administration of Justice Act 1970 s40(3).

require borrowers to hand over social security benefit books, most commonly for child benefit.

It is a criminal offence to carry on a credit business or a debt collection business without a licence.[100] Where the creditor is a company, a director of the company can be convicted of the offence.[101] The maximum penalty on a Crown Court trial is two years' imprisonment and an unlimited fine. A prosecution can be taken by the Director General of Fair Trading, the local authority trading standards department, the police or the Crown Prosecution Service. In practice, initial complaints should be made to the trading standards department.

If a criminal prosecution is begun against a creditor, or a debt collector, and the proceedings are begun either by the creditor being charged or by a magistrates' court granting an arrest warrant, the court will be in a position to grant bail pending the hearing of the trial. Amongst the bail conditions that can be imposed are conditions requiring that the person concerned does not return to the client's home and continue the harassment.

The client him or herself will have several options available to obtain an injunction restraining further harassment including:

– an action for trespass if there are any private premises, eg, a garden or house into which the person has to gain entry in order to harass the client;
– assault if the client has been assaulted or threatened with assault;
– nuisance if the collector has stood outside the client's home or garden on the street shouting or pestering the client, impeding anyone trying to visit the client's home or waiting for the client to come out.

The procedure will be identical to that involved in obtaining an injunction to restrain entry to premises and/or a nuisance where the creditor is threatening to come and remove goods because of non-payment. See page 55 above.

Court bailiff expected to seize goods under a warrant of execution

Application to set aside the judgment

In the vast majority of cases, a judgment will have been obtained by the creditor against the client 'by default', ie, because the client has failed to file a defence. If the client has a defence then s/he can apply to set aside the

100   Consumer Credit Act 1974 s39.
101   Consumer Credit Act 1974 s169.

judgment. In addition, where the credit has been supplied under a regulated agreement under the Consumer Credit Act 1974, the client could have asked the court in those proceedings to make a time order rather than giving judgment for the sum claimed.[102] The client can therefore apply for the judgment to be set aside in order to have it replaced by a time order.

In case the application to set aside judgment is unsuccessful, an application to set aside should always be combined with an application to suspend or stay the judgment which will prevent the court bailiff enforcing a warrant of execution.

The procedure for applying to set aside and/or stay a judgment for debts covered by this chapter is identical to the procedure in cases of debt for water charges (see pages 107 and 115). Precedents 10 and 13 in Part III are of a notice of application to set aside or suspend judgment with an affidavit in support. Precedent 11 shows a letter to a water company asking it to confirm that it will not disconnect pending a hearing. A similar letter can be written to a creditor asking it to confirm that the bailiff will not be used to levy execution pending a hearing of an application to set aside or stay judgment.

Precdent 12 shows a letter to the court asking for judgment to be suspended pending the hearing to set aside. A similar letter should be written in the cases of consumer debts and other civil debts.

Where the client seeks a time order on an application to set aside the judgment, the notice of application to set aside should include both the information shown in precedent 10 in Part III and the information shown in the originating application seeking a time order in precedent 2.

Application to suspend or stay judgment

The grounds upon which the court can grant such an application in relation to arrears of water charges are discussed on p 107 and the position in relation to debts covered by this chapter is identical. A stay of the judgment has the effect of preventing the creditor from sending the bailiffs to collect the debt.

Safeguarding belongings and refusing entry to the bailiff

Methods of safeguarding belongings from the bailiff and the client's right to refuse entry in relation to community charge or council tax are discussed on pages 123–4. The procedure for preventing bailiffs or

102   Consumer Credit Act 1974 s129.

sheriffs operating under a county court or High Court order from removing goods, is identical. Court bailiffs do not have the right to enter by breaking into property and the client can prevent entry by keeping all the doors and windows shut and locked.

Application for an administration order

The procedure for applying for an administration order is described in chapter 2.

The effect of an administrative order is to prevent a creditor having any remedy 'against the person or property of the debtor'. The creditor will therefore be prevented from instructing the bailiff to levy execution unless it has permission from the court which made the administration order.

Application for a bankruptcy order or interim order

These remedies and their effects are also discussed in chapter 2.

Ensuring that family members have proof of ownership of any of their goods

Under the court judgment, only the debts of the defendant in the proceedings can be seized. Jointly owned goods of which the defendant is one of the owners can also be seized. If there are goods in the house which do not belong to the named defendant at all and execution is threatened, anyone else who owns goods in the house should either remove them or alternatively ensure that they have adequate paperwork available, as there is a risk that the bailiff will seize that person's belongings. Experience shows that bailiffs often make assumptions as to ownership of goods within a person's home and place the onus of proof upon the righful owner. If steps can be taken at an early stage to prove ownership, this will be advantageous.

Ensuring that exempt goods are clearly identified

Under the rules relating to execution against a client's goods by a court, certain goods are exempt (see page 46). The categories of goods that are exempt will be clear in most cases but there will always be some goods that could be considered to be on the borderline. Where there is a risk that execution will be levied, it is advisable to prepare the client to be able to argue that certain goods are exempt. If necessary, a letter should be prepared for the client to give to the bailiff explaining why certain items within the home are exempt because they are necessary for the client and/ or his family or her family. See p 62 below for the strategy that should be adotped if exempt goods are actually seized.

Court bailiffs have already levied execution and sale of the goods is imminent

Apply to set aside the judgment

The procedure is identical to that described on p 58 above. If the bailiff has already collected the goods from the person's home, the matter will be extremely urgent and an immediate *ex parte* application will need to be made to the court in person for a stay of the judgment pending a hearing. If this is not done, there is a substantial risk that a sale will take place before an application to set aside can be heard.

Apply to suspend or stay the judgment

See p 58 above.

Apply for an administration order

This is discussed on p 14 above. Unless it is possible to convince the court of the need for an expedited hearing for the purposes of making an administration order, it is unlikely that sufficient time will be available to obtain an administration order before a sale takes place.

Apply for a bankruptcy order or interim order pending a voluntary arrangement

In many courts a bankruptcy order will be immediate and an application should be made to stay execution (see chapter 2).

Delay removal of goods

Bailiffs will usually enter into a walking possession agreement with the client rather than remove the goods straight away. A 'walking possession agreement' is an agreement between the bailiff and the client whereby the client agrees to keep the goods safely at his or her home and to allow the bailiff access when he or she returns to collect the goods and in exchange the bailiff allows the client to keep the goods for the time being rather than remove them straight away. If the debt is paid before the bailiff returns, the goods are released.

If a walking possession agreement has been signed, the client cannot lawfully remove the goods. However, if there are goods which do not belong to the client but which are included within the walking possession agreement, any third party who owns those goods can remove them. Bailiffs usually assume that the person named as the debtor is the owner of all goods found in that person's home unless a third party, including the debtor's spouse, has paper evidence of his or her ownership. It is therefore common practice for the bailiffs to levy execution on goods that do not belong to the person whose goods they are supposed to be seizing.

If goods have been seized under a walking possession agreement which do not belong to the named defendant, the owner of those goods can remove them from the home so that the bailiff cannot obtain them when he or she returns.

It is important that the client is absolutely certain about ownership when carrying out this procedure, since to remove goods which *do* belong to the client against whom the execution is to be levied will amount to a criminal offence.

Take interpleader proceedings

If goods belonging to a third party have been removed which do not belong to the person named in the warrant, the owner can take interpleader proceedings. These are described in full in the County Court Rules 1981.[103] The problem with interpleader proceedings in general is that in order to take those proceedings, the person who owns the goods has either to pay the bailiff the value of the goods claimed, give the bailiff security for that value or pay to the bailiff the sum which the bailiff is allowed to charge as costs for keeping possession of the goods until the decision of the court has been made as to who owns them.[104] That money will be returnable if the applicant succeeds, but nevertheless it amounts to a substantial disincentive and will prohibit many people from using interpleader proceedings.

Inform the district judge of dispute over title

The County Courts Act 1984 provides that the district judge is not liable to pay compensation to a person whose goods are sold having been wrongly removed by the bailiff unlawfully unless it is proved that the

103   County Court Rules 1981 Ord 33.
104   County Courts Act 1984 s100.

district judge and/or bailiff had notice or might from reasonable enquiry have ascertained that the goods are not the property of the person named in the warrant of execution.[105] It follows that if the district judge and/or the bailiff is informed of a dispute over title to the goods, then the district judge and/or bailiff may become liable for damages for selling those goods. It may therefore be possible to persuade the district judge and/or the bailiff of the need to return the goods to the rightful owner without taking interpleader proceedings simply by writing to the district judge explaining the circumstances and providing some evidence of ownership. It is important that such a letter is written at the earliest possible opportunity and the district judge should have his or her attention drawn to the provisions of s98 of the County Courts Act 1984. A specimen letter is shown in precedent 6 in part III.

Apply for a declaration that goods are exempt

Although certain goods are now exempt from seizure, there is no procedure set up in the court rules for challenging the decision of the bailiff over whether particular items are exempt. It therefore appears that such an application needs to be made within the court proceedings by a notice of application to the district judge. The application should be supported by an affidavit stating quite clearly the reasons why the items stated fall within the exempt categories referred to on p 46. A specimen notice of application is shown in precedent 7 in Part III.

A garnishee order has been obtained

The process of obtaining a garnishee order was explained on p 46. In most cases, the client will first discover that a garnishee order has been made either because he or she is unable to draw money from a bank or building society account or when the court papers are served a week or so after the garnishee order *nisi* has been made.

A client who has reason to believe that a garnishee order may be made in the future can defeat that order either by transferring his or her bank or building society account into joint names or alternatively shutting down that account and transferring any funds to a different bank or building society of which the creditor is unaware.

The freezing of a client's bank or building society account by the making of a garnishee order *nisi* will cause many clients severe difficulties. It may therefore be necessary to apply for an expedited hearing of the

105   County Courts Act 1984 s98.

application for a garnishee order so that the application can be opposed at the hearing. Precedent 8 in part III is a letter amounting to an application for an expedited hearing. An alternative and more reliable method of seeking an expedited hearing is to make a personal application before the district judge on an *ex parte* basis. Whichever method is chosen, whether by letter or by personal application, an affidavit should be filed in support wherever possible explaining the reason why the client will be severely prejudiced if the hearing does not take place immediately. Precedent 3 in part III is of an affidavit in support of an application for an expedited hearing to obtain a time order.

The strategies listed below are available if a garnishee order *nisi* has already been made.

Apply to set aside and/or stay or suspend judgment

The procedure for either setting aside the judgment or suspending or staying the judgment is described on pages 107 and 115. In particular it should be noted that the client may be able to apply to set aside a judgment if the court could have made a time order. Whenever an application is made to set aside the judgment this should always be combined with an application to stay the judgment as an alternative remedy.

The effect of an order to stay the judgment is that whilst it remains stayed or suspended, a garnishee order cannot be made.[106] If a suspension or stay is made upon terms, eg, as to payment of instalments, a garnishee order cannot be made as long as those instalments are kept to.[107]

Apply for an adminstration order

Chapter 2 deals with administration orders. The effect of an administration order is to prevent a creditor having any remedy against the 'person or property of the debtor' and the creditor would therefore not be able to obtain a garnishee order.

Apply for a bankruptcy order or interim order pending a voluntary arrangement

This is dealt with in chapter 2.

---

106 County Courts Act 1984 s71.
107 See *Mercantile Credit Co Ltd v Ellis* (1987) *The Times*, 1 April.

Oppose the making of a garnishee order at the hearing

A garnishee order is a discretionary remedy.[108] There are no specific factors that the court is required to take into account. However, in practice the following are the most likely defences and/or arguments that will be available to persuade a court that a garnishee order should not be made.

Money in a joint account

If the creditor is enforcing a judgment against one of two parties who hold a joint bank or building society account, a garnishee order cannot be obtained against that account.[109] In practice the fact that an account may be in joint names may therefore amount to an absolute defence to an application for a garnishee order.

The interests of other creditors

Where the interests of other creditors may be prejudiced, it should be possible to convince the court that a garnishee order should not be made. In particular, in cases where there are multiple debts and the client has been advised to make payment by instalments to a number of different creditors, the effect of a garnishee order will often be to destroy this kind of arrangement, thereby seriously prejudicing other creditors. It is therefore a tremendous advantage to the client if a properly worked-out package has been prepared in time for the hearing where it can be clearly shown what sums will be available to the creditor claiming the garnishee order and also to other creditors and where details can be provided of the other debts that are due.

The small amount of the debt

There is no specific rule stating that a garnishee order should not be made for a small debt except where it is below £25.[110] Nevertheless, where the amount claimed is small it should be possible to argue that a garnishee order should not be made for two reasons. First it is a fairly draconian remedy which is particularly unsuited for small amounts of money. Secondly in any event if instalments are being paid, the judgment creditor will be paid off within a reasonable time.

---

108   County Court Rules 1981 Ord 30 r1.
109   *Hirschhorn v Evans* [1938] 2 KB 801.
110   County Court Rules 1981 Ord 30 r1.

Personal circumstances of the creditor and family

It is particularly important to stress any hardship that may be caused to a client and members of his or her family if a garnishee order is made. In practice, the inability to use a bank account will, for most people, potentially give rise to the inability to pay certain crucial debts, eg, the mortgage, life insurance, gas and electricity charges, community charge or council tax, which will lead to serious consequences for the client in the future. In addition, the money in a bank or building society may have been saved for a specific purpose, eg, to buy an essential item such as a child's school uniform. The consequences of a garnishee order for the client and his or her family should therefore be explained in detail.

Alternative remedies available

Another strong argument against the making of a garnishee order is that an alternative remedy is available. In practice, a client is not going to want to suggest a charging order as an alternative, so the alternatives will either be the making of an attachment of earnings order or the payment by the client of sufficiently high instalments to discharge the debt within a reasonable time.

A charging order has been obtained

The process under which a creditor obtains a charging order is explained on p 47. As with a garnishee order *nisi*, the first that the client is likely to hear of the application is when he or she is served with the charging order *nisi* saying that his or her home has been charged.

If the client is in the process of selling the home and has exchanged contracts to sell, the making of a charging order *nisi* will prevent the sale being completed if the creditor has taken steps to register the charge properly. This can have catastrophic effects for the client. Many people's homes are now worth less than their mortgages. If the amount of other outstanding charges already outweighs the value of the home, it will usually be possible to persuade the creditor to withdraw any charging order to allow sale to proceed. If there is likely to ba a value left in the home (known as an 'equity') after the discharge of all other mortgages, the creditor is unlikely to be prepared to release the charging order *nisi* unless there is some guarantee that some funds will be paid to reduce the debt when the sale is completed. It may therefore be imperative to apply for an expedited hearing of the charging order application. See p 63 above for details of the appropriate procedure for obtaining an expedited hearing.

It is imperative that a client defends an application for a charging order at the earliest available opportunity. Once a charging order has been made, a creditor may apply for an order for sale. Although many county courts are prepared to lean over backwards to avoid making an order for sale, the appeal courts have heavily restricted the circumstances in which an order for sale at the request of the creditor can be refused even when the property is jointly owned. For example, where a property is jointly owned by a husband and wife and a charging order has been obtained against the husband's share of the home and not the wife's and where the couple are divorcing, the courts have held that, save in the most exceptional circumstances, an order for sale will have to be made. The fact that the wife and children may be made homeless is not considered to be an exceptional circumstance.[111] The options for opposing an order for sale once a charging order has been made will therefore be extremely limited.

The same strategies are available to oppose an application for a charging order as are available to oppose an application for a garnishee order (see p 63).

As far as the grounds for opposing an application for a charging order are concerned, the arguments that can be used are almost identical to those in the case of a garnishee order. However, the following additional points should be made.

Personal circumstances of the debtor

In the case of a garnishee order, there are no specific factors that the court is required to take into account in deciding whether to make the order. However, in the case of a charging order the court is specifically required to take particular account of the 'personal circumstances of the debtor' before deciding whether or not to make an order.[112]

When arguing against making a charging order absolute great emphasis should therefore be placed on the effect of a charging order on the client and his or her ability to deal with other debts.

Prejudice to other creditors

The courts are also required to take account of any prejudice that other creditors may face.[113]

Small debt

In the case of charging orders, the courts have specifically stated that it would not be a proper exercise of their discretion to make a charging order

---

111   *Lloyds Bank Plc v Byrne* (1991) 23 HLR 472.
112   Charging Orders Act 1979 s1(5).
113   Charging Orders Act 1979 s1(5).

where the debt is very small but the asset to be charged is of a substantial value.[114]

Property jointly owned

Care must be taken when a property is jointly owned. As explained above, as a result of a 1991 court decision, once a charging order has been made the court has virtually no discretion to refuse an order for sale even if this means making a spouse who jointly owns the property homeless together with his or her children.

In the past, district judges have made charging orders absolute on the basis that the court has a wide discretion to refuse an order for sale. In the light of the Court of Appeal decision this is no longer the case and when arguing against making a charging order absolute the district judge must be made aware that if the order is made absolute and the creditor decides to apply for an order for sale, the chances of such an order being refused are slim.

Where a charging order application is made in respect of a home which is jointly owned and only one of the joint owners is liable under the court judgment, the district judge may direct that the proceedings are served on the other joint owners.[115] In any event, the joint owner should be named in the creditor's affidavit filed in support of the charging order application and the joint owner is entitled to make representations to the court as to why a charging order should not be made. Wherever property is jointly owned, a joint owner who is not the debtor should attend court and make representations on a personal basis in all possible cases. The court is far more likely to be persuaded by arguments based on the hardship of someone who does not owe the debt at all than by arguments put forward on behalf of the debtor personally.

Time order

It is particularly important to consider an application to set aside judgment and seek a time order when a creditor under a regulated agreement is seeking a charging order (see p 66).

Power to make charging orders subject to conditions

Even if it is not possible to persuade the district judge to refuse to make a charging order absolute, it can be argued that any charging order should be made subject to conditions which as far as possible protect innocent parties. For example, the courts have been prepared to make charging orders on similar bases to the kinds of orders made in ancillary relief

114 *Robinson v Bailer* [1942] Ch 268.
115 County Court Rules 1981 Ord 31 r1(6).

proceedings connected with divorce such as an order that the sale cannot be enforced until the youngest child of the family is 18.[116] The court has express power to make the charging order 'subject to conditions as to notifying the debtor or as to the time when the charge is to become enforceable, or as to other matters'.[117]

116   See, for example, *Austin-Fell v Austin-Fell* [1990] Fam 172.
117   Charging Orders Act 1979 s3(1).

CHAPTER 4

Fuel debts

Introduction

Typical problems requiring emergency action include:
-   where the fuel supplier threatens disconnection for arrears, for failure to pay a deposit or for tampering;
-   where the fuel supplier refuses to connect or has already disconnected and refuses to reconnect.

Liability to pay

Since fuel is provided under statutory provisions, one would expect the statutes to make clear in what circumstances a person will be responsible for fuel charges; in fact, the law is far from clear. Different views are expressed by consumer advisors, the suppliers, OFFER and OFGAS. Since there is no case law, it is not possible to be certain which interpretation is correct.

In practice, electricity and gas suppliers use the threat of disconnection as their main weapon to collect charges. Since they need no court order to disconnect, they can use their interpretation of the law to justify disconnecting a client's supply without the need to subject their interpretation to scrutiny by the courts. The consumer threatened with disconnection is then faced with paying a bill of perhaps a few hundred pounds under protest or engaging in full-scale litigation against a company with limitless resources. Unsurprisingly, in most cases people pay and the law remains unclear!

Electricity

Before the Electricity Act 1989, the electricity suppliers relied on the 1984 unreported county court case *Jackman v Yorkshire Electricity Board*[1] as authority for saying that any person who was the occupier of the house to which electricity was supplied and who benefitted from the electricity that was supplied was equally liable for the debt, whether or not s/he initially requested the supply and whether or not s/he was named on the bill. Thus where the person named in the bill had failed to pay or left (eg, on relationship breakdown), that person's partner and any other members of the household could be held equally responsible.

The Electricity Act 1989 entitles any owner or occupier of premises to require a supply of electricity, eg, where premises are being used for the first time or have been disconnected and reconnection is sought.[2] The Act also allows an owner or occupier to require the continuation of a supply eg, where a person moves into a home which is already connected.[3] In practice both requests are often made by signing an agreement to be responsible for the charges. Sometimes, someone moving into a home and taking over an existing supply only needs to make a telephone request for the supply to be continued.

Under the Electricity Act 1989, the 'tariff customer' is responsible for the payment of fuel charges.[4] The electricity company can disconnect the supply if the 'tariff customer' fails to pay the bill.[5] A tariff customer is defined as 'a person who *requires* a supply of electricity . . . and is supplied by the public electricity supplier . . .'[6] The Electricity Act 1989 provides that if the tariff customer does not give at least two working days advance warning that he or she is leaving the premises supplied, then his or her liability for charges for the supply of electricity still continues even after he or she has left until the first of the following dates:
– the second working day after the tariff customer has given notice to the supplier that he or she has left;
– the next day on which the meter would normally be read;
– the day on which a subsequent occupier requests a supply to those premises.[7]

Liability for electricity charges: the author's view
Although the law remains uncertain, the legal liability of those living in

1   August 1986 *Legal Action* 107; see also article in March 1993 *Legal Action* 19.
2   Electricity Act 1989 s16(1).
3   Ibid, s16(1) and (5)(b).
4   Ibid, Sch 6 para 1.
5   Ibid, Sch 6 para 1(6).
6   Ibid, s22(4).
7   Ibid, Sch 6 para 3.

the dwelling, based on the legislation, would appear to be as set out below.

a) *A client who has requested a supply*

The client is liable as long as he or she remains living in the dwelling. If he or she leaves his or her liability ceases on the day of departure if two days' advance notice has been given. Otherwise, his or her liability continues until two days notice is subsequently given, the meter should have been read or someone else requests a supply.

b) *A client who has not requested a supply*

(i) *Where some other person has requested a supply*

If someone has requested a supply and that person is still liable for charges, he or she remains the 'tariff customer' and responsible for the bill under the Electricity Act 1989. There is no legal principle under which any other person should be held responsible.

(ii) *Where no-one has actually requested a supply*

In this situation neither the Electricity Act 1989 nor the general law makes clear who is liable for charges. Since liability cannot be determined by the statutory provisions, it must be determined on the basis of the general law. The principle usually adopted is that of 'unjust enrichment'. This will mean that the client may be required to pay for the fuel that he or she has used. The fact that a client is named on the bill is not conclusive; it is merely an indication whom the supplier considers should pay. In practice, liability can be expected to be based upon the degree of interest the client has in the dwelling. If he or she is a joint occupier of the whole dwelling supplied, he or she may be jointly liable for all the fuel consumed, eg a couple with children living in a house. If he or she occupies part only of the dwelling supplied, he or she may only be liable for the amount of fuel consumed by him or her, eg a multi-occupied house with separate bedsits but one bill.

The legal position is therefore far from clear. In addition, according to the facts, a client may be liable for part of a bill and not for the remainder.

Example

A married couple lived in a house and the husband requested a supply when they moved in. The bills were in his name. The couple split up and he left. When he left, there were outstanding bills, he did not give notice and his wife did not request a supply. Under the statute he remains liable until the date the next meter reading should take place. Up until then he remains the tariff customer and his wife should not be liable for the charges. Once his liability ends, his wife will probably assume legal responsibility on the basis that if she did not do so she would be unjustly enriched.

Liability for electricity charges: the view of OFFER

OFFER has not formally published any position statement which clearly sets out its view on legal liability despite the fact that it acknowledged that it is a common cause of problems among the 14,000 customers seeking its help during 1991/2. However, in a letter to *Adviser* magazine (No. 29, January/February 1992) the Director of Consumer Affairs at OFFER, Tony Boorman, said:

> . . . the law is in fact by no means clear cut . . . generally where people have equal status as occupants (for example husband and wife) then any one or more of those occupants can be held liable for electricity used during their occupancy, regardless of who is named on the account . . .

He did not explain the legal basis for this view. The note of uncertainty in his view is significant.

Liability for electricity charges: the view of the electricity suppliers

The electricity suppliers essentially operate on the basis that all occupiers are equally responsible for the cost of fuel supplied whilst they are in occupation. They use their interpretation of the law to justify disconnecting a supply if there are arrears and if any person who was the occupier at the time the fuel was supplied is still living in the premises.

Gas

Before the Gas Act 1986, the gas boards also operated on the basis that all occupiers were liable for gas supplied to premises whilst they were in occupation. There was no authority — not even a county court decision — to support that view.

The Gas Act 1986 entitles any owner or occupier of premises to require a supply of gas, eg, where premises are being used for the first time or have been disconnected and reconnection is sought.[8] The Act also allows an owner or occupier to require the continuation of a supply, eg, where a person moves into a home which is already connected. In practice British Gas rarely requires a written application, relying upon telephone requests or letters.

Under the Gas Act 1986, the 'tariff customer' is responsible for the

8   Gas Act 1986 s10(1).

payment of fuel charges.[9] British Gas can disconnect the supply if the 'tariff customer' fails to pay the bill within 28 days of a demand in writing.[10] 'Tariff customer' is defined in the Gas Act 1986 as meaning 'a person who is supplied with gas by a public gas supplier.'[11] Whereas liability for electricity is limited to the person who has actually required the supply, there is no provision expressly stating that a tariff customer must have required a supply under the Gas Act.

The Act provides that if the tariff customer does not give at least 24 hours' advance warning that he or she is leaving the premises supplied, then his or her liability for charges for the supply of gas still continues even after he or she has left until the first of the following dates:
- 28 days after the tariff customer has given written notice to the supplier that he or she has left;
- the next day on which the meter would normally be read;
- the day on which a subsequent occupier requests a supply to those premises.[12]

Liability for gas charges: the author's view
The law on liability for charges for gas supply is even more uncertain than that for electricity. Nevertheless, based on the legislation, the legal liability of those living in the dwelling would appear to be as set out below.
a) *A client who has requested a supply*
   The client is liable as long as he or she remains living in the dwelling. If he or she leaves, his or her liability ceases on the day of departure if 24 hours' advance notice has been given. Otherwise, his or her liability continues until 28 days' subsequent notice has expired, the meter should have been read or someone else requests a supply, whichever is the earliest.
b) *A client who has not requested a supply*
   (i) *Where some other person has requested a supply*
        If someone has requested a supply and that person is still liable for charges, he or she remains the 'tariff customer' and responsible for the bill under the Gas Act 1986. The client can only be held liable if he or she can also be considered within the definition of a tariff customer because he or she 'is supplied with gas by a public gas supplier'. There are two bases upon which it is possible to argue that the client is not liable. The first argument is that as a matter

9   Ibid, Sch 5 para 7.
10 Ibid, Sch 5 para 7(5).
11 Ibid, s14(5).
12 Ibid, Sch 5 para 7(2).

of fact the person who requested the supply is the only person being supplied by British Gas. The gas belongs to that person only and she or he can choose to use it all or share it with others living in the premises. British Gas are not supplying gas to the client as he or she has no need of it, being able to share the gas provided to the person who originally requested it. Just as, for example, the husband of a tenant may be his wife's licensee and be allowed by his wife to use and occupy and obtain the benefit of the home though not liable for rent, so the husband of a person who has requested and is receiving a gas supply can be allowed by his wife to use her gas and obtain the benefit of the gas supplied to her, even though he is not supplied directly with gas by British Gas. The second argument is that on looking at the overall scheme of the Gas Act 1986, it is apparent that what is meant by the words 'tariff customer' is not just a person supplied with gas, but someone supplied with gas *after he or she has required a supply.* In other words, although the words 'who has required a supply' are missing from the statutory definition, they should be implied. If the legislation had meant an 'occupier' to be liable for gas supplied to premises (and note that liability for the old general rates and water rates falls on the occupier), then this would have been specifically stated.

If these arguments are valid, the position for gas charges is the same as that for electricity, and only the person who requested the supply can be held liable.[13] If these arguments are not valid, anyone who occupies the premises supplied could be liable.

(ii)   *Where no-one has requested a supply*
The position here will be identical to that for electricity (see p 71 above).

Liability for gas charges: the view of OFGAS

The Director General of Gas Supply has issued a position paper which deals, amongst other things, with liability for payment of charges for the supply of gas,[14] in which OFGAS's position is stated as follows:

> There are many cases where two or more persons are together legally entitled to occupy premises and, in such cases, *it may be* (emphasis added) that each of them can properly be regarded as being supplied with gas. It is thought that

13   See May/June 1992 *Adviser* 35 for two examples of county court decisions where these arguments have been accepted.
14   OFGAS Position Paper about matters arising from British Gas Plc's duty under s 10(1) of the Gas Act 1986 to continue to give a gas supply to tariff customers. Available from OFGAS, Southside, 105 Victoria Street, London SW1E 6QS.

the proper criterion is the nature of the control exercised by any persons over the activities at the premises and, in particular, the use of the gas supplied to them. This could, for example, justify regarding each of two spouses or a number of sharing students as persons to whom gas is supplied but not regarding young adults resident in premises with their parents as such persons.

OFGAS therefore essentially consider that anyone who can be considered to be occupying premises may be liable for gas charges. It is important to note the uncertainty in that view.

Liability for gas charges: the view of British Gas
OFGAS accept that the law is uncertain, stating that 'it may be' that two or more persons who are the occupiers can be regarded as being supplied with gas, even though only one is named in the bill. British Gas is categoric that anyone occupying the premises is liable for the charges regardless of whether they are named in the bill and will threaten to disconnect, and indeed will disconnect, the supply to a person who is left in the home after the person named in the bill has left, if he or she refuses or fails to pay the bill.

Threatened disconnection for arrears

In practice, both gas and electricity companies recover arrears by threatening and/or carrying out disconnection. Only if forced to do so, will they take county court proceedings to recover outstanding charges.

Arguments on liability[15]
No power to disconnect for the charges due
The power to disconnect electricity only relates to charges in respect of the supply of power to any premises or the hiring charges for any meter. Meters may be provided by way of sale, hire or loan though, in practice, hiring of the meter to domestic premises is extremely rare so that it is only likely to be the charges for the supply of electricity that will give rise to the power to disconnect.[16] Charges for the supply of electricity only become overdue 20 working days after the making by the supplier of a demand in writing for payment of the charges, and the electricity company must give two working days' notice of an intention to disconnect.[17]

Disconnection for failing to pay charges to a gas supplier can only be made in respect of charges for the supply of gas and can only take place

15 See also above p 69.
16 Electricity Act 1989 Sch 6 para 1(6) and Sch 7 para 1(2).
17 Electricity Act 1989 Sch 6 para 1(6) and (7).

after the expiry of 28 days from the making of a demand in writing for payment and seven days' notice of intention to disconnect must be given.[18]

Since the power to disconnect applies only to charges for the supply of gas or electricity, there is no power to disconnect for charges relating to hire-purchase.

Estimated bills

Some gas and electricity bills are based on estimates of consumption usually calculated by the supplier's computer using consumption over the previous year or so. Sometimes these estimates are based on occupation by a previous householder and bear no relation to the real consumption. If the bill is high because it has been estimated, the client can read the meter and notify the supplier of the correct amount or ask the supplier to read the meter. Payment should be made of the amount that is not disputed to avoid the power to disconnect arising.

Faulty meter

If the consumer suspects that the meter is faulty (eg, because bills are much higher than seems reasonable) s/he can require that the meter is tested by a meter examiner appointed by the Secretary of State.[19]

When required to do so either by the supplier or by the consumer, a meter examiner must inspect a meter that has been used to supply electricity. The examiner must ascertain whether the meter is in proper order and whether it has been registering correctly at any time when there has been a dispute about the amount of electricity consumed. A written report must be made of the conclusions.[20] If the meter examiner decides that a meter was operating outside the prescribed margins of error then s/he must, if possible, give an opinion as to any period for which the meter may have been operating outside those margins and the degree of accuracy within which it was operating.[21]

Unless the meter is proved to be defective, the meter is presumed to have been registering correctly.[22] Essentially, therefore, there is no way of challenging the register on the meter on the basis that it is faulty except by getting the meter examined by a meter examiner. If that is not done, the reading on the meter is conclusively presumed to be correct.[23] On the other hand, if the meter examiner reports that the meter is faulty and provides

18   Gas Act 1986 Sch 5 para 7(5).
19   Electricity Act 1989 Sch 7 para 7 and Gas Act 1986 s17(2).
20   Electricity Act 1989 Sch 7 para 7(1).
21   Electricity Act 1989 Sch 7 para 7(2).
22   Electricity Act 1989 Sch 7 para 9(3).
23   Electricity Act 1989 Sch 7 para 9(4).

an opinion on the degree of accuracy of the meter, that opinion is presumed to be correct unless the contrary can be proved.[24]

There is a danger that a defective meter may be removed and destroyed before it has been tested. However, where there is a genuine dispute about the accuracy of a meter and notice of the dispute has been given to the electricity supplier by the customer or any other person interested, then the meter cannot be removed or altered except with the approval of a meter examiner until after the dispute is resolved by agreement or the meter is examined and tested, whichever occurs first.[25] This is an important provision enabling an adviser to ensure that evidence is preserved but action must be taken to give notice of the dispute to the electricity supplier, if necessary by telephone and/or fax.

Although there is power to charge for a meter test, in practice no fee is required for an initial test of a meter, though the meter examiner has power to require a fee to be paid if it turns out that the test was unnecessary.

A meter examiner must inspect a gas meter if required to do so by any person on payment of the prescribed fee.[26] The fee for inspection of a gas meter is £26.64, which is refundable if the meter proves to be defective.

The register on a gas meter is *prima facie* evidence of the quantity of gas supplied.[27] Where the meter is inspected and found by a meter examiner to be incorrectly registering to an extent specified by the meter examiner, the meter is deemed to have registered incorrectly to that degree since the occasion when the meter was last read unless it is proved to have begun to register wrongly on some later date.[28] This means that it is only possible to argue that a meter has been incorrect since the last meter reading. Where there is any question that a meter is incorrect, serious consideration should be given to having it tested as soon as possible.

There is no provision that a gas supplier is prevented from removing a meter without the permission of a meter examiner if there is a dispute about the amount of money owed for gas. As for electricity, the meter examiner can award the costs of the examination. If the meter is found to be defective but the meter examiner is unable to estimate the extent to which it is inaccurate, there will be no alternative but for the bill to be assessed. See below for challenging such an assessment.

24   Electricity Act 1989 Sch 7 para 9(5).
25   Electricity Act 1989 Sch 7 para 8.
26   Gas Act 1986 s17(2).
27   Gas Act 1986 Sch 5 para 5.
28   Gas Act 1986 Sch 5 para 5(2) and (3).

Bill has been assessed

If the meter has not been registering correctly, the supplier will usually remove the meter and send a bill based on its assessment of likely consumption. This will also occur if the supplier believes that the meter has been tampered with or bypassed. The suppliers usually use information about average bills for certain family compositions, house sizes, installations etc which may or may not be appropriate for a particular client. The consumer does not have to accept the assessment without question. If a consumer admits to tampering with or bypassing the meter, he or she should consider very carefully whether it is to his or her advantage to challenge the assessment. There is always the risk of a prosecution for bypassing or tampering. The supplier may exercise its discretion not to pursue a prosecution if the client pays an assessed bill without question.

If an electricity meter has been tampered with, the meter reading is conclusive unless the meter has been referred to an independent meter examiner who has found the meter to be faulty. If the meter examiner has concluded the extent to which the meter was faulty that will be the binding assessment unless the contrary is proved. If a meter examiner has said that it is impossible to ascertain the degree to which it has been faulty, then an assessment will have to be carried out.

The meter reading is only conclusive as to the 'quantity of electricity supplied through it'. If the meter has been bypassed then clearly the electricity has not been passed through it. This then gives the supplier the opportunity to estimate the amount of supply by way of assessment.

If a consumer does not accept an assessed bill, then to avoid disconnection he or she should at least pay the sum accepted by him or her as the amount of fuel consumed based on his or her own assessment. This sum is not in dispute so that the supplier has the power to disconnect for failure to pay this amount.

Professional advice may be required to make an assessment of the quantity of electricity or gas consumed. A heating or electrical engineer is usually the best expert to use and the cost can be met under a legal aid green form if the client is financially eligible. It is possible to make rough and ready calculations by assessing the number of appliances in use, the hours which they are used and the amount of electricity or gas they consume and this should give some general indication of the likely scale of the bill.

Apart from the amount of electricity or gas being consumed, the consumer can also still dispute the length of time for which a meter has not been properly recording though, as explained above, it is not possible to argue that a gas meter has been recording incorrectly prior to the date of the last meter reading. A sudden change in the size of bills may be an indication of a faulty meter. A consumer should state when he or she believes the defects began and offer to pay an amount based on the meter reading up to and until this time and on the basis of an assessment afterwards. The remainder of the bill should be disputed.

If the consumer does not accept the amount assessed by the supplier, a request should be made for a written breakdown of the assessment. The supplier may have inaccurate information about the types of appliances, the family composition and its consumption or may claim that the meter has been faulty, tampered with or bypassed of years. In these circumstances an accurate assessment of the fuel consumption is needed and this requires clear information from the consumer and professional advice from an expert on the likely amount of consumption.

Consumer is not liable for the bill

If the consumer is the person named in the bill having requested a supply, there will be no argument about liability. However, if the person from whom payment is sought has never specifically requested the supply, the points made at pages 69 to 75 should be considered to establish whether or not there is a good argument on liability. As explained above, there is some uncertainty about whether liability extends to other joint 'occupiers'.

It is certainly the case that the present occupier cannot be ordered to pay or required to pay the arrears of gas charges of a previous occupier unless s/he was a joint occupier at the time the gas charges were incurred. Where the client has been a joint occupier for only some of the time over which the arrears are claimed, the supplier certainly cannot claim for charges arising before the date when the client moved in.

Slot meter theft

The general rule is that once money has been put into a slot meter, the money belongs to the supplier and in those circumstances if the money is stolen, it is the supplier who bears the loss.[29] This is because electricity and gas are supplied under a statutory duty. The fact that the consumer may have signed a document agreeing to certain conditions of supply does not alter this position. No contract is created whether or not the agreement that the consumer signs is described as a contract or has terms and conditions. This is because consideration is required to form a valid contract and the supplier gives no consideration by providing a supply which it is under a statutory duty to provide.[30]

29   *Martin v Marsh* [1955] Crim LR 781.
30   *Willmore and Willmore v South Eeastern Electicity Board* [1957] 2 Lloyds Rep 375.

However, the courts have held that it is possible for energy to be supplied under a special agreement with a consumer made to avoid disconnection. In exchange for the supplier postponing disconnection, the consumer can be asked to agree to certain conditions upon which supply will be continued. These can include conditions making the consumer liable for the contents of any slot meter.[31] In practice, many consumers will only have electricity or gas meters using coins because they have previously been in arrears and in those circumstances it will have been legitimate for the board to impose conditions that the consumer take responsibility for the contents if they are stolen. If, on the other hand, a consumer moves into premises where there is already a slot meter and continues to use it, he or she cannot be made responsible for the contents.

Preventing disconnection

No disconnection can take place for sums due to an electricity or gas supplier when the amount is 'genuinely in dispute'.[32]

Some of the strategies suggested below are only available where arrears are disputed. Where the client disputes part of the arrears and admits the remainder, these strategies can only be used for the part of the arrears disputed. The power to disconnect for any undisputed part of arrears will remain and may be exercised by the supplier unless the undisputed part of the arrears are paid.

Reaching agreement by negotiation

Whenever disconnection is threatened, attempts should be made to reach an agreement with the supplier by negotiation. The supplier may be prepared to accept instalments or to accept a down payment towards the arrears followed by instalments.

In addition, two methods exist which will guarantee the supplier a regular contribution towards the arrears as well as the cost of the current supply. These are the installation of a prepayment meter and direct deductions from benefits.

There are a number of kinds of prepayment meter:

- Slot meters where the consumer puts in cash.
- Token meters where the consumer buys plastic tokens from a showroom or from vending machines. The token is inserted into the

---

31   *R v Midlands Electricity Board, ex parte Bushby* (1987) *Guardian*, 29 October 1987, *The Times*, 28 October 1987.
32   Electricity Act 1989 Sch 6 para 1(9) and Gas Act 1986 Sch 5 para 7(5A) added by Competition and Services (Utilities) (CSU) Act 1992 s19.

meter and is cancelled but credits the meter with a certain amount of consumption.

- Credit key meters which operate in the same way as token meters but the consumer has a key which can be recharged in a showroom or vending machine.
- Card meters which are similar to token meters but operate by stiff cards.

Condition 19 of the licences for all public electricity suppliers requires them to have approved by the Director General of Electricity Supply methods for dealing with tariff customers who, through misfortune or inability to cope with electricity supplied for domestic use on credit terms, incur obligations to pay for electricity which they find difficulty in discharging and in particular to include methods for:

a) providing for such a tariff customer who has failed to comply with such arrangements a prepayment meter where safe and practicable to do so; and

b) calibrating any prepayment meter so provided so as to take into account the tariff customer's ability to pay any of the charges due from the customer under such arrangements in addition to the other charges lawfully being recovered through the prepayment meter.[33]

Each electricity supplier should therefore have a policy requiring it to provide prepayment meters wherever possible for customers who are unable to pay and those meters should be calibrated taking into account the customer's ability to pay back any arrears. The condition also requires that the board has methods for distinguishing between tariff customers who are unable to pay and those who are unwilling to pay.

The authorisation given to British Gas also requires that it must have methods for dealing with tariff customers who cannot afford to pay for gas supplied and for providing such customers with a prepayment meter where safe and practical to do so.[34]

There is nothing specific in the licence conditions or authorisation which deals with breaches of policy by the suppliers, eg, refusing to supply a prepayment meter, and nothing specific that authorises the Director General of Gas or Electricity Supply to intervene. Nevertheless, where a policy is being breached all available methods should be used to complain both through the supplier's internal hierarchy, by reference to the Director General of Electricity or Gas Supply, through the local Gas or Electricity Consumers Council or a MP.

---

33   *Successor Company Licences in England and Wales* vol. 1 Public Electricity Supply Licence, HMSO, condition 19.

34   Modification of the Conditions of British Gas plc's Authorisation, condition 12A.

Both electricity and gas suppliers are now required to have a complaints procedure approved by the relevant Director General and to supply a copy of the procedure by post to anyone who requests it.[35]

The Benefits Agency has power to make direct deductions from income support for payment of fuel debts. This includes a power to make deductions where income support is payable with other benefits, eg, as a top-up to unemployment benefit, invalidity benefit etc.[36]

The Benefits Agency can make the deduction 'if in its opinion it would be in the interests of the family to do so'.[37] The maximum amount of the deduction for each fuel debt is £2.20 per week towards the arrears. If there is more than one fuel debt, the total amount that can be deducted in respect of all the debts is £4.40 per week. In addition to making a deduction for arrears of fuel consumption, the Benefits Agency can also deduct an amount for current consumption 'equal to the estimated average weekly costs necessary to meet the continuing needs for that fuel item'.[38] The amount for current consumption can be varied if it proves to be insufficient or too much.[39] Where the original debt is discharged, the Benefits Agency can continue paying for current consumption.

It will sometimes be the case that the amount the Benefits Agency wants to deduct for current consumption is substantial. It can often cause hardship because the claimant is receiving a substantially reduced amount. Where it is considered that the estimate of current consumption is too high, an appeal can be lodged with the social security appeals tribunal. Alternatively a request for a review can be made. No deduction should be made for current consumption if there is already a prepayment meter fixed.

The joint statement of intent on direct payment for fuel subscribed to by British Gas and the electricity suppliers states that the supplier will on request from the Benefits Agency supply details of how it arrives at its estimate for the future fuel consumption.

The joint statement makes clear that the whole purpose of the statement of intent is to ensure that where direct deductions are available as a method of paying off a debt, the fuel suppliers will accept a direct deduction rather than disconnect.

Where the supplier indicates that it will not accept a direct deduction,

---

35   Gas Act 1986 s33E as inserted by Competition and Service (Utilities) (CSU) Act 1992 s14; Electricity Act 1989 s42B as inserted by CSU Act 1992 s22.
36   Social Security (Claims and Payments) Regulations 1987 SI No. 1968 Sch 9 para 6.
37   Social Security (Claims and Payments) Regulations 1987 SI No. 1968 Sch 9 para 6(1).
38   Social Security (Claims and Payments) Regulations 1987 SI No. 1968 Sch 9 para 6(2)(b).
39   Social Security (Claims and Payments) Regulations 1987 Sch 9 para 4(a).

a complaint should be made through the supplier's internal hierarchy, using its complaints procedures, through the Gas or Electricity Consumers Councils, to the Director General of Gas or Electricity Supply and/or to MPs.

Paying off an undisputed debt

Where a debt is undisputed, the client may have little or no alternative but to pay off the debt in full if it is not possible to arrange a direct deduction from benefits or to install a prepayment meter. There are a number of ways in which the client may obtain assistance to pay the bill.

First, under the Children Act 1989, a 'child in need' is defined to include a child whose health or development is likely to be significantly impaired or further impaired unless services are provided to him or her under the Act.[40] Assistance under the Act can include, in exceptional circumstances, assistance in cash.[41] There will be many cases where disconnection of fuel is likely to lead to the health of a child being impaired and it will therefore be open to the Social Services Department to interpret the Children Act 1989 as giving them power to assist with the payment of the fuel arrears.

Secondly, a crisis loan under the Social Fund may be available to assist with the payment of a fuel debt if this is the only means by which serious damage or serious risk to health or safety of the client or a member of the family can be prevented.[42] An application should be made to the local office of the Benefits Agency. For further details see the *National Welfare Benefits Handbook*, 23rd ed., Child Poverty Action Group.

Thirdly, if the landlord has failed to pay the bill, a tenant or licensee can request a local authority (London or metropolitan borough council or district council) to make arrangements with the fuel supplier for the continuation of the supply if disconnection is threatened. The important requirement is that it was the owner or former owner who failed to pay the charges and not the occupier.[43]

Pay disputed charges and seek to recover them

If all or part of the charges claimed are disputed, and if the client has the financial means, s/he can pay the debt which is disputed but then seek recovery of the sum that has been paid through the county court by way of proceedings for restitution.

The process of claiming restitution is an old-established remedy but

40   Children Act 1989 s17(10).
41   Children Act 1989 s17(6).
42   Social Fund Directions, direction 3(a).
43   Local Government (Miscellaneous Provisions) Act 1976 s33.

the parameters are by no means certain because it is not often used. It is also called 'unjust enrichment' and 'quasi-contract'.

Generally, where a person makes a voluntary payment to someone after he or she has been asked to pay, then that payment is taken to have been voluntary and cannot be reclaimed. However, that rule is changed where the payment is made under duress or some form of compulsion other than legal compulsion. In that case the sum paid is recoverable as money 'had and received'.[44] No cases have been reported where money paid under threat of disconnection has been recovered in this way but money has been recovered where it has been paid in order to recover goods that have wrongly been detained.[45] In *Woolwich Equitable Building Society v Inland Revenue Commissioners* in the House of Lords it was suggested that the law of restitution could now go further:

> The nature of the demand for tax or similar impost on the citizen by the state with the perceived economic and social consequences of non-payment stemming from the inequality of the parties' respective position and the unjust enrichment falling on the state where the citizen paid the demand to avoid these consequences, warrant a reformulation of the law of restitution so as to recognise a *prima facie* right of recovery based solely on the payment of money pursuant to an *ultra vires* demand by a public authority.

In practice, the absence of effective and easily used remedies against electricity or gas suppliers to prevent disconnection and their quasi-public nature should justify the ability to reclaim the sums paid by way of restitution. Action will be in the county court and can be commenced in the court covering the district in which the action arose, ie, the court covering the district in which the sum was paid to the supplier.[46] In many cases, the action will be a small claim and may be dealt with by arbitration, though it is possible that the action will be referred for a full hearing on the grounds that 'a difficult question of law' is involved.[47] If the matter is referred to a full hearing, legal aid may be available, although there may be some difficulty in obtaining it given the small amount of money involved.

A suggested model letter to be written to an electricity or gas supplier when payment is to be made under protest which reserves the possibility of reclaiming the sum at a later date is shown in precedent 9 in Part III. Precedent 21 in Part III is of particulars of claim seeking the recovery of

---

44   See generally *Halsbury's Laws of England* vol 9, 3rd ed., paras 660–4.
45   *Halsbury's Laws of England* vol 9, 3rd ed., para 663 and *Woolwich Equitable Building Society v Inland Revenue Commissioners* [1992] 3 WLR 366, HL.
46   County Court Rules 1981 Ord 4 r2.
47   County Court Rules 1981 Ord 19 r2(4)(a).

money paid under duress which can be adapted for recovery of fuel charges.

Refer the dispute to arbitration

The Competition and Service (Utilities) Act 1992 contains provisions allowing regulations to be made for an arbitration scheme to deal with disputes with tariff customers about charges for gas and electricity supply.[48] At the time of writing the provisions are not in force and no regulations have been made. The regulations can provide for decisions of the arbitrator to be final and enforceable as if they were county court judgments and prevent court action to resolve the dispute when one party has requested arbitration.[49]

Even when the provisions are in force it is unlikely they will deal with the situation where a client denies liability on the ground that s/he is not a tariff customer, eg, where there is joint occupation and one occupier has left or where payment is being sought by the supplier under the principle of unjust enrichment (see pp 83–4). The provisions are more suited to dealing with disputes over the amounts of assessed bills.

There is an alternative arbitration mechanism which arguably should cover all disputes over liability but where the provisions are already in force. Both the Gas Act 1986 and the Electricity Act 1989 allow the relevant Director General to determine a dispute or appoint an arbitrator to do so where the dispute concerns the supplier's duty to give and continue to give a supply of gas or electricity to a person who has required one.[50] Since the duty to continue the supply exists until a valid power arises to disconnect for arrears which are genuinely due, the Director General must have power to determine whether any such arrears are due and thus whether the client is legally liable for them.[51] If he does not determine this issue, he cannot determine a dispute about giving or continuing to give a supply.

The Director General can decide what the practice and procedure should be to decide the dispute and can give directions as to the circumstances in which and the terms on which the supplier must give or continue to give a supply pending the determination of the dispute.[52] The decision of the arbitrator or the Director General is final and can include a

---

48   CSU Act 1992 ss16 and 23.
49   CSU Act 1992 ss17 and 23.
50   Gas Act 1986 s14A as inserted by CSU Act 1992 s16 and Electricity Act 1989 s23(1).
51   Gas Act 1986 ss10(1), 15 and Sch 5 para 7(5); Electricity Act 1989 s16(1) and (5)(a), s24 and Sch 6 para 1(6).
52   Electricity Act 1989 23(2) as amended by CSU Act 1992 s25 and Gas Act 1986 s14A(3) and (4) inserted by CSU Act 1992 s16.

requirement requiring either party to pay a sum in respect of the costs and expenses incurred by the arbitrator (but not the other party). However, when deciding whether to make an award of costs and expenses, the arbitrator must have regard 'to the conduct and means of the parties and any other relevant circumstances'.[53]

The procedure might provide an effective mechanism for resolving a dispute between a supplier and a consumer. No legal aid will be available for any kind of hearing before the arbitrator, but green form assistance should be available for preparation of written representations. It is difficult to predict the kind of costs that an arbitrator might award but the Act clearly intends that these should be based on the conduct of the person making the complaint. Bearing in mind the possible risk as to costs, if the client has finances available it may be more sensible for the client to pay the bill which is disputed and then seek to recover the amount in the small claims court where there is no risk as to costs.

The effect of the order being final is that as far as the facts are concerned, they cannot be disputed by taking the matter to court. However, it does not prevent an appeal being lodged with the Court of Appeal against the decision of the arbitrator on the basis that the law has been wrongly applied.

Applications should be made by letter to the Director General of Electricity Supply or of Gas Supply. It should set out clearly the factual position as seen by the consumer as well as the legal position where relevant. It is recommended that the letter should also state what directions the Director is being asked to give to the supplier regarding continuity of supply pending the determination of the dispute.

Request an enforcement order from the Director General of Gas or Electricity Supply

This mechanism is available both for gas and electricity where a debt is disputed.

Both the Director General of Gas Supply and the Director General of Electricity Supply have a duty to investigate any matter which appears to them to be 'an enforcement matter' if it is the subject of a representation made to the Director by or on behalf of a person appearing to have an interest in the matter.[54] This means that the Directors have no choice but to act when a client or an adviser writes complaining that the gas or electricity supplier has or is about to disconnect the supply when it has no legal power to do so.

53   Electricity Act 1989 s23(5) and (6) and Gas Act 1986 s14A(7) and (8) inserted by CSU Act 1992 s16.
54   Electricity Act 1989 s45 and Gas Act 1986 s31.

Both Directors can require the supplier to produce any documents or provide any information requested and the power to require production of documents applies both to the supplier and to the consumer or indeed to an advice agency, though it does not apply to documents that would be privileged in court proceedings.[55]

The power of the Director General of Electricity Supply to make an order applies if the Director General is satisfied that a supplier 'is contravening, or is likely to contravene any relevant condition or requirement'.[56] The power of the Director General of Gas Supply to make an order applies if the Director General is satisfied that a supplier is likely to contravene any relevant condition or requirement.[57]

The Director Generals clearly have power to prevent disconnection before it has occurred. Whenever disconnection is threatened, a provisional order should always be asked for (see below). A breach of the duty to supply is one of the relevant requirements; the breach gives rise to the Director Generals' powers.[58]

Both Directors can make either a final or a provisional order. These are orders requiring the supplier either to do or not to do specific things stated in the order or of a description specified in the order.[59] Where a Director has powers to make a final order, a provisional order can be made if it appears to be required.[60] In deciding whether to make a provisional order, they must take particular account of the extent to which any person is likely to sustain loss or damage in consequence of any breach of statutory duty or licence condition which is likely to occur before a final order can be made and of the fact that the consumer has no other effective remedy to prevent disconnection.[61]

Both the Directors have a duty to exercise their functions in a manner which they consider is best calculated to protect the interests of consumers in respect of, amongst other things, 'continuity of supply'.[62] When seeking an order, the Director should be reminded of these responsibilities.

To get either Director General of Supply to intervene, the Director should be contacted immediately in writing setting out the circumstances of the case, the reason why the debt is disputed and other factors such as the family circumstances. It will be necessary to convince the Director:

---

55   Electricity Act 1989 s28 and Gas Act 1986 s38.
56   Electricity Act 1989 s25(1).
57   Gas Act 1986 s28 as amended by CSU Act 1992 s48(2).
58   Electricity Act 1989 s25(8) and Gas Act 1986 s28(8).
59   Electricity Act 1989 s25(7) and Gas Act 1986 s28(7).
60   Electricity Act 1989 s25(2) and Gas Act 1986 s28(2).
61   Electricity Act 1989 s25(3) and Gas Act 1986 s28(3).
62   Electricity Act 1989 s3(1)(a)(ii) and Gas Act 1986 s3(2)(a).

- that the debt is genuinely disputed;
- that it is likely that the dispute would be resolved in favour of the consumer;
- that the consumer is going to suffer significant loss or damage if the electricity or gas is disconnected.

Where the dispute concerns the question of liability of occupiers (see pages 69 to 75), the acknowledgement by both OFGAS and OFFER that the law is unclear should be quoted as a justification for preventing disconnection, leaving liability to be established properly where it should be, in the courts.

Injunction

It is unlikely that the remedy of injunction is available to prevent disconnection of electricity or gas. Generally, an injunction can only be granted if it is ancillary to some other form of relief claimed through the court, or in respect of some recognised cause of action. The only kind of relief that could be claimed against an electricity or gas supplier which would give rise to the power to seek an injunction would be an action for damages for breach of statutory duty.

Where a statute such as the Electricity Act 1989 or the Gas Act 1986 sets out a duty which must be followed by a supplier, this does not necessarily mean that a breach of that duty will give rise to a claim for damages. The court will look at the whole structure of the Act and in particular at the extent to which other alternative remedies are put in the Act by way of criminal prosecution or other enforcement methods before deciding whether breach of statutory duty gives rise to damages. Similar principles are considered by the High Court when deciding whether to exercise its inherent jurisdiction.[63] In the case of electricity and gas, both the Acts contain enforcement procedures exercisable by the Director Generals and require a Director General to consider the fact that 'the effect of the provisions [of the Act] is to exclude the availability of any remedy . . . in respect of any contravention of a relevant condition or requirement'.[64] It is therefore difficult to see how the courts could interpret these Acts other than by deciding that the intention of Parliament was to exclude an action for breach of statutory duty or for an injunction. However, this view is not shared by the authors of the *Fuel Rights Handbook*, 8th ed., published by Child Poverty Action Group.

In the author's view no injunction will be available against a supplier for failure to supply electricity or gas or to restrain disconnection.

63   See generally *Halsbury's Laws* 4th edn vol 21 para 824.
64   Electricity Act 1989 s25(3)(b) and Gas Act 1986 s28(3)(b).

Declaration

There is uncertainty about the availability of a declaration. In general, it is not possible to apply to a court for a declaration that you do not owe someone any money. The general rule is that you have to wait for them to take action to recover the debt and then defend the proceedings.[65] However, it appears that the issue has been addressed in cases where the potential creditor has not made a demand for payment.[66] In at least one case, the courts have left open the possibility that in exceptional circumstances the court would grant a declaration that no money was due even though no court action had been taken to enforce the debt.[67]

It may therefore be the case that it is possible to seek a declaration against an electricity or gas supplier to the effect that the client does not owe the supplier any money if disconnection is threatened for a sum that has been demanded. An application for a declaration would have to be made in the High Court, and this means that there will be significant problems with getting legal aid. The costs will be high and the amount in dispute is likely to be extremely low. It is unlikely that the legal aid authorities would be prepared to grant legal aid for such an action, particularly bearing in mind that an application for a declaration will not, in itself, prevent disconnection. It will only be a mechanism for resolving the dispute about the bill.

Wherever possible, the alternative remedy of paying the debt and then seeking to recover it by way of a claim for restitution should be used as an alternative.

Future developments

Section 13 of the Courts and Legal Services Act 1990, when it is brought into force, will amend the County Courts Act 1984 by adding a new s112A. This will allow the court to make an order restricting enforcement by electricity, gas and water suppliers by disconnection. At the time of writing, the Government is proposing to bring these provisions into force at the end of 1994.

Threatened disconnection for failing to pay a deposit

Power to require a deposit

Both electricity and gas suppliers can require a deposit before connecting a consumer to the supply. In addition, both can demand a deposit at a later

---

65   *Midland Bank plc v Laker Airways Ltd* [1986] QB 689.
66   *Re Clay* [1919] 1 Ch 66.
67   *Guaranty Trust Co of New York v Hannay and Co* [1915] 2 KB 536, CA, per Pickford LJ at pp555, 565.

stage either if the consumer has not given security or where the security has become invalid or insufficient.[68]

Power to disconnect if deposit is not paid

The electricity supplier can disconnect seven days after demanding payment of a deposit but the security required must be 'reasonable security for the payment of all money which may become due in respect of the supply'. In addition, any notice demanding a deposit when the electricity is already being supplied, must state the effect of s23 of the Act.[69] Section 23 deals with the ability of the Director General to resolve disputes or to appoint an arbitrator to resolve disputes (see p 85 above).

British Gas can also disconnect seven days after demanding a deposit but again can only demand 'reasonable security for the payment of all money which may become due to him in respect of the supply'.[70] As with electricity the client can ask the Director General to arbitrate on a dispute about a deposit or other security.[71]

'Reasonable security'

There is no specific definition of what would be considered to be a 'reasonable security'. The implication of the Act is that the supplier is entitled to require security that is enough to cover any arrears that might arise before disconnection could occur. The maximum that is likely to arise is something in the region of four to five months' payment, ie, the time it takes to enforce one quarterly bill. This therefore should be the maximum deposit that a supplier could require.

However, it is worth noting that the obligation is for the consumer to provide 'security', not a deposit. Security could include an undertaking by some relative of the consumer to pay any arrears of charges.

Essentially, the grounds upon which a client may be able to challenge a security deposit are as follows:

- that his or her track record shows that no deposit of any kind is required, eg, s/he has paid bills regularly for some time;
- in particular that any problems with fuel arrears arise from the actions of some other member of the household who was liable for the bill;
- that s/he is offering security though not a deposit, eg, from some other member of the family;

---

68   Electricity Act 1989 s20(2) and Gas Act 1986 s11(3).
69   Electricity Act 1989 s20(2).
70   Gas Act 1986 s11(3).
71   Gas Act 1986 s14A inserted by CSU Act 1992 s16.

– that the amount of the deposit requested is far in excess of the likely fuel consumption over a four to five-month period.

Preventing disconnection

Installation of a prepayment meter

A prepayment meter removes any need for a deposit or other security. The principles for the collection of domestic cash debt issued by British Gas state that it will only disconnect for non-payment of a security deposit where a prepayment meter cannot be installed or has been refused by the customer, or where there is no contact with the customer at a disconnection visit.[72]

Similar policies will be applied by many electricity companies. It is helpful to be aware of the local company's policy.

Where suppliers fail to agree the installation of a prepayment meter in breach of their own policies, all available steps should be taken to seek to persuade them to change their decision, eg, by complaint through the internal hierarchy of the supplier, using the complaints procedure, complaint to the Gas or Electricity Consumers Council, complaint to the Director Generals of Supply, MPs etc.

Paying the deposit

If the deposit claimed is reasonable, the client may have little or no alternative but to pay it. There are a number of ways in which the client may obtain assistance with that payment.

First, assistance may be obtained from the local authority social services department. British Gas states that it will disconnect for non-payment of a security deposit only where social services, where appropriate, have been informed of the proposed disconnection and there is no offer of assistance from the DSS or any other agency which might help the customer either financially or with counselling.[73]

Assistance may be available from social services under the provisions of the Children Act 1989 (see page 83). Where a request has been made to social services, advisers should be in a position to argue that disconnection should not take place until it is apparent whether or not social services are going to assist.

Similar policies may be applied by the electricity companies.

Secondly, help may be obtained from the Social Fund. To obtain a

---

72 British Gas, *Principles for the Collection of Domestic Gas Debt*, January 1989, para 15.

73 British Gas, *Principles for the Collection of Domestic Gas Debt*, January 1989, para 15.

crisis loan, a person must be without sufficient resources to meet his or her immediate short-term needs or the needs of his or her family at the time the application is determined.[74] To qualify for a crisis loan, the Social Fund payment must be awarded to assist an eligible person to meet expenses in an emergency or as a consequence of a disaster provided that the provision of the assistance is the only means by which serious damage or serious risk to health or safety of that person or to a member of his or her family may be prevented.[75] A crisis loan can be awarded to anyone even if they are not on income support.

A budgeting loan is only available to someone who is on income support. It cannot be paid for 'the cost of mains fuel consumption and associated standing charges'. This means that a budgeting loan cannot be obtained for fuel arrears but can be obtained for a deposit, fuel meter installation and reconnection charges.[76]

Families or those moving out of institutional or residential care who are receiving income support may be able to obtain a community care grant to pay for a deposit.[77]

Paying the deposit when it is disputed and then seeking to recover all or part of the sum paid

As explained on page 83, it is possible to pay a disputed sum under protest and then seek to recover it by way of a claim in restitution in the county court which will usually be a small claim. This can equally well be done for a security deposit where the full amount demanded is paid and then court proceedings are taken, either to recover all the security if the client is able to show that no security should have been required or, alternatively, to require payment back of part of the security if the amount demanded was unreasonably high. Precedent 9 in Part III can be adapted as a covering letter for payment of a deposit in these circumstances.

Asking the relevant Director General to resolve a dispute

As explained on page 85, s23 of the Electricity Act 1989 and s14A Gas Act 1986 allow the Director Generals to resolve disputes. Note that in effect the decision of the Director General on the amount of the deposit (if any)

---

74   Social Fund Directions, direction 14. For general information relating to the Social Fund see the *National Welfare Benefits Handbook 1993/1994*, Child Poverty Action Group, part 9 from p 352.
75   Social Fund Directions, direction 3.
76   Social Fund Officers Guide para 306.1 states fuel deposits to be high priority for budgeting loans.
77   Social Fund Directions, directions 4 and 29. For further information see *National Welfare Benefits Handbook*, (CPAG, annual).

is likely to be final, since the law is fairly clear and an appeal can only be made on a point of law (see page 86).

Whilst the dispute is being resolved, the Director can give directions as to the circumstances in which and the terms on which the supplier is to give or to continue to give the supply pending the determination of the dispute.[78] This may include a requirement for the consumer to give a limited amount of security whilst the dispute is resolved, particularly if the client is not arguing that no security should be given at all but that a smaller security should be supplied. In those circumstances, the client may be asked to give whatever security he or she considers to be reasonable. Where the argument is that no security should be given at all, it is necessary to persuade the Director General that no security should be provided at all pending the resolution of the dispute.

Injunction

The author's view is that no injunction will be available to prevent disconnection for the reasons explained on page 88.

Declaration

It will be possible to take action for a declaration in the High Court as to the amount that would be a reasonable security. However, for the reasons explained on page 89, it would be extremely difficult to obtain legal aid for such an application and the alternative remedy of paying the amount claimed and then seeking to recover it throught the county court small claims proceedings is preferable if it is possible to make use of it. So, too, is the use of the relevant Director General as an arbiter.

Threatened disconnection for alleged tampering with or bypassing of a meter

Power to disconnect

Both gas and electricity suppliers have power to disconnect the supply of gas or electricity to a person who intentionally or by 'culpable negligence' has damaged or allowed to be damaged any gas or electricity fittings

---

78   Electricity Act 1989 s23(2) as amended by CSU Act 1992 s25 and Gas Act 1988 s14A(4), inserted by CSU Act 1992 s16.

including meters, has altered the index to any meter or is preventing a meter from registering, eg, bypassing it.[79]

The power to discontinue the supply of electricity or gas to the premises and to remove the meter only continues 'until the matter has been remedied'.[80]

Standard of proof

The legislation makes it a criminal offence to damage fittings or to bypass or tamper with a meter. The power to disconnect applies only when such an offence has been committed. If a person were prosecuted for the offence, the court would have to be satisfied 'beyond reasonable doubt' that the person charged had committed the acts required. It is not clear what level of proof is required to give rise to the power to disconnect. The view of British Gas and the Director General of Gas Supply is that only proof on the balance of probabilities is required. They point out that in other similar kinds of cases even where an appropriate criminal offence is necessary to give rise to a civil action, the proper standard of proof in civil actions should be based on the balance of probabilities rather than the standard required for criminal proceedings.[81] This view is probably correct but it is still possible to argue that proof beyond reasonable doubt is required to give rise to the power to disconnect until such time as the courts have determined the issue and set a binding precedent.

How was the meter damaged?

The power to disconnect only arises where the person to whom the supply is made has committed the offence. The power to disconnect therefore only arises if the person to whom the supply is made:

-   intentionally damaged, bypassed or tampered with the meter;
-   damaged the meter by 'culpable negligence', eg, by dropping something on it or damaging it whilst trying to get a coin out that was stuck;
-   was an active participant in deliberate damage by somebody else, eg, by getting his or her partner to damage the meter or bypass it.

---

79   Gas Act 1986 Sch 5 para 10, Electricity Act 1989 Sch 6 para 4 and Electricity Act 1989 Sch 7 para 11.
80   Electricity Act 1989 Sch 7 para 11(3) and Gas Act 1986 Sch 5 para 10(2).
81   OFGAS Position Paper about Matters arising from British Gas plc's Duty under Section 10(1) of the Gas Act 1986 to Continue to Give a Gas Supply to Tariff Customers, section A para 6, quoting *Hornal v Neuburger Products Ltd* [1957] 1 QB 247.

It is difficult to see how a person could 'allow' a meter to be damaged or bypassed by 'culpable neglect'.

Where it is uncertain who was responsible for damaging the meter and there are several members of the household who could have done so, it is more difficult to establish whether the power to disconnect arises. The person who receives the supply must have been present or actively participating in the damage or tampering with the meter. On the other hand, bypassing is a continuous state of affairs and it is going to be extremely difficult for the person who received the supply of electricity to argue that he or she was not aware that the meter was bypassed and therefore did not actively allow that state of affairs to continue.

Culpable negligence

To give rise to a power to disconnect, the person receiving the supply must have 'allowed' the meter to be damaged or bypassed. It is not clear to what extent the consumer must have had the power to sanction or otherwise the bypassing of the meter or the damage to it. Since the legislation gives rise to the possibility of criminal proceedings, the word 'allow' should be interpreted as requiring some positive step on the consumer's part to have been taken to authorise the damage or tampering that occurred.

The legislation also does not define the meaning of the words 'culpable negligence'. Again because the words are used in the definition of a criminal offence they must require some seriously improper conduct deserving a punishment. This is a view shared by OFGAS.[82]

As explained on pages 72 and 75, British Gas and electricity suppliers argue that all occupiers of the household are persons to whom gas and electricity are supplied. They may therefore argue that whoever is responsible for any damage caused to a meter, they have power to disconnect. The contrary argument is that if there is any one person in the household who can be considered to be an 'occupier', suppliers have a continuing duty to provide that person with a supply and have no power to disconnect the supply to that person. It is submitted that the argument that all occupiers of the household are equally liable for the charges means that to justify disconnection all occupiers of the household must have been responsible for the tampering or damage.

The supplier of electicity or gas has power to remove, inspect and reinstall any meter which is measuring the quantity or gas or electricity supplied but when removing the meter must fix a substitute unless the power to disconnect has arisen.[83]

---

82   OFGAS Position Paper, para 4.
83   Electricity Act 1989 Sch 7 para 10(3) and Gas Act 1986 sch 5 para 4(3).

Preventing disconnection for tampering or bypassing a meter

Paying the sum due

The electricity and gas suppliers have power to discontinue the supply only 'until the matter has been remedied'. They interpret this as a power to disconnect until the consumer has paid the cost of repairing any damage to the meter, the cost of installing a meter that is working satisfactorily and any sums due for fuel that was used but which was not recorded on the meter. If damage was caused to a coin meter in order to remove the contents, they argue that the power to discontinue the supply continues until the suppliers have been recompensed for any money that has been taken.

The alternative view is that the phrase 'the matter has been remedied' involves only a power to disconnect for as long as it takes to repair the damage to the meter, eg, to rewire so that there is no bypassing, correcting any alteration that has been made by the consumer or removing any obstruction to the meter satisfactorily operating. This is the more logical interpretation of the legislation and this interpretation is shared by OFGAS.[84]

It is therefore unclear whether in order to prevent disconnection for tampering, bypassing etc. the consumer need only pay the cost of repairing any damage to the meter or replacing the meter with one that is functioning properly or whether he or she will also have to pay for any bill based on an assessment of the amount of fuel that he or she has been using without it being properly recorded on the meter.

If it is possible to ascertain the cost of repairing the meter and/or replacing the meter with one that is functioning correctly and the client is able to pay this sum, he or she may then be able to obtain an enforcement order from the Director General of Electricity or Gas Supply requiring the supplier not to disconnect.

Change the supply into a new customer's name

As explained above, the power to disconnect only relates to tampering, bypassing etc. by the person who is supplied with electricity or gas. A request for a continuous supply by any other person who is an occupier of the premises gives rise to a duty owed by the supplier to supply that person with fuel. If there is any one occupier who was not responsible for the tampering, bypassing etc. he or she is owed a continuing duty to supply and it should be that person who seeks an Enforcement Order from the Director General requiring the continuation of the supply (see page 87).

---

84   OFGAS Position Paper (see note 81), part A, paras 7 and 8.

A formal written request should be made by a person who is not involved in the damage or tampering or bypassing for a supply to those premises followed by a request for the Director General to make an enforcement order.

Paying the cost and recovering it
Even if it is disputed that the meter has been bypassed, tampered with or damaged, it is open to the client to pay off the sums requested by the supplier if he or she has the finance to do so and then seek to recover the money paid on the basis of a claim in restitution (see page 83). It will then be open to the court to decide whether or not the sums are due.

Refer dispute to Director General
As for disputes over arrears or deposits, the consumer can refer any dispute about whether he or she is responsible for tampering and whether the right to disconnect arises to the relevant Director General. The consumer will not be able to argue that the supplier has no power to enter and replace the meter which is damaged and to rewire where appropriate because there is a separate power to do so.[85] However, when exercising this power, the suppliers have a responsibility to replace the meter if it is removed.

If the power to disconnect is disputed, the Director can give directions as to the circumstances in which and terms on which the supplier must continue to give supply pending determination of the dispute.[86]

Obtaining an order or provisional order from the Director General
The relevant Director General can make an order preventing disconnection or requiring the supplier to replace the meter but maintain continuation of the supply if satisfied that the supplier is likely to be going to exceed its powers by disconnecting.[87]

Declaration
It is possible to apply to the High Court for a declaration that the consumer has not damaged a meter or allowed it to be damaged as a method of resolving a dispute about whether or not this has occurred. For the reasons explained on page 89, this is unlikely to be an effective remedy.

85   Electricity Act 1989 Sch 7 para 10(3) and Gas Act 1986 Sch 5 para 4(3).
86   Electricity Act 1989 s23(2) and Gas Act 1986 s14A(4) inserted by CSU Act 1992 s16.
87   Electricity Act 1989 s25 and Gas Act 1986 s28(1) as amended by CSU Act 1992 s48(2).

Refusal to connect supply

Because of outstanding arrears

The strategies suggested on pages 80–9 above are all relevant as a means of getting a supply reconnected for arrears that are outstanding or are alleged to be outstanding. These include:

- reaching agreement by negotiation and in particular encouraging the supplier to install a prepayment meter or accept direct deductions from benefits (see page 80);
- paying off any undisputed arrears with or without assistance from the social services department under the Children Act 1989, the Social Fund or with assistance from the local authority if the arrears were those of the landlord (see page 83);
- paying arrears that are disputed and taking action to reclaim that sum by way of claiming restitution or seeking an arbitration on the dispute and if successful requiring reimbursement (see pages 83–5);
- requesting arbitration on a dispute by the relevant Director General (see page 85) – where it is apparent that a genuine dispute exists, the Director General may be prepared to direct that the supplier reinstates the supply whilst the dispute is pending;
- obtaining an enforcement order against the supplier requiring reconnection (see page 86) – it is possible that the Directors will not be prepared to intervene unless the client is taking some active steps to challenge the disputed arrears, eg, by request for arbitration, by inviting the supplier to take court action against him or her for the debt by which the matter can be resolved or by applying for a declaration;
- applying for a declaration that no money is due (see page 89).

In addition, where there is any occupier of the dwelling who could not be liable for the arrears, s/he should request a supply. This will apply to an occupier who did not live in the dwelling at the time the arrears arose or to a person who has a lesser interest in the dwelling, eg, as a licensee. In all such cases, a request for a supply should be made in writing to the supplier and a copy sent to the Director General with a request for intervention and an enforcement order. The application to the Director General should include a statement of the personal circumstances of the client and the reason why intervention is necessary as a matter or urgency in the form of a provisional order in order to have the supply reconnected as soon as possible. An explanation should be given as to why the applicant is not liable for the debt.

Any other occupier whose liability is unclear because liability depends upon which of the legal arguments on pages 69 to 75 are correct may also apply, but reconnection is not then guaranteed. S/he can seek arbitration on the dispute and an order requiring connection of supply whilst the dispute is resolved.

If s/he has the money available to clear the debt, this can be offered as security pending the determination of the dispute and will be repaid if the person concerned is not found to be liable. Alternatively, if s/he has the money and the supplier maintains s/he is liable for the debt which is disputed, the debt can be paid under duress and then recovery of the sum can take place through a county court action under the law of restitution (see page 83).

Refusal to connect because of a lack of reasonable security

The remedies listed on pages 91–3 above will all be relevant. These include:

- removing the need for a security deposit by arranging for the installation of a prepayment meter (see page 91);
- paying the deposit with help from the Social Fund or from social services under the Children Act 1989 (see pages 91–2);
- paying the amount requested as a deposit then taking action in the county court by way of a claim for restitution for any disputed part of the deposit (see pages 83 and 92);
- requesting arbitration by the Director General of Electricity or Gas Supply without paying the deposit, though this may lead to considerable delay while the matter is arbitrated before the supply is reconnected (see page 93);
- seeking an enforcement order from the Director General of Electricity or Gas Supply on the basis that the deposit claimed is unreasonable (see page 86). Note that the Directors may be reluctant to intervene unless the client is taking some steps to challenge the deposit, eg, by reference to arbitration or by applying for a declaration.

Refusal to reconnect because of previous tampering, bypassing or damage to a meter

The strategies explained on pages 96–7 should all be considered as possible methods of obtaining reconnection of the supply when there is an allegation of tampering of bypassing or there has been tampering or bypassing. These include:

- arranging for a different person to request a supply (see page 96);

–   paying the full cost of repairs to the meter, reinstatement of a new meter and any assessed bill then making a claim in restitution for any part of the assessed bill which is disputed (see page 83);
–   paying the full cost of repairs to the meter and the cost of replacing the meter and any assessed bill then making a claim in restitution for recovery of the cost of repairing the meter and replacing it if the tampering or damage to the meter did not occur because of failure by the consumer to take proper care of the meter (see page 97);
–   paying the cost of repairs to the meter and replacement with an effective meter and then seeking an enforcement order against the supplier on the basis that the supplier only has power to discontinue the supply until 'the matter has been remedied' and by paying the cost of repairs and replacement, the matter has been remedied (see page 97).

CHAPTER 5

Arrears of water charges

Introduction

Typical problems requiring emergency action are:
- where the water company threatens disconnection of the water supply;
- where the water company has already disconnected and refuses to reconnect.

Where water rates are collected as part of the rent, arrears of these charges will be considered to be arrears of rent (see chapter 11).

Water supply

Water supplies and sewerage services are now provided by private-sector companies under the Water Industry Act 1991. These companies are appointed by the Secretary of State to provide water or sewerage services for a particular area of the country.[1] The Secretary of State appoints the water companies by what is known as an 'instrument of appointment'.[2] The instrument of appointment can include conditions.[3] Once appointed, the company supplying water must comply with any conditions of appointment, has an obligation to perform any duties placed on water undertakers under the Act and can use any of the powers given to undertakers by the Act.[4]

It is possible for separate companies to be appointed to provide sewerage services and water supplies.[5] In practice, the same companies usually do both and the bill that most people call 'water rates' includes

1 Water Industry Act 1991 s6.
2 Water Industry Act 1991 s6(3).
3 Water Industry Act 1991 s11.
4 Water Industry Act 1991 s6(2)(a) and (b).
5 Water Industry Act 1991 s6(4).

charges for the supply of water and separate charges for sewerage services.

Since privatisation, water charges have increased drastically. The number of people finding difficulty in paying their water charges is steadily increasing. Water companies annually issue hundreds of thousands of county court summonses for non-payment of charges and over 7,500 disconnections took place in the period from 1 April 1991 to 30 September 1991.

At present, most water companies charge domestic customers on the basis of the rateable value which applied to the premises they occupied on 31 March 1990. This method must be phased out completely by 31 March 2000.[6] Different water companies may adopt different methods of charging in future but water metering seems likely. Charges based on rateable values are levied in advance. Once metering takes place, charges will have to be levied in arrears as they are for electricity and gas.

Liability for water charges

With one or two limited exceptions,[7] the occupier or occupiers of any premises supplied are liable for payment of the charges for supplies of water and for sewerage services.[8]

Who is an occupier?

The Water Industry Act 1991 does not define 'occupier'. The word 'occupier' is used in a variety of different legislation and can have a different meaning according to the purpose of that legislation. There have been no reported cases in which the word has been interpreted by the courts for the purposes of water charges.

However, the basis of charging the occupier derives from the system for general rates formerly contained in the General Rate Act 1967 which was abolished when the community charge was introduced.

The courts might therefore be expected to follow the interpretation of the word 'occupier' under the law relating to general rates. Three relevant

---

6 Water Industry Act 1991 s145.
7 The exceptions are contained in the Water Industry Act 1991 s144. A person who has made an agreement with the water supplier for the supply of water is responsible for charges. If water is metered, an occupier who leaves but fails to notify the water supplier remains liable for a short period after leaving. In some cases where premises have been rented since before September 1989, the owner is liable for the charges.
8 Water Industry Act 1991 s144(1).

requirements had to be satisfied under rating law for a person living in domestic premises to be considered to be the 'occupier'.[9]

A person must be in actual occupation or possession

This is a question of fact. Legal title is relevant but is not conclusive.[10]

The person must be in exclusive occupation or possession for the person's own purposes

This again is a question of fact. The law of landlord and tenant regarding the meaning of 'exclusive occupation' is not relevant. What matters is whether, in practice, the person concerned occupies the premises rated without sharing them with anyone else other than with another joint occupier.[11] The case-law relating to this issue establishes liability in certain kinds of cases.

Where there are two or more occupiers of parts of premises, liability is based upon an assessment of whose occupation is paramount and whose is subordinate.[12] This will involve examination of the title to explain the circumstance of occupation. If a landlord retains control of occupied parts then the landlord will be the person liable to pay water charges. What matters is the degree of control that the owner or landlord has over the use of the premises.

If there is only one occupier then that occupier is responsible for water charges for the whole premises unless the description of the rated property in the valuation list includes explicitly property which he or she does not occupy. In practice, a description of a person's home in the valuation list is usually by one word eg, 'dwellinghouse'.[13]

Several people may be joint occupiers of premises. However, it does appear that it is not possible to have two separate occupiers of premises unless they are joint occupiers of the whole premises.[14] It is therefore

9   For a detailed discussion of the meaning of the word 'occupier' for general rates purposes see Duncan Forbes, 'General rates on residential accommodation: 1 Liability', September 1986 *Legal Action* 119.

10   *Westminster City Council v Southern Railway Co.* [1936] AC 511, HL; *Re Briant Colour Printing Co. Ltd* [1977] 3 All ER 968, CA; *Holywell Union Assessment Committee v Halkyn District Mines Drainage Co.* [1895] AC 117, HL.

11   *John Laing and Son Ltd v Kingswood Assessment Area Assessments Committee* [1949] 1 KB 344, CA.

12   *Westminster City Council v Southern Railway Co.* [1936] AC 511, HL.

13   *Camden London Borough Council v Herwald* [1977] 1 WLR 100, DC; [1978] QB 626, CA.

14   *Verral v Hackney London Borough Council* [1983] QB 444, CA and *Re Briant Colour Printing Co. Ltd* [1977] 3 All ER 968, CA.

arguable that tenants or licensees of a house in multiple occupation are not occupiers for the purposes of water charges.

The person's occupation must be reasonably permanent

Occupation must not be too transient if the person concerned is to be an 'occupier'.[15]

Examples of liability

–   A tenant in a multi-occupied house where his or her premises are separately rated will be the occupier of those premises.
–   A tenant occupying one flat in a house divided into two flats where the other flat is vacant but where the house is rated as one unit will be considered to be the occupier of the whole house for water charges.
–   The landlord where lodgers and/or tenants live in the house but it is rated as one unit will be considered to be the occupier of the whole house.
–   An unmarried partner of a tenant or owner will probably not be an occupier when s/he first moves in but may become an occupier when effectively s/he takes over joint occupation of the premises with the tenant or owner on a permanent basis.
–   A joint owner or tenant who has left the premises permanently, eg, on relationship breakdown, will not be the occupier.

Recovery methods

As private-sector companies, the water and sewerage undertakers can recover their charges in the same way as any other private-sector company by taking civil proceedings in the county court. However, in addition, water companies have power to disconnect the water supply if charges due to them in respect of the supply of water have not been paid within seven days beginning the day after service of a notice requiring payment.[16] There is no power to disconnect for failing to pay sewerage charges so these charges will not be further considered.

If the occupier of the premises is liable for the payment, the power is to disconnect the supply to the premises occupied. If the occupier who is liable for charges has left, there is no power to disconnect the supply to those premises. If, on the other hand, someone has voluntarily taken

---

15   *Moore v Williamson* [1973] RA 172, LT and *K. H. Tawell and Son v Buckingham* (1963) 10 RRC 123.
16   Water Industry Act 1991 s61(1).

responsibility for payment of water charges, the power to disconnect is a power to disconnect the supply to the premises s/he occupies provided that the same water company supplies water to those premises.[17] For example, if the son of an elderly person voluntarily takes on responsibility for payment of his parent's water charges, it would be the supply to the son's home that would be disconnected if he failed to pay the bill. There would be no power to disconnect the supply to the parent's home.

The power to disconnect ceases if within seven days of receiving the notice demanding payment, the person served with the notice serves a counter-notice disputing liability to pay the charges.[18] In those circumstances, the water company only has statutory power to disconnect when it has obtained a court judgment for the sums due.

In addition to the limitations on the statutory power to disconnect, the instrument of appointment of water companies sets out in condition H para 7.4 a requirement that no supply of water to domestic premises should be disconnected:

- except at a time when the person liable to pay relevant charges is the occupier of those premises; and
- except where the water company has obtained an enforceable judgment against that person for the payment of those relevant charges but they remain unpaid for any reason (other than by virtue of compliance with the terms of the judgment).

However, this protection does not apply where a judgment has been obtained for some previous arrears and that judgment has not been satisfied or has not been complied with.

Examples of circumstances where the water company should not disconnect are:

- where the only outstanding charges are for sewerage services;
- where the water company has not obtained any county court judgment against the person concerned for water charges;
- where the water company has obtained a judgment but the judgment requires payment of the arrears by instalments and those instalments have been paid on or before the date they were due (and this judgment may be in respect of the current arrears or previous arrears);
- where the person liable to pay has entered into an agreement with the water company and that agreement has been maintained;
- where the water company has obtained a judgment and the client was previously in breach of the terms of any instalments but the court has

17   Water Industry Act 1991 s61(1)(a).
18   Water Industry Act 1991 s61(2).

suspended the judgment on different terms after an application by the client and the client has complied with those terms;
- where the client has obtained an administration order and is maintaining payments required under the order (see page 31);
- where the occupier liable for water charges has left the premises;
- where the landlord has been responsible for the payment of water charges and has failed to pay, unless the landlord lives on the premises and is therefore an occupier.

Examples of circumstances where the water company may disconnect are:
- where it has obtained a judgment requiring payment by a specified date or dates, eg, within 28 days or by instalments, and that order has not been complied with;
- for this year's water charges where the company obtained a judgment in respect of last year's water charges and the judgment was not complied with.

Right to supply

The owner of any premises may demand a supply of water to those premises from the mains.[19] Provided there are pipes the water company then has a duty to supply water to those premises for domestic purposes.[20] Where a demand is made as a consequence of the supply having been cut off by reason of the person's failure to pay any charges, it can be a condition of reinstating the supply that the person making the demand has paid any amount due from him or her in respect of the supply of water and in respect of the expenses of cutting off the supply.[21] Other conditions may be made in relation to the condition of the water apparatus.

Threatened disconnection for undisputed arrears

The client may dispute part of the arrears claimed by a water company. For example, the sum claimed may be the water charges for the whole financial year when the client argues that he or she only moved in halfway through that year and only became the occupier from that time. Where part of the arrears is disputed and part undisputed, then, for the undisputed part, the strategies in this section should be followed, and the

---

19   Water Industry Act 1991 s52(5).
20   Water Industry Act 1991 s52(1).
21   Water Industry Act 1991 s53(2) and (1).

strategy on page 112 should be adopted for the disputed part of the arrears.

Removing entitlement to disconnect

As stated above, the water company has statutory powers to disconnect if water charges are unpaid seven days after a demand is made. However, the instrument of appointment for water companies requires that they do not disconnect unless a court judgment has been obtained, either for the current arrears or previous arrears, and the client is in breach of the judgment. In practice, the first stage in preventing disconnection should therefore be to ensure that the client comes within the protection provided by the instrument of appointment.

Application to the court to suspend the terms of the judgment

A county court has the power at any time to suspend or stay a judgment or order for such time and on such terms as the court thinks fit.[22] The power is exercisable if it appears to the satisfaction of the court that the client 'is unable from any cause to pay any sum recovered against him . . . or any instalment of such a sum'. Suspension of the judgment can continue until it appears that the cause of an inability to pay has ceased.

This gives a general discretionary power to the court at any time to suspend a judgment on terms (eg, that a weekly sum is paid) or completely for a fixed period (eg, for six months to enable the client to overcome a financial crisis).

As a first stage to preventing disconnection the adviser should establish what court judgment the water company has obtained against the client, the name of the county court and the case number and date of judgment. The water company should be able to provide the name of the court and the case number, and the court will be able to provide the date of judgment. It should be noted that most water companies use summons distribution centres, ie, a company issues all its summonses in one county court. It must not be assumed that the proceedings will have been issued in the county court covering the area where the particular client lives.

The entitlement to disconnect may arise from a judgment for the current year's arrears or a previous year's arrears. An application can be made to suspend either of these judgments.

If part of the arrears is disputed, an application to set aside the judgment should be made in respect of the disputed part of the arrears and to suspend the judgment in respect of the balance. In practice, these

---

22   County Courts Act 1984 s71(2).

applications should be combined and precedent 10 in Part III shows a combined application, both to suspend and set aside a judgment. The supporting affidavit is in precedent 13. Three copies of the notice of application should be filed in court together with the affidavit in support of the application and a copy of that affidavit for service on the water company.

In the period between the lodging of the application to suspend the judgment and the hearing, the water company will continue to have the right to disconnect. It may therefore be necessary to make an emergency (*ex parte*) application to suspend the judgment pending the hearing.

Before making an *ex parte* application to suspend the judgment pending a hearing, a request should be made to the water company to see whether it is prepared voluntarily to agree not to disconnect pending the hearing of the application (see precedent 11 in Part III). In many circumstances it is likely that it will. If it refuses, contact should be made with the Director General of Water Services (see below) and a request should be made for OFWAT to intervene to request the water company not to disconnect pending the hearing of the application. Water companies are now required to have complaints procedures.[23] If there are mechanisms for urgent complaints to be dealt with it may be possible to use the complaints procedure to halt disconnection temporarily. Only if these approaches are unsuccessful will it be necessary to make an *ex parte* application pending the hearing of the application. The Director General has no formal power to intervene to prevent disconnection in the period between making an application to the court and the hearing, but nevertheless a request should be made for such intervention where necessary.

In some courts, an application to suspend the judgment pending the hearing can be done in writing explaining the circumstances and precedent 12 in Part III shows such an application. In other courts, an application will need to be made in person. In those circumstances there will have to be an attendance before the district judge to make the application. If a judgment is suspended on an *ex parte* basis, pending the hearing, the water company will be in breach of the terms of its instrument of appointment if it disconnects during that period.

Apply for an administration order (see chapter 2)

There must be a judgment for water charges due if the water company is intending to disconnect. This judgment gives the county court jurisdiction

---

23   Water Industry Act 1991 s86A inserted by Competition and Service (Utilities) Act 1992 s29.

to make an administration order if the total unsecured debts are less than £5,000.

An administration order will provide a new scheme of payment of debts and any county court proceedings will be *automatically* stayed.[24] This should include any judgment which then becomes payable under the terms of the administration order. As long as the client maintains payments under the terms of the order, the right to disconnect should cease.

Apply to social services for assistance

Condition H para 7.3 of the instrument of appointment of water companies states that they must not disconnect a supply at any time when the debtor has made an application to social services for assistance with the debt and a request has been made by social services that disconnection should not take place.

No time-limit is placed on this provision so that a delay by social services in making a decision whether to assist a client should not lead to any prejudice.

An application should be made to social services and a request for such a letter should be made in all circumstances where disconnection is threatened where social services intervention is possible. eg, where there are children, people with disabilities, elderly people, people with severe learning difficulties or mental illness. A model letter from social services to the water company which could be given to social services for them to use is shown in precedent 14 in Part III.

Reach agreement by negotiation

Condition H para 7.3. of the instrument of appointment of water companies requires that the water company must not disconnect as long as it has made an agreement with the debtor which is still being complied with. If it is possible to negotiate an agreement, this will then remove the water company's entitlement to disconnect.

Where the client is claiming income support, it can be suggested to the water company that a direct deduction should be made from benefit for the arrears of water charges including sewerage and environmental services.[25] Deductions can be made from income support and any other benefits payable with income support, eg, unemployment benefit and invalidity benefit.[26] The maximum amount payable towards arrears is

24   County Courts Act 1984 s114(2).
25   Social Security (Claims and Payments) Regulations 1987 SI No. 1968 (SSC&P Regs) Sch 9 para 7.
26   SSC&P Regs Sch 9 para 1.

£2.20 per week (1993/4 rates) but in addition a deduction must be made to cover the current consumption.[27]

The Benefits Agency has power to make direct deductions, either when at least half the annual water charges are in arrears or if they consider it in the interests of the family to do so.[28] For further details of these provisions, see the *National Welfare Benefits Handbook*, 23rd ed., Child Poverty Action Group.

Action to prevent disconnection

In practice, no action should be necessary to prevent disconnection if the entitlement to disconnect has gone. Most water companies can be expected to comply with the terms of their instrument of appointment. However, the application to suspend a judgment may be unsuccessful leaving the water company with the power to disconnect, social services may refuse to intervene and negotiations may break down. It is therefore necessary to consider what steps may be possible to prevent disconnection.

Assistance with payment of a debt

The social services department of the local authority has power to make payments to assist the families of children in need.[29] The definition of a 'child in need' includes a child whose health is likely to be significantly impaired or further impaired unless assistance is provided.[30] Disconnection of a water supply prevents washing and the use of sanitary facilities. It leads to a risk of drinking contaminated water. It would therefore be open to the social services department to interpret the meaning of the words 'child in need' to include any child who lives in a household at risk of water disconnection and to make a payment under the Act.

Complaint to the Director General of Water Supply (OFWAT)

This remedy will only be available where the disconnection will be in breach of the licence conditions, eg, where social services have requested the water company not to disconnect or the client is not in breach of a county court judgment or where an agreement has been reached which the client has maintained.

The Director General of Water Supply (OFWAT) has certain powers to require compliance with the terms of an instrument of appointment.

27   SSC&P Regs Sch 9 para 7(3).
28   SSC&P Regs Sch 9 para 7(1).
29   Children Act 1989 s17(6).
30   Children Act 1989 s17(10).

However, the Director's powers only come into effect when a condition of the company's appointment or certain statutory duties are being contravened or the water company has contravened those requirements or conditions and is likely to do so again.[31] Technically, until disconnection has actually occurred, there is no breach of condition nor of statutory duties so that the Director General has no formal power to intervene, even to prevent a disconnection which is in breach of the licence conditions.

However, as soon as such a disconnection has occurred, the Director General has formal power to require reconnection.

In practice, if a disconnection is threatened which is going to be in breach of the terms of the instrument of appointment, OFWAT should be contacted immediately to seek intervention to prevent such a breach.

Injunction

Where the arrears are not disputed, an injunction will not be available because the water company has statutory power to disconnect even though the company will be in breach of the terms of its instrument of appointment.

Threatened disconnection for disputed arrears

Removing entitlement to disconnect

In practice, the water company will have a judgment which entitles it to disconnect. This judgment is a declaration that the client is liable for the water charges and it is therefore essential that this judgment is set aside in order to be able to dispute the liability.

Application to set aside judgment

Precedent 10 in Part III shows an application to set aside judgment combined with an application to suspend the judgment as an alternative remedy or for that part of a debt which is undisputed. As soon as the application is to be made, a request should be made to the water company not to disconnect pending the hearing of the application. If that request is refused, an application should be made to the Director General of Water Services to intervene, to request the water company not to disconnect pending the hearing of the application. If intervention by the Director General does not lead the water company to agree not to disconnect pending the hearing, an *ex parte* application to suspend the judgment until

---

31   Water Industry Act 1991 s18(1).

the hearing should be made as soon as possible. See precedent 12 in Part III.

Other steps

If social services intervene or an agreement is reached for payments pending the hearing of an application to set aside, eg, of a weekly sum, these both remove entitlement to disconnect (see above page 109).

Action to prevent disconnection

Payment of the debt

As with undisputed arrears, assistance may be obtained to pay the debt from the social services department. However, where disconnection is threatened, payment of the debt can be made under protest pending a hearing of the application to set aside judgment. As explained on page 83, money paid under duress can be recovered subsequently in court action though in practice a water company might be expected to return the amounts voluntarily if payments have been wrongly made. The letter shown in precedent 9 in Part III can be adapted to be sent with any payments made under protest for water charges.

Complaints to Director General

Technically, as long as the court judgment is in place, the water company still has power to disconnect. However, as a matter of good practice if there is a serious dispute about the debt, it should not disconnect until such time as the application to hear that dispute has been dealt with. A request should therefore be made to the Director General to request his or her intervention to prevent disconnection pending the hearing of the application. The Director General has no formal powers to prevent disconnection.

Injunction

As long as a court judgment is in force, no injunction will be available against the water company to restrain disconnection. Once the court judgment has been set aside, it is very unlikely that the water company will seek to disconnect since it would be in breach of the terms of its instrument of appointment. If a water company were to threaten to disconnect in these circumstances and the Director General refused to intervene, it would be possible to apply for an injunction to restrain disconnection on the grounds of breach of statutory duty. This situation is so unlikely to arise that a model application has not been included.

Arbitration of a billing dispute

The Competition and Service (Utilities) Act 1992 includes provisions enabling regulations to be made allowing OFWAT to arbitrate or appoint an arbitrator to do so in respect of any dispute over charges.[32] These provisions are not in force at the time of writing. When they are introduced, it will be possible to resolve disputes about bills between suppliers and customers by this mechanism. Unfortunately the remedy is not available where the main dispute over liability is on the question of whether the client is or is not a 'customer'. Arbitration will only be available where there is no existing county court judgment for the debt concerned. If a judgment has already been entered, to avoid disconnection it will still have to be set aside and the court will have to determine liability.

Refusal to connect supply

Where the occupier of premises demands a supply, the water company has a duty to provide a supply of water sufficient for domestic purposes.[33] However, where such a request is made after the disconnection of the supply for failing to pay any charges, the water company can require as a condition of connection that the person making the demand has paid any amount owed by that person to the water company in respect of the supply of water to the relevant premises and in connection with the expenses incurred in cutting off the supply.[34]

No outstanding arrears

It is extremely unlikely that the water company will refuse to turn on the supply to domestic premises which are already connected to the mains where the supply has been turned off unless there are arrears which have not been paid. If it does refuse in these circumstances, a complaint should initially be made to the Director General of Water Services which will almost certainly lead to connection taking place. If the Director General does not intervene, an application can be made for an injunction on the grounds of a breach of statutory duty. The procedure for this is dealt with further below.

---

32   Water Industry Act 1991 s150A, inserted by CSU Act 1992 s36.
33   Water Industry Act 1991 s52.
34   Water Industry Act 1991 s53(2)(a).

Reconnection where the arrears are not disputed

There are two strategies for dealing with the situation where the arrears are not disputed.

First, supply could be requested by a person who is not liable for the debt. The water company has power to impose conditions requiring payment of the debt including arrears of water charges and disconnection costs before reconnecting. However, it can only make this a condition where the person requesting the supply was liable for the debt.[35] This means that the person requesting the supply must have been an occupier of the premises at the time at which the debt arose.

If there is someone living in the household who is an occupier but who is not the person who was liable for the original debt, then he or she can make the request for the supply and the water company has no right to refuse. The person making the request must therefore not have been an 'occupier' at the time at which the debt arose but must be an 'occupier' at the time the request for the reconnection of the supply is made.

The new 'occupier' should make a demand for a supply in writing to the water company and if there is a failure to supply, a complaint should be made to the Director General. If the Director General is not prepared to intervene, an application can in these circumstances be made to the county court for an injunction. The terms upon which the injunction can be sought and the procedure together with a model form of particulars of claim are shown in precedent 15 in Part III.

Secondly, if it is not possible to change the identity of the occupier who is requesting the supply, there will be little alternative but to pay the debt or to negotiate an agreement whereby connection is made immediately upon terms as to the discharge of the debt. For example, the water company might be prepared to reconnect upon a down payment followed by deductions of £2.20 per week (1993/4 rates) from income support. Assistance may be available from the social services under the Children Act 1989 to obtain reconnection.

Where there is someone who is partly liable for the debt, eg, a relatively new occupier who moved in part-way through the period for which arrears are due, s/he can pay the part of the debt for which s/he is liable and can then require reconnection. If a dispute arises as to whether s/he has paid the correct amount, the Director General can be asked to determine the dispute or the dispute can be resolved in proceedings seeking an injunction requiring connection.[36] Unfortunately the Director is given

---

35 Water Industry Act 1991 s53(2A).

36 Water Industry Act 1991 s30A and s53(2A) inserted by the Competition and Service (Utilities) Act 1992 s34 and s35(5).

no power to require a connection of supply whilst the dispute is being resolved; so unless a speedy resolution is likely, an injunction may still remain the only mechanism for obtaining an immediate supply.

Arrears disputed

Request for supply by a person who is not liable for the disputed arrears

This remedy is available in the same circumstances as where the arrears are not disputed and again it will be possible to obtain an injunction if the water company then refuses to reconnect.

Payment of the debt followed by recovery at a later stage

As explained in chapter 4 payment of a debt can be made under protest where there is duress which can be recovered at a later stage through an action in the county court. Though there have been no decided cases, it seems likely that this strategy will be available for water charges where the water company is refusing to reconnect until the debt is paid. It is therefore possible for the client to pay the debt under protest, apply to set aside the judgment (see below) and subsequently reclaim the amount paid if it is not voluntarily returned by the water company. Precedent 9 in Part III shows a letter drafted to make a payment under protest for electricity or gas charges. A similarly worded letter can be sent for water charges.

Applying to set aside judgment

As long as the judgment is in force, the water company is entitled to say that the debt is due. It is therefore essential that an application is made at the earliest opportunity to set aside the judgment which gave rise to the disconnection. An application to set aside judgment and supporting affidavit are shown in precedents 10 and 13 in Part III and although the factual circumstances contained in the affidavit will differ, the procedure is identical.

However, in this case, an *ex parte* application to suspend the judgment will be of no use since it will not give rise to a duty to reconnect. Instead, the adviser should take steps to obtain an early hearing of the application to set aside from the court. It may be necessary to make an *ex parte* application for an expedited hearing and a letter requesting such a hearing is shown in precedent 16 in Part III. In some courts, this application would be dealt with more speedily if made in person.

Once the judgment has been set aside, the water company may voluntarily reconnect. If it does not do so, a request can be made for the Director General to intervene, which may lead to a successful reconnection. If the Director General does not intervene or the water company does not comply with the request for reconnection, an application can be made for an injunction on the grounds of breach of a statutory duty. The particulars of claim will be identical to those in precedent 15 in Part III though the affidavit filed in support of the injunction will have to make clear that the water company is arguing that the client is liable for water charges but that these are disputed. The grounds on which the client disputes liability will have to be made clear and the court will need to be convinced that the client has an arguable case.

CHAPTER 6

Council Tax and Community Charge Arrears

Introduction

Typical problems requiring emergency action are:

- where the client receives a court summons because the local authority is seeking a liability order;
- where a bailiff is due to call to levy distress;
- where the bailiff has called and levied distress but has not yet removed the client's goods;
- where goods have been removed by the bailiff but not yet sold;
- where the client receives a summons requiring him or her to attend a means enquiry to show cause why he or she should not be committed to prison;
- where a means enquiry has already been held and the client is now under immediate threat of imprisonment for breaching the terms of a suspension or adjournment;
- where the client has already been imprisoned.

The community charge (poll tax) and the council tax are considered together because enforcement mechanisms for them are almost identical. The legislation relating to the community charge is contained in the Local Government Finance Act 1988 and the Community Charges (Administration and Enforcement) Regulations 1989 (as amended). The legislation relating to the council tax is contained in the Local Government Finance Act 1992 and the Council Tax (Administration and Enforcement) Regulations 1992 (as amended).[1]

The council tax came into force on 1 April 1993. At the time of writing the way in which local authorities will administer the tax is not clear, but it is likely that similar if not identical problems to those encountered with the community charge will arise.

---

1 The Community Charges (Administration and Enforcement) Regulations 1989 SI No. 438 (CCA&E Regs) and the Council Tax (Administration and Enforcement) Regulations 1992 SI No. 613 (CTA&E Regs).

Stages of enforcement

Stage 1.   *Local authority obtains a liability order*

To have power to take any enforcement action, the local authority must first obtain a liability order from the magistrates' court confirming that a person is liable to pay the community charge or council tax. If liability for the debt is to be disputed, it is at or before the liability order hearing that this must occur. Once a liability order is made, the existence of the debt cannot be challenged in subsequent enforcement proceedings. The defence that may be available to an application for a liability order is discussed on page 120.

Stage 2.   *Local authority chooses which enforcement method to use*

Once the local authority has obtained a liability order in respect of either the council tax or the poll tax, the options for enforcement are as follows:

- instructing a bailiff to distrain the debtor's goods;[2]
- requiring the employer to deduct specified sums from the earnings of the debtor;[3]
- for the council tax where over £1,000 is owing, applying for a charging order against the dwelling in respect of which the council tax was payable;[4]
- applying to make the debtor bankrupt;[5]
- applying to the Benefits Agency for direct deductions from income support;[6]
- if distress by the bailiffs has taken place or has been attempted, and the debt has not been cleared, the local authority can also apply to the magistrates' court for a summons for the debtor to attend a means enquiry to enquire whether the failure to pay which led to the liability order concerned being made was due to wilful refusal or culpable neglect.[7]

In practice, in the vast majority of cases where enforcement action is taken, local authorities use bailiffs and thereafter apply for a summons for

2   CCA&E Regs reg 39 and CTA&E Regs reg 45.
3   CCA&E Regs regs 32 and 38 and CTA&E Regs regs 37 and 43.
4   CTA&E Regs regs 50 and 51.
5   CCA&E Regs reg 43 and CTA&E Regs reg 49 but note that the minimum amount payable must be £750.
6   Community Charge (Deduction from Income Support) Regs 1990 SI No. 107 and Council Tax (Deductions from Income Support) Regs 1992 SI No. 494.
7   CCA&E Regs reg 41(2) and CTA&E Regs reg 47(2).

a debtor to attend a means enquiry to show cause why he or she should not be imprisoned. Comparatively little use is made of deductions from income support or attachment of earnings orders. The two primary enforcement methods will therefore be considered further.

Stage 3.   Local authority instructs bailiffs to levy distress

The Regulations for the poll tax and council tax say little about the rights of bailiffs so it is necessary to try to deduce their rights from old case-law on distraint for rent dating back several centuries. This shows that their rights are as follows:

- they may not break in but they can enter through any open or unlocked window or door;
- only goods may be distrained, not fixtures;
- money can be distrained as well as goods;
- the debtor's goods may be distrained anywhere, not only on the premises in which s/he lives;
- only the debtor's goods can be distrained but this includes goods owned jointly with someone else (not therefore goods solely owned by other members of the family);
- certain goods are exempt from distress for both taxes.[8]

Stage 4.   If the bailiff fails to recover the sum due, the local authority applies for a summons for a means enquiry

If the bailiff is unable to recover sufficient goods to raise the money to pay off the arrears and the bailiff's costs, he or she will inform the local authority.

A local authority then has power to apply for a warrant of commitment of the debtor to prison.[9] Before the magistrates' court can issue a warrant of commitment, it must carry out a means enquiry of the debtor in his or her presence to establish whether the failure to pay the poll tax or council tax and the costs of recovery was due either to wilful refusal or culpable neglect.[10]

---

8   The Community Charges (Administration and Enforcement) (Amendment) Regulations 1993 SI No 775 amend the CCA&E Regs, and the Council Tax (Administration and Enforcement) (Amendment) (No 2) Regulations 1993 SI No 773 amend the CTA&E Regs (both from 1 April 1993) to allow the same exemptions from distress as apply to seizure by county court bailiffs (see page 46).

9   CCA&E Regs reg 41(1) and CTA&E Regs reg 47(1) and Local Government Financial Act Sch 4 para 8 as amended by Local Government Finance Act 1992 s102(3).

10   CCA&E Regs reg 41(2) and CTA&E Regs reg 47(2).

Summons for liability order hearing received

Arguments on liability: the community charge

If a person is registered as being liable for the community charge, it is not open to the magistrates to question this registration. It is beyond the scope of this book on emergency procedures to look at the circumstances in which a person must register for community charge and the exemptions. If a person considers they have been wrongly registered, then they have to appeal against their registration to the community charge registration officer and thereafter to the Community Charge & Valuation Tribunal.[11] Registration for community charge is quite separate from the enforcement procedure.

Because entry on the community charge register cannot be questioned in liability order proceedings, in practice there is rarely a defence. The only exception to this rule applies in the case of joint liability between married or unmarried partners.

Joint liability

Community charge is payable on a daily basis. There is joint liability during every day that:

– a man and woman are married to each other and are members of the same household, or
– a man and a woman are not married to each but are living together as husband and wife.[12]

It will be a question of fact for the magistrates' court considering an application for a liability order whether the parties are married together and living in the same household or living together as man and wife.

A checklist of factors the court will take into account in deciding joint liability is contained in appendix 2.

Arguments on liability: the council tax

If a person is summonsed for non-payment of the council tax it is not open to the magistrates' court to question:

– whether the defendant is correctly being held responsible for the council tax;
– whether any tax should be paid in respect of that dwelling or the dwelling should be exempt; nor

---

11   Local Government Finance Act 1988 s23.
12   Local Government Finance Act 1988 s16.

- how much council tax should be payable.[13]

If a person feels he has been wrongly summonsed, he must appeal to a Valuation Tribunal.[14]

For the council tax, even a dispute about joint liability cannot be raised in the magistrates' court. So there will virtually never be any defence to the proceedings other than that the debt has been paid.

How the council tax works

Someone is liable to pay the council tax for every dwelling which is self-contained and which is not exempt.[15]

Order of liability

The general rule is that the first person in the following list who exists is liable on any particular day for the council tax in respect of a dwelling which is not exempt:

- a resident of the dwelling who has a freehold interest in the whole or any part of it;
- a resident of the dwelling who has a leasehold interest in the whole or any part of the dwelling which is not inferior to another such interest held by another such resident;
- a person who is both a resident and a statutory or secure tenant of the whole or any part of the dwelling;
- a resident of the dwelling who has a contractual licence to occupy the whole or any part of the dwelling;
- a resident of the dwelling; or
- the owner of the dwelling.[16]

Essentially the list breaks down in order of priority as follows:

- a freehold owner-occupier;
- a leaseholder owner-occupier;
- any kind of tenant who is living in the dwelling;
- a licensee who is living in the dwelling;
- anyone else living in the dwelling regardless of their legal position;
- if no one is living there, the owner.

13   Council Tax (A&E) Regs reg 57 and Local Government Finance Act 1992 s16.
14   Local Government Finance Act 1992 s16.
15   Local Government Finance Act 1992 s3(2) defined a dwelling as meaning a hereditament for rating purposes if rates were still in existence and which is not subject to business rates. For practical purposes a hereditament is rateable if it is self-contained. Exempt dwellings are prescribed by the Council Tax (Exempt Dwellings) Regulations 1992 SI No. 558.
16   Local Government Finance Act 1992 s6.

The normal priority of order of payment referred to above is only disturbed where the dwelling falls into a particular class that has been prescribed by regulations. The regulations can prescribe who is liable in particular cases, eg, they state that the owner is liable for the tax for certain houses in multiple occupation.[17]

Joint liability

Where liability in order of priority falls on a person in a particular category above, there is joint and several liability of every person within that category.

In addition, there is joint liability between spouses and unmarried partners in the same circumstances as for the community charge.[18]

Amount payable

Generally the amount payable depends on the tax band within which the dwelling falls. However, in addition, a discount of 25 per cent is allowed if there is only one resident of the dwelling or there is more than one person resident but all but one fall to be disregarded for the purposes of the discount.[19] There is a list of people who have to be disregarded for the discount including, for example, those detained in prison or hospital, severely mentally impaired, young people for whom child benefit is being received, students, hospital patients, etc.[20]

Representation

There is no form of legal aid available for a person to be represented in proceedings for a liability order by a solicitor who has been instructed in advance. The green form scheme will be available to carry out preliminary advice and assistance but not for representation. However, the client will be entitled to attend court with a 'McKenzie friend' who will be able to advise and assist him or her during the course of the proceedings but not to represent him or her.[21] A McKenzie friend can be excluded only if his or her behaviour is disruptive.

---

17 Local Government Finance Act 1992 s8 and Council Tax (Liability of Owner) Regulations 1992 SI No. 551.
18 Local Government Finance Act 1992 s9.
19 Local Government Finance Act 1992 s11.
20 Local Government Finance Act 1992 Sch 1.
21 *R v Leicester City Justices ex parte Barrow* [1991] 2 QB 260, CA and *R v Wolverhampton Stipendiary Magistrate ex parte Mould* (1992) 4 November, December 1992 *Legal Action* 14

Bailiff due to levy distress

If a bailiff is due to call, the local authority will have obtained a liability order from the magistrates' court. A liability order authorises the local authority to instruct bailiffs to levy distress.

The strategies in this section are relevant where the bailiff has not yet succeeded in levying distress, eg, where the bailiff is threatening to call and has written an initial letter, where the bailiff has called but the client was out or where the bailiff has called and was not allowed entry.

It used to be the common practice for bailiffs to argue that they did not need to gain access to a house to levy distress. When they visited and the person was out, they used to put a note through the door stating that they had levied distress on all the goods within the house. This practice was found to be unlawful.[22] It is also insufficient to identify goods through a window and then put a list of the goods through the letter-box stating that they have been distrained. Entry is essential for the purposes of levying distress.

Safeguarding belongings

There are various precautions the client can take when distress is threatened:

a) Hide items of value. When the bailiff gains entry s/he is unlikely to make a thorough search of the dwelling. It is therefore possible to hide items of value. There is nothing unlawful about hiding items which the client wishes to keep safe.

b) Park cars well away from home. Distress can be levied on the client's goods wherever they are.

c) Do not bring items of value into the home from elsewhere.

d) Remove items of value from the home to alternative venues for the time being. Again this is not unlawful. The bailiff can still impound those items if s/he can find out where they are, but this is very unlikely to occur unless the client tells the bailiff where they are. There is no obligation to answer the bailiff's questions.

e) Where appropriate, transfer ownership of property to a friend or family member. There are two problems with transferring ownership. The first is that there is an argument that in order to avoid distress by this method, the transfer of property must have occurred before the distress warrant was issued to the bailiff. The second problem is that bailiffs in practice do not distinguish between the various members of the household but tend to distrain anything of value within the house,

---

22 *Evans v South Ribble Borough Council* [1992] 2 WLR 429.

leaving the onus of proof on the non-debtors to prove that they own any items that have been removed or distrained.

Refusing entry to the bailiff

By far the most effective method of dealing with bailiffs is to ensure that the windows and doors are kept shut and locked and that the door is not opened to them. Since the bailiff has no right to break in, s/he is unable to carry out the distress without gaining access unless there is some item on the premises which can be reached without gaining access. Note that there is an argument that bailiffs are entitled to break into outside sheds and they will be able to remove a car unless it is in a locked garage which is attached to the house.

People often find it very difficult to refuse access. It has been known for the bailiff to call at half past six in the morning, catching clients by surprise. The bailiff can return to the premises as many times as s/he wishes.

Injunction

There will be few cases where an injunction is appropriate. In practice, it will only be appropriate where the bailiff calls at the wrong address, ie, an address at which the client has no goods. Otherwise, the bailiff will have the right to call under the provisions of the liability order and the distress warrant.

If a letter threatening distress is received at an address where the debtor no longer lives, the bailiff should be sent a letter making clear that the debtor no longer resides at the address and has no belongings in the property. Bailiffs should be asked to confirm within a fixed period that they will not return to the property and will not seek to levy distress there. If such an undertaking is not forthcoming, this may give rise to an application for an injunction restraining a trespass (see below).

Overturning a liability order

Once a liability order has been made, it is extremely difficult to overturn because there is no right of appeal. The only methods of challenge are by way of judicial review and/or case stated in the divisional court. In most cases, the client will not have been present at the hearing and this makes the client's ability to apply for case stated or judicial review almost impossible because he or she will not have the essential information to form a basis for challenge.

Essentially, the grounds for challenging a liability order are as follows:
- that no reasonable magistrates' court would have made the liability order on the evidence presented;
- that the magistrates' court took into account irrelevant considerations or failed to take account of relevant considerations;
- breach of the rules of natural justice; for example, a refusal to allow a McKenzie friend;[23]
- lack of evidence upon which a liability order could be made.

Clearly, if the client was not present, it is going to be difficult to know what factors the magistrates took into account when reaching their decision. In any event, they do not give reasons. It will also be difficult, in most cases, to argue that there was not a fair hearing if the client was not present. It may be possible to argue that there was insufficient evidence if a relative or friend of the client was present and took notes.

Apply for an administration order

An administration order (see chapter 2) prevents the local authority from using bailiffs to levy distress. If a county court or High Court judgment has been obtained, this should therefore be considered as a remedy.

If there is no judgment against the client, there are two ways the client may try to ensure that such a judgment is obtained in order to give grounds for an administration order:
- stop paying for any consumer or credit debts to encourage the creditors to try and take action to recover the debt and to obtain a judgment;
- if money is owed to relatives or friends, invite them to take court action for the debt and obtain a judgment.

Apply for an interim order

An interim order with a view to a voluntary arrangement or for bankruptcy (see chapter 2) prevents the local authority from enforcing a liability order by levying distress or seeking the client's committal to prison.

Complaint to the magistrates' court

The administration and enforcement regulations provide any person aggrieved by a levy or an attempt to levy a distress the right of appeal to a

---

23   *R v Leicester City Justices, ex parte Barrow* [1991] 2 QB 260.

magistrates' court. This mechanism has been used unsuccessfully by complainants who have been visited by bailiffs who have failed to gain access. The magistrates' courts considering those applications have held that this first visit did not constitute 'an attempt to levy' distress and have dismissed the applications, sometimes with substantial costs orders against the complainant.[24]

Distress levied but goods not yet removed

Once bailiffs gain access to the home, in practice they identify items of the client's property which they propose to remove. They do not remove them straight away but enter into what is known as a 'walking possession' agreement with the client. Under this agreement, the client agrees not to dispose of the property and in return the bailiff agrees to leave the items in the home for the time being giving the client an opportunity to pay before the goods are removed.

The community charge and council tax regulations require that any walking possession agreement is in writing and that a copy of any walking possession agreement entered into is handed to the client.[25]

Once a walking possession agreement has been entered into, costs of 10p per day start to clock up.[26] Any money paid will first of all go to discharge this 10p daily rate and will go to the bailiff rather than to discharging the debt. The sooner the debt is paid, therefore, the better. The same categories of goods are exempt from distress from the council tax as are exempt from execution by bailiffs executing county court warrants (see page 46).[27]

The bailiff has power to levy distress on goods even though they are of little or no value on the second-hand market.

---

24   For example, *Charlton v Cheltenham Borough Council* (Cheltenham Magistrates' Court, 28 March 1991, unreported).
25   CCA&E Regs reg 39(5) and CTA&E Regs reg 45(5).
26   Community Charges (Administration and Enforcement) (Amendment) Regulations 1993 SI No 775 (CCA&E(A) Regs) reg 10 and Sch, and Council Tax (Administration and Enforcement) (Amendment) (No 2) Regulations 1993 SI No 775 (CTA&E(A No 2) Regs) reg 7 and Sch.
27   Local Government Finance Act 1992 s102(3) amending Sch 4 para 8 of the Local Government Finance Act 1988; 1992 Act Sch 4 para 7(4); CTA&E(A No 2) Regs reg 5; and CCA&E(A) Regs reg 6.

Safeguarding belongings

If the bailiff has called and a walking possession agreement has been signed, it is too late to safeguard belongings by moving them elsewhere. To do so could amount to a criminal offence. However, if the client refused to sign a walking possession agreement, or there is an argument that the walking possession agreement is invalid because it was signed by some other person (see below) then this strategy may still be available. It is only available if it can be successfully argued that the distress has been 'abandoned' because the bailiff did not remove the goods at the time and did not have a walking possession agreement. There is no clear law on what constitutes an abandonment but there is a strong argument that the bailiff can only levy distress either by removing the goods immediately, leaving a person on the premises in possession of the goods (this is called 'close possession') or leaving with a signed walking possession agreement.

Refusing entry

If the bailiff has once gained entry and levied distress, then the bailiff has a right to break into the house on returning to remove the goods. The strategy of refusing entry is therefore not available.

Challenging a walking possession agreement

If it is possible to argue that a walking possession agreement is invalid, the bailiff will not have effectively levied distress. The bailiff would therefore have no right to break in when returning to collect the goods. No charges will accrue to the bailiff under the walking possession agreement. The rights of the client will be the same as if the bailiff had never visited (see page 123). The four grounds for challenging a walking possession agreement are set out below.

Signature by non-debtor

Bailiffs will always operate on the basis that a signature by any member of the household is sufficient for a walking possession agreement to be valid. In fact, an agreement can only be valid if the person who signed the agreement had express or implied authority from the client to do so. Express authority is unlikely. There is no general rule that a spouse of other family member has implied authority to sign agreements on another person's behalf.

Agreement not signed at the time of the bailiff's visit
Some bailiffs post agreements through the letter-box, having failed to gain access, asking for them to be signed and returned. When they are returned, they argue that they have a walking possession agreement. Enforcement regulations require that the agreement is signed 'at the time that the distress is levied'.[28]

Agreement does not identify the goods distrained
The legislation does not make clear precisely how much information the bailiff has to provide as to the goods that have been distrained. However, the whole basis upon which distress has operated over centuries is that bailiffs must identify goods in order to distrain them effectively. If this has not been done, it is possible to argue that the walking possession agreement is invalid.

Agreement includes goods that do not belong to the client
If the agreement refers to goods that do not belong to the client, the walking possession agreement will be ineffective only so far as those goods are concerned. The bailiff has no power to levy distress on these goods so that the owner of the goods is entitled to deal with them in any way whatsoever regardless of the walking possession agreement. Certainly, so far as these goods are concerned, steps can be taken to prevent them being removed by the bailiff if he or she returns, eg, by moving them elsewhere.

Complaint to the magistrates' court

Now that regulations have been introduced to exempt certain items from distress, a complaint may be made to the magistrates' court (see page 125) by the debtor where the bailiff has gained entry and levied distress against exempt goods.

A non-debtor can also use this mechanism to complain that goods that do not belong to the debtor have been distrained. However, removing the goods from the home is probably a more effective and less risky strategy.

A draft complaint is shown in precedent 17 in Part III.

Injunction

An injunction will be appropriate either to prevent the bailiff from breaking into the premises when he or she is threatening to do so or to prevent the bailiff removing goods which cannot be distrained because

---

28   CCA&E Regs Sch 5 para 2(3) and CTA&E(A No 2) Regs Sch para 2(2).

they belong to other members of the family. It should be noted that goods that are jointly owned with the debtor and some other person are liable to distress. Wherever it can be argued that a walking possession agreement is not valid (see page 127) and the bailiff is threatening to break in upon his or her return to collect the goods, an injunction may be the only way to prevent this occurring.

Under the amendments to the County Courts Act 1984 introduced by the Courts and Legal Services Act 1990, injunctions and declarations can now be obtained in the county court where the matter involves a contract or a tort independently of any claim for damages.[29]

A specimen particulars of claim seeking an injunction on several grounds is shown in precedent 18 in Part III.

An affidavit in support of an application for an injunction will be required dealing with the following issues:

- the identity and ownership of any goods involved;
- the initial threat to levy distress issued by the bailiff, a copy of the walking possession agreement and any correspondence or telephone contact with the bailiff about the right to return and remove the goods;
- the reason why some or all of the money demanded is not due if applicable;
- the steps taken to persuade the bailiff that he or she has no right to distrain;
- the bailiff's response;
- the likely detriment to the owner if distress takes place.

The court will grant an interlocutory injunction if satisfied that:

- there is a serious question to be tried (ie, the applicant has an arguable case);
- the balance of convenience is in favour of granting the injunction;
- damages for wrongful distress would be an inadequate remedy;
- there is a real likelihood of the distress taking place;
- grave damage to the plaintiff would result if distress takes place.[30]

Notice of an application for an injunction must generally be served on the defendant at least two clear days before the hearing.[31] Where there is a genuine fear that the bailiff will seek to levy distress before the hearing and the bailiff refuses to postpone distress, an *ex parte* application should be made.

29   County Courts Act 1984 s38.
30   *American Cyanamid Co v Ethicon Ltd* [1975] CA 396, HL, and *Redland Bricks Ltd v Morris* [1970] AC 652, HL.
31   County Court Rules 1981 Ord 13 r1.

Disputing the bailiff's charges

Even if the bailiff has successfully levied distress and a walking possession agreement has been properly signed, it may be that the bailiff is seeking to recover greater charges than he or she is entitled to.

Charges which can be disputed

The charges which bailiffs can make are governed by regulations.[32] Bailiffs have charged for a large number of matters under a general heading in the schedule of charges relating to community charge which provides 'for other expenses incurred in connection with the proposed sale where there is no buyer in relation to it' and that allows them to charge 'reasonable costs and fees incurred'.

Using this provision, bailiffs have made charges for letters written before they have made any visits at all, charges for direct debit and standing order facilities and charges for processing cheques.

There is a very strong argument that these charges cannot be made under this provision. There is no 'proposed sale' at the time at which the bailiffs are writing their first letter before even visiting. There is no 'proposed sale' at the time the bailiffs make their first visit. Nor is there a 'proposed sale' when arrangements have been made for payment by instalments, direct debits, standing orders etc. In addition, the government has announced that this head of charge will be removed from the administration and enforcement regulations.

There may therefore be significant sums which the client can argue that s/he is not liable to pay to the bailiff by way of costs. Under the walking possession agreement, costs are incurred at the rate of £0.10 per day until the debt and charges *legally* due are cleared. If the undisputed part of any debt and costs is cleared, then the client should not only dispute the remainder but also any walking possession fees that accrue from the date that the last undisputed sum is cleared.

Taxing the bailiff's costs

In case of any dispute as to charges due to bailiffs, the amount of their charges can be taxed by the county court for the district in which the distress is or is intended to be levied.[33] The court can award the costs of taxation. The application is made by originating application and a specimen of such an application is shown in precedent 19 in Part III. It is possible that the client cannot apply for taxation once the bailiff's costs have actually been paid. A copy of the demand for payment should be

---

32   See page 126 and SIs cited there.
33   CCA&E Regs Sch 5 para 3; CTA&E(A No 2) Regs Sch para 3.

attached to the application.[34] The fee for an originating application is £40 which will be a substantial deterrent to any applicant. An application can be made to the Lord Chancellor's Department for the fee to be waived.

Paying the bailiff and claiming back disputed sums

An alternative remedy, which is more attractive to most people, is to pay the debt under protest and then to take action in the small claims court to recover the debt. Where a payment is made under duress to a person who is not entitled to it, the money can be recovered under the law of restitution.[35]

The sum being claimed will inevitably be less than £1,000 so the procedure for claiming it is by way of a small claim. A specimen letter to be sent to the bailiff when paying a disputed sum is shown in precedent 20 in Part III and a specimen particulars of claim for reclaiming the sum due is shown in precedent 21.

Overturning liability order

See page 124 above.

Applying for an administration order

See page 125 above and chapter 2.

Applying for a bankruptcy order or an interim order with a view to a voluntary arrangement

See page 125 and chapter 2.

Goods removed but not yet sold

The options for challenging the bailiff become more limited when goods have already been removed. There is no statutory time-limit within which the bailiff has a right to sell. Sale can take place immediately. It is therefore crucial to move extremely swiftly to deal with the situation.

---

34 County Court Rules 1981 Ord 35 r22.
35 See *Woolwich Equitable Building Society v Inland Revenue Commissioners* [1992] 3 WLR 366, HL and page 83 above.

Injunction[36]

An injunction will be available in two circumstances:

- where goods belonging to a non-debtor which do not belong to the client have been removed;
- where the undisputed part of the debt has been paid and the balance owing is disputed upon the grounds that the bailiff is not entitled to certain costs (see page 130).

See page 128 for the details and grounds. The specimen particulars of claim in precedent 18 in Part III will require minor amendment.

Complaint to magistrates' court

See page 125.

Pay the debt and costs

Once the bailiff has taken away goods and is about to sell them, the client may have little choice but to pay the debt and recover the goods.

If any sum is disputed, then payment should be made under protest using the form of letter shown in precedent 20 in Part III. The client can then seek to recover the disputed sums paid by action in the small claims court. See precedent 21 in Part III for draft particulars of claim.

Apply for an administration order

Since an administration order (see page 125 and chapter 2) prevents the creditor from having any remedy against the property of the debtor, this must include the right to sell property which has been distrained.

Apply for a bankruptcy order or interim order

See page 34 in chapter 2. These will have the same effect as an administration order.

Summons for means enquiry received

If the bailiff has failed to get the debt repaid and/or cannot gain access or cannot find any goods to distrain, s/he should report to the local

---

36   See *Davidson v Roach and Co. (Revenues) Ltd* (1991) July 1991 *Legal Action* 21 as an example of a similar kind of application for an injunction.

authority which then applies for a summons for a warrant of commitment. The right to apply for a warrant applies when the bailiff reports to the authority that no or insufficient goods of the client can be found on which to levy the amount due.[37]

The rules require the magistrates' court to carry out a means enquiry in the client's presence and enquire whether the failure to pay which led to the liability order concerned being made against the client was due to his or her 'wilful refusal or culpable neglect'.[38]

The proper procedure is that the court should decide two issues as soon as it has the necessary information: the first is whether the non-payment of the debt due under the liability order was due to wilful refusal or culpable neglect; the second is to decide what order should be made in the light of the first finding. The sum due will include any bailiff's costs for visiting the premises.

Many magistrates' courts ignore the statutory requirement to consider these questions. Generally, they obtain brief details of the client's means, order him or her to repay the arrears by fixed instalments and adjourn the means enquiry. Sometimes they fix a future hearing but inform the client that s/he need not attend if s/he has kept to the order. Thus the threat of imprisonment hangs over the client until the arrears are discharged. If s/he does not keep to the order made, the court is unlikely to be sympathetic when the matter returns. The practice of most courts is, arguably, unlawful and persists only because few, if any, debtors are represented.

Representation at the hearing

No legal aid is available for the hearing despite the risk of imprisonment. A client has the right to a McKenzie friend (see page 122).

Disputing culpable neglect or wilful default

It is only at this stage in the enforcement process that there is any power to remit any arrears of poll tax or council tax. Only the magistrates' court has such power but it also has the power at this stage to imprison the client. In practice, on the first occasion, it is unlikely that the client will be imprisoned. It is far more likely that he or she will have a sentence of imprisonment imposed which is suspended upon terms. Nevertheless, this places the client concerned at serious risk of being imprisoned in the future if s/he breaches the terms of the suspension.

---

37   Local Government Finance Act 1988 Sch 4 para 8(1)(a) as amended by Local Government Finance Act 1992 s102(3) and Local Government Finance Act 1992 Sch 4 para 8(1)(a).
38   CCA&E Regs reg 41(2) and CTA&E Regs reg 47(2).

A full statement of means should be prepared and presented using the checklist shown on page 8. Stress should be laid either on the client's present financial circumstances or on the history of the financial circumstances which led to the arrears, whichever is the more favourable to the client. When the client is not represented, courts frequently consider only the present means of the non-payer although the statutory criteria suggest that the past means are more important.

It is not unusual for the court or presenting officer to suggest a ludicrous method of raising money, for example, that the client should sell his or her home. In the one reported case that has reached the High Court regarding the imprisonment of debtors for culpable neglect, the court held that an unemployed person with no assets who had a potential to earn money could not be found guilty of culpable neglect for failing to pay the community charge unless there was clear evidence that gainful employment was on offer but had been refused.[39]

A client can be found guilty of 'wilful default' only if s/he had the money to pay the debt and deliberately failed to pay. The more difficult question is whether a client is guilty of 'culpable neglect'. For practical purposes, the only cases in which the question of possible 'culpable neglect' is going to arise is where there is an allegation that a source of income or capital is available to a client which s/he has failed to use to pay the debt. The case of *R v Poole Justices, ex parte Benham* (1991) 156 JP 177 in the Divisional Court makes clear that the onus of proof is not on the client to disprove all potential sources of income unless there is some evidence to suggest that a source of income or capital is available (and this can include a small surplus of income after essential expenditure). At court, therefore, it is necessary to be prepared to deal with any suggestions that sources of income or capital, including small surpluses of income over essential expenditure, are available to pay the debt.

Mitigation

If the court finds the client guilty of wilful default or culpable neglect it can deal with the case in one of four ways:

- Issue a warrant of commitment immediately so that the client is imprisoned for a period of up to three months.
- Issue a warrant of commitment but suspended on terms as to payment, eg, a sum off the arrears each week.
- If no warrant of commitment is issued, remit all or part of the debt.
- Make no order at all.

Even if it finds culpable neglect or wilful default, the court has total

39   *R v Poole Justices, ex parte Benham* (1991) 156 JP 177, DC.

discretion as to which of these options to choose. When a finding of culpable neglect or wilful default has been made, a plea in mitigation should be presented to convince the court that imprisonment is inappropriate or that at the very least a suspended term of imprisonment should be imposed. It is worth arguing that the local authority is better served by a suspended warrant of commitment because if the client is imprisoned, the poll tax or council tax debt will never be paid. In addition it should be pointed out that imprisonment is intended as a weapon to extract payment not a punishment.[40]

The courts have responsibility to consider all alternatives to issuing a warrant for immediate commitment to prison before deciding to do so.[41]

Powers of the court where the client is found not guilty of wilful refusal or culpable neglect

If the court finds there was no wilful refusal or culpable neglect, or is not satisfied that there was wilful refusal or culpable neglect, it may:

– remit all or part of the poll tax or council tax due;
– make no order at all.[42]

Apply for an administration order, bankruptcy order or interim order

All these orders prevent the local authority from seeking an order for committal.

Breach of suspended order or terms of adjournment

Challenging the adjournment

If the court had all the necessary information to carry out a means enquiry, it should have made a decision and if the matter was adjourned this was probably unlawful. The client could challenge the adjournment by judicial review, but the Divisional Court would probably order the matter to be reheard. There is a risk that, on a rehearing, the court might impose a period of immediate or suspended imprisonment. The best tactic, therefore, is simply to go back to the court at the next hearing and treat this as the first means enquiry, inviting the court to make a finding that

---

40   R v Wolverhampton Stipendiary Magistrate ex parte Mould December 1992 Legal Action 14.
41   R v Poole Justices, ex parte Benham (1991) 156 JP 177, DC.
42   CCA&E Regs regs 41 and 42 and CTA&E Regs regs 47 and 48.

there was no culpable neglect or wilful default. A full statement of means should be prepared and presented.

Challenging the suspended order

The decision to issue a suspended warrant may be challenged by judicial review in the same way as the decision to imprison immediately (see below). This should be seriously considered if it is totally impossible for the client to comply with the terms of the suspension, since the court is more likely to impose immediate imprisonment at the next hearing. However, if the client was not represented, a full statement of means at the next hearing may persuade the court that the instalments were too high.

Making representations why imprisonment should not take place for breach of suspension

If the client does not comply with the terms of the suspension, imprisonment is not automatic. In a recent case the Divisional Court quite clearly stated that the client has a further right of rehearing before a warrant of committal is issued even if he or she is in breach of a suspended order.[43] More recently, the court has indicated that magistrates are obliged to have a second hearing for a means enquiry to discover why the payments have not been kept up and at that hearing the test they must use to decide whether to issue a warrant of commitment is whether the failure of the client to keep up the payments was due to 'wilful refusal or culpable neglect'.[44] Even if the magistrates' court is not obliged to hold a rehearing, when a complaint is made by the local authority, the court should at the very least warn the client that s/he is in breach of the terms of suspension and invite the client's comments. It is therefore imperative to contact the court by telephone immediately to state that representations are to be made and then follow the call up with a letter making representations. A full statement of means will be required and the court's attention should be drawn to any changes of circumstances since the date of the decision to fix a term of imprisonment. At this second hearing, the justices no longer have the power to remit any part of the community charge but do have a

---

43 *R v Faversham and Sittingbourne Justices, ex parte Ursell* (1992) *Independent*, 19 March, QBD.

44 *R v St Albans Justices, ex parte Pointer* (14 July 1992 QBD) unreported but see September 1992 *Legal Action* 17. It should be noted that leave for judicial review was refused in this case and the remarks of Rose J are not binding.

discretion not to issue a warrant and are bound to give the debtor an opportunity to address them prior to the exercise of that discretion.

Apply for an administration order, bankruptcy order or interim order

See page 125 and chapter 2.

Client imprisoned

If the client has been sent to prison there are two possible courses of action.

- payment of the debt and all the costs, thus securing his or her immediate release;[45]
- judicial review.

Judicial review may be available on any of the following grounds:

- a proper means enquiry was not carried out;
- the court's decision is perverse;[46]
- the magistrates were 'functus officio'. If at a previous hearing the court has already made a finding on the issue of culpable neglect or wilful default, but then adjourned and ordered the client to pay instalments, its jurisdiction had ceased and therefore it cannot consider the matter at all unless a fresh application is made by the local authority. The original finding of wilful default or culpable neglect gave rise to the need to decide what to do to dispose of the case and the case has been completed.

45   CCA&E Regs reg 41(6) and (7) and CTA&E Regs reg 47(6) and (7).
46   *R v Faversham and Sittingbourne Magistrates' Court, ex parte Ursell* (1992) 156 JP 765, QBD.

CHAPTER 7

Arrears under magistrates' courts orders

Introduction

Typical problems requiring emergency action are where:

- the client expects a visit from the bailiff collecting arrears;
- the bailiff has called and levied distress but has not yet removed the client's goods;
- goods have been removed by the bailiff but not yet sold;
- the client receives a summons requiring him or her to attend a means enquiry to show cause why he or she should not be committed to prison;
- a means enquiry has already been held and the client is now under immediate threat of imprisonment for breaching the terms of suspension or adjournment or a suspended term of imprisonment was imposed at the time of a conviction.

Debts recoverable in a magistrates' court

There are essentially three categories of financial orders which can be enforced by the magistrates court: (1) fines and other orders made in criminal proceedings; (2) magistrates' court maintenance orders; and (3) sums recoverable as a civil debt.

The first category includes:

- fines imposed by the magistrates' court on conviction;
- fines imposed by the Crown Court which are dealt with by a magistrates' court named by the Crown Court or alternatively by the magistrates' court which committed the defendant for trial;[1]
- compensation orders made by either the magistrates' court or the Crown Court;[2]

---

1 Powers of Criminal Courts Act 1973 s32.
2 Administration of Justice Act 1970 Sch 9 part I para 10.

- costs orders made by the magistrates' court or Crown Court at the time of trial and on most appeals;[3]
- orders for the payment by a parent or guardian of a juvenile of fines, compensation orders, costs etc;[4]
- recognisances (for example, a bind-over or a recognisance by a parent or guardian to take proper care of a child or keep proper control of him or her) ordered to be forfeited;[5]
- unpaid national insurance contributions following a conviction for failing to pay those contributions.[6]

In the rest of this chapter, these kinds of debts will be referred to as 'orders in criminal proceedings'.

The second category includes:

- orders for maintenance under the Domestic Proceedings and Magistrates' Courts Act 1978;
- orders for maintenance that were made under the Guardianship of Minors Acts 1971 and 1973;
- affiliation orders which are still in force;
- High Court and county court maintenance orders which are registered in the magistrates' court;
- orders made under the Children Act 1989.[7]

In this chapter, these debts will be referred to as 'orders in matrimonial proceedings'. Maintenance assessments under the Child Support Act 1991 will gradually replace orders for maintenance of children in the period 1993–1997 (see chapter 8).

The third category includes:

- unpaid tax and employees' national insurance contributions of less than £500;[8]
- orders for legally aided defendants to contribute to the cost of their defence;[9]

---

3 Administration of Justice Act 1970 Sch 9 paras 1 to 9.
4 Administration of Justice Act 1970 Sch 9 para 12.
5 Magistrates' Courts Act 1980 s120(4).
6 Social Security Act 1975 ss150 to 152.
7 Magistrates' Courts Act 1980 s150. Technically, orders under the Children Act 1989 are not magistrates' court maintenance orders but are stated to be enforceable as such by virtue of the Children Act 1989 Sch 1 para 12(3). Otherwise, the full list of magistrates' court maintenance orders is in the Adminstration of Justice Act 1970 Sch 8.
8 Taxes Management Act 1970 s65.
9 Legal Aid Act 1988 ss23 and 24 and Sch 3.

- charges or contributions payable to social services authorities for community care services.[10]

In this chapter, these debts will be referred to as 'orders in civil proceedings'.

Types of court order

Orders in criminal and civil proceedings

In criminal and civil proceedings the total sum payable will be fixed.

Allowing time for payment

The magistrates' court may make an order:

- requiring payment immediately;
- allowing time for payment, eg, payment within 28 days; or
- ordering payment by instalments, eg, a certain amount per week.[11]

Applying for deduction from income support

When a fine is imposed or some other sum is required to be paid in criminal proceedings the court can request the Benefits Agency to make a deduction from income support payable to the defendant.[12] Before doing so, it must carry out a means enquiry.[13] Deductions can also be made where income support is payable with other benefits such as unemployment or invalidity benefit.

The Benefits Agency will make a deduction from income support for payment towards the fine provided the defendant would be left with at least 10p income support after the deduction has been made and provided that the total weekly deductions for all debts do not exceed £4.40.[14] If there are other debts, deductions for fines take the lowest priority, so that these other debts may prevent a deduction being made.[15]

Issuing a warrant of distress

Magistrates' courts have powers to issue warrants of distress authorising bailiffs or police officers to collect sums outstanding. In the case of criminal and civil proceedings, they may issue a warrant of distress at the time of making an order for payment of money, eg, at the time of fining a

---

10   Health and Social Services and Social Security Adjudications Act 1983 s17(4).
11   Magistrates' Court Act 1980 s75.
12   Fines (Deduction from Income Support) Regulations 1992 (SI No 2182) reg 2(1).
13   Ibid reg 2(2).
14   Ibid reg 4(2).
15   Ibid reg 4(1)(b).

person who has been convicted, and they may postpone the issue of the warrant.[16] Postponement may be made until a specific time or on conditions, eg, as to payment of instalments.[17] A distress warrant can only be issued where there is a default in making a payment under the terms of the order.[18]

Immediate imprisonment for failing to pay a sum due

In criminal proceedings but not in civil proceedings, the court can in some circumstances impose an immediate sentence of imprisonment for failing to pay a fine or other sum due on conviction.[19] This power is only exercisable:

a)   in the case of an offence punishable with imprisonment if the defendant appears to the court to have sufficient means to pay the sum due 'forthwith';

b)   if it appears to the court that the defendant is unlikely to remain long enough at a place of residence in the UK to enable payment of the sum to be enforced by methods other than immediate imprisonment; or

c)   the defendant is sentenced to a term of immediate imprisonment or detention in any event.

On the face of it, this would appear to be a very limited power to impose imprisonment in default. It would clearly apply to people who are currently homeless or are likely to become homeless in the near future as well as people who are in any event sentenced to imprisonment or detention. Otherwise, the power to order imprisonment in default is limited to defendants who 'appear to the court to have sufficient means to pay the sum forthwith'. *Stone's Justices' Manual*[20] suggests that the word 'forthwith' means a 'reasonable time thereafter' and could be as long as six months. However, the wording of the statute suggests that at the time the order is made, ie, the time at which the fine is imposed, the magistrates must be satisfied that the defendant immediately has the finances to pay the debt. In practice, this would appear to mean that a sentence of imprisonment in default of payment should only be imposed if the defendant is given a relatively short time to pay, eg, 14 or 28 days simply to arrange for the cheque or cash to be deposited with the court. If instalments are ordered, then by definition the magistrates' court is unlikely to be satisfied that the defendant immediately has in his or her possession the means to discharge the whole debt.

16   Magistrates' Courts Act 1980 ss76 and 77.
17   Magistrates' Courts Act 1980 s77(1).
18   Magistrates' Courts Act 1980 s76(1).
19   Magistrates' Courts Act 1980 s82(1).
20   *Stone's Justices' Manual* 1991 ed para 2–744.

Before making an order for immediate detention for non-payment of a fine of a person aged 17 to 20, the court must be of the opinion that no other method of dealing with him or her is appropriate.[21] The court must take into account all aggravating and mitigating circumstances, can take into account any other information and must give reasons for detention in open court.[22]

Subsequent imprisonment in default

In criminal proceedings, if the magistrates' court does not make an order for imprisonment immediately in default of immediate payment, the court can instead impose a subsequent sentence of imprisonment to be served only if default is made in payment. However, it can only do so on the same grounds as it could have imposed an immediate sentence of imprisonment, ie, the defendant has means to pay, defendant will not remain at his or her place of residence long enough to enforce the order, or a sentence of imprisonment or detention is to be imposed. Before imposing a sentence of imprisonment in default of payment of a fine against a person aged 17 to 20, the court must be of the opinion that no other method of dealing with him or her is appropriate.[23] Otherwise, the powers of the court to deal with a 17 to 21 year old in default of payment are the same as for a person over 21.[24]

Where a sentence of imprisonment is fixed in default, the issue of a warrant of commitment (ie, the warrant under which a person can be arrested and sent to prison or detention) is postponed.[25] Postponement can be made until a particular time or on conditions.

The maximum term of imprisonment which can be imposed for default in making a payment in criminal proceedings depends either on the amount required to be paid by the order or the number of units imposed by the conviction if it led to a unit fine.[26]

Fixing a further hearing

Where a court allows time for payment of an order made in criminal proceedings, it can at that stage or at a later stage fix a day on which, if

21   Criminal Justice Act 1982 s1(5) as amended by Criminal Justice Act 1991 Sch 11 para 30.
22   Criminal Justice Act 1982 s1(5) and (5A) as amended by Criminal Justice Act 1991 Sch 11 para 30.
23   Criminal Justice Act 1982 s1(5) and (5A) as amended by Criminal Justice Act 1991 Sch 11 para 30.
24   Criminal Justice Act 1982 s9.
25   Magistrates' Court Act 1980 s77(2).
26   Powers of Criminal Courts Act 1973 s31(3A) as amended by Criminal Justice Act 1988 s60 and Criminal Justice Act 1991 s22.

certain conditions are satisfied, the offender must appear in person before the court either to enable a means enquiry to be held or for the court to consider whether to activate a term of imprisonment imposed in default.[27] The condition is that any part of the sum due remains unpaid on the day fixed by the court or an instalment is overdue.[28]

Money payment supervision order

At the time of imposing a fine or other order in criminal proceedings, or at a later stage, the court can make an order known as a 'money payment supervision order' placing the person under the supervision of a probation officer. The power cannot be exercised if an immediate sentence of imprisonment in default of payment is imposed.[29]

Orders in matrimonial proceedings

Generally an order in matrimonial proceedings will be that the respondent pays periodical payments to the complainant. The court has a general discretion to order that the payment should be made to the clerk of the court.[30] However, orders under the Domestic Proceedings and Magistrates' Courts Act 1978, under the old provisions in the Guardianship of Minors Acts 1971 and 1973 and new orders under the Children Act 1989 must be made through the court unless, after hearing representations expressly made by the applicant for the order asking for payments to be made direct, the court is satisfied that it is undesirable to make payment through the clerk to the court.[31] No distress warrant can be issued and suspended at the time that an order in matrimonial proceedings is made because there will be no default in payment until at least some instalment is overdue.

Default in payment

Orders in criminal and civil proceedings

When one instalment of an order made in criminal proceedings or an order made in civil proceedings is overdue, the whole sum becomes payable immediately.[32] In civil proceedings, proceedings to recover arrears must be

27 Magistrates' Courts Act 1980 s86(1).
28 Magistrates' Courts Act 1980 s86(1)(a) and (b).
29 Magistrates' Courts Act 1980 s88.
30 Magistrates' Courts Act 1980 s59(1).
31 Magistrates' Courts Act 1980 s59(2).
32 Magistrates' Courts Act 1980 s75(3).

begun by way of complaint by the person in whose favour an order is made.[33]

Orders in matrimonial proceedings

In all cases the person in whose favour an order is made may take action to recover any arrears. However, in addition, if the order is being paid through the court, the person in whose favour the order is made can ask the clerk to the court to enforce the sum on his or her behalf. The clerk must then recover the payments unless the clerk considers that it is unreasonable in the circumstances to do so.[34] The procedure for dealing with arrears of payments under an order made in matrimonial proceedings is by way of complaint.[35]

Powers to vary orders

Orders in criminal proceedings and civil proceedings

Where a court has allowed time for payment, eg, payment within 28 days, or has allowed payment by instalments, eg, £5 per week, it can at any stage allow further time or order payment by instalments on application by or on behalf of the person liable to make the payment.[36] The application may be made in writing unless the court requires the applicant to attend.[37] The court cannot vary the amount of the fine, compensation order, costs etc originally imposed but only the terms of payment. The court can vary the number of instalments payable, the amount of any instalment payable and the date on which any instalment becomes payable.[38]

Orders in matrimonial proceedings

Where a person ordered to make a payment applies by way of complaint to the magistrates' court, the court may revoke, revive or vary the order. Under the Child Support Act 1991 s8 magistrates' courts' powers to revive or vary orders for child maintenance are further restricted. No new orders for child maintenance can be made since 5 April 1993 when the Act came into force. Parents have to use the Child Support Agency instead (see

33   Magistrates' Courts Act 1980 s96.
34   Magistrates' Courts Act 1980 s59(3) and (4).
35   Magistrates' Courts Act 1980 s93.
36   Magistrates' Courts Act 1980 s75(2).
37   Magistrates' Courts Act 1980 r51.
38   Magistrates' Courts Act 1980 s85A.

chapter 8). A magistrates' court cannot revive an order after that date.[39] During the transitional period 1993–7 cases where existing orders for child maintenance are in force will progressively come within the ambit of the 1991 Act and the courts will then lose their power to vary such orders.[40] The powers to revoke orders remain.[41] Subject to the above a court also has power to suspend the operation of any provisions of an order temporarily and to revive the operation of any provision suspended at a later date.[42]

Collection of arrears by bailiffs

In the past, many magistrates' courts did not use bailiffs to a large extent in the collection of debts. However, they are now being encouraged to do so because it is considered to be a cheap and effective method of recovering sums due. It can therefore be expected that the remedy of distress will be used far more widely by magistrates' courts in the future.

Orders in criminal proceedings

The court has power to issue a warrant of distress where there has been any default in paying a sum ordered to be paid in criminal proceedings.[43] The court also has power to postpone the issue of the warrant of distress until a particular time and on such conditions as it thinks just.[44] The court may require positive evidence that the defendant actually has some goods worth distraining before issuing a distress warrant.[45]

The warrant authorises the bailiff to collect both property and money but clothes and bedding are exempt as are tools and implements of the trade up to the value of £150.[46] Goods cannot be removed from the house until the date of sale and there must be at least six days between the making of the distress and the date of the sale which must take place by public auction.[47]

It is possible that the court may have issued a warrant at the time that the order for payment was made and then postponed it upon terms which

---

39   Child Support Act 1991 s8(3).
40   Ibid. s8(3).
41   Ibid. s8(4).
42   Magistrates' Courts Act 1980 s60.
43   Magistrates' Courts Act 1980 s76(1).
44   Magistrates' Courts Act 1980 s77(1).
45   *R v German* (1891) 61 LJ MC 43 and see also *R v Mortimer* (1906) 70 JP 542.
46   Magistrates' Courts Rules 1981 r54(2) and (4).
47   Magistrates' Courts Rules 1981 r54(5) to 8.

have now been breached. If that is the case, the decision to activate the warrant of distress is a judicial one and natural justice requires that the defendant is given an opportunity to be heard and to make representations why a warrant should not be issued.[48] The court will have a continuing power to postpone the issue of the warrant on different terms if it sees fit and to vary the number of instalments payable, the amount of any instalments payable or the date upon which the instalments become payable.[49]

If a warrant of distress was not made at the time the order for payment was imposed, then again it is a judicial decision whether or not to issue a warrant of distress and the defendant should be given an opportunity to be heard and make representations why a warrant should not be issued.[50]

Orders in matrimonial proceedings

The same rules apply as for orders in criminal proceedings.

Orders in civil proceedings

The same rules apply as for orders in criminal proceedings save that there is a specific requirement that a warrant of distress cannot be issued for a sum enforceable as a civil debt unless the defendant has previously been served with a copy of the order or the order was made in his presence and a warrant was issued on that occasion.[51] Service is effected by delivering it to the defendant or by sending it to him by post in a letter addressed to him or her at his or her last known or usual place of residence.[52]

Imprisonment and youth detention

Orders in criminal proceedings

Term of imprisonment fixed in default at the time the order was made

When the court orders a fine or other payment to be made, it can also fix a period of imprisonment in default subject to the conditions referred to on page 141 above.

Before issuing a warrant of committal, even if a term of imprisonment

---

48   *Re Wilson* [1985] AC 750, HL.
49   Magistrates' Courts Act 1980 ss77(1) and 85A.
50   *Re Wilson* [1985] AC 750, HL.
51   Magistrates' Courts Rules 1981 r53(1).
52   Magistrates' Courts Rules 1981 r53(3).

has previously been fixed, the magistrates' court must first serve on the offender at least 21 days' notice in writing stating that the court intends to hold a hearing to consider whether to issue such a warrant and giving the reason why the court intends to do so.[53] The notice must state the time and place appointed for the hearing and should inform the offender that if he or she considers that there are grounds why the warrant should not be issued, he or she may make representations to the court in person or in writing but the court can exercise its powers in relation to the issue of the warrant whether or not the person makes representations.[54] The court must consider whatever information it has about the offender's means available to it unless it has previously enquired into the offender's means before postponing the issue of the warrant of commitment.[55]

At the hearing, the court has the following powers:

- to postpone further the issue of the warrant of commitment or to vary any of the conditions on which its issue was previously postponed if it thinks it is just to do so having regard to a change of circumstances since the previous postponement;[56]
- to remit a fine but not any other order for payment if it thinks just to do so having regard to a change of circumstances which has occurred since the previous time when the warrant was postponed.[57]

No term of imprisonment fixed in default

If a term of imprisonment is not fixed at the time the order is made, far more conditions have to be satisfied before the magistrates can imprison a debtor for non-payment.

First, the court cannot issue a warrant of commitment for any default or for want of sufficient distress to satisfy a sum ordered to be paid unless the defendant is already serving a sentence of custody or the court has since the conviction enquired into his or her means in his or her presence on at least one occasion.[58] Having carried out the means enquiry, the court still cannot imprison unless the offence was one punishable by imprisonment and the offender appeared to have sufficient means to pay the sum forthwith or:

- the court is satisfied that the default is due to the offender's wilful refusal or culpable neglect; and

---

53   Magistrates' Courts Act 1980 s82(5A) and (5D).
54   Magistrates' Courts Act 1980 s82(5C).
55   Magistrates' Courts Act 1980 s82(5B).
56   Magistrates' Courts Act 1980 s77(3) and (4).
57   Magistrates' Courts Act 1980 s85(1).
58   Magistrates' Courts Act 1980 s82(3).

- the court has considered or tried all other methods of enforcing payment of the sum and it appears to the court that they are inappropriate or unsuccessful.[59]

The court must consider the following alternative methods:

- issuing a warrant of distress (see above);
- using the High Court or county court for enforcement and therefore using enforcement methods available through those courts, eg, garnishee orders or charging orders (see chapter 3) (the clerk has power to take High Court or county court proceedings for enforcement under the Magistrates' Courts Act 1980 s87);
- making a money payment supervision order;
- making an attachment of earnings order;
- if the offender is under 21, making an attendance centre order;[60]
- applying to the Benefits Agency for a direct deduction from income support payable to the offender.[61]

There is a further condition if the defendant is under 21 years old. In this case, he or she cannot be committed to detention for default in payment unless he or she has first been placed under supervision in respect of the sum due or the court is satisfied that it is undesirable or impracticable to place him or her under supervision.[62]

The court has power to remit any fine (but not an order for any other kind of payment) but can also issue a warrant of commitment and suspend it on terms.[63]

The court can issue a summons requiring the defendant to attend for a means enquiry or issue a warrant of arrest. If the offender fails to appear before the court in answer to the summons, the court can issue a warrant to arrest him or her and bring him or her before the court.[64] The court can order the person concerned to furnish to the court within the specified period such statement of his or her means as the court may require and it is an offence to fail to comply and an offence to provide a false statement.[65]

---

59   Magistrates' Courts Act 1980 s82(4).
60   Magistrates' Courts Act 1980 s82(4A);
61   Criminal Justice Act 1991 s24 and Fines (Deduction from Income Support) Regs 1992 (SI No 2182).
62   Magistrates' Courts Act 1980 s88(4).
63   Magistrates' Courts Act 1980 s85 and s77(3).
64   Magistrates' Courts Act 1980 s83.
65   Magistrates' Courts Act 1980 s84.

Orders for payment in a matrimonial proceedings

If there are arrears under a magistrates' court maintenance order, a complaint can be issued by the clerk to the magistrates' court (if payment is being made through the court) or by the person in whose favour the order is made. The court has power to imprison for non-payment under a magistrates' court maintenance order.[66]

The court may not impose imprisonment in respect of a default unless the court has enquired in the presence of the defendant whether the default was due to the defendant's wilful refusal or culpable neglect and must not impose imprisonment if it is of the opinion that default was not due to wilful refusal and culpable neglect. In addition, the court must not impose imprisonment:

– in a case in which the court has power to make an attachment of earnings order unless the court is of the opinion that it is inappropriate to make such an order;
– in any case in the absence of the defendant.[67]

Imprisonment does not discharge the defendant from liability to pay under the order but during the time the person is in custody, no arrears are accruing.[68] The maximum period of imprisonment is six weeks.[69] A statement by the person in whose favour an order is made that any specific sums have not been paid to him or her in the form of a statutory declaration is admissible evidence unless the court requires that person to be called as a witness.[70] Where payments should have been made through the clerk to the court, a certificate purporting to be signed by the clerk is evidence.[71]

On the hearing of the complaint for the enforcement, the court may remit the whole or any part of the sum due by way of arrears.[72] Before remitting all or any part of a sum due under a magistrates' court maintenance order the court must inform the person in whose favour the order is made or if that person is a child the person with whom the child has his or her home of its intention and afford that person a reasonable opportunity to make representations to the court either orally at an adjourned hearing or in writing except when it appears to be unnecesary or impracticable to do so. Written representations can be considered by the

66   Magistrates' Courts Act 1980 s92.
67   Magistrates' Courts Act 1980 s93(6).
68   Magistrates' Courts Act 1980 s93(8) and s94.
69   Magistrates' Courts Act 1980 s93(7).
70   Magistrates' Courts Act 1980 s99.
71   Ibid.
72   Magistrates' Courts Act 1980 s95.

court it they purport to be signed by or on behalf of the person in whose favour the order is made or if that person is a child by or on behalf of the child or the person with whom the child has his or her home.[73]

The procedure for enforcement of a magistrates' court maintenance order is by the issue of a judgment summons which must be served personally on the debtor unless the court orders substituted service because it considers that prompt personal service of the summons is impracticable.[74]

Orders in civil proceedings

Imprisonment can only be imposed where there is default in certain kinds of orders recoverable as civil debts in the magistrates' courts. These include orders for legally aided or assisted defendants to make contributions to their defence costs and orders for the payment of taxes or national insurance contributions.[75] The court cannot commit to prison for default in payment or for want of sufficient distress to satisfy payment except by an order made on complaint and on proof to the satisfaction of the court that the person has, or has had since the date on which the sum was adjudged to be paid, the means to pay the sum or any instalments of it on which s/he has defaulted and refuses or neglects or, as the case may be, has refused or neglected to pay it.[76]

If the debtor is committed to prison, the complainant's costs are added to the sum due for the purposes of obtaining release from prison by payment.[77]

Obtaining release

In all cases, a person imprisoned by a magistrates' court for non-payment can obtain release by paying off the sum due including any costs and charges (if any) of the commitment and distress.[78] If there is a part payment, the period of detention is reduced by a proportionate amount.[79]

73   Magistrates' Courts Rules 1981 r44.
74   Magistrates' Courts Rules 1981 r58.
75   Magistrates' Courts Act 1980 s92(1).
76   Magistrates' Courts Act 1980 s96(1).
77   Magistrates' Courts Act 1980 s96.
78   Magistrates' Courts Act 1980 s79(1).
79   Magistrates' Courts Act 1980 s79(2) and (3).

Enforcement of young offenders fines

Where a fine is imposed on someone under the age of 17, he or she can be committed to detention in an attendance centre for non-payment in the same circumstances as a 17–21-year-old can be committed (see page 141).[80]

Instead of enforcing the order against the offender, if there would have been power to commit the person to prison if over the age of 21, the court may make one of the following orders:

- an order requiring the defaulter's parent or guardian to enter into a recognisance to ensure that the defaulter pays any part of the sum remaining unpaid; or
- an order directing that however much remains unpaid should be paid by the defaulter's parent or guardian instead of by the defaulter.[81]

The consent of the defaulter's parent or guardian is required before an order requiring a recognisance is made. An order can only be made directing the defaulter's parent or guardian to pay the fine if the court is satisfied in all the circumstances that it is reasonable to make the order.[82]

The court can make neither order unless it has enquired into the means of the juvenile in his or her presence on at least one occasion and the court is satisfied that the defaulting juvenile has, or has had since the date on which the sum was ordered to be paid, the means to pay the sum or any instalment of it on which s/he has defaulted and refused or neglects or, as the case may be, has refused or neglected to pay.[83] An order requiring the parent or guardian to pay the fine can be made if the parent or guardian has been given an opportunity to attend but fails to do so. Once a sum is ordered to be paid by the parent or guardian, it can be enforced as if it had been ordered to be paid in the first place on conviction.[84]

Appeals

In respect of all kinds of orders made by magistrates' courts it may be possible to appeal on the grounds that the order should not have been made, eg, that a fine is too excessive or than an order for periodical payments in matrimonial proceedings is too large. It is beyond the remit of this book to deal with questions of appeal.

---

80   Criminal Justice Act 1982 ss1, 9 and 17.
81   Magistrates' Courts Act 1980 s81(1).
82   Magistrates' Courts Act 1980 s81(2).
83   Magistrates' Courts Act 1980 s81(4).
84   Magistrates' Courts Act 1980 s81(7).

Bailiff due to levy distress

Bailiffs collecting fines and other orders payable to the magistrates' court have almost identical powers to bailiffs collecting the community charge (see chapter 6). The strategies of safeguarding belongings and of refusing entry to the bailiff described on pages 123–4 are equally applicable to bailiffs collecting fines and other orders payable under orders made by magistrates' courts. As with the community charge and council tax, if the bailiff is unsuccessful in collecting the sum due, in most cases the client will be summonsed for a means enquiry to show cause why he or she should not be committed to prison for non-payment.

The client may face a difficult choice in deciding whether to refuse entry to the bailiff or safeguard belongings. If the bailiff reports that distress cannot be levied, a means enquiry will be held at which the client is at risk of imprisonment. On the other hand, in the case of fines and orders in matrimonial proceedings, the court has power to remit the arrears. If the client wants the arrears to be remitted, he or she must also face the possibility that imprisonment will be imposed instead. It is only at this stage of the means enquiry that the court has power to remit arrears. It seems likely that magistrates will be more reluctant to remit a fine than a maintenance order unless they can be convinced that the defendant has been suitably punished.

In addition to the possibility of safeguarding belongings and refusing entry the following strategies are available.

Applying for time to pay

Orders in criminal and civil proceedings

As stated on pages 144–5 above, the court has power at any stage to allow further time for payment or to order payment by instalments on an application by or on behalf of the person liable to make payment. The application can be made in writing unless the court requires the applicant to attend.

Whenever distress is threatened for non-payment of an order made in criminal or civil proceedings, an application should be made for further time to pay, for payment by instalments or for different instalment arrangements to those that originally applied.

The request should be made in writing to the local magistrates' court and the court should be provided with the following information:

- a statement of income and expenditure showing the client's financial position;

- an explanation of any changes in circumstances which have taken place since the original order was imposed;
- an explanation why the client was unable to keep to the terms of the original order;
- any other circumstances justifying the request that is now being made for changes in payment arrangements.

If a unit fine was imposed originally, it is particularly important to draw attention to any error there may have been in assessing the client's means.

If there is insufficient time for a written application to be considered before the bailiff is likely to call, a personal application should be made. In practice, experience shows that many courts are reluctant to accept an application when the bailiff has already been instructed and pressure may have to be put on a reluctant court to accept an application and to consider it. In the event that the court refuses to consider an application, a personal application will have to be made to the magistrates. If the clerk refuses to allow access to the magistrates, a telephone complaint should be made to the Lord Chancellor's Department and consideration should be given to initiating proceedings for judicial review.

No legal aid is available to make an application for the variation of an order, though a McKenzie friend may assist in the application.

Matrimonial proceedings

Assistance by way of representation is available to make an application to revoke or vary an order made in a magistrates' court in matrimonial proceedings where the client is financially eligible. An application to vary or revoke an order is made by way of complaint and where the client is unable to afford the terms of the payment an application should be made as soon as possible.

The client must provide written particulars:

- of the nature of the evidence s/he proposes to adduce at the hearing of the complaint and the names and addresses and if known to him or her the occupations of his or her witnesses; and
- of the occupations of the client and defendant and the address of the client and last address of the defendant known to the client.[85]

In addition, the client should provide:

- a statement of income and expenditure showing the client's financial position;
- an explanation of any changes in circumstances that have taken place since the order was made;

85   Magistrates' Courts Rules 1981 r41(3).

- an explanation of why any arrears have arisen;
- any other circumstances explaining why the variation order or revocation is requested.

Making representations against the issue of a warrant of distress

As indicated on page 146, the issue of a warrant of dstress is a judicial act. In all cases the defendant should therefore be given an opportunity to be heard and to make representations why a warrant should not be issued.

At any time up to the time of issue of the warrant of distress, representations should be made to the court in writing as to why a distress warrant should not be issued.

The representations should include:

- a statement of income and expenditure of the client showing his or her financial position;
- where the client has no goods of any value to distrain, an explanation that this is the case;
- an explanation of why the debt has not been paid based on the financial circumstances of the client;
- the effect of the removal of goods on other family members, eg, children;
- an explanation of why the client was unable to keep to the original terms of the order.

Wherever possible, representations on the issue of making a distress warrant should be combined with an application for time to pay.

Applying for administration order, bankruptcy order or interim order prior to a voluntary arrangement

See chapter 2. An administration order can only be applied for if a county court judgment has already been obtained against the client. No such restriction applies to a bankruptcy order or interim order. Any such order probably prevents a court issuing a distress warrant or warrant of committal.

Distress levied but goods not yet removed

Safeguarding belongings

The points made on page 127 relating to the position of bailiffs collecting the community charge are equally applicable here.

Refusing entry to the bailiff

The points made on page 127 relating to the community charge are equally applicable.

Challenging a walking possession agreement

In many cases, bailiffs will not remove a client's goods immediately but will enter into what is known as a 'walking possession' agreement with the client. Under this agreement, the client agrees not to dispose of the property that has been distrained and in return the bailiff agrees to leave the items in the home for the time being, giving the client an opportunity to pay up instead of having the goods removed.

If it is possible to argue that a walking possession agreement is invalid, and the bailiff leaves the premises, it is possible to argue that the bailiff abandoned distress and therefore the goods are no longer effectively distrained. The bailiff would therefore have no right to break into the premises on returning to collect the goods as would otherwise be the case.

For bailiffs collecting sums due from a magistrates' court there are three grounds for challenging a walking possession agreement:

- signature by non-debtor;
- agreement does not identify the goods distrained;
- agreement includes goods that do not belong to the client.

Each of these grounds is dealt with in more detail on pages 127–8.

If it is possible that a walking possession is invalid on these grounds, the rights of the client are identical to the position where distress has not yet been levied (see page 152). For example, a non-debtor can remove his or her goods from the premises or hide them.

Apply for time to pay or variation

This remedy is equally applicable even after the bailiff has called. See page 152 above.

Apply for administration order, bankruptcy order or interim order

This remedy is only available if a county court judgment has been obtained against the debtor. In practice, there may be insufficient time to obtain an administration order before the bailiff returns to collect the goods and sell them. A bankruptcy order or interim order can be obtained more quickly. See chapter 2 for a discussion of their effects.

Injunction

An injunction will be appropriate in the same circumstances as in the case of community charge, ie, where it is argued that the bailiff has abandoned distress because a walking possession agreement is invalid or where the bailiff is threatening to remove goods belonging to some other family member (see page 128). The procedure for obtaining an injunction is identical to that for the community charge so that precedent 18 in Part III will be relevant. The defendants will be the clerk to the justices for the court which instructed the bailiff and the bailiff's firm itself.

Goods removed but not yet sold

Injunction

An injunction will be available where goods belonging to a non-debtor which do not belong to the person liable for the fine or other order made in magistrates' court proceedings have been removed. See page 128. The grounds upon which the court will grant an injunction are identical to those referred to in chapter 6 and the specimen particulars of claim shown in precedent 18 in Part III will require minor amendment. The defendants will be the clerk to the justices and the bailiffs.

Pay the debt under protest

In most cases there will be no dispute about the liability for the debt but if goods belonging to a family member are threatened, he or she may pay the debt under protest and then seek to recover the amount from the magistrates' court by taking proceedings in the county court under the law of restitution.[86] The model letter to be sent with the payment of a debt under protest shown in precedent 20 in Part III can be adapted for these purposes as can the model particulars of claim shown in precedent 21.

---

86   See *Woolwich Equitable Building Society v Inland Revenue Commissioners* [1992] 3 WLR 366, HL, page 84 above and generally Halsbury's Laws of England, 3rd ed., vol. 9, paras 660 to 663.

Administration order, bankruptcy order or interim order

An administration order will only be available if a county court judgment has already been obtained against the client. It may be extremely difficult to obtain an order in sufficient time to prevent goods being sold. It should be possible to obtain a bankruptcy order or interim order more quickly. See chapter 2 for a discussion of their effects.

Summons to attend a means enquiry

Avoiding the means enquiry

An administration order, bankruptcy order or interim order will all, it is submitted, prevent the court from imprisoning the client for non-payment of an order in criminal, civil or matrimonial proceedings. Furthermore, the debt may be reduced or even discharged by the order (see chapter 2).

Representation at the hearing

There is no legal aid available to represent a defendant at a means enquiry. However, the client will be entitled to attend with a McKenzie friend who may advise and assist the client during the course of a hearing.[87] In addition, 'where necessary' the duty solicitor available in all magistrates' courts has a responsibility to represent a defendant who is before the court as a result of a failure to pay a fine or other sum ordered on conviction where such failure may lead to the defendant being at risk of imprisonment.[88] Either an adviser who has no right of audience in the court or a solicitor who is not prepared to represent free of charge can ask the duty solicitor to represent the client at the hearing and indeed instruct him or her with the relevant information in the same way that a solicitor would instruct a barrister. In practice, in many courts the duty solicitor does little or no representation of clients in means enquiries, normally because the court staff do not request the duty solicitor's assistance. This does not prevent an adviser or solicitor asking the duty solicitor to represent.

The hearing

The precise criteria which the court has to consider in respect of criminal proceedings, matrimonial proceedings and civil proceedings are slightly

87   *R v Leicester City Justices, ex parte Barrow* [1991] 2 QB 260, CA.
88   Legal Aid Board Duty Solicitor Arrangements 1992 clause 52(2)(b).

different (see page 146) but essentially the court must consider three issues at a means enquiry:

- whether or not default in payment was due to the defendant's wilful refusal or culpable neglect;
- alternative methods of enforcing payment and whether they are appropriate or likely to be successful;
- whether in the interests of justice a warrant of commitment ought to be issued.

Wilful refusal or culpable neglect

In a case involving the community charge regarding the imprisonment of debtors for culpable neglect, the High Court held that an unemployed person with no assets who had a potential to earn money could not be found guilty of culpable neglect for failing to pay the community charge unless there was clear evidence that gainful employment was on offer but had been refused.[89]

The solicitor of the client (with the help of an adviser) should be in a position to make representations on the following:

- the client's present financial circumstances or the history of the financial circumstances which led to the arrears, whichever are the more favourable to the client;
- the reason why the client failed to comply with the terms of the original order;
- any changes in financial circumstances since the order was made;
- any information about which the court was not aware at the time the order was made;
- any efforts made by the client to raise the money to pay the debt.

If the court decides there is no wilful refusal or culpable neglect it cannot order imprisonment. It can, however, make use of one of the alternative enforcement methods available.

Alternative methods of enforcing payment

As far as alternative remedies are concerned, it is necessary to discuss with the client which particular remedy he or she would prefer to have adopted. In particular, in criminal proceedings, attachment of earnings orders, deductions of sums from income support or money payment supervision orders should be considered and if the defendant is under 21, the court is under an obligation to make a money payment supervision order unless satisfied that it is undesirable or impracticable. It is best, therefore, to be

---

89 R v Poole Justices, ex parte Benham (1991) 156 JP 177, DC and R v Wolverhampton Stipendiary Magistrate ex parte Mould December 1992 Legal Action 14.

in a position to make representations that it is not undesirable or impracticable to make such an order, leaving the court with little option.

Mitigation

If the court decides there has been wilful refusal or culpable neglect and considers that no alternative methods of enforcement are appropriate, a plea in mitigation should be made, explaining the particular personal circumstances of the client and why he or she should not be imprisoned. If necessary, a request should be made for the warrant of commitment to be postponed on different terms or at the very least suspended for a fixed period, eg, 14 days, to allow payment to be made in full.

Immediate threat of imprisonment

Even if an order for imprisonment in default was made at the time criminal proceedings were concluded or a term of imprisonment has been imposed but suspended after a means enquiry, the court must still give the defendant notice of its intention to issue a warrant because the making of a warrant is a judicial act. This must invite the defendant to make representations.[90]

Representations should be made in all cases, whether or not the time-limit for making representations has expired and should include information:

- on the income and expenditure of the client showing his or her financial position;
- explaining why the fine or other order was not paid in accordance with the terms that the court imposed;
- explaining any information which was not available to the court which imposed the order;
- explaining any changes in financial circumstances since the order was made;
- explaining what alternative order the defendant could comply with bearing in mind his or her financial position and relating this to the financial information made available.

The court has power to postpone the issue of the warrant of commitment on terms and also to remit a fine but no other order for payment.

Careful consideration should be given to an application to remit a fine but it should always be borne in mind that the court will still wish to

---

90 *R v Faversham and Sittingbourne Magistrates' Court ex parte Ursell* (1992) 156 JP 765, QBD, a case on the community charge where the legislation is identical.

ensure that the defendant has in some way been punished for the offence for which he or she was convicted and a fine is unlikely to be discharged in its entirety. It is therefore often sensible to apply to remit the fine on the basis that the reduced fine that is left has the same punitive effect as the fine that was imposed would have had at the time the order was made.

CHAPTER 8

Child support maintenance debts

Introduction

Typical problems requiring emergency action will arise:

- where the client receives a summons from the court because the Child Support Agency is seeking a liability order;
- where the Child Support Agency has obtained a garnishee order nisi;
- where the Child Support Agency has obtained a charging order nisi;
- where a bailiff is due to call to levy distress;
- where the bailiff has called and levied distress but has not yet removed the client's goods;
- where goods have been removed by the bailiff but not yet sold;
- where the client receives a summons requiring him or her to attend a means enquiry to show cause why he or she should not be committed to prison;
- when a means enquiry has already been held and the client is now under immediate threat of imprisonment for breaching the terms of suspension or adjournment;
- where the client has already been imprisoned.

Child support maintenance

From 5 April 1993 the Child Support Act 1991 and regulations made under the Act will gradually bring into effect a new scheme for child maintenance.

Who will be affected?

The Act will be brought into effect in phases. Currently the following phases are planned.

a)   April 1993

The Act will apply:[1]

- on a phased basis between 1993 and 1996 to any case where the parent with care of any child is already claiming income support, disability working allowance or family credit;
- immediately to any case where a parent with care of a child begins claiming income support, family credit or disability working allowance after 5 April 1993;
- immediately if the parent with care of a child applies for maintenance under the Act and no maintenance arrangements are in existence on 5 April 1993 (the courts will be prevented from making maintenance orders in almost all such cases, so a parent who needs maintenance will have no choice but to use the Act).

b)   1994

There are provisions in the Act allowing the courts to make awards of maintenance for children with disabilities, for school fees and in cases where parents have particularly high incomes.[2] From 1994, parents who are receiving basic maintenance for a child under the Act will also be able to arrange for the Child Support Agency to collect any additional maintenance ordered by the courts. The courts retain jurisdiction about the level of that additional maintenance.

c)   1996

There are provisions in the Act allowing the Child Support Agency to collect other maintenance, eg, maintenance for the caring parent herself or himself as well as maintenance for any children.[3] From 1996, any parent receiving child maintenance under the Act can request that other maintenance is collected at the same time. The courts retain the ability to fix the level of that other maintenance.

d)   1996–7

On a phased basis the Act will be brought into force for all other groups of parents caring for one or more children, according to the first letter of the surname of the caring parent. When it is brought into force, the courts will

---

1   Child Support Act 1991 (Commencement No 3 and Transitional Provisions) Order 1992 (SI No 2644). See also generally M Street *Money and Family Breakdown* (Legal Action Group 1993) chs 17–19.
2   Child Support Act 1991 s8.
3   Child Support Act 1991 s30.

lose the power to vary any existing court order for maintenance of such children.[4]

Who must use the Act?

In theory, no parent caring for a child has to make use of the provisions of the Act. However, the courts will lose their powers on 5 April 1993 to award child maintenance so that the only method of obtaining maintenance in new cases will be by applying under the Act. Where parents caring for children are receiving income support, family credit or disability working allowance, they will be required to give authorisation to the Child Support Agency to calculate and recover maintenance under the Act unless the Child Support Agency considers that there are reasonable grounds for believing that if the parent were required to give such authorisation there would be a risk of the caring parent or any child suffering harm or undue distress as a result.[5] A parent who fails to give authorisation can have his or her benefit reduced by up to £8.50 per week for 6 months and £4.25 for 12 months (1993/4 rates) after that unless she or he has good cause.[6] An appeal against such a reduction can be made to a Child Support Appeal Tribunal.[7]

How much will the maintenance be?

The amount of maintenance will be fixed by a rigid formula. It will be possible to seek a review of the amount payable if circumstances change and to appeal an assessment if it is based on the wrong information. No appeal will be possible on the grounds that the formula is unfair.[8]

Disputes over parentage

The courts will still deal with disputes over parentage. The Child Support Agency may apply to the magistrates' court, county court or High Court for a declaration as to parentage.[9]

---

4   Child Support Act 1991 s8(3).
5   Child Support Act 1991 s6.
6   Child Support Act 1991 s46 and Child Support (Maintenance and Assessment Procedures) Regs 1992 (SI No 1813) reg 36.
7   Child Support Act 1991 s46(7).
8   Child Support Act 1991 ss11–20 and Sch 1.
9   Child Support Act 1991 s27.

Collection

The Child Support Agency is responsible for deciding the method by which any maintenance will be collected.[10]

Payments can be required to be made direct to the person caring for the child, through the Child Support Agency or through any other third party.[11] The Child Support Agency can decide the frequency of payments and the method, eg, direct debit, cheques, standing order or cash, after consulting the parties.[12]

The Child Support Agency can make a deductions from earnings order requiring the employer of the person required to pay maintenance to make deductions from his or her wages or salary for current instalments, arrears or both.[13]

Where the parent required to pay maintenance is him or herself receiving income support, payment will be recovered by deduction from that person's benefit entitlement unless the parent comes within an exempt category.[14]

Enforcement

If the parent liable to pay fails to do so, the Child Support Agency may apply to the magistrates' court for the area in which that parent lives for a liability order.[15]

Once a liability order has been made, the Child Support Agency may enforce the order by the use of bailiffs to levy distress or by seeking a garnishee or charging order through the county court.[16] The rules relating to bailiffs levying distress are almost identical to those for the community charge and council tax and, as for those debts, if distress is ineffective to collect the debt, the client can be summonsed before the magistrates' court for a means enquiry and may be imprisoned if a failure to pay was due to culpable neglect or wilful default (see chapter 6).[17] If the county court is used, the collection procedure becomes the same as for any other civil debt (see chapter 3).

10   Child Support Act 1991 s29.
11   Child Support Act 1991 s29(3) and the Child Support (Collection and Enforcement) Regs 1992 (SI No 1989) reg 2.
12   Child Support (Collection and Enforcement) Regs regs 3, 4 and 6.
13   Child Support Act 1991 s31 and Child Support (Collection and Enforcement) Regs regs 8–12.
14   Child Support Act 1991 s43 and Child Support (Maintenance Assessment and Special Cases) Regs 1991 (SI No 1815) regs 13, 26 and 28, Sch 1 Pt II and Sch 4.
15   Child Support Act 1991 s33.
16   Child Support Act 1991 ss35 and 36.
17   Child Support Act 1991 s40.

Dealing with emergencies

1)   *Where the client receives a summons from the court because the Child Support Agency is seeking a liability order*

The magistrates' court considering an application for a liability order cannot question the amount of maintenance assessed to be paid. This is a matter that must be raised with the Child Support Agency and on appeal to the Child Support Appeal Tribunal.[18] An adjournment can be sought if there is a genuine dispute about the amount of the assessment or where a court application is needed to resolve a dispute over parentage. Otherwise, there is unlikely to be a defence to a liability order application unless it is that the money due has already been paid.

2)   *Where the Child Support Agency has obtained a garnishee order nisi*

Garnishee orders are explained on page 46. The strategies for dealing with a garnishee order nisi discussed in chapter 3 on pages 62 to 65 are equally applicable to a garnishee order for the collection of child maintenance, save that it is not possible to set aside and/or stay or suspend enforcement of a liability order, unlike a civil court judgment (see page 63).

3)   *Where the Child Support Agency has obtained a charging order nisi*

Charging orders are explained on page 47. The strategies for dealing with a charging order nisi discussed in chapter 3 on pages 65 to 68 are equally applicable to a charging order for the collection of child maintenance, but it is not possible to set aside and/or stay or suspend enforcement of a liability order, unlike a civil court judgment.

4)   *Where a bailiff is due to call on levy distress*

The powers of bailiffs collecting maintenance under a liability order are identical to those for bailiffs collecting community charge or council tax arrears, save that there are slightly different regimes for the bailiffs' costs. The strategies for obstructing bailiffs collecting the community charge or council tax described on pages 123 to 124 are therefore equally applicable. There is an equivalent procedure to that for the council tax and community charge enabling a person aggrieved by any distress to appeal to the magistrates' court.[19] The grounds for such an appeal are likely to be limited to an irregularity in the levy.

---

18   Child Support Act 1991 s33(4).
19   Child Support (Collection and Enforcement) Regs reg 31.

5)   Where the bailiff has called and levied distress but has not yet removed the client's goods

The strategies under this heading in chapter 6 (pages 126 to 131 are equally applicable where bailiffs are collecting maintenance, subject to the following points:

- The fees for a walking possession agreement are 45p per day rather than 10p per day.
- It is still possible to challenge any walking possession agreement on the basis that it is signed by a third party.
- It may be more difficult to challenge a walking possession agreement on the basis that it is not signed at the time that distress is levied. A walking possession agreement is not defined for child support maintenance purposes and there is no express requirement that such an agreement must be made at the time distress is levied, nor that it need be signed at all (see page 128). The regulations for child support maintenance only require that a memorandum is left at the premises 'of any arrangement entered into regarding the taking of possession of goods distrained'.[20] Nevertheless there is still a good argument that for there to be an arrangement, details of which are left at the premises, there must have been two parties to make the arrangement.
- Bailiffs' charges which can be disputed. At the time of writing, the practices which bailiffs will adopt are unclear. Nevertheless if they repeat their practice when collecting the community charge, they will seek to charge for numerous items which are not included in the schedule of charges. Though the wording of the schedule of charges is slightly different from that for the council tax and community charge, bailiffs are prevented from collecting the same kinds of charges.[21]

6)   Where goods have been removed by the bailiff but not yet sold

The strategies available at this stage of the process of recovery are identical to those in the similar stage of recovery of community charge and council tax debts (see page 131).

7)   Where the client receives a summons requiring him or her to attend a means enquiry to show cause why he or she should not be committed to prison

As with the council tax or community charge (see page 133):

- The magistrates' court before which a client appears must carry out a

---

20   Child Support (Collection and Enforcement) Regs reg 30(2)(c).
21   Child Support (Collection and Enforcement) Regs reg 32 and Sch 2 and see p130.

means enquiry in the client's presence and enquire whether the failure to pay was due to his 'wilful refusal or culpable neglect'[22]

- The court should operate on a two-stage process: first establishing whether there is culpable neglect or wilful default, and second deciding what steps to take as a result of the first finding.

Unlike the case for the community charge or council tax, there is no power for the court to remit arrears outstanding.

The points made about preparation for the hearing and the case law on community charge will be equally applicable to enforcement or child support maintenance (see pages 133–5.

If the court finds the client guilty of wilful default or culpable neglect, it can deal with the case in one of three ways:

- issue a warrant of commitment immediately so that the client is imprisoned for a period of up to 6 weeks;
- issue a warrant of commitment but suspended on terms as to payment, eg, a certain sum off the arrears each week; or
- make no order at all.

Even if it finds culpable neglect or wilful default, the court has total discretion as to which of these options to choose. When a finding of culpable neglect or wilful default has been made, the adviser should be prepared to make a plea of mitigation to convince the court that imprisonment is inappropriate or that at the very least a suspended term of imprisonment should be imposed. It is worth arguing that the parent with care is better served by a suspended warrant of commitment because if the client is imprisoned, the maintenance will arguably be discharged. This is because there is no provision authorising a repeat application for imprisonment if imprisonment was imposed on the first occasion.[23]

If the court finds there was no wilful refusal or culpable neglect, or is not satisfied that there was wilful refusal or culpable neglect, it cannot make any order. The application can be renewed if the client's circumstances change.[24]

8)   When a means enquiry has already been held and the client is now under immediate threat of imprisonment for breaching the terms of suspension or adjournment

The strategies and case law applicable to this stage in the recovery process

---

22   Child Support Act 1991 s40.
23   See Child Support Act 1991 s40(11)(b) which specifically authorises repeat applications when no imprisonment is imposed.
24   Child Support Act 1991 s40(11)(b).

for community charge and council tax will be equally applicable here (see pages 135 to 137).

9)   Where the client has already been imprisoned

The same strategies are available at this stage of the recovery process as for council tax and community charge arrears (see page 137).[25]

---

25   Child Support Act 1991 s40(8) and Child Support (Collection and Enforcement) Regs 1992 reg 34.

Part II

Housing emergencies

CHAPTER 9

Harassment and unlawful eviction

Introduction

Tenants and licensees (residential occupiers) have remedies in both the criminal and civil law. The appropriate remedy will depend on the complaint and the status of the residential occupier. In an emergency (for example, attempted or actual unlawful eviction), civil proceedings can provide a very quick remedy. An application to the court for an injunction must be made with all speed, and delay will prejudice the occupier's chances of obtaining an injunction.

Checklist for instructions

1 *Client*
   Full name, address, occupation and date of birth
2 *Any person with whom client lives*
   Details as in 1 above
3 *Children*
   Names and dates of birth
4 *Premises*
   Address and brief description of premises which are the subject of dispute
5 *Status of occupier*
6 *Brief details of tenancy or licence*
   Eg, date of commencement
   Nature of premises
   Rent and whether weekly, monthly or fixed term
   Notice: whether given, and if so whether valid
   Category of protection
7 *Landlord*
   Name, address and telephone number
8 *Any person harassing or evicting*

Details as in 7 above
9 *Details of behaviour complained of*
As specific as possible, ie, what has been done, by whom, to whom
with dates and times
10 *Witnesses*
Including tenancy relations officer and police, if appropriate
11 *Effect on occupier*
Eg, severe stress, no cooking facilities, no heating, nowhere to sleep.
Include number of people affected
12 *Details of claim for special damages*
Eg, damaged goods, hotel costs, additional cost of travel to work
13 *Evidence of right to occupy premises*
Eg, rent book, tenancy agreement, correspondence addressed to
occupier at premises
14 *Doctor*
Where assault is alleged or health affected: name, address and
telephone number. Signed authority for medical details to be released.

Local authority powers

Protection from Eviction Act 1977, as amended by Housing Act 1988

Introduction
Unlawful eviction and harassment are criminal offences as defined by the
Protection from Eviction Act 1977, as amended (all subsequent references
in this chapter refer to this Act unless stated otherwise). Local authorities
have express powers to prosecute offences under the Act[1] and most local
authorities employ tenancy relations officers (or harassment officers) to
deal with disputes in the private sector.

In the event of harassment or eviction, the tenancy relations officer
should be contacted as soon as possible. In an emergency s/he will
normally call at the premises without delay and endeavour to resolve the
dispute. Often, the threat of a prosecution is sufficient to ensure that the
evicted occupier is permitted to re-enter.

If a prosecution is proposed, the case will usually be referred to the
legal department of the local authority, which is often slow to take action.

In principle, there is no reason why an individual cannot bring his or

1 Protection from Eviction Act 1977 s6.

her own prosecution, but the fact that legal aid is not available is a deterrent.[2]

Offences under the Act

If any person unlawfully deprives the residential occupier of any premises of his occupation of the premises or any part thereof, or attempts to do so, he shall be guilty of an offence unless he proves that he believed, and had reasonable cause to believe, that the residential occupier had ceased to reside in the premises.[3]

If any person with intent to cause the residential occupier of any premises—
(a) to give up the occupation of the premises or any part thereof; or
(b) to refrain from exercising any right or pursuing any remedy in respect of the premises or part thereof;
does acts likely to interfere with the peace or comfort of the residential occupier or members of his household, or persistently withdraws or withholds services reasonably required for the occupation of the premises as a residence, he shall be guilty of an offence.[4]

The landlord of a residential occupier or an agent of the landlord shall be guilty of an offence if—
(a)   he does acts likely to interfere with the peace or comfort of the residential occupier or members of his household; or
(b)   he persistently withdraws or withholds services reasonably required for the occupation of the premises in question as a residence,
and (in either case) he knows, or has reasonable cause to believe, that that conduct is likely to cause the residential occupier to give up the occupation of the whole or part of the premises or to refrain from exercising any right, or pursuing any remedy in respect of the whole or part of the premises.[5]

'Residential occupier'.   Section 1(1) defines a residential occupier as:

a person occupying the premises as a residence, whether under a contract or by virtue of any enactment or rule of law giving him the right to remain in occupation or restricting the right of any other person to recover possession of the premises.

This is a very wide definition and includes:
– all tenants and licensees (including service tenants and occupiers) whose tenancies and licences have not been brought to an end;

---

2   For procedure, see Carrott and Hunter *Arden and Partington on Quiet Enjoyment* 3rd ed., LAG, 1990.
3   S1(2).
4   S1(3), as amended by Housing Act 1988 s29(1). The amendment substituted the word 'likely' for 'calculated' as from 10 January 1989.
5   S1(3A).

- protected tenants whose contractual tenancies have been brought to an end, and who occupy as statutory tenants;
- secure tenants;
- all other former tenants who are residential occupiers because s3 restricts 'the right of any other person to recover possession of the premises';
- restricted contractual licensees where the licence was created after 28 November 1980;[6]
- former service occupiers who were granted exclusive occupation of at least some of their accommodation;[7]
- anyone lawfully living with either such a service occupier or a former unprotected tenant or restricted contractual licensee at the end of the tenancy or occupancy, even if the former tenant or occupier has him or herself left the premises.[8]

This list is not exhaustive – for a full list see the annotations to the Protection from Eviction Act 1977 in Arden (ed.) *Encyclopedia of Housing*, Sweet & Maxwell.

Acts of harassment.   The act must be done with one of the two types of intention described in s1(3). The offence may be expressed in one charge with alternative intention.[9] In *R v Burke* [1991] 1 AC 135 the House of Lords held that it was not necessary for the acts complained of to be actionable in civil law in order for an offence to be made out under s1(3). In *R v Burke*, the landlord had padlocked a lavatory, disconnected the front door bells and cut off the water supplies to one of the toilets and to one of the bathrooms. See too *R v Yuthiwattana* (1984) 80 Cr App R 55. Other examples of such types of harassment are withholding or withdrawing services, or refusing to allow the occupier use of the facilities, eg, the bathroom, or continually entering the occupier's premises without permission. The word 'acts' includes a single act[10] However, the words of s1(3) do not impose a responsibility to rectify damage which the landlord has caused by an act done without intention necessary to constitute an offence, even if s/he has rendered a tenant's premises uninhabitable.[11]

Section 1(3A) creates a new offence of harassment introduced by the Housing Act 1988. It applies to the same conduct as the offence under

---

6   S3(2A).
7   S8(2).
8   S3(2).
9   *Schon v London Borough of Camden* (1986) 18 HLR 341.
10 *R v Policarpou* (1978) 9 HLR 129.
11 *R v Ahmad* (1986) 84 Cr App R 64.

s1(3), but the difference in practice between the two offences of harassment is likely to lie in the different tests of intention. For the new offence, it is not necessary to prove that the defendant acted with 'intent to cause' – actual knowledge or a reasonable cause to believe will be sufficient.

Acts of eviction. Eviction can be from the whole or part of the premises. The offence may be committed by a successful or by an attempted eviction.

The eviction need not be 'permanent' but exclusion for a short, finite period of time, eg, overnight, is harassment, not eviction.[12]

For the accused to defend a prosecution successfully, s/he must show that s/he believed *and* had reasonable cause to believe that the residential occupier had ceased to reside in the premises.

Who may be prosecuted? Anyone can be charged with an offence under s1(2) or (3), but in most cases it is the landlord or his or her agents. An offence under s1(3A) may be committed only by a landlord, a superior landlord or an agent of the landlord.

Penalties

In the magistrates' court, the accused can be fined up to the prescribed sum (now £5,000) and/or imprisoned for six months. In the Crown Court, s/he can be fined an unlimited amount and/or sent to prison for up to two years. The criminal courts have no power to order the accused to allow the occupier to re-enter his or her home although it may be made a condition of a landlord's bail that he or she does not go to the premises in question.

Local Government Act 1972

Where a local authority considers it expedient for the promotion or protection of the interests of the inhabitants of its area:
- it may prosecute or defend or appear in any legal proceedings, and, in the case of civil proceedings, may institute them in its own name;[13] and
- in an emergency, it may be persuaded to take out a civil injunction (see below) to remedy or prohibit harassment or illegal eviction. This is a speedier and more effective weapon than criminal proceedings but unless the local authority has an unusually efficient legal department, it is likely to be slower than the tenant instructing solicitors to apply for emergency legal aid and then taking county court proceedings.

---

12   *R v Yuthiwattana* (1984) 80 Cr App R 55.
13   Local Government Act 1972 s222(1)(a)

If occupiers are unlawfully evicted, they will qualify for advice and assistance under the homelessness provisions of the Housing Act 1985 (see pages 262–3). The use of the local authority's powers under the Local Government Act 1972 might be the most effective means of assistance for a person who is homeless or threatened with homelessness by remedying or preventing the homelessness.

Civil proceedings

Introduction

In view of the limitations to many local authorities' resources the quickest way for residential occupiers to prevent harassment or to secure reinstatement after an illegal eviction is often to take action in the county court. *Ex parte* injunctions (see page 186) can, if necessary, be obtained very quickly.

Occupiers who have suffered illegal eviction or harassment can sue in a civil court for breach of contract or in tort. The appropriate cause of action will depend on the status of the occupier and the behaviour complained of. Here follows a brief outline of the most common causes of action: for a comprehensive list, see Carrott and Hunter *Arden and Partington on Quiet Enjoyment* 3rd ed., LAG, 1990.

Tenants' representatives should include reference to all relevant causes of action in particulars of claim which they draft.

Contract

Breach of covenant for quiet enjoyment

Every tenancy agreement contains a covenant by the landlord to allow the tenant 'quiet enjoyment' of the premises for as long as the tenancy lasts. The covenant is either expressly written into the agreement, or implied by law.

Examples of breach of covenant for quiet enjoyment are:
– unlawful eviction, attempted unlawful eviction or acts of harassment; physical eviction is not necessary;[14]
– cutting off gas, electricity or water supplies;[15]
– building works so substantial that the tenant is unable to remain in the premises undisturbed due to noise, dust, lack of safety and/or withdrawal of services and facilities;[16]

14   *Sampson v Floyd* [1989] 2 EGLR 49.
15   *McCall v Abelesz* [1976] QB 585.
16   *Guppy's (Bridport) Ltd v Brookling* (1983) 14 HLR 1.

 - building works adjacent to premises causing loss of privacy and noise;[17]
 - erection of scaffolding around a building.[18]

Who may sue?   All tenants, including service or statutory tenants, and members of the tenant's family, provided that they are parties to the contract, may sue.

Trespassers or licensees (including service occupiers) may not sue for breach of the covenant for quiet enjoyment (although a licensee may have an action for breach of a term of the contract, see below).

Who may be sued?   The landlord may be sued; this includes a new landlord who buys the property from the previous landlord.

Breach of term of contract
If the terms of an agreement to occupy premises are broken, there is a breach of contract. The terms will usually be expressed (even if only orally), but may be implied by the court as being necessary to give effect to the intention of the parties.

Examples of breach of term of contract are:
 - cutting off gas, water or electricity;[19]
 - removal of furniture

where it is an express or implied term that the landlord would supply these services.

Who may sue?   All the categories of tenants who may sue for breach of the covenant for quiet enjoyment (see above) may sue for breach of term of contract (although they will usually sue for breach of the covenant).

Licensees may sue if the harassment is of such an order that the licensee cannot reasonably be expected to use the premises for the purpose for which the rights of occupation were granted.[20]

A contractual licensee may not sue for a breach which has occurred *after* the date on which the contractual licence ended. Equally, a restricted or unprotected tenant may not sue for a breach which occurred *after* the tenancy came to an end.

17   *Mira v Aylmer Square Investments Ltd* (1989) 21 HLR 284.
18   *Queensway Marketing Ltd v Associated Restaurants Ltd* [1988] 2 EGLR 49.
19   *McCall v Abelesz* [1976] QB 585.
20   *Smith v Nottinghamshire County Council* (1981) *The Times*, 7 November 1981.

Tort

Breach of Protection from Eviction Act 1977 s3 as amended by Housing Act 1988 ss30 and 31

Where a tenancy or licence which is neither 'statutorily protected' (as defined in s8(1)) nor 'excluded' has come to an end but the former tenant or licensee continues to reside on the premises, s/he may not be evicted without a court order.

Breach of the provisions of this section gives rise to a cause of action which applies only to acts of eviction or attempted eviction and not to acts of harassment short of actual or attempted eviction (see page 174).

Who may sue?   The following occupiers may sue:
(a) restricted contract licensees where the licence was created after 28 November 1980;
(b) service occupiers who have exclusive occupation of at least some of their accommodation;
(c) secure tenants;
(d) statutory tenants; and
(e) any person lawfully residing in the premises or part of them when the tenancy as in (a) to (d) above comes to an end which includes members of the tenant's family, lawful subtenants and licensees;
(f) rental purchasers (Housing Act 1980 s88); and
(g) tenants who lack security of tenure because of the exceptions in the Rent Act 1977 ss4 to 16 and the Housing Act 1988 Sch 1, provided that they do not have excluded tenancies (see below).

Rent Act protected tenants (which includes protected shorthold tenants) cannot use this cause of action.[21]

Similarly the section cannot be used by assured or assured shorthold tenants. The intention of Parliament seems to have been that this section was only required by occupiers who could not rely on covenants for quiet enjoyment because their tenancies had been terminated.

Section 30 of the Housing Act 1988 denies the protection of s3 to occupiers with 'excluded tenancies' or 'excluded licences' which were created after the Housing Act provisions came into force on 15 January 1989.

Section 31 provides that tenancies and licences are 'excluded' if:
– the occupier shares with the landlord or licensor accommodation which is part of the owner's 'only or principal home' (unless this shared accommodation consists only of storage areas or means of access);

21   Protection from Eviction Act 1977, ss3(1) and 8(1)(a).

- the occupier lives in the same building as the landlord or licensor and shares accommodation with a member of the landlord's or licensor's family;[22]
- the tenancy or licence is granted as a temporary expedient to a person who entered the premises or any other premises as a trespasser;
- the tenancy or licence confers the right to occupy for a holiday only; or
- a licensee occupies a hostel provided by a local authority, development corporation, housing action trust, the Housing Corporation, a housing trust etc;
- the tenancy or licence is granted otherwise than for money or money's worth.

Who may be sued?   The 'owner of the premises',[23] ie, the person who, as against the occupier, is entitled to possession of the premises, may be sued.

Trespass to land

An unlawful entry onto land or unlawful placing of something on the land constitutes the tort of trespass to land. In view of the fact that a tenancy confers rights to exclusive possession and to exclude all other persons, including the landlord,[24] this tort may be committed by the landlord on the land of his or her tenant.[25] It is not necessary to prove actual harm in order to sue; it is sufficient to show that there has been a trespass.

Examples of trespass to land are:

- nailing up a door or blocking up a lock;
- entering without permission;
- entering without permission, harassing the tenant and refusing to leave;[26]
- purporting to grant a new tenancy to another person whilst an existing tenancy persists.[27]

Who may sue?   Any person in legal possession of the land may sue for trespass to land. This includes:

- protected tenants;
- statutory tenants;
- assured and assured shorthold tenants;
- secure tenants;

22 For definition of 'member of the family', see the Housing Act 1985 s113.
23 Protection from Eviction Act 1977 s8(3).
24 See *Street v Mountford* [1985] AC 809.
25 *Shah v Givert* (1980) 124 SJ 513.
26 *Hillden v ICI (Alkali) Ltd* [1936] AC 65.
27 *Shah v Givert* (1980) 124 SJ 513.

- subtenants including illegal subtenants as long as the mesne tenancy exists;[28] and
- licensees with exclusive occupation may be able to sue.[29]

Who may be sued?   Anyone may be sued for trespass to land, and if the agent is carrying out the trespass on behalf of the landlord, both the agent and the landlord should be sued.

Trespass to the person and assault and battery

A battery is any *intentional* application of direct physical force on another person without lawful excuse. An assault is any act which puts another person in immediate *reasonable* fear of battery. There must be some threatening *act*; threatening words alone are not usually enough. It is not necessary to prove actual damage or harm to sustain an action.

Examples of assault and battery are:

- a gesture which suggests a physical attack;
- a physical attack, which could include an occupier being pushed around.

Who may sue?   Anyone who is assaulted may sue. This includes trespassers, although a landowner who only uses reasonable force to evict a trespasser will have a defence to such an action.

Who may be sued?   Anyone who commits an assault may be sued. Where an agent is involved both the agent and the landlord should be sued.

Trespass to goods and conversion

Trespass to goods is a direct interference with another person's belongings. Conversion occurs where a person entitled to possession of goods is permanently deprived of that possession and the goods are converted to the use of someone else. An action may be brought under the Torts (Interference with Goods) Act 1977 for the return of the goods, or their value, or for damages.

Examples of trespass to goods and conversion are:

- interference with the occupier's belongings either in the premises or by removing them outside the premises;
- where the landlord gives a tenant's belongings to someone else.

Who may sue?   Anyone may sue for trespass to goods or conversion if s/he has suffered the interference described above. However, in the case of

28   *Mellor v Watkins* (1874) LR 9 QB 400.
29   *McPhail v Persons Unknown* [1973] Ch 447.

trespassers, there will be a good defence if the defendant has moved the goods in a reasonable manner and the trespasser had no permission to have the goods in the premises.

Who may be sued? Anyone who is responsible for the trespass or conversion may be sued.

Nuisance

Nuisance is interference with the reasonable use or enjoyment of land; it must be a state of affairs that is either continual or recurring, or a condition or activity which interferes with the use of land. There are alternative tests which have been used to decide whether a nuisance exists:

– whether the act complained of is one which could be considered a nuisance according to the standards of the average person, and not one of undue sensitivity;[30] or
– if a course of conduct is engaged in with the intention of annoying the occupier and which actually succeeds in so doing to the extent that harm (including loss of enjoyment) follows.[31]

Examples of nuisance are:

– harassment by the landlord or his or her agent by causing excessive noise/disturbance, eg, loud music;[32]
– unlawful eviction, but it is usually more appropriate to sue in contract unless exemplary damages are sought;[33] and
– keeping rubbish in the common parts of a block of flats (which remain in the landlord's possession) until it causes a smell or danger to health.

Who may sue? A tenant or someone in actual possession or occupation of land (which includes licensees with exclusive possession)[34] and his or her licensee or spouse[35] may sue.

The person suing must suffer actual harm, even if only loss of enjoyment.[36]

Who may be sued? Whoever causes the nuisance may be sued, including the landlord and his or her agent if s/he is party to it.

---

30 *Robinson v Kilvert* (1884) 41 Ch D 88.
31 *Christie v Davey* [1893] 1 Ch 316.
32 *Charles v Trott* (1973) 227 EG 1857.
33 *Guppy's (Bridport) Ltd v Brookling* (1983) 14 HLR 1.
34 *Foster v Warblington Urban District Council* [1906] 1 KB 648
35 *Malone v Laskey* [1907] 3 KB 141.
36 *Malone v Laskey* [1907] 3 KB 141.

Unlawful eviction under Housing Act 1988 s27

If after 9 June 1988 the landlord or any person acting on his or her behalf commits an act which amounts to a criminal offence under the Protection from Eviction Act 1977 s1, this constitutes the tort of unlawful eviction.

Damages are based on the profit which the landlord gains by obtaining vacant possession.[37] No damages are recoverable if the residential occupier is reinstated in the premises by the time of the disposal of any civil proceedings, or if the landlord has offered to reinstate the tenant and it was unreasonable for the tenant to refuse the offer.

The tort can be committed by the landlord or someone acting on his or her behalf, who actually evicts the residential occupier, or causes the residential occupier to leave the premises as a result of his or her conduct. The essential precondition of liability is the departure of the residential occupier from the premises in question.

Who may sue?   A 'residential occupier' as defined in the Protection from Eviction Act 1977 s1(1) (see page 173) may sue.

Who may be sued?   The landlord and any superior landlord under whom that person derives title may be sued. This definition includes someone who has contracted to purchase the landlord's interest in the premises, even if completion has not taken place.[38]

Remedies

Damages

When dealing with harassment or unlawful eviction, the primary object is to prevent further harassment and/or to gain re-entry to the home, which will be achieved by obtaining an injunction. In the long term, the occupier may also be entitled to damages. It is beyond the scope of this book to discuss all the types of damages available, but the following points should be considered when deciding which cause of action to pursue.

Contract

The court will endeavour to put the occupier in the position into which s/he would have been if the contract had been fulfilled. Thus if the occupier cannot be reinstated in his or her home, the court will seek to ensure that s/he is compensated financially for this loss.

---

37   See, eg, *Tagro v Cafane* [1991] 1 WLR 378.
38   *Jones v Miah* (1992) 24 HLR 578.

Who may sue?   The following may sue in contract:

- the parties to the contract;
- their assignees; or
- a tenant who is a statutory successor.

The person who sues is able to claim on behalf of him or herself and those for whose benefit the contract of tenancy was made, eg, his or her family.[39]

Tort

The basic principle of damages in tort is that the plaintiff should be put in the same position as s/he would have been had the tort not occurred. The damage must, however, be such that it is a reasonably foreseeable consequence of the tort. General damages in tort are available for pain and suffering, nervous shock and personal injury but not usually for discomfort, embarrassment or disappointment.[40]

As a general principle, a person should not receive damages which will place him or her in a better position than before, simply because s/he suffered harm.

Who may sue?   The following may sue in tort:

- anyone who has suffered damage; and
- a cohabitee, flat sharer or visitor may sue personally, or may join the proceedings as a joint plaintiff if the occupier has suffered harm.

The occupier cannot claim in tort on behalf of others.

Types of damages

General damages   General damages are available in both contract and tort and are unquantified damages which can be claimed for, *inter alia*, harm, loss of enjoyment, pain and suffering, shock, physical injury and inconvenience.

Special damages.   Special damages are available in contract and tort and are compensation for an identifiable and quantifiable loss.

Exemplary damages   Exemplary damages are available in a claim in tort

---

39   *Jackson v Horizon Holidays Ltd* [1975] 1 WLR 1468; *Jarvis v Swans Tours Ltd* [1973] QB 233; *McCall v Abelesz* [1976] QB 585 and *Calabar Properties Ltd v Stitcher* [1984] 1 WLR 287; but cf *Wooder Investment Development Ltd v Wimpey Construction Ltd* [1980] 1 WLR 277.
40   *Branchett v Beaney* [1992] 3 All ER 910.

but not for breach of contract.[41] They are available where the defendant's conduct has been calculated by him or her to make a profit which may well exceed the compensation payable to the plaintiff.[42] If it can be shown that the landlord was seeking vacant possession and that this would result in an increase in the value of the property, then the necessary element of calculation may be present. In one case on exemplary damages for unlawful eviction, the court held the correct approach to the assessment of damages was to quantify damage to property or person, any aggravated damages for damage to feelings, and only then exemplary damages.[43] Exemplary damages of £1,000 have been awarded where a tenant and his family were evicted and an interlocutory injunction ignored.[44]

Aggravated damages.   Aggravated damages are available in a claim in tort but not for breach of contract (but note that Denning MR's comments in *Drane v Evangelou* (above) apply equally to aggravated damages). Aggravated damages will be awarded as compensation for especially severe suffering, outrage and indignation at the way a person has been handled.[45] Aggravated damages may be claimed where the eviction or harassment was particularly unpleasant and will be awarded where the court wishes to register its disapproval of the defendant's actions. In *Asghar v Ahmed*, aggravated damages of £500 were awarded.

Damages under the Housing Act 1988 ss27 and 28.   For the special method of calculating damages for illegal eviction under these sections, see page 182.

Mitigation

A person who has suffered damage is under a duty to mitigate the loss if it is possible so to do. For example, if the occupier's belongings are put out on the road by the landlord or his or her agents, the occupier must endeavour to find somewhere to store his or her belongings.

---

41   *Guppy's (Bridport) Ltd v Brookling* (1983) 14 HLR 1 but see *Drane v Evangelou* [1978] 1 WLR 455, where Denning MR commented that, if the *facts* disclose a cause in tort as well as in contract, exemplary damages can be recovered even where a claim in contract only was pleaded.
42   *Rookes v Barnard* [1964] AC 1229.
43   *McMillan v Singh* (1985) 17 HLR 120.
44   *Asghar v Ahmed* (1984) 17 HLR 25.
45   *Cassell & Co Ltd v Broome* [1972] AC 1027.

Injunctions

Where there has been harassment or unlawful eviction, the occupier should apply to the court for an interlocutory injunction restraining the landlord and/or his or her agents from further harassment and/or ordering him or her or them to readmit the occupier to the premises. There is authority for the issue of a mandatory injunction where an occupier has been unlawfully ejected.[46]

Grounds for injunction

The occupier will be required to satisfy the usual prerequisites for interlocutory relief:
- there must be a serious question to be tried;
- damages alone would not be adequate compensation (eg, because the occupier has nowhere else to live);
- the occupier must give an undertaking in damages to compensate the landlord if it is later found that the order should not have been made; and
- the balance of convenience must be in favour of granting the injunction and restoring or maintaining the status quo for the time being rather than awaiting a full trial of the case.[47]

In most cases of harassment and unlawful eviction, the balance of convenience will be very heavily tilted in favour of restoring or maintaining the status quo and thus obtaining an interim injunction should normally present no problem. However, interlocutory relief is entirely in the discretion of the court and the onus will be on the occupier to show that the injunction is necessary. The old equitable rules apply to injunctions so that the applicant must have 'clean hands' (eg, if an occupier is in breach of his or her obligations an injunction may be refused) and an order must be capable of supervision by the court.

An interlocutory application should be made on notice if possible, but in an emergency an *ex parte* application may be appropriate. Breach of an injunction is punishable by committal to prison (see page 190). Any delay in making the application, and events in the intervening period, will be relevant considerations.[48]

Undertakings

The service of a notice of application for an interlocutory injunction may result in the landlord offering an undertaking to readmit the occupier

---

46   *Luganda v Service Hotels Ltd* [1969] 2 Ch 209.
47   *American Cyanamid Co v Ethicon Ltd* [1975] AC 396.
48   *Lindsay Petroleum Co v Hurd* (1874) LR 5 PC 22.

and/or to refrain from harassment. The occupier can be properly protected only if the landlord's undertaking is incorporated in a court order, which can then be enforced in the same way as an injunction if necessary.

Procedure on application for interlocutory injunction

Initial steps

In view of the provisions of the High Court and County Courts Jurisdiction Order 1991 and Housing Act 1988 s40, applications for injunctions in cases involving harassment or eviction are now inevitably made in a county court.

The adviser should, after taking full instructions, either fax a letter to, or telephone the prospective defendant, setting out the position in law and informing him or her that legal aid has been granted and that court proceedings are about to be issued. S/he should ask if the landlord will permit re-entry. A detailed attendance note of any conversation should be kept.

Details of the proposed application to court, emphasising that a claim for costs will be made, should be given and the right to refer to the letter at court reserved. If it is not possible to fax a letter, one should be delivered by hand. Do not wait for a reply, and commence drafting court documents.

If making an *ex parte* application, ie, an immediate application without issuing and serving documents, the court should be informed by telephone of the proposed proceedings. It should be ascertained that a judge is available. In the vacation it may be necessary to go to another county court or to the High Court.

If the emergency arises outside court hours, it is possible to apply to the High Court duty judge for an injunction by telephoning the gatekeeper at the Royal Courts of Justice (tel: 071-405 7641), who will contact the judge's clerk. In a case of extreme urgency, an injunction may be granted over the telephone on an undertaking by the solicitor, or a condition imposed by the judge, to issue a writ within a certain time. An unjustified failure to comply with the condition will amount to contempt of court.[49]

Documents to be filed

The action must be commenced by filing:

– a request for the issue of a summons;[50]

---

49   *Refson & Co Ltd v Saggers* [1984] 1 WLR 1025.
50   Practice form N203 available from the court; CCR Ord 3 r3(1).

- the original particulars of claim;
- a copy of the particulars of claim for each defendant;[51]
- notice of application for an interlocutory injunction and copy;[52]
- affidavit in support of application;[53]
- court fee;[54]
- legal aid certificate (if available).[55]

Particulars of claim. The particulars of claim must specify:[56]

- the cause of action;
- the relief or remedy sought; and
- the material facts on which the plaintiff relies.[57]
- where there is a claim for aggravated or exemplary damages, a statement to this effect and details of the facts relied on in support of that claim (CCR Ord 6 r1B).

The following information should also be included:

- full names of plaintiff(s) and defendant(s) – if the full name of the landlord is not known, sufficient information must be given to identify him or her (eg, Grubbins (male));
- status of plaintiff (eg, protected tenant) and relationship to defendant;
- address of premises and description of the accommodation occupied;
- date of occupation of premises and rent payable and whether or not registered rent;
- details of the tenancy agreement;
- obligation on which it is intended to rely or the tort which it is alleged has been committed;
- particulars of the breach of contract or tort;
- particulars of damage;
- claim for injunction;
- claim for damages including details of special damage suffered (but see below);
- claim for interest on damages; and
- claim for costs.

If the plaintiff has a claim for injury to health, a medical report should be attached to the particulars of claim unless leave has been given to dispense with this requirement.

51   CCR Ord 3 r3 and Ord 6 r1
52   Practice form N16A available from the court; CCR Ord 13 r6.
53   CCR Ord 13 r6(3).
54   County Court Fees (Amendment) Order 1985.
55   Civil Legal Aid (General) Regulations 1989 reg 50(2).
56   CCR Ord 6 r1(1).
57   CCR Ord 6 r1(1).

Notice of application.   The notice of application should set out the order requested and the grounds upon which the application is made.[58]

Affidavits.   The occupier's affidavit should:
- verify the contents of the particulars of claim;
- add details about the incidents relied on;
- include precise dates and times of incidents relied on – vague allegations are not sufficient and will prejudice the application; and
- include details of attempts made by the occupier and/or his or her adviser to gain re-entry by telephone calls or letters to the defendant.

There should be exhibited to the affidavit copies of any of the following which are available:
- written agreement and/or rent book/card;
- medical report;
- police report;
- photographs; and/or
- letters to defendant relevant to application.

There should also be affidavits from witnesses to the unlawful eviction, including one from the tenancy relations officer where appropriate.

Draft order.   This should be in form N16 and specify the terms of the injunction sought.[59]

Service of documents

Unless the application is being made *ex parte*, the defendant must be served personally with the court documents not less than two days before the hearing of the application.[60] Personal service should be arranged by the solicitor, not by the court, as this might cause a delay.

The documents to be served are:
- the application for an injunction in form N16A;
- a sealed copy of the summons;
- a sealed copy of the particulars of claim; and
- a copy of the affidavit(s).

Service may not take place on Sunday, Good Friday or Christmas Day except with the leave of the court.[61]

If the defendant is not present at the hearing, an affidavit of service

---

58   CCR Ord 13 r6(3).
59   CCR Ord 13 r6(6).
60   CCR Ord 13 r1.
61   CCR Ord 7 r3.

will be necessary to show service of the documents, or that serious attempts have been made to serve the documents.[62] A copy of the documents which have been served should be exhibited to the affidavit and the affidavit must contain information as to how the defendant's identity was established and when, where and how the documents were served.[63]

Notice

All interlocutory applications must be made on notice unless they are allowed or authorised to be made *ex parte*.[64]

The notice must be at least two days.[65]

The court has power to abridge the time between service and hearing if necessary.[66]

Ex parte *applications*

In a case of real emergency, a court will hear an application without the defendant having been notified (*ex parte*),[67] but initially the court will make an order only for a few days so that the defendant may be served with the papers and given an opportunity to be heard.

In a case of urgency, the application may be made on affidavit alone, but the affidavit must show that the court has jurisdiction to hear the action and the injunction will be granted on the condition that a summons is issued within a certain time.[68]

If an *ex parte* application is made it is good practice to ensure that the defendant and/or his or her solicitors have been notified of the hearing, and even if s/he cannot be served personally with the papers, s/he should be notified by letter, telephone or telemessage.

Hearing

An application for an injunction will usually be made to the judge in open court.[69] It is essential that both the occupier and witnesses should attend court and be ready to give oral evidence.[70] They should be warned that they may be cross-examined.

---

62   CCR Ord 8 r11.
63   CCR Ord 7 r6.
64   CCR Ord 13 r1.
65   CCR Ord 13 r4.
66   CCR Ord 13 r4.
67   CCR Ord 13 r6(3).
68   CCR Ord 13 r6(4).
69   CCR Ord 13 r6(2) and (5).
70   CCR Ord 20 r4.

Draft order

A draft order should be prepared before the hearing and submitted to the judge if the application is successful.[71]

Mandatory injunction.   If a mandatory injunction is sought (eg, an injunction ordering the landlord to re-admit the occupier to his or her house), the draft order should always set out the time within which the order must be carried out and the time should run from service of the order if the landlord is not in court, eg, 'within 24 hours of service of this order'. If a date is incorporated in the order and the order is not served by that date, the order will become ineffective and a fresh application will be necessary.[72]

Prohibitory injunction.   If an injunction is sought restraining the defendant from harassment or unlawful eviction, the order should run 'until further order' or 'until trial of the action'.

Penal notice.   An injunction should always be endorsed with a penal notice by the court. It is not possible to apply for committal to prison for contempt of court unless the order is endorsed with a penal notice.[73]

Service of order

The order must be served personally on the defendant before it can be enforced, except in certain circumstances (see page 191).[74] The order should be collected from the judge's clerk immediately after the hearing and served as soon as possible.

Enforcement

If the defendant breaches the order or fails to comply with it after it has been served on him or her, the plaintiff may apply for the defendant's committal to prison for contempt of court.[75]

The following documents should be filed when an application for committal to prison for contempt of court is made:

– notice to show cause why an order of committal should not be made and a copy[76] – the notice must set out details of the original order and specify details of the alleged breach;[77]

---

71   CCR Ord 13 r6(6); prescribed form N16.
72   CCR Ord 29 r1(2).
73   CCR Ord 29 r1(3).
74   CCR Ord 29 r1(2).
75   CCR Ord 29 r1(4).
76   CCR Ord 29 r1(4); prescribed form N78.
77   CCR Ord 29 r1(4)(a); *Williams v Fawcett* [1986] QB 604.

- affidavit of occupier in support of the application – the affidavit must verify the alleged breach of the injunction;[78] and
- affidavit of service of the original order. The court has discretion to dispense with personal service of the original order if the landlord was in court when the order was made or was subsequently notified by telephone, telemessage or otherwise, or if the court thinks it just to do so.[79] There is no need for an undertaking to be served before taking action to enforce it.[80]

Great care must be taken to follow the correct procedure. If these requirements are not strictly complied with, it is likely that the court will not make a committal order.[81]

The defendant must be given a minimum of two clear days' notice of the hearing, and it is unlikely that the court will abridge the time where the defendant's liberty is at stake.[82]

The defendant must be served personally with the notice to show cause,[83] but the court has power to order substituted service[84] or to dispense with service altogether if there is a flagrant and deliberate breach of the court's orders.[85] Personal service is necessary in all but exceptional circumstances.[86] An application to commit should not be adjourned pending criminal proceedings against the defendant arising out of the same incident.[87]

County courts have power to order imprisonment for contempt of court for a fixed term of not more than two years (County Courts (Penalties for Contempt) Act 1983). They have power also to suspend the operation of a committal order and to impose consecutive committal orders where more than one contempt has been proved.[88] If the court decides not to make a committal order, there is power to order an enquiry into damages sustained as a result of the breach of the injunction or undertaking.[89]

The committal order must be served personally on the defendant.

---

78   *Chakravorty v Braganza* (1983) *The Times*, 12 October 1983.
79   CCR Ord 29 r1(6) and (7).
80   *D v A and Co* [1900] 1 Ch 484.
81   See, eg, *Parsons v Nasar* (1990) 23 HLR 1; *Clarke v Clarke* [1990] 2 FLR 115 and *Temporal v Temporal* [1990] 2 FLR 98.
82   CCR Ord 13 r1(2).
83   CCR Ord 29 r1(4).
84   CCR Ord 7 r8(1).
85   *Lamb v Lamb* [1984] FLR 278.
86   *Phonographic Performance Ltd v Tsang* (1985) *The Times*, 17 May 1985.
87   *Caprice v Boswell* (1985) *The Times*, 24 June 1985.
88   *Lee v Walker* [1985] QB 1191.
89   *Midland Marts Ltd v Hobday* [1989] 1 WLR 1148.

CHAPTER 10

Disrepair

Introduction

Generally

Non-owner occupiers of residential accommodation whose premises are in a state of disrepair have a variety of remedies. Local authorities have extensive powers to prevent or remedy disrepair. Occupiers may take their own action where local authority powers are unavailable, inappropriate or inadequate. Here we are concerned only with ways to deal with emergency disrepair, and the legal remedies included in this chapter are necessarily selective.

Occupier's status

It is essential to check the occupier's status when advising on remedies for disrepair. Any occupier who complains about disrepair and tries to enforce his or her rights runs the risk of harassment. The risk to an occupier who does not have security of tenure or a long contractual licence is much greater. Reporting the matter to the environmental health officer, or commencing individual action, may well result in eviction before any repairs are carried out. This is true even where tenants have security of tenure if they are in serious arrears with their rent or have breached the tenancy agreement in some other way.

The legal status of the occupier must be established and s/he must be warned of the possible consequences of his or her action. Occupiers without security of tenure are very vulnerable and many reluctantly opt to remain living in poor conditions rather than risk becoming homeless.

Checklist for instructions

1 *Occupier*
   Full name and address
   Date of birth

Occupation

Income and capital

Status, eg, protected tenant, secure tenant etc

2 *Details of accommodation*

Size, shared facilities, location in house and whether other occupiers

3 *Children living with occupier*

Names and dates of birth

4 *Others sharing premises with occupier*

Names

Relationship with occupier

5 *Rent*

Whether registered

Any arrears

Rent book

6 *Date of commencement of occupancy*

7 *Written agreement*

8 *Landlord and/or agent*

Name, address and telephone number

9 *Details of disrepair*

Including date disrepair commenced

10 *Environmental health officer*

Name

Dates of any visits/inspections

11 *Housing Act and Public Health Act notices*

12 *Notice of disrepair to landlord*

Written or oral?

Dates

13 *Has landlord/agent seen disrepair?*

Dates

14 *Correspondence relating to disrepair*

15 *Details of damage to goods*

16 *Medical effects of disrepair*

With names and addresses of GP and hospitals and signed authority to doctor to provide information

17 *Details of general inconvenience etc*

18 *Photographs*

19 *Witnesses*

Names and addresses

20 *Any previous court proceedings*

21 *Surveyor's report*

Local authority proceedings

Role of local authorities

Local authorities have extensive powers to ensure that housing is kept in a proper state of repair. These powers are vested in them by the Environmental Protection and Housing Acts. The enforcement of public health and housing legislation is usually delegated to environmental health officers employed by the local authority.[1] Environmental health officers can serve notices requiring repairs to be carried out and in some circumstances can arrange for the work to be carried out in default if the landlord refuses to comply with the notice.

An environmental health officer cannot serve notices on his or her own authority[2] so local authority tenants must use civil proceedings (see page 197), prosecute the local authority in the magistrates' court if a statutory nuisance exists (for definition see below)[3] or make a complaint to a magistrate if the premises are unfit for human habitation (Housing Act 1985 s606).

Emergency procedures

Urgent statutory nuisance

A statutory nuisance is defined in the Environmental Protection Act 1990 s79.

Only s79(1)(a) is relevant here, which defines a statutory nuisance as 'any premises in such a state as to be prejudicial to health or a nuisance'. The limbs are in the alternative. 'Prejudicial to health' is defined as meaning 'injurious or likely to cause injury to health'.[4] A 'nuisance' means a nuisance at common law and it follows that the nuisance must emanate from one set of premises and create an effect in another.[5] This definition includes a nuisance emanating from common parts in a house or building in multiple occupation, having effect in an individual unit, as the common parts are different 'premises' from those suffering the nuisance.

The authority has the power to adopt a special speedy procedure if it appears to it that premises are in such a defective state as to be prejudicial to health or a nuisance and unreasonable delay in remedying the state of

---

1 Local Government Act 1972 s101.
2 *R v Cardiff City Council ex parte Cross* (1982) 1 HLR 54.
3 Environmental Protection Act 1990 ss79 and 82.
4 Environmental Protection Act 1990 s79(7).
5 *National Coal Board v Thorne* [1976] 1 WLR 543.

affairs would be caused if normal procedures were to be followed.[6] The most common example of an urgent statutory nuisance is a leaking roof.

'Unreasonable delay' is to be decided on the facts, but a difference between four weeks under urgent procedures and 11 to 12 weeks under normal procedures has been held unreasonable.[7]

The procedure permits an authority to serve, usually on the landlord, a notice of its intention to come in and do the work necessary to remedy the defective state of the premises.[8] The notice must specify what defects the authority intends to remedy. The authority may go in and do the work necessary to remedy the statutory nuisance when nine days from the service of the notice have expired, unless a counter-notice is served by the landlord.[9]

The person served has seven days from service within which to serve on the authority a counter-notice indicating his or her intention to remedy the defects him or herself.[10] If such a counter-notice is served, then the authority may not proceed to carry out the works in default itself unless the works are not commenced by the person served within a reasonable time, or progress towards completion of the work within a reasonable time is not maintained.[11]

An authority may not serve a notice, or proceed with the execution of the works in accordance with the notice, if the execution of the works would, to its knowledge, be in contravention of a building preservation order under the Town and Country Planning Act 1947 s29.[12]

The authority may serve a notice under s26, notwithstanding that it might instead have proceeded under the Housing Act 1985 part IX.[13]

Dangerous buildings

Authorities have powers to deal with dangerous buildings by normal or urgent procedures. Normal procedure is by way of application to the magistrates' court for an appropriate order.[14]

If it appears to an authority that immediate action should be taken in respect of a dangerous building, it may take such steps as may be necessary to remove the danger.[15]

6 Environmental Protection Act 1990 s80.
7 *Celcrest Properties v Hastings Borough Council* (29 October 1979) unreported.
8 Environmental Protection Act 1990 ss80(1) and 81(3); Building Act 1984 s76.
9 Building Act 1984 s76(2).
10 Building Act 1984 s76(3).
11 Building Act 1984 s76(3).
12 Building Act 1984 s86(6).
13 Building Act 1984 s86(7).
14 Building Act 1984 s77(1).
15 Building Act 1984 s78.

There is no restriction on the local authority's power and the whole building may be demolished if necessary.

A surveyor or other proper officer of the authority can exercise these powers without first being expressly authorised by the authority itself.[16]

There is no specific provision for rehousing an occupier of the premises.[17]

Occupier's proceedings

Courses of action for occupiers

A non-owner occupier of residential accommodation has three courses of individual action if his or her premises are in a state of disrepair. An occupier may wish to use individual action because the environmental health officer cannot or will not exercise his or her powers (see page 194) and/or because s/he wishes to obtain financial compensation for disrepair and/or because s/he wishes to have more control over the procedure for getting repairs carried out.

Environmental Protection Act 1990 s82

Where a statutory nuisance exists (see page 194), an individual may prosecute the landlord in the magistrates' court. Twenty-one days' written notice of intention to take proceedings has to be given.[18] This is not a speedy procedure and is not advisable in cases of emergency, particularly if the landlord is likely to deny that there is a statutory nuisance. Legal aid is not available for these proceedings.

Housing Act 1985 s606

Where premises are unfit,[19] an occupier may make a complaint to a magistrate. If the magistrate is satisfied that the complaint is correct, s/he will report to the local authority's medical officer of health or other appropriate officer. That officer then has a duty to report to the authority, which will consider what (if any) action to take. The procedure is too slow and uncertain to be of any immediate assistance in an emergency, although it could be used in conjunction with civil proceedings.

16 Building Act s78(8).
17 But see generally Housing Act 1985 part III.
18 Environmental Protection Act 1990, s82(7).
19 Housing Act (HA) 1985 s604.

Action for breach of contract or in tort

An occupier may in some circumstances sue the landlord or his or her agent for breach of contract or in tort and, where an urgent repair is required, obtain an injunction requiring the defect to be remedied. The first place to look for the landlord's repairing obligations is in the agreement between landlord and occupier. If the agreement is silent or the landlord has sought to exempt him or herself from a duty to repair, the repairing obligations may be found in the Landlord and Tenant Act (LTA) 1985 (see page 198). In the absence of a contractual obligation, a remedy may be available in tort (page 203). There is no higher obligation to repair on a local authority than on a private landlord.[20] An obligation to effect repairs carries with it an obligation to make good any consequential damage to decorations.[21]

Contract

Introduction

An occupier's contractual right to have his or her premises kept in good repair will be found as an express term of the agreement or as a term implied by law or, in the case of a tenant only, implied by statute.

There follows a brief outline of some of the contractual provisions governing an occupier's right to repairs. The list is not comprehensive but will suffice for straightforward cases of emergency (for a more detailed exposition see Luba *Repairs: Tenants' Rights*, LAG, 2nd edn 1991).

Breach of contract

A written agreement usually sets out the repairing obligations of a landlord and occupier. It is rare for a licensee to be responsible for repairs (see page 201). A landlord cannot unilaterally exempt him or herself from obligations imposed on him or her by statute (for example, by LTA 1985 s11 or HA 1985 s190). A landlord may be sued under this head only in respect of the obligations contained or implied in the agreement.

Who may sue?   The following may sue:

- the original occupier who signed the agreement;
- an assignee of a tenant who signed the agreement;
- a statutory tenant;[22] and

---

20   *Wainwright v Leeds City Council* (1984) 82 LGR 657.
21   *Bradley v Chorley Borough Council* (1985) 83 LGR 623.
22   Rent Act (RA) 1977 s3(1)

- members of the occupier's family provided that they were a party to the agreement.

Who may be sued?   The following may be sued:
- the original landlord who signed the agreement; and
- assignees of the original landlord.

Landlord and Tenant Act 1985 s11, as amended by Housing Act 1988 s116

There is a repairing covenant implied if the tenancy agreement is granted after 24 October 1961 for a term of less than seven years.[23] LTA 1985 s11 supersedes HA 1961 s32, and has been amended by HA 1988. It applies to both public and private sector tenancies but does not bind the Crown.[24]

The covenant requires the landlord to:
- keep in repair the structure and exterior of the dwelling-house (including drains, gutters and external pipes);
- keep in repair and proper working order the installations in the dwelling-house for the supply of water, gas and electricity and for sanitation, including basins, sinks, bathroom sanitary conveniences, but not other fixtures and fittings and appliances for making use of the supply of water, gas and electricity;
- keep in repair and proper working order the installations in the dwelling-house for space heating and heating water.

However, HA 1988 s116 amends s11 in its application to leases entered into on or after 15 January 1989 (except for those entered into pursuant to a contract made before that date).[25]

It modifies the covenant where the lease in question is of a dwelling-house which forms part of a building. The modified covenant requires the landlord:
- to keep in repair the structure and exterior of any parts of the building in which s/he has an estate or interest;
- keep in repair and proper working order installations (as listed in s11) which directly or indirectly serve the flat and which either form part of any part of a building in which the landlord has an estate or interest or which are owned by him or her or are under his or her control.

Scope of covenant   'Repair' means to 'put and keep in repair'.[26] A repair

---

23   LTA 1985 ss11 and 13
24   *Department of Transport v Egoroff* (1986) 18 HLR 326.
25   HA 1988 s116(4).
26   *Proudfoot v Hart* (1890) 25 QBD 42.

as opposed to an improvement is a question of fact and degree, having regard in particular to the cost relative to the value of the property.[27] Thus, design or construction defects may come within the covenant if the remedial work is not so extensive that the premises would be improved rather than repaired.

Examples include:

- the insertion of expansion joints have been held to come within the covenant;[28]
- the rebuilding of a back addition at a cost representing more than one-third of rebuilding the whole premises does not come within the covenant;[29]
- the covenant will not extend to a replacement roof unless it can be shown that piecemeal repair has become impracticable;[30]
- rising damp attributable to an ineffectual damp-proof course constitutes a breach of covenant to repair even if the remedy is replacement of the damp-proof course by a different and modern method.[31]

'Structure' has been widely defined as 'something appertaining to the fabric of a building so as to be part of the complex whole'[32] and 'those elements of the overall dwelling-house which give it its essential stability and shape'.[33] There must be disrepair related to the physical condition of the structure and/or exterior, not merely a condition causing internal damage. Thus, condensation caused by design or inherent defects where there was no physical harm to the structure or exterior does not come within the covenant,[34] but where the condensation is so bad that the wall plaster has become saturated, there may be actionable disrepair under s11.[35] An inherent design defect causing water ingress through the front door of the property resulting in warping and rotting to the door does come within the covenant because the disrepair relates to the physical condition of the door.[36]

The structure and exterior include:

---

27 *McDougall v Easington District Council* (1989) 21 HLR 310.
28 *Ravenseft Properties Ltd v Davstone (Holdings) Ltd* [1980] QB 12
29 *Halliard Property Co v Nicholas Clarke Investments* (1984) 269 EG 1257.
30 *Murray v Birmingham City Council* (1988) 20 HLR 39.
31 *Elmcroft Developments Ltd v Tankersley-Sawyer* (1984) 270 EG 140.
32 *Granada Theatres Ltd v Freehold Investment (Leytonstone) Ltd* [1959] Ch 592.
33 *Irvine v Moran* [1991] 1 EGLR 261.
34 *Quick v Taff Ely Borough Council* [1986] QB 809.
35 *Staves v Leeds City Council* (1991) 23 HLR 95.
36 *Stent v Monmouth District Council* (1987) 19 HLR 269.

- the roof if it is part of the premises to which the covenant applies[37] and skylights in the roof;[38]
- a partition wall with another set of premises;[39]
- windows;[40]
- essential means of access to the premises;[41]
- a blocked pipe;[42] and
- the walls[43] and doors.[44]

A landlord is not obliged to lag water pipes unless the pipes are especially prone to bursting.[45] Repairs to the 'exterior' may include external redecoration.[46]

The covenant obliges a landlord to repair defective toilets, sinks and baths and water heaters.

With regard to the modified covenant contained in HA 1988 s116, the tenant will be able to complain of disrepair to the structure and exterior of a part of a building other than his or her own flat or disrepair or malfunctioning of an installation outside his or her own flat only where s/he can show that his or her enjoyment of the flat or the common parts of the building has been affected as a result.

In addition, the landlord has a statutory defence to an action where s/he needs to carry out repairs or works outside the flat if s/he does not have sufficient right in the part of the building or the installation concerned to enable him or her to carry them out. S/he must prove (the burden of proof is on the landlord) that s/he used all reasonable endeavours to obtain the rights s/he required to do the works, but that s/he was unable to obtain them.

The covenant does not extend to works for which the tenant is liable under the duty imposed by common law on all tenants to use the premises in a tenant-like manner.[47] This includes 'the little jobs about the place which a reasonable tenant would do',[48] eg, unblocking a sink, turning off the water if the tenant is going away for the winter.

---

37   *Douglas-Scott v Scorgie* [1984] 1 WLR 716.
38   *Taylor v Webb* [1937] 2 KB 283.
39   *Pembery v Lamdin* [1940] 2 All ER 434; *Campden Hill Towers Ltd v Gardner* [1977] QB 823.
40   *Boswell v Crucible Steel Co* [1925] 1 KB 119 and *Irvine v Moran* [1991] 1 EGLR 261.
41   *Brown v Liverpool Corporation* [1969] 3 All ER 1345.
42   *Bishop v Consolidated London Properties* (1933) 102 LJ KB 257.
43   *Elmcroft Developments Ltd v Tankersky-Sawyer* (1984) 270 EG 140.
44   *Stent v Monmouth District Council* (1987) 19 HLR 269.
45   *Wycombe Area Health Authority v Barnett* (1982) 5 HLR 84.
46   *Irvine v Moran* [1991] 1 EGLR 261.
47   LTA 1985 s11(2)(a)
48   *Warren v Keen* [1954] 1 KB 15.

There is no duty on the landlord to rebuild or reinstate the premises in the case of destruction or damage by fire, tempest, flood or other inevitable accident.[49]

Who may sue? The following may sue:

- a tenant where the tenancy was granted after 24 October 1961 for a term of less than seven years;
- assignees of such a tenant;
- a statutory tenant;[50] and
- members of the tenant's family provided that they are party to the contract.

Where a landlord is not statutorily liable to perform the repairing covenants contained in s11, s/he may be estopped from denying such liability if s/he has accepted rent on the basis of a registration of a fair rent which states that the landlord's repairing obligations are contained in s11.[51]

In cases where s11 does not apply, it may be possible to imply such a requirement to give business efficacy to the lease.[52]

If the tenancy is of local authority accommodation, the authority will have determined it by notice to quit after 1961 in order to increase the rent, and regranted a fresh tenancy, to which s11 applies.[53]

Who may be sued? The following may be sued:

- the original landlord; and
- assignees of the original landlord.

Implied term in licences

There is an implied term in licences that premises will be kept fit for the purpose for which they were granted.[54] Thus, if the premises become uninhabitable through disrepair, the licensor is under an obligation to carry out remedial works.

It is rare for a licensee to be responsible for repairs and it may be evidence of the existence of a tenancy if s/he is, though not necessarily in the case of a short-life licensee, or in the case of a licence that was granted or is a licence *because* of disrepair or redevelopment proposals.

49   LTA 1985 s11(2)(b).
50   RA 1977 s3(1).
51   *Brikom Investments Ltd v Seaford* [1981] 1 WLR 863 (decided on HA 1961 s32, which s11 supersedes).
52   *Barrett v Lounova (1982) Ltd* [1990] 1 QB 348.
53   *Benson v Liverpool City Council* (1988) March 1989 *Legal Action* 22.
54   *Smith v Nottinghamshire County Council* (1981) *The Times*, 7 November 1981.

Who may sue?   The following may sue:
- the licensee; and
- members of the licensee's family if they are party to the contract.

Who may be sued?   The following may be sued:
- the licensor; and
- assignees of the licensor.

Common parts

The landlord is usually responsible for the upkeep of the common parts[55] and must keep them reasonably safe.[56]

In a block of flats, it may be implied, in the absence of express provisions to the contrary, that the landlord is under an obligation to use reasonable care to ensure that lifts are kept in repair and proper working order and that lighting, rubbish chutes, stairs and corridors are similarly maintained. This obligation can only be avoided by express exclusion in the contract of letting.[57]

The courts may also be prepared to imply a covenant to repair essential means of access to houses.[58]

Who may sue?   The following may sue:
- the original occupier;
- assignees of an original tenant;
- a statutory tenant;[59] and
- members of the occupier's family if they are party to the contract.

Who may be sued?   The following may be sued:
- the original landlord; and
- assignees of the original landlord.

Notice of defect

The landlord's liability in contract only arises after s/he has notice of, or at least actual knowledge of, a defect.[60] Notice should be given as soon as possible as delay may affect the damages awarded.[61]

There is no requirement that the notice be in writing, nor does the

---

55   *Cockburn v Smith* (1968) 112 SJ 631.
56   *Dunster v Hollis* [1918] 2 KB 795.
57   *Liverpool City Council v Irwin* [1977] AC 239.
58   *King v South Northamptonshire District Council* (1991) 90 LGR 121 – garden paths.
59   RA 1977 s3(1)
60   *O'Brien v Robinson* [1973] AC 912; *McGreal v Wake* (1984) 13 HLR 107.
61   *Minchburn v Peck* (1988) 20 HLR 392.

tenant have to give notice him or herself. Thus, if the environmental health officer has served a statutory notice, or written a letter to the landlord, that will suffice.[62] A surveyor's report for valuation purposes sent to the landlord will also suffice.[63]

Actual knowledge by the landlord, in the absence of express notice, is sufficient, eg, where a plumber, sent by the landlord, inspected the water tank which burst six weeks later, the inspection by the plumber was sufficient to fix the landlord with notice.[64] Similarly, where a technical officer employed by the landlord local authority visited premises and was notified of a defect, this notice was sufficient, and where the chief executive received a report, even though it was not for the purpose of complaining about defects, it nevertheless put the local authority on enquiry and constituted notice.[65]

However, the landlord must have sufficient information about the defect to put a reasonable man on enquiry as to whether repairs were needed.[66] If the tenant specifically states that s/he will ascertain what works are necessary and submit estimates, then the landlord's obligations do not arise until s/he is specifically told what is necessary.[67]

If a landlord fails to carry out the repairs within a reasonable time after notification (which will depend on the facts of the case), then an action for damages and other relief will lie for breach of covenant to repair.[68]

The notice requirement does not apply to those parts of the building retained in the landlord's own possession and control, which includes the common parts.[69]

If notice has not been given, it may still be possible to sue in tort (see below).

Tort

Where the contractual provisions are not relevant, either because they do not exist, or because notice has not been given, the landlord may be liable to the occupier in tort. This is a brief outline of the most common causes of action in tort in respect of disrepair (for further guidance see Luba *Repairs: Tenants' Rights*, LAG, 1991).

62 *McGreal v Wake* (above).
63 *Hall v Howard* (1988) 20 HLR 566.
64 *Sheldon v West Bromwich Corporation* (1984) 13 HLR 23.
65 *Dinefwr Borough Council v Jones* (1987) 19 HLR 445.
66 *O'Brien v Robinson* [1973] AC 912.
67 *Al Hassani v Merrigan* (1988) 20 HLR 238.
68 *Calabar Properties Ltd v Stitcher* [1984] 1 WLR 287.
69 *Melles & Co v Holme* [1918] 2 KB 100.

Negligence

It must be shown that a duty of care is owed (by the landlord to the occupier), that that duty has been broken, and that the damage suffered was caused by a negligent act or omission.[70]

Examples.   The duty of care has been considered in the following cases:

a) Landlords who design or build dwellings for occupation owe a duty of care to ensure that the premises are constructed free from defects which might cause personal injury or damage to the property of the occupiers.[71] In *Rimmer v Liverpool City Council* the defect complained of was a panel of thin glass set in the wall of the hallway. The flat had been designed by the City Council's architects department and built by its direct works department. In *Targett v Torfaen Borough Council*,[72] the defects were stone steps which had been constructed without a handrail or lighting.

b) A landlord may be liable in negligence if his or her repairing obligations have not been properly carried out by others, or for failure to take remedial action.[73]

c) Where a landlord lets premises, but retains in his or her control other premises (including common parts) which s/he knows to be dangerous and which s/he negligently fails to render safe, s/he will be liable for any damage to the occupier or members of the occupier's family caused by that part of the building which remains in the landlord's control. This will be so whether the occupier (or his or her family) is injured on the premises which have been let, or on the land adjacent to those premises (eg, a backyard).[74]

d) A landlord has been held not liable in negligence for injury caused to a baby as a result of accidental contact with unlagged central heating pipes; in this particular case the baby fell off a bed, became trapped on the pipes and was burned. It was held that the risk was slight and the landlord was entitled to rely on precautions taken by the parents.[75]

e) It must be reasonably foreseeable that the damage would arise from the act or omission, eg, there was no liability where vacant premises were insecure and there had been a burglary to an adjacent property.[76]

---

70   *Donoghue v Stephenson* [1932] AC 562.
71   *Rimmer v Liverpool City Council* [1985] QB 1.
72   [1992] 3 All ER 27.
73   *Sharpe v Manchester District Council* (1977) 5 HLR 71.
74   *Cunard v Antifyre Ltd* [1953] 1 KB 551.
75   *Ryan v London Borough of Camden* (1982) *The Times*, 16 December 1982.
76   *P. Perl (Exporters) Ltd v Camden London Borough Council* [1984] QB 342.

f) A contractor is not liable for negligence committed by a subcontractor.[77]

g) An occupier of premises owes a duty of care to his or her neighbours to take reasonable care to refrain from acts or omissions which a reasonable and prudent person would have known were likely to damage the neighbours' premises. It would impose too great a duty on an occupier to require him or her to run water every two or so months to see whether the waste pipe was blocked *in the absence of previous blockages.*[78]

h) A landlord, including a local authority, of unfurnished premises does not owe a duty of care to a tenant as to the state of the premises when they were let.[79]

Who may sue?
- any lawful occupier;
- any member of the lawful occupier's family.

Who may be sued?   The landlord and his or her agent if s/he has been party to the negligent act may be sued.

Defective Premises Act 1972 s4

A landlord who is under a repairing obligation (see page 198):

> owes to all persons who might reasonably be expected to be affected by defects in the state of the premises a duty to take such care as is reasonable in all the circumstances to see that they are reasonably safe from personal injury or from damage to their property caused by a relevant defect.[80]

For these purposes, the landlord is treated as being under an obligation to repair or maintain whenever s/he is in a position to exercise a right of entry to carry out a particular class of repair.[81] A right of entry may be expressly provided for in a tenancy agreement, or may be implied by statute.[82]

The defect must arise from an item of disrepair which falls within the premises, but need not fall within the landlord's obligations pursuant to s11.[83]

This duty is owed if the landlord knows of the defect or should have

---

77   *D & F Estates Ltd v Church Commissioners for England* [1989] AC 177.
78   *Hawkins v Dhawan and Mishiku* (1987) 19 HLR 232.
79   *McNerny v Lambeth Borough Council* (1989) 21 HLR 188.
80   Defective Premises Act 1972 s4.
81   Defective Premises Act 1972 s4(4).
82   For example, the Landlord and Tenant Act 1985 ss8 and 11.
83   *McAuley v Bristol City Council* [1992] QB 134 – a defective garden step.

known of it.[84] Thus, the landlord can be sued if s/he is in breach of a repairing obligation, even if no notice has been given.[85]

Such care as is reasonable in all the circumstances may include failure to make regular or more general inspections when visiting to carry out repairs, particularly where, because of the age of the premises and/or type of construction it is foreseeable that a defect (eg, wet or dry rot) may occur.[86] Thus, this cause of action may be appropriate where a ceiling collapses because of a leaking roof.

Who may sue?   The following may sue:
- all occupiers where the landlord is under a repairing obligation;
- all weekly tenants;[87] and
- all other persons who might reasonably be expected to be affected by defects, eg, members of the occupier's family and visitors.

Who may be sued?   The following may be sued:
- the original landlord; and
- assignees of the original landlord.

Nuisance

In order for an action in nuisance to lie, there must be some act or state of affairs in one set of premises which adversely affects the use and enjoyment of another.

A landlord's control of neighbouring property may be such that it interferes with the occupier's reasonable use of his or her premises, eg, where an adjacent flat has been designed in such a way that normal user will adversely affect the use and enjoyment of the premises because of noise.[88]

The landlord will be liable if a nuisance emanates from the common parts, eg, where a landlord failed to deal with an infestation of cockroaches in the common parts which spread to the tenant's premises.[89]

If the claim is based on the act of a trespasser, it must be shown that the landlord had adopted or continued the nuisance.[90]

---

84   Defective Premises Act 1972 s4(2).
85   *Smith v Bradford MC Metropolitan City Council* (1982) 80 LGR 713.
86   *Clarke v Taff Ely Borough Council* (1980) 10 HLR 44.
87   *Mint v Good* [1951] 1 KB 517.
88   *Sampson v Hodson-Pressinger* [1981] 3 All ER 710.
89   *Sharpe v Manchester District Council* (1977) 5 HLR 71.
90   *King v Liverpool City Council* [1986] 1 WLR 89.

Who may sue? Anyone with a right to occupy the premises suffering the nuisance[91] may sue, but not a mere visitor.

Who may be sued? The person in control of the premises from which the nuisance emanates should be sued.

Remedies

Damages

The long-term remedies for breach of contract or tort include mandatory and prohibitory injunctions and damages, ie, monetary compensation for the loss caused by the breach of contract or the tort. As this book deals with emergencies only, it is inappropriate to deal with damages in detail. However, long-term considerations are relevant when deciding which cause of action to pursue. Thus, a brief outline of the types of damages available has been included.

Contract
The court will endeavour to put the occupier into the position s/he would have been in if the repairing obligation had been carried out. There is no one set of rules as to how this should be calculated. However, damages will be awarded for:
– the cost of alternative accommodation while the premises were uninhabitable;
– the costs of redecoration; and
– discomfort, loss of enjoyment, ill health and inconvenience.

Special damages must be specifically pleaded.[92]

Only the parties to the contract, or their assignees or a tenant who is a statutory successor, may sue for breach of contract. However, it is now well established that the occupier is able to claim on behalf of those for whose benefit the contract was made, eg, his or her family.[93]

Tort
The basic principle of damages in tort is that the plaintiff should be put in the same position as s/he would have been if the tort had not occurred.

91   *Read v J Lyons & Co* [1947] AC 156.
92   *Calabar Properties Ltd v Stitcher* [1984] 1 WLR 287.
93   *Jackson v Horizon Holidays Ltd* [1975] 1 WLR 1468; *Jarvis v Swans Tours Ltd* [1973] QB 233; *McCall v Abelesz* [1976] QB 585 and *Calabar Properties Ltd v Stitcher* [1984] 1 WLR 287; but cf *Woodar Investment Development Ltd v Wimpey Construction UK Ltd* [1980] 1 WLR 277.

The damage must, however, be damage that is a reasonably foreseeable consequence of the tort. General damages in tort are available for pain and suffering, nervous shock and personal injury, but not usually for discomfort, embarrassment or disappointment.

An occupier cannot claim in tort on behalf of others, but a cohabitant, flat sharer or visitor could him or herself sue or join in the proceedings as a joint plaintiff if the occupier has also suffered harm.

Types of damages

General, special, exemplary and aggravated damages may be available depending on the cause of action and the facts of the case. These heads of damages have been considered on page 183. Aggravated damages should be sought in cases where the landlord is in blatant breach of his or her repairing obligations and fully aware of the effect of the breach on the occupier.

Mitigation of loss

A person who has suffered damage is under a duty to mitigate the loss if it is possible to do so. For example, if a roof is leaking and belongings are not removed after the leak becomes apparent it may not be possible to claim damages for these items. Notice of the defect must be given as soon as possible.[94] A tenant will not be disentitled to damages because the rent has been reduced by a rent officer to take account of disrepair.[95]

Specific performance and injunctions

Introduction

Where there is disrepair causing interference with the occupier's enjoyment of the property, s/he will be entitled, at the trial, to specific performance of any contractual term or to an injunction. Here, however, we are concerned with emergency relief, which will mean an interim injunction. If the disrepair is serious enough to merit interlocutory relief, ie, it is severe, causing substantial continuing interference or damage, the occupier should issue a summons and make an interlocutory application for an order that the disrepair be remedied. The occupier may make an application for an injunction if s/he does not wish to claim damages or any other relief.[96] An application for an injunction should be made only on the advice of a surveyor or other expert who has inspected the property and who can give evidence at court, at this stage by affidavit. If an

94   *Minchburn v Peck* (1988) 20 HLR 392.
95   *Sturolson & Co v Manroux* (1988) 20 HLR 332.
96   County Courts Act 1984 s22.

unsuccessful application for an interim injunction is made, it is very
unlikely that the tenant will recover costs. In those circumstances, if the
tenant is legally aided, the costs incurred by his or her lawyers will be
deducted from any damages eventually awarded in accordance with the
provisions of the Legal Aid Board's statutory charge.

Criteria for grant of injunction

The occupier will be required to satisfy the usual prerequisites to the grant
of interlocutory relief, ie:[97]

- that there is a serious question to be tried;
- that damages alone would not be adequate compensation (eg, because
  of danger to health or because the landlord would not be in a position
  to meet the damages to which the occupier would be entitled);
- that the occupier can give an undertaking in damages to compensate
  the landlord if it is later found that the order should not have been
  made; and
- that the balance of convenience favours the tenant.

To obtain a mandatory injunction, ie, requiring work to be carried out
before trial, the occupier will also have to show:

- the imminent danger of further serious harm;
- that the harm outweighs the cost of the remedial works (unless the
  landlord has acted unreasonably or with wanton disregard of the law);
  and
- the order sought is sufficiently precise that the landlord knows exactly
  what remedial work has to be executed and by what date.[98]

A mandatory injunction will be issued at an interlocutory stage only in
urgent cases where there is a clear breach of contract causing major
discomfort and damage to health, eg, where the services for space heating
and water heating require repair.[99]

Interlocutory relief is in the discretion of the court[100] and the onus will
be on the occupier to show that the order is necessary. The old equitable
rules apply to injunctions, so that the applicant must come to court with
'clean hands' (eg, if an occupier is in breach of his or her obligations, an
injunction may be refused) and 'an order must be capable of supervision
by the Court'.

The injunction must be relevant to the subject-matter of the

---

97   *American Cyanamid Co v Ethicon Ltd* [1975] AC 396.
98   *Redland Bricks Ltd v Morris* [1970] AC 652.
99   *Parker v Camden London Borough Council* [1986] Ch 162.
100 County Courts Act 1984 s38.

proceedings,[101] so the particular item of disrepair which the injunction will remedy must be pleaded in the particulars of claim.

An injunction will be granted against the landlord, even if the landlord can show want of financial capacity to comply with the order.[102]

An action for breach of a landlord's repairing obligations, including a claim for an injunction, cannot be protected by a caution on the Land Register because it is not a claim to an 'interest' in the land.[103]

Appointment of receiver

If the landlord cannot be found, or if it can be shown that s/he will not carry out the repairs, a receiver (who may be a surveyor) may be appointed by interlocutory order to collect the rents and manage the property, including carrying out repairs.[104] This remedy is not available against local authorities or other public sector landlords or against resident landlords.[105] This procedure is set out in LTA 1987 ss22 to 24.

Undertakings

Service of a summons and an application for a mandatory injunction may result in the landlord offering to carry out work. The occupier can be properly protected only by having the landlord's undertaking to carry out the work by a specific date incorporated in a court order. The undertaking can be enforced in the same way as an injunction if the landlord does not comply with his or her promise.[106]

Declarations

The county court has full power to grant a declaration relating to rights in housing, even if that is the only relief sought.[107]

If the occupier can, him or herself, afford to carry out the repairs, a declaration can provide a speedy remedy.

The court should be invited to make a declaration incorporating the following terms:

- that the landlord is in breach of a specified repairing obligation;

---

101   *Winstone v Winstone* [1960] P 28.
102   *Francis v Cowcliffe* (1976) 33 P & CP 368.
103   *Regan and Blackburn Ltd v Rogers* [1985] 1 WLR 870.
104   LTA 1987 Pt II; *Hart v Emelkirk Ltd* [1983] 1 WLR 1289; *Daiches v Bluelake Investments* (1985) 17 HLR 543; *Clayhope Properties Ltd v Evans* [1986] 1 WLR 1223.
105   LTA 1987 s21.
106   CCR Ord 29 r1.
107   County Courts Act 1984 s22.

- that the occupier is entitled to do the necessary works of repair in default;
- that the work may be financed by deduction of the future rent; and
- that carrying out the work and deducting the cost from the rent will not constitute a breach by the occupier of an express term of the agreement, eg, to pay rent or not to do works to the building.

There are, however, risks involved in following this course of action. For example, the tenant may end up being liable for any defects caused by his or her builders.

Direct action

In cases where the environmental health officer cannot (or will not) intervene and court proceedings would be too expensive or cumbersome, a tenant may, in some circumstances, carry out repairs him or herself and recoup the costs from future rent payments[108] or from accumulated arrears.[109]

This remedy is useful where the repairs needed are not expensive and the tenant has the necessary finance.

There is direct authority only for the use of the procedure by tenants, but in principle it would seem to be equally available to contractual licensees, but the absence of long-term security of tenure may make it risky.

The procedure should be used with caution and only where the landlord is in clear breach of his or her repairing obligations. It is particularly important to check the tenant's status and to ensure that there is security of tenure. The following steps must be followed:

a) The landlord should be informed in writing of the disrepair and advised of the occupier's intention to carry out the remedial work and to deduct the cost from the rent if the landlord does not have the repairs done within a reasonable time.

b) The occupier must then allow a reasonable time for the landlord to comply with his or her repairing obligations. 'A reasonable time' will depend on the type and extent of disrepair.[110] The onus is on the occupier to show that delay has occurred; a delay of one week to repair an exterior door was not unreasonable.[111]

c) If the work is not carried out, the occupier should obtain estimates for the cost of carrying out the remedial works and submit copies of these to the landlord with a final warning.

108 *Lee-Parker v Izzet* [1971] 1 WLR 1688.
109 *Asco Developments Ltd v Gordon* (1978) 248 EG 683.
110 *Calabar Properties Ltd v Stitcher* [1984] 1 WLR 287.
111 *Morris v Liverpool City Council* (1988) 20 HLR 498.

d) If the works are still not carried out the occupier should engage the contractor of the lowest tender and have the work done.

e) If no money is forthcoming, the occupier should inform the landlord that s/he intends to recoup the cost by deduction from future rent, or from arrears already accrued. A time-limit for a response should be placed on the landlord, and if there is still no reimbursement when that time has expired the occupier should deduct the cost from rent or from arrears as appropriate. The right to recoup from rent is confined to the actual cost and expenses of remedial work.

Provided that the occupier has followed this procedure, s/he will have a defence if s/he is sued for the rent which remains unpaid after repairs have been carried out.[112]

It has also been held that a tenant is entitled to raise a defence to an action for arrears of rent on the ground that the rent money has been expended on remedial work following the landlord's default in carrying out repairing obligations.[113]

Secure tenant's right to repair

A secure tenant's right to repair is contained in HA 1985 s96(1) and (2). This permits the Secretary of State to make regulations for a right to repair scheme, which will allow secure tenants to execute works for which the landlord is responsible, and to recoup the cost from the landlord. The scheme is confined to repairs to the dwelling-house itself, ie, it does not extend to the common parts.[114]

Procedure

Negotiation with landlord

Where repairs need to be carried out urgently, the landlord should be contacted first in an attempt to obtain his or her agreement to carry out the work. In some cases the landlord may not know of the immediate crisis or may not be aware of his or her obligation to remedy the defect. In a case where notice is required (see page 202) and none has been given, a letter or a telephone call will put the landlord on notice. Direct negotiations may be more effective than court proceedings which may be delayed for procedural reasons, but it is important to be on guard against

---

112   *Lee-Parker v Izzet* [1971] 1 WLR 1688.
113   *Asco Developments Ltd v Gordon* (1978) 248 EG 683.
114   Secure Tenants (Right to Repair Scheme) Regulations 1985.

false promises of repair work: a date by which the work must be done should be incorporated in the agreement.

The landlord (or his or her agent where appropriate) should be telephoned if possible. If the occupier is a local authority tenant, both the housing officer and a solicitor in the legal department should be telephoned. The position in law should be set out and the landlord should be asked to carry out the repair work immediately. A detailed note should be kept of the conversation, including the date and the time and the person with whom the conversation was held.

The next step is to follow this immediately with a letter to the landlord confirming the details of the disrepair and its effect on the occupier. The landlord should again be asked to carry out the necessary work or to confirm any agreement which has been reached, making it clear that legal action will be taken if the defect is not remedied within a reasonable time.

In the meantime, an application should be made for emergency legal aid in readiness for an application to court if the repairs are not carried out.

Environmental health service

If negotiations with the landlord are unsuccessful, the environmental health officer should be telephoned and asked to inspect the premises immediately. The best time to telephone is usually between 9am and 10am before the officers leave the office to make inspections. If possible, there should be a meeting with the environmental health officer at the premises to discuss with him or her the appropriate remedy.

Although environmental health officers cannot serve or enforce notices against their own authority,[115] there is no reason why they should not inspect properties belonging to the authority for which they work, and inform the housing department of the defect and the remedy required.

If the environmental health officer will not visit, the request should be made in writing immediately setting out the details of the disrepair, the effect on the occupier and the reason why it is urgent. This should be followed with another telephone call in order to try to arrange an inspection.

If the environmental health officer does serve a notice (see page 194) on the landlord, a copy should be requested so that the occupier can be advised of the situation and informed what works are to be carried out and by what date.

115 *R v Cardiff City Council ex parte Cross* (1982) 1 HLR 54.

If the landlord will not (or cannot) carry out his or her obligations and the environmental health officer cannot (or will not) serve a notice to force him or her to do so, the occupier must pursue his or her private remedies. In a serious emergency civil court proceedings can provide a speedy remedy for which legal aid is usually available.

Application for interim injunction in county court

Applications for interim injunctions in illegal eviction cases have been considered above. Where procedural requirements are the same, references are given to the relevant pages in that chapter.

Which court?

The county court now has jurisdiction to hear all claims for breach of repairing obligations.[116] Although proceedings may be issued in any county court, it may be wise to issue in the court where the landlord's address is situated in order to avoid any delays caused by automatic transfer if the landlord files a defence.[117]

Documents to be filed

The documents to be filed are the same as where action is to be taken for harassment or illegal eviction, and are listed on page 186.

Particulars of claim

The particulars of claim must specify:[118]

- the cause of action;
- the relief or remedy sought; and
- the material facts on which the plaintiff relies.

The particulars must contain the following information:[119]

- full name of plaintiff and defendant – if the full name of the landlord is not known, sufficient information must be given to identify him or her;
- status of plaintiff and status of defendant and the relationship between the two;
- address of the premises and precise description of accommodation occupied;

---

116 County Courts Act 1984 s21, as amended by High Court and County Courts Jurisdiction Order 1991.
117 CCR Ord 1 r13.
118 CCR Ord 6 r1(1).
119 CCR Ord 6 r1(1).

- date of occupation of premises and rent payable and whether or not registered rent;
- details of occupancy agreement;
- the repairing obligation on which it is intended to rely and/or the tort which it is alleged has been committed;
- particulars of the breach of contract or tort, ie details of the disrepair;
- particulars of the notice given in respect of the disrepair (where appropriate);
- particulars of damage;
- claim for injunction;
- claim for damages (including schedule of special damage suffered);
- claim for interest on damages; and
- claim for costs.

If the tenant's health has been affected by the disrepair, a medical report should be attached to the particulars of claim.[120]

Notice of application

The notice of application should set out the order requested and the grounds upon which the application is made.[121]

Affidavits

The occupier's affidavit should:

- verify the contents of the particulars of claim; and
- add details about the incidents relied on.

Where possible precise dates and times of any incident relied on should be included, eg, where a ceiling has collapsed. Details of all attempts made by the occupier and/or his or her adviser to have repairs carried out since the emergency arose must be given.

There should be exhibited to the affidavit copies of any of the following which are available:

- written agreement and/or rent book or card;
- letters written to the defendant about the disrepair;
- surveyor's report;
- Environmental Protection Act or Housing Act notices served by the local authority;
- photographs;
- medical report; and
- plan.

---

120   CCR Ord 6 r1(5).
121   CCR Ord 13 r6(3) and form N16A.

The surveyor who has inspected the property and written a report should also swear an affidavit exhibiting his or her report and explaining why s/he thinks an injunction is necessary, setting out the works which are necessary and giving an estimate of the costs.

Service

Provisions governing service have been dealt with on page 188.

Notice

All interlocutory applications must be made on notice unless they are allowed or authorised to be made *ex parte*.[122]

The notice must be at least two days.[123] (Weekends and bank holidays are excluded.)

The court has power to abridge the time between service and hearing if necessary.[124] If it has not been possible to give the landlord the required amount of notice, provided that s/he has been served with the documents, the court should always be asked to abridge the notice requirement if there is an emergency.

In cases of real emergency a court will hear an application without the defendant having been notified.[125] However, it is very unlikely that the court will hear an application for a mandatory injunction for repair works to be carried out without the landlord being given an opportunity to be heard.

Hearing

An application for an injunction will usually be made to a judge in open court.[126]

It is essential that both the occupier and other witnesses (including a surveyor) attend court and be prepared to give oral evidence and to be cross-examined.[127] If an environmental health officer has been involved with the property, s/he should be served with a witness summons and requested to bring with him or her all documents in his or her possession relating to the property.

---

122   CCR Ord 13 r1.
123   CCR Ord 13 r4.
124   CCR Ord 13 r4.
125   CCR Ord 13 r6(3).
126   CCR Ord 13 r6(2) and (5).
127   CCR Ord 20 r4.

Draft order

A draft order should be prepared before the hearing and submitted to the judge if the application is successful.[128]

For mandatory injunctions, eg, ordering the landlord to carry out repair work, the draft order should always set out the time within which the order must be carried out and the time should run from the service of the order if the landlord is not in court, eg, 'within 14 days of service of this order'. The importance of this is that if an actual date is incorporated in the order by which the works must be carried out and the order is not served by that date, the order will become ineffective and a fresh application will be necessary.[129]

The draft order should also contain a realistic schedule of works and where appropriate should be drawn up in conjunction with the surveyor. A request that the landlord make good any consequential damage to decorations should also be included.[130]

Penal notice

See above page 190.

Service of order

See above page 190.

Enforcement

See above page 190.

Application for committal for contempt of court

See above page 191.

---

128   CCR Ord 13 r6(6); prescribed form N16.
129   CCR Ord 29 r1(2).
130   *Bradley v Chorley Borough Council* (1985) 17 HLR 305.

CHAPTER 11

Possession proceedings

Introduction

This chapter deals with the most common emergencies that arise from the time when possession proceedings are commenced to the issue of a warrant for possession. The list is not comprehensive but should give guidance in most cases. For more detailed coverage, see Luba, Madge and McConnell *Defending Possession Proceedings* 3rd ed., LAG, 1993, and see also page 254 for possession proceedings for mortgage arrears.

Summary proceedings: unauthorised occupiers

Introduction

A summary process for claiming possession of land is available in the county court[1] and in the High Court.[2] To simplify, all references here are to county court proceedings unless otherwise stated. For details of High Court proceedings (which are, in principle, the same), see the notes in the *Supreme Court Practice* to RSC Ord 113.

The proceedings are commonly known as 'squatters proceedings' and may be used against trespassers,[3] ex-licensees,[4] and unlawful subtenants.[5]

The person seeking possession must be able to demonstrate that s/he has an immediate right to possession[6] and the summary process should not be used where it is clear that there is a serious issue as to whether a tenancy or holding over existed.[7]

---

1 CCR Ord 24.
2 RSC Ord 113.
3 *Bristol Corporation v Persons Unknown* [1974] 1 WLR 365.
4 *GLC v Jenkins* [1975] 1 WLR 155.
5 *Moore Properties (Ilford) Ltd v McKeon* [1976] 1 WLR 1278.
6 *Wirral Borough Council v Smith and Cooper* (1982) 43 P&CR 312.
7 *Henderson v Law* (1985) 17 HLR 237.

The procedure is simple and speedy, requiring only five days' notice (less in exceptional circumstances). It is brought by originating application in the county court (originating summons in the High Court); evidence is given by affidavit and there is normally no order for discovery. If the original entry on the land was unlawful, possession will be ordered forthwith. It is important to take immediate and detailed instructions to establish if there is a valid defence.

Order 24 proceedings

Circumstances in which proceedings may be issued

Where a person claims possession of land which s/he alleges is occupied solely by a person or persons (not being a tenant or tenants holding over after the termination of a tenancy) who entered into or remained in occupation without his or her licence or consent or that of any predecessor in title, the proceedings may be brought by originating application in the county court.[8]

No relief other than possession can be claimed in these proceedings, ie, no money claim can be attached, nor an application for an injunction or declaration.[9]

The county court has jurisdiction to hear any action for the recovery of land, whatever the rateable value.[10]

The summary procedure is available only in a limited number of cases.[11] It should not be used where there is a serious or complicated issue to be tried. In such cases, formal pleadings and discovery are necessary, as well as oral evidence and cross-examination at the hearing.[12]

The procedure is not appropriate where there is a genuine dispute as to whether the occupier has a licence or a tenancy,[13] or where there is a dispute regarding surrender of a tenancy.[14] In such cases the summary hearing should be adjourned for a further hearing, or the application should be dismissed.[15]

However, the fact that the respondent has chosen, without warning, to

---

8   CCR Ord 24 r1.
9   CCR Ord 24 r1; RSC Ord 113 r1 and notes thereto in the *Supreme Court Practice 1988*.
10   County Courts Act 1984 s21, as amended by High Court and County Courts Jurisdiction Order 1991.
11   *Filemart Ltd v Avery* [1989] 2 EGLR 177.
12   *Cudworth v Masefield* (1984) *The Times*, 16 May 1984.
13   *Islamic Republic of Pakistan v Ghani* (1976) 121 SJ 86; *Henderson v Law* (1985) 17 HLR 237.
14   *Cooper v Varzdari* (1986) 18 HLR 299.
15   *Henderson v Law* (1985) 17 HLR 237.

assert that there is a tenancy or a holding over is not in itself sufficient to say that the use of CCR Ord 24 is inappropriate.[16] In *Fryer v Brook*,[17] a judge's refusal to grant an adjournment to allow the occupier of property to put in a defence to an application for possession of that property did not amount to a miscarriage of justice where there appeared to be no triable defence and the occupier had not substantiated his claim that he had a valid defence, either by making an affidavit or by giving oral evidence of what the defence was. The procedure may be used even if there is a triable issue, but only where the matter is clear and straightforward.[18] However, it is not appropriate where there is a written agreement which is arguably a sham or where there is evidence of a prior oral agreement which raises issues that cannot properly be resolved without the process of trial.[19]

The procedure may be used against:

a) A person who entered into occupation without the consent of the person entitled to possession, whether or not s/he can be identified[20] and whether or not the person entitled to possession has been ousted from the whole of the premises.[21]

b) A person who entered into occupation with the consent of the person entitled to possession but who remains in occupation without such consent or licence.[22] This will include former service occupants, licensees who had restricted contracts which have been terminated and former licensees under rental purchase agreements.

c) Unlawful subtenants when the eviction is by the head landlord and the mesne tenancy has been determined.[23]

d) A person let into occupation of a tenant's premises by the landlord in the tenant's absence.[24]

e) A bankrupt who has refused to give up possession of premises required for sale by his or her trustee in bankruptcy.[25]

The procedure may not be used against:

---

16   *Henderson v Law* (1985) 17 HLR 237.
17   (1984) 81 LS Gaz 2856.
18   *Shah v Givert* (1980) 124 SJ 513; CCR Ord 24 r5 and note thereto in the *County Court Practice*; RSC Ord 113 and notes thereto in the *Supreme Court Practice*.
19   *Crancour Ltd v Da Silvaesa* (1986) 18 HLR 265.
20   CCR Ord 24 r1.
21   *Wiltshire County Council v Frazer (No 2)* [1986] 1 WLR 109.
22   *Bristol Corporation v Persons Unknown* [1974] 1 WLR 365.
23   *Moore Properties (Ilford) Ltd v McKeon* [1976] 1 WLR 1278; *Henderson v Law* (1985) 17 HLR 237.
24   *Borg v Rogers* (1981) 132 NLJ 134.
25   *Fryer v Brook* (1984) 81 LS Gaz 2856.

a) A person who has a subsisting tenancy whether or not s/he is in occupation of the premises or a former tenant holding over after the termination of his or her tenancy.[26]

b) A purported licensee who is in fact a tenant protected under the Rent Act. Where a person is granted exclusive use of residential accommodation for a fixed or periodic term at a stated rent, where neither attendance nor services are provided, the premises are held on a tenancy rather than a licence. This is so notwithstanding the use of the word 'licence' in the occupancy agreement.[27] In the case of premises occupied by more than one person with a purported licence agreement, a joint tenancy will have been created if the agreements are interdependent, eg, where two occupiers have sought exclusive possession of the whole flat and the landlord has allowed them jointly to enjoy exclusive possession and accepted a single sum of rent from both.[28] However, where licence agreements are not dependent on each other and are made at different times on different terms, where separate amounts of money are paid by each licensee for use and occupation and where licensees cannot exclude a new person nominated by the licensor, then such an agreement cannot be construed as a joint tenancy.[29]

In order to establish whether a licence or tenancy has been granted, it is essential to consider the surrounding circumstances including any relationship between the prospective occupiers, the course of negotiations and the nature and extent of the accommodation and the intended and actual mode of occupation of the premises.[30]

c) A licensee who has a secure licence by virtue of the Housing Act (HA) 1985 s79(3). The occupation as a licensee must be in such circumstances that if the licence were a tenancy it would be a secure tenancy.[31]

d) An occupier who has moved in with the permission of the tenant who subsequently has died, but where the landlord has not terminated the tenancy.[32]

---

26 CCR Ord 24 r1; *Cooper v Varzdari* (1986) 18 HLR 299.
27 *Street v Mountford* [1985] AC 809.
28 *Antoniades v Villiers* [1990] 1 AC 417.
29 *AG Securities v Vaughan* [1990] 1 AC 417.
30 *AG Securities v Vaughan* [1990] 1 AC 417.
31 HA 1985 s79(3). For the conditions necessary to fulfil the requirements of a secure tenancy see the HA 1985 ss79 to 82.
32 *Wirral Borough Council v Smith* (1982) 80 LGR 628; *Preston Borough Council v Fairclough* (1982) *The Times*, 15 December 1982.

e) A secure tenant who has exchanged his or her home without the landlord's permission.[33]
f) A licensee whose licence has not been properly determined before the issue of the proceedings.[34] Notice terminating a licence must be not only of reasonable length and comply with any agreed terms which were part of the licence, eg, that it should be in writing or of a particular length, it must also comply with the provisions of Protection From Eviction Act 1977 s5, unless the licence is an excluded licence (see below). A licence does not end until both these conditions are fulfilled.
g) Occupiers of premises, some of whom are trespassers and one or more of whom has been granted a right of occupation.[35]
h) A trespasser who has acquired a term of ownership in the land by adverse possession. An action to evict a trespasser is statute-barred after 12 years.[36]

This is not an exhaustive list. See Luba, Madge and McConnell *Defending Possession Proceedings* 3rd ed., LAG, 1993, for a fuller treatment.

Procedure

The proceedings are initiated by originating application.[37] A special form is prescribed by the County Court Rules.[38] Originating applications must now state whether possession is claimed in respect of residential premises or other land.

The originating application must be supported by an affidavit. The affidavit must state:[39]

- the nature of the applicant's interest in the land;
- the circumstances in which the land came to be occupied; and
- that the applicant does not know the name of any person occupying the land who is not named in the originating application.

Any person in occupation who is not named in the originating application or summons and who wishes to be heard on the question of whether an order for possession should be made, may apply at any stage in the proceedings to be joined as respondent.[40] Generally it is not wise to

33   *Warwick District Council v Smith* (1982) March/April *Roof* 5.
34   *Greater London Council v Jenkins* [1975] 1 WLR 155.
35   *Wiltshire County Council v Frazer (No 2)* [1986] 1 WLR 109.
36   Limitation Act 1980 s15(17).
37   CCR Ord 24 r1.
38   Form N312.
39   CCR Ord 24 r2.
40   CCR Ord 24 r4.

apply to be joined as a party to the proceedings unless there is a reasonable prospect of defending the action or postponing the making of a possession order, since otherwise an order for costs will almost certainly be made against any named respondents. No order for costs can be made against 'persons unknown'.

The originating application, notice of return day and affidavit must be served on any person named in the originating application:

- by personal service; or
- by an officer of the court leaving the documents at, or sending them to, the premises; or
- by service on the person's solicitors; or
- in such other manner as the court may direct.

In addition, copies must be served by:[41]

- pinning the documents to the main door of the premises or other conspicuous part of the premises; and
- if practicable, inserting the documents through the letter-box in a sealed envelope addressed to 'the occupiers'; or
- otherwise in such manner as the court may direct.

Placing the documents through the letter-box but not affixing them to the door will not nullify the proceedings if the respondent has knowledge of the proceedings.[42]

The burden is on the applicant to prove service, but the method of service is his or her choice.[43]

The hearing must be not less than five days after the day of service of the documents except in the case of urgency and by leave of the court.[44] In the county court, Saturday and Sunday may be included in the period of five days.[45] This is not so in the High Court. (If the claim does not relate to residential premises, the minimum period between service and the hearing is two days.[46])

Where less than five days have elapsed between service and the hearing, if the applicant establishes a right to possession but not a case of urgency, the proper procedure is not to dismiss the application but to adjourn it so that at least five days may elapse before the final order is made.[47]

The normal order is for possession to be given forthwith.[48] If the

41   CCR Ord 24 r3.
42   *Westminster City Council v Chapman* [1975] 1 WLR 1112.
43   *Crosfield Electronics Ltd v Baginsky* [1975] 1 WLR 1135.
44   CCR Ord 24 r5(1).
45   *Croydon LBC v Curtin* (1974) 118 SJ 297.
46   CCR Ord 24 r5(1)(b).
47   *Westminster City Council v Monahan* [1981] WLR 698.
48   CCR Ord 24 r5(3).

respondent's original entry on the land was unlawful, the court has no power to postpone the possession order otherwise except with consent of the applicant.[49]

Where the original entry was lawful, the court can postpone the possession order if it would have had such power in an ordinary possession action.[50] This will apply to service occupants, licensees with certain restricted contracts and licensees under rental purchase agreements. The period for which the order is to be suspended must be defined.[51]

The court has full power to set aside or vary the order for possession on such an application.[52]

The possession order is enforceable by warrant.[53]

Where an immediate possession order is made, a warrant for possession may be issued at any time after the possession order is made.[54] However, the county court has an inherent jurisdiction to allow a reasonable time before execution, which may be up to 28 days.[55]

If the possession order has been postponed to a specified date,[56] the warrant cannot be issued until after the specified date.[57]

Leave is not required for a warrant of possession to be issued, unless three or more months have elapsed from the date of the possession order. An application for such leave may be made *ex parte* unless the court otherwise directs.[58]

On execution of the warrant, anyone who is in the premises who cannot raise an independent right of occupation will be evicted. Anyone who is not a party to the judgment and can raise an independent right of occupation should be given the opportunity to apply to the court.[59]

Procedure when defending

An adjournment for a further hearing or dismissal of the application should be sought if there is a genuine defence to the application for possession. Such an application will be granted only if the defence raised is

49   *Department of the Environment v James* [1972] 1 WLR 1279.
50   CCR Ord 24 r5(4).
51   *Royal Trust Company of Canada v Markham* [1975] 1 WLR 1416.
52   CCR Ord 24 r7.
53   CCR Ord 26 r17(1).
54   CCR Ord 24 r6(1).
55   *Kelly v White* [1920] WN 220.
56   CCR Ord 25 r5(4).
57   CCR Ord 24 r3.
58   CCR Ord 24 r6(2).
59   *R v Wandsworth County Court ex parte Wandsworth London Borough Council* [1975] 1 WLR 1314.

substantial.[60] A frivolous application may prejudice the respondent, particularly where the court has discretion to postpone the possession order, and may result in an order for costs against the respondent.

The court may grant an adjournment of the hearing[61] and give directions for the future conduct of the case.[62] Usually, directions in respect of delivery of pleadings and discovery will be given.

Where the respondent is seeking to strike out the action on the basis of a public law right, because the applicant has no authority to bring the action, the correct procedure is to apply for an adjournment to enable judicial review proceedings to be taken.[63] The fact that a county council is in breach of its statutory duty to provide accommodation is not in itself a defence to proceedings for possession against trespassers.[64]

The applicant (or his or her solicitors if they are on the court record) should be advised by telephone that the proceedings will be defended, and an adjournment requested. This telephone conversation should be followed with a letter setting out the basis of the defence, requesting an adjournment and proposing appropriate directions for the future conduct of the case. A threat to apply for an order for costs if an adjournment is not agreed is often effective. The letter should be faxed or delivered by hand if possible.

The next step is to prepare and file at court an affidavit setting out the respondent's answer to the application for possession. The affidavit must be drafted with care as it will form the basis of subsequent pleadings.

The affidavit should include the following:

- date and circumstances in which the agreement to occupy was made;
- if there was a written agreement between the parties, even if it is only a letter or a note, a copy of this should be exhibited to the affidavit;
- copies of any other documents on which the occupier intends to rely, eg, correspondence between tenant and subtenant should also be exhibited;
- a reply, from the occupier, to each paragraph of the applicant's affidavit;
- the status which the occupier claims and a brief outline of the law on which the claim is based; and

60 *Shah v Givert* (1980) 124 SJ 513; *Henderson v Law* (1985) 17 HLR 237; *Fryer v Brook* (1984) 81 LS Gaz 2856.
61 CCR Ord 13 r3(1).
62 CCR Ord 13 r2(1).
63 *Avon County Council v Buscott* [1988] QB 656; *South Hams DC v Shough* (1992) *Times* 8 December.
64 *West Glamorgan County Council v Rafferty* (1986) 18 HLR 375; *R v London Borough of Barnet ex parte Grumbridge* (1992) 24 HLR 433.

– any other information which is relevant to the occupier's defence.

Guidance on the drafting of affidavits can be found on pages 319, 337 and 345.

If shortage of time means that all the necessary details cannot be obtained, the affidavit should explain this. The affidavit can be filed at court on the day of the hearing if necessary, but it is advisable to serve a copy on the applicant in advance.

The respondent should attend court and be represented on the hearing date. This is so even if an adjournment has been agreed, as the sanction of the judge is required for an adjournment.[65] If the application for an adjournment is opposed, the judge may wish to hear oral evidence.

If representation is not possible, the respondent should attend in person with a letter to the court from his or her solicitors setting out the reason for the request for an adjournment and details of prior notice which has been given to the applicant. The applicant should be provided with a copy of this letter.

Procedure where possession order granted

If a possession order is made under CCR Ord 24 and the occupier either did not know of the proceedings or did not know s/he had a defence, the judge may, on such terms as s/he thinks fit, set aside or vary an order made in the proceedings.[66]

Occupier named in judgment.   Where the occupier is named in the judgment, immediate action should be taken by making an application to the court. The application should be on notice to the applicant.[67] Two days' notice is required but in an emergency an ex parte application may be allowed with leave of the court.[68] The application should be on county court Form N244 and supported by an affidavit showing why the occupier had not taken part in the proceedings earlier, eg, s/he did not receive the originating application because s/he was away on holiday, and must contain facts showing a defence on the merits or the respects in which the order complained of is prejudicial to the occupier.

In addition, an application should be made for a stay of execution of the possession order (see page 227 below).

Occupier not named in judgment.   If the occupier is not named in the judgment, an immediate application should be made for the occupier to

---

65   *Morgan v Rees* (1881) 6 QBD 508.
66   CCR Ord 24 r7.
67   CCR Ord 13 r1(2).
68   CCR Ord 13 r1(2).

be joined as a respondent[69] and for the possession order to be set aside or varied.[70] The procedure is as set out above.

As above, an application should be made for a stay of execution of the possession order.

Procedure where warrant of possession issued

The warrant of possession may be issued at any time after the making of the possession order[71] but will not be issued after the expiry of three months without leave of the court.[72] The application for leave may be made *ex parte* unless the court otherwise directs. If the possession order has been postponed to a specified date,[73] then the warrant cannot be issued until after the specified date.[74]

An occupier who was named in the judgment should follow the procedure set out below and, in addition, in the notice of application should request that the warrant be suspended.

Any occupier who is not a party to the judgment and can raise an independent right of occupation should be given the opportunity to apply to the court.[75] The occupier should follow the procedure set out above, and should include in the application an application for the warrant to be suspended.

Procedure where warrant executed

An application to set aside or vary the possession order[76] can be made after execution of the warrant for possession in appropriate circumstances, eg, where the accommodation is still vacant. Obviously, such an application would have to be made with all speed. Alternatively, a claim for damages should be made.

Procedure where no defence

Negotiations should be made with the applicant to obtain his or her consent to a postponement of the possession order. The applicant will often agree to give an occupier time to leave in return for the certainty of a possession order. A telephone call or letter before the hearing is advisable

---

69   CCR Ord 24 r4.
70   Ord 24 r7.
71   CCR Ord 24 r6(1).
72   CCR Ord 24 r6(2).
73   CCR Ord 24 r5(4).
74   CCR Ord 24 r3.
75   *R v Wandsworth County Court ex parte Wandsworth London Borough Council* [1975] 1 WLR 1314.
76   CCR Ord 24 r7.

but, if shortage of time precludes this, negotiations can take place outside the court on the day of the hearing.

Where the original entry on the land was lawful, the court can postpone the date of the possession order (see page 224). If agreement has not been reached before the hearing, an affidavit should be filed at court requesting that the court postpone the order and setting out the facts relied on. The affidavit should include:

- the terms of the occupation including the date it commenced;
- details of notice to leave given by the applicant to the respondent; and
- family circumstances and the reason why the postponement is needed, eg, because the occupier will be homeless.

Where the original entry on the land was unlawful, the court has no power to order anything other than immediate possession. However, the court may exercise its inherent jurisdiction to allow a reasonable time before execution, which may be up to 28 days.[77]

If a large number of occupiers make applications to be joined, in a busy court the matter may have to be adjourned to another date for hearing. This may be another reason why the applicant will agree to postpone the possession order.

It is important to check that the correct procedure has been followed, particularly in relation to service and notice. It may be possible to obtain an adjournment if an irregularity has occurred,[78] but it is unlikely that a procedural irregularity will nullify the proceedings, as the court has power to give appropriate directions.[79]

Summary proceedings: mandatory grounds for possession

Introduction

The Rent Act (County Court Proceedings for Possession) Rules (RACCPP Rules) 1981 enable a private landlord to seek possession by speedy summary proceedings where the mandatory grounds for possession apply, subject to certain conditions.[80]

Mandatory grounds for possession are provided in the Rent Act (RA) 1977 Sch 15 Cases 11 to 20, as amended by the Rent (Amendment) Act 1985:

---

77   *Kelly v White* [1920] WN 220.
78   *Westminster City Council v Monahan* [1981] 1 WLR 698.
79   CCR Ord 37 r5.
80   RACCPP Rules r2(2).

case	grounds
11	lettings by owner-occupiers
12	retirement homes
13	winter holiday lets
14	student lettings during vacation
15	ministers of religion
16	agricultural employees
17	farmhouses redundant on amalgamation
18	other redundant farmhouses
19	protected shorthold lettings
20	lettings by members of the services.

Special conditions for use of the summary procedure

The conditions: Cases 11, 12 and 20

For an application under Case 11 (lettings by owner-occupiers), the tenant must have been given notice that possession might be recovered under the Case, and the dwelling-house must be required as a residence for:[81]

- the owner; or
- a member of the owner's family who resided with him or her at his or her death; or
- a member of the owner's family who resided with him or her when s/he last occupied the dwelling-house as a residence.

A landlord who wishes the court to dispense with the requirement of notice cannot rely on this procedure.[82] However, where the notice has been sent by the landlord, even if not received by the tenant, the summary procedure is appropriate.[83]

For an application to be made under Case 12 (retirement home) or under Case 20 (lettings by members of the services), the tenant must have been given notice that possession might be recovered under the Case, and the dwelling must be required as a residence for:[84]

- the owner; or
- a member of the owner's family who resided with him or her at the owner's death.

The conditions regarding notice set out above in relation to Case 11 apply to Cases 12 and 20 also.

---

81   RACCPP Rules r2(1)(a).
82   *Minay v Sentongo* (1983) 6 HLR 81.
83   *Minay v Sentongo.*
84   RACCPP Rules r2(1)(a).

Procedure governing issue

Procedure is governed by the Rent Act (County Court Proceedings for Possession) Rules 1981 (RACCPP Rules) and the County Court Rules 1981.

The originating application must be in the prescribed form, which will depend upon the Case relied on.[85]

An affidavit in support of the originating application must be filed. The affidavit must:[86]

- verify the statements in the application;
- depose to any other material matters; and
- exhibit any material documents.

The originating application, copy of exhibits and notice of return day must be served on each respondent. The onus is on the applicant to prove service.[87]

Notice must be given as follows:[88]

- Cases 11, 12 and 20: each respondent must be served at least seven clear days before the return day;
- Cases 13 to 19: each respondent must be served at least 14 clear days before the return day.

The originating application may be heard by a circuit judge or district judge.[89]

Judgment

A time must be specified within which possession is to be delivered up.[90]

Where possession is granted under Cases 11 to 20, the order for possession must be no more than 14 days from the date of judgment,[91] but in cases of exceptional hardship the court has a discretion to postpone the date on which possession is to be delivered to a maximum of six weeks from the date of the order.[92]

Defences

It is beyond the scope of this book to set out all the possible defences to claims for possession under Cases 11 to 20. For full details, see Luba,

85   RACCPP Rules r3.
86   RACCPP Rules r4.
87   CCR Ord 3 rr4 and 7.
88   RACCPP Rules r5.
89   RACPP Rules r6.
90   CCR Ord 22 r3.
91   HA 1980 s89(1).
92   HA 1980 s89(1).

Madge and McConnell *Defending Possession Proceedings* 3rd ed., LAG, 1993. Examples are:

- Case 11: the landlord has never occupied the premises.
- Case 20: the landlord was not in the armed forces at the time of the acquisition of the property, or was not in the armed forces at the time of the letting.
- Cases 11, 12 and 20: no notice was given that possession might be recovered under one of these Cases.[93] (If notice was given, the court retains its full discretionary powers in respect of notice.)[94]

Procedure when defending

Application for an adjournment. An application for an adjournment should be made if time is required to prepare the case properly. The court has power to grant an adjournment,[95] and to give any directions necessary for the future conduct of the case.[96] The application should be made on notice to the applicant.[97] Two days' notice is required, but in an emergency an *ex parte* application may be allowed.[98] The application should be made on county court form N244 and supported by an affidavit setting out the framework of the respondent's defence and the reason why an adjournment is required, eg, the need to find witnesses or documents, or respondent awaiting determination of his or her legal aid application. The need for a direction relating to discovery may also be an important factor.

Every effort should be made to agree an adjournment with the applicant by telephone followed by a letter setting out the defence and the reasons for the adjournment. A threat to apply for an order for costs if the adjournment is not agreed is often effective.

The respondent should attend court and be represented on the return date. This is so even if the adjournment is agreed, as the sanction of the judge is required for an adjournment.[99] If the application for an adjournment is opposed, the judge may wish to hear oral evidence.

If representation is not possible, the respondent should attend in person with a letter to the court from his or her solicitors setting out the details of the defence and the reasons for the application for an

93 *Minay v Sentongo* (1983) 6 HLR 81.
94 *Minay v Sentongo*.
95 CCR Ord 13 r3(1).
96 CCR Ord 13 r2.
97 CCR Ord 13 r1(2).
98 CCR Ord 13 r1(2).
99 *Morgan v Rees* (1881) 6 QBD 508.

adjournment. The letter should refer to requests made directly to the applicant for an adjournment. A copy of a letter to the court should be given to the applicant.

Where no adjournment is required.   An affidavit should be filed setting out full details of the defence and a copy served on the applicant as far in advance of the hearing as possible. Any documents upon which the respondent intends to rely at the hearing should be exhibited to the affidavit.

The respondent and other witnesses should be told that they must attend court to give oral evidence.

Procedure where no defence

An attempt should be made to persuade the applicant to consent to the postponement of the possession order. Although the court can postpone possession only for up to six weeks,[100] there is no reason why a longer period cannot be ordered by consent. Negotiations can be conducted by telephone and/or letter before the hearing and/or at court.

If the applicant refuses to consent to a period longer than the minimum 14 days,[101] and the respondent will suffer hardship as a result, s/he should file an affidavit requesting postponement of the order and setting out the reasons for this request. The affidavit should include:

–   the terms of the occupation including the date it commenced;
–   details of how much notice to leave the respondent received; and
–   family circumstances and the reason why the postponement is needed, eg, because the occupier and his or her family will be homeless.

Ordinary possession proceedings

Introduction

This section deals with possession proceedings in respect of private sector tenancies granted prior to 15 January 1989,[102] public sector tenancies and housing association tenancies granted prior to 15 January 1989 (secure tenancies)[103] and private and housing association tenancies granted on or after 15 January 1989 (assured tenancies).[104]

Possession proceedings are brought by way of a fixed-date action in the

100   HA 1980 s89(1).
101   HA 1980 s89(1).
102   RA 1977.
103   HA 1985.
104   HA 1988.

county court.[105] The tenant will be served with a summons either personally or by post[106] at least 21 days before the return date.[107] The return date will usually be the date fixed for the hearing of the claim for possession, unless there is a claim for some relief other than mesne profits or arrears of rent, in which case it will take the form of a pre-trial review.[108]

It is not uncommon for a tenant to seek advice a day or two before the hearing, because s/he did not know about legal aid, or was frightened of losing his or her home, or had not received or did not understand the summons. Immediate action must be taken to prevent a possession order being made against the tenant.

Procedure when defending

Full instructions should be taken regarding the claim for possession and the reasons for the delay in seeking advice. If the claim is based on the ground that rent lawfully due from the tenant has not been paid,[109] check if the amount of arrears is admitted, in full or in part, and if so take full instructions as to the reasons (eg, failure to receive housing benefit, recent unemployment, tax difficulties, matrimonial dispute). Instructions should also be taken in respect of disrepair in the premises and/or harassment with a view to a counterclaim for damages for breach of covenant to repair or of quiet enjoyment which may be set off against all or some of the arrears of rent.

Particulars to be checked
The following points in the particulars of claim must be checked:

a) Do they comply with the County Court Rules for recovery of land?[110] The particulars of claim must include a full description of the land, the net annual value of the land, the rent and the ground on which the claim is founded.

b) Does the court have jurisdiction to deal with the claim? Proceedings

---

105   CCR Ord 3 r2(1); RA 1977 s141; HA 1985 s110; HA 1988 s40.
106   CCR Ord 7 r10(1).
107   CCR Ord 7 r10(5).
108   CCR Ord 3 r3(3) and (4) and notes thereto in the *County Court Practice*.
109   RA 1977 s98 and Sch 15 Case 1; HA 1985 s84 and Sch 3 Ground 1; HA 1988 s7 and Sch 2 Grounds 8, 10 and 11.
110   CCR Ord 6 r3. Proposed rule changes due to be introduced in 1993 are expected to require plaintiffs to include far more information in rent arrears cases.

for the recovery of land may be commenced only in the court for the district in which the land or any part thereof is situated.[111]

c) Has a proper notice been served?

– *Private sector tenancies entered into before 15 January 1989* – the tenancy must have been properly determined before possession proceedings are issued. A periodic tenancy requires notice to quit to bring it to an end. A notice to quit must be both validly drawn up and properly served. An invalid notice does not determine the tenancy. A statutory tenancy need not be determined by a notice to quit where it follows a fixed-term tenancy which has expired or a periodic tenancy which has formally been determined by a notice to quit.[112]

– *Public sector tenancies* – a proper notice must be served and if a tenancy is a periodic tenancy the proceedings must begin after the date specified in the notice. It should be in the correct form as prescribed by the Secure Tenancies (Notices) Regulations 1987, or be in a form substantially to the same effect. A copy of the correct form appears in Precedent 30. The notice lapses 12 months after the date specified in it.[113] The notice must state the ground on which possession is sought and give particulars of that ground, in sufficient detail to enable the tenant to know and meet the case against him or her. In rent arrears cases, it should specify the amount of rent due on a particular date.[114] Minor inaccuracies due to an honest error will not render a notice invalid if the landlord has, in good faith, stated the grounds and particulars to be relied upon.[115] Other requirements are that it should be signed (although a copy signature will suffice), be properly served (although postal service is adequate) and give at least four weeks' notice.[116]

– *Private and housing association tenancies entered into on or after 15 January 1989* – before proceedings are commenced the landlord must serve on the tenant a notice, which must be in prescribed form, must inform the tenant of the grounds on which possession is to be sought, and must set out the time-scale of the action. If the

---

111   CCR Ord 4 r3.
112   See generally Woodfall *Law of Landlord and Tenant* 28th ed., paras 1-1967 et seq; Protection from Eviction Act 1977 s5; Notices to Quit (Prescribed Information) Regulations 1988.
113   HA 1985 s83(3).
114   *Torridge District Council v Jones* (1985) 18 HLR 107.
115   *Dudley Metropolitan Council v Bailey* (1990) 89 LGR 246.
116   HA 1985 s83(3).

landlord fails to serve such a notice, the court will not consider the proceedings, although it does have discretion to dispense with the notice requirement if it considers it just and equitable to do so, provided that the possession is not sought on Ground 8 of Sch 2 to HA 1988.

Proceedings should not commence earlier than two weeks from the service of the notice, unless possession is sought under Grounds 1, 2, 5, 6, 7, 9 or 16, in which case proceedings should not commence earlier than two months from service and, if the tenancy is periodic, the date on which the tenancy could be terminated by a notice to quit given on the date of service of the notice. The proceedings should not commence later than 12 months after service of the notice.[117]

– HA 1988 s32 alters the scope of the Protection from Eviction Act 1977 s5. Section 5 lays down various requirements for notices to quit: they must contain statutorily prescribed information and allow a minimum period of four weeks' notice. The 1988 Act extends these provisions to periodic licences of residential properties. However, the Act also ensures that s5 does not apply to excluded tenancies or licences – only to tenants entering into agreements on or after 15 January 1989. For definitions of 'excluded tenancies' and 'licences', see page 178.

Defences

It is beyond the scope of this book to deal in detail with defences to claims for possession under RA 1977, HA 1985 and HA 1988 (see generally Luba, Madge and McConnell *Defending Possession Proceedings* 3rd ed., LAG, 1993) but the following points should be considered:

a) Is the rent claimed irrecoverable? See RA 1977 s44(2) (landlord claiming more than the registered rent), s46(2) (need for valid notice of increase in some circumstances), ss51, 54 and 57 (need for valid rent agreements) and LTA 1987 ss47 and 48 (need for demand for rent to include landlord's name and address).[118] In the public sector, it may be possible to challenge the rent level charged by a local authority, although such challenges are rarely successful.[119]

---

117 HA 1988 s8.
118 *Dallhold Estates (UK) Pty Ltd v Lindsey Trading Properties Inc.* [1992] 1 EGLR 88; *Hussain v Singh* (1992) *Independent* 19 December CA.
119 *Wandsworth London Borough Council v Winder* [1985] AC 461 but cf *R v London Borough of Ealing ex parte Lewis* (1992) 24 HLR 484.

b) Is there a defence of set-off and counterclaim for breach of repairing obligations?[120]

Advisers should never make hasty admissions on behalf of the tenant. It is not difficult in an emergency, when time is short, to overlook a crucial point. Generally, further time should always be sought in order to obtain full and proper instructions. It will be difficult to get a possession order set aside if the tenant has had the benefit of independent legal advice before the hearing.

c) Are there any other grounds for disputing rent claimed by local authority landlords? If any of the following situations arise, there may, arguably, be a defence to the claim for possession:
   - Rent arrears include arrears from a previous tenancy. These can be recovered only as an ordinary civil debt.
   - Rent arrears include adjustments for overpaid housing benefit.
   - Proper notices of increase of rent have not been served. The express terms of the tenancy agreement should be checked for any reference to increases of rent or charges.
   - Rent arrears include amounts that are not 'rent'. Water rates, heating charges etc may not be rent if the tenancy agreement does not expressly make them so.
   - Rent records are incorrect.

With the exception of adjustments for overpaid housing benefit, all the possible defences for local authority tenants apply equally to other tenants. However, the provisions allowing landlords to increase rent are different; for details of these statutory requirements see Luba, Madge and McConnell *Defending Possession Proceedings* 3rd ed., LAG, 1993.

For assured tenancies under HA 1988, substantial rent arrears are now a mandatory ground for possession. In the case of a weekly tenancy, such a ground exists when at least 13 weeks' rent is owing at the time notice of seeking possession is served and at the date of the hearing.[121] The ability to dispute the actual rent owing may, therefore, be the only possible defence to the proceedings, and it will be crucial to check precisely how the rent claimed is calculated.

Reasonableness.   Where possession is sought under RA 1977 on the ground that suitable alternative accommodation is available or under Sch 15 Cases 1 to 10 inclusive, the court must be satisfied that it is reasonable

---

120   See *British Anzani (Felixstowe) Ltd v International Marine Management (UK) Ltd* [1980] QB 137; *Asco Developments v Gordon* (1978) 248 EG 683; *Chiodi v De Marney* (1989) 21 HLR 6; *Davies v Peterson* (1989) 21 HLR 63 and *Trevantos v McCulloch* (1990) 23 HLR 412, CA.
121   HA 1988 s7 and Sch 2 Pt 1 Ground 8.

to make an order and/or for possession.[122] Where possession is sought under HA 1985, the court must consider it reasonable to make the order and/or be satisfied that suitable alternative accommodation is available for the tenant.[123] Also the court has extensive powers to adjourn the hearing of the claim for possession, postpone the date of possession and to stay or suspend the execution of the possession order. These powers are available where possession is sought under RA 1977 Sch 15 Cases 1 to 10 or HA 1985 Sch 3 Grounds 1 to 8 or 12 to 16 or HA 1988 Sch 2 Grounds 1 to 8.[124]

Other defences to a possession order. The following points should be considered for arguing that it is not reasonable to make a possession order:

- tenant has made payments off the arrears at a reasonable level since the notice was served and therefore proceedings were unnecessary;
- mitigating circumstances;
- landlord failed to respond to queries about the rent.

In addition, the court has powers to suspend possession orders in the case of a restricted contract entered into on or after 28 November 1980,[125] a rental purchase agreement[126] and where premises have been let to a person who is employed in agriculture but who is not a protected occupant or statutory tenant.[127]

Legal aid

If there is a valid defence, an application for emergency legal aid should be made, or, if time is very short, the legal aid area office must be telephoned immediately to obtain emergency legal aid. The area office will require a full explanation for any delay and may refuse legal aid on that ground. The defences available to the tenant should be stressed and it should be emphasised that non-representation at court may result in a possession order against the tenant. If it is a case where the court must be satisfied that it is reasonable to make a possession order, the need for representation on this point should also be emphasised. Good reasons for delay in making an application for legal aid are illness, absence on business or on holiday when a summons was served, failure of previous solicitors to advise about legal aid, or the respondent having just received a summons because of late service.

122   RA 1977 s98.
123   HA 1985 s84.
124   RA 1977 s100; HA 1985 s85; HA 1988 s9.
125   RA 1977 s106A(1) and (2).
126   HA 1980 s88.
127   Protection from Eviction Act 1977 s4.

Adjournment

In view of the pressures on courts to list cases, very little time will normally be allotted to the first hearing of a possession summons. If the case is likely to be defended and to take more than a few minutes, it may well be that the court will only have time to give directions, eg, as to discovery.

However, if the issues are apparently straightforward, eg, in a rent arrears case where there is no dispute about the amount or arrears and the main issues are the nature of the possession order sought and the time for repayment of the arrears, the case will probably be dealt with at the first hearing. In those circumstances, it may be wise to apply for an adjournment of the hearing. The court has power to adjourn the hearing[128] and to give directions for the future conduct of the case.[129] The application should be made on county court prescribed form N244 and the plaintiff should be given at least two days' notice.[130] In an emergency this will not be possible and the court should be asked to abridge the notice so that the application may be heard on the return day of the fixed-date summons.[131]

The plaintiff should be telephoned and asked to agree to an adjournment. Details of the defence should be given and the reason for any delay in the tenant seeking advice. It should be suggested that the hearing be treated as a pre-trial review.[132] If emergency legal aid has been granted, the plaintiff must be informed and advised that an order for costs will be sought if the adjournment is refused by the plaintiff but granted by the court. This telephone call should be followed by a letter, either faxed or delivered by hand if possible, confirming the contents of the telephone conversation. In this kind of situation a tenant's representative is always in a stronger position if it has been possible to file and serve a defence. Another useful tactic in cases involving rent arrears is to serve a request for further and better particulars (see, eg, precedent 32 in Part III).

If no agreement has been reached, an attempt should be made to negotiate outside the court (see above). If the plaintiff still refuses to agree to an adjournment, an application must be made to the judge for an adjournment[133] and for directions giving time to file a defence.[134] The tenant should be available to give oral evidence as to the reasons for the

---

128   CCR Ord 13 r3(1); RA 1977 s100; HA 1985 s85; HA 1988 s9.
129   CCR Ord 13 r2(1).
130   CCR Ord 13 r1(2).
131   CCR Ord 13 r4(1).
132   CCR Ords 1 r3 and 17 r1.
133   CCR Ord 13 r3; RA 1977 s100; HA 1985 s85; HA 1988 s9.
134   CCR Ord 13 r2.

delay. If this is not possible, an affidavit must be filed. The judge will also require an outline of the defence. If a tenant cannot attend because of illness, a doctor's certificate should be submitted to the judge.[135] It will not be a miscarriage of justice if an adjournment is refused where the occupier has not substantiated his or her claim that s/he had a valid defence either by giving oral evidence or making an affidavit of what the defence was.[136]

Payment of rent

If the claim for possession is based on non-payment of rent, and some or all of the arrears are admitted, the tenant should be advised to pay as much rent as possible before the hearing. Payment or tendering of rent after the action has started does not deprive the court of jurisdiction, but in practice such action will render it unreasonable for the court to make an order for possession unless there is a long history of default.[137] Where there are arrears which cannot be paid before the hearing, it is likely that if an adjournment is granted it will be on condition that current rent is paid in future and appropriate arrears paid by lump sum or instalments.[138] Alternatively, a possession order may be granted but execution suspended on the condition that current rent and instalments of the arrears are paid.[139]

Where legal aid refused

If legal aid is refused on the telephone, a written application must be submitted immediately, with a letter in support setting out the reason for the delay in making the application and details of the defence. If possible, a defence should be drafted under the green form scheme. If this is not possible letters should be sent to the court and the plaintiff setting out details of a defence, the reasons for the delay in filing the defence and the position regarding legal aid, and requesting an adjournment and time to deliver a defence. These letters must be faxed or delivered by hand before the hearing if time permits. In any event, the tenant must attend court and should have copies of the letters to submit to the court if necessary. The tenant should be advised that s/he may have to give oral evidence in a crowded court, and should take an interpreter if s/he has difficulty speaking or understanding English.

---

135   *Dick v Piller* [1943] KB 497; notes in *County Court Practice* to CCR Ord 13 r3.
136   *Fryer v Brook* (1984) 81 LS Gaz 2856.
137   *Dellenty v Pellow* [1951] 2 KB 858.
138   CCR Ord 13 r1(8); RA 1977 s100(3); HA 1985 s85(2); HA 1988 s9.
139   RA 1977 s100(2) and (3); HA 1985 s85(2) and (3).

Procedure where no defence

If it is quite clear that there is no defence (and the points made on page 235 above are repeated) or the tenant does not wish to defend the proceedings but needs time to leave, a postponement of the possession order should be negotiated with the plaintiff.

It is unwise to agree to a possession order 'by consent' as this may mean that the tenant is considered homeless intentionally under the HA 1985 (see page 269). In any event there is no jurisdiction to make a consent order unless the judge has obtained from the tenant or his or her legal representative the concession that the tenant is not entitled to the protection of the Rent Act (and by analogy the Housing Acts).[140] There must be a plain admission that the qualifying conditions for whichever ground is relied on are met and that it is reasonable for the order to be made.[141] If negotiations are unsuccessful, an application should be made to the court at the hearing for postponement of the possession order. The court has wide powers to postpone in some cases (see page 224), but in other cases the court's power is fettered by HA 1980 s89(1). In most cases the court may not postpone the order to a date later than 14 days after the making of the order, unless there is exceptional hardship, when it may be postponed for up to six weeks from the date of the order. The tenant should file an affidavit and/or give oral evidence as to hardship, eg, s/he will be homeless and needs time to find alternative accommodation.

Setting aside or varying the possession order

If the tenant does not seek legal advice until a possession order is made, it may in some circumstances be possible to get the possession order set aside[142] or to obtain an order for a rehearing.[143]

Set aside

It may be possible to have a possession order set aside and the claim heard again if the order was made:[144]

– without the tenant being notified of the proceedings; or
– without the tenant being in court; or

---

140   *R v Bloomsbury and Marylebone County Court ex parte Blackburne* (1985) 275 EG 1273.
141   *R v Newcastle upon Tyne County Court ex parte Thompson* (1988) 20 HLR 430.
142   CCR Ord 37 r2.
143   CCR Ord 37 r1.
144   CCR Ord 37 rr2 and 3; *Tower Hamlets London Borough Council v McCarron* (unreported, see September 1988 *Legal Action* 13); *London Borough of Tower Hamlets v Abadie* (1990) 22 HLR 264.

- without the tenant knowing s/he had a defence; and if there is a proper defence to the claim.

The opposite party must be given at least two days' notice of the application.[145]

If there has been a failure to comply with the requirements of the County Court Rules, the court may set aside the proceedings wholly or in part or exercise its powers to give any such directions as it thinks fit.[146] This may be appropriate where there has been an irregularity in respect of service.[147] The application must be made in reasonable time and must state the grounds of objection.[148] This remedy is discretionary, but it has been held[149] that the court must allow the application where failure to set aside would lead to a miscarriage of justice – for example, where the tenant was unable to attend at the last minute because of an accident, or where the landlord advised the tenant not to bother to attend, or where the tenant went to the wrong court through a genuine mistake. The application is made to the district judge if s/he made the original order but otherwise to the circuit judge.[150]

Rehearing

The judge has power on application to order a rehearing when no error of the court at the hearing is alleged.[151] An application for a rehearing should be made on notice stating the grounds of the application and the notice should be served on the opposite party, not more than 14 days after the day of the trial and not less than seven days before the day fixed for the hearing of the application.[152] The application must usually be to the judge by whom the proceedings were tried. The principles governing the grant of a new trial are set out in the *County Court Practice* in the notes to CCR Ord 37 r1. The most likely reason for applying for a rehearing in this context is default or misconduct of the opposite party.

Varying possession orders

In addition to the powers of the court described above, there are other ways in which a possession order may be varied, namely:

- by the tenant applying to pay any debt (eg, arrears of rent in a

---

145   CCR Ord 13 r1.
146   CCR Ord 37 r5(1).
147   CCR Ord 37 r3(1).
148   CCR Ord 37 r5(2) and (3).
149   *Grimshaw v Dunbar* [1953] 1 QB 408.
150   CCR Ord 37 r2(2).
151   CCR Ord 37 r1(1).
152   CCR Ord 37 r1(5).

suspended possession order) by smaller instalments if the debtor
cannot pay at the existing rate;[153]
- by applying to extend the time to make any payment (eg, a lump sum
  which is a condition of a suspended possession order);[154]
- by the tenant applying for a suspension (or further suspension) of a
  possession order – see below.

If a tenant thinks that s/he will be unable to comply with the terms of
a possession order, it is far better to make such an application before the
terms have been breached, rather than waiting for the landlord to apply
for a warrant of execution (ie, an application to send the bailiffs in). The
procedure for making any of these applications is the same as for an
application to suspend a possession order – an application in form N244
or N245 and an affidavit in support – see below.

Stay of execution where warrant has not been issued

If the landlord has applied for a warrant of execution, the tenant should
also make an application for a stay of execution of the possession order, as
notice of application in any of the above provisions does not in itself
operate as a stay of execution on the order to which it relates. The court
may order a stay of execution pending the hearing of the application or
any rehearing or new trial ordered on the application.[155]

The application for a stay of execution should be made immediately
and may be included on the same notice of application. Two days' notice
is usually required, but in an emergency, where the warrant for possession
is about to be issued, the application should be made *ex parte*.[156]

If the application is to be made *ex parte*, the adviser should make every
effort to contact the plaintiff and advise him or her of the application. It
may be that the plaintiff will agree not to issue the warrant of execution,
but a court order is necessary in order to protect the occupier properly, as
leave is not required to issue a warrant for possession.[157]

Procedure

An application to set aside the possession order, or for a rehearing or for a
stay of execution (see above), should be made by notice of application
(prescribed form N244), which should state the order requested and the
grounds of the application.

153   CCR Ord 22 r10.
154   CCR Ord 13 r4.
155   CCR Ord 37 r8(2).
156   CCR Ord 13 r1(2).
157   CCR Ord 26 r17(2).

The application should be made personally at the court office so that the earliest possible hearing date can be arranged. The notice should then be served personally on the plaintiff so that service can be proved if the plaintiff does not attend court. The application for a stay of execution should normally be made on an earlier date.

An application to set aside should be supported by an affidavit covering the following points:

- the reason why the tenant did not attend the hearing (if appropriate);
- as much information as possible about the likely defences to the claim for rent (full information may not be available until discovery has taken place);
- as much information as possible about the defence to the possession claim;
- any proposals from the tenant for paying off the arrears if the order is set aside;
- any other factor likely to persuade the court.

See precedents 35 and 36 in Part III for an application to set aside and an affidavit in support.

Suspended possession orders and warrants of execution

Introduction

An emergency can arise where a possession order has been suspended on conditions (see below). If a tenant fails to comply with the terms of the suspended order, the suspension terminates automatically.[158] Unless the original order provided that it was not to be enforced without the leave of the court, no further court order is necessary and the landlord may file a request for a warrant for possession, for which leave is not required.[159] Thus, the tenant may simply receive a few days' notice that s/he is to be evicted. An immediate application must be made for the warrant of execution to be suspended or stayed.

Circumstances in which an order may be suspended

A county court judge has power to suspend possession orders where the premises are let:

---

158   *Yates v Morris* [1951] 1 KB 77; *Thompson v Elmbridge BC* (1987) 19 HLR 526; *Leicester City Council v Aldwinckle* (1992) 24 HLR 40, CA.
159   CCR Ord 26 r17(2).

- on a protected tenancy or subject to a statutory tenancy[160] where possession is granted under RA 1977 Sch 15 Cases 1 to 10 (the 'discretionary' grounds);[161]
- under a secure tenancy[162] where possession is granted under HA 1985 on any of the Sch 3 Pt I Grounds 1 to 8 or 12 to 16;
- under a restricted contract entered into on or after 28 November 1980[163] in this case the court can delay possession for a period of up to three months only;[164]
- on a rental purchase agreement;[165]
- to a person who is employed in agriculture but who is not a protected occupant or statutory tenant; or[166]
- on an assured tenancy[167] where possession is granted under the grounds in HA 1988 Sch 2 Pt II.[168]

In all six cases the court must impose conditions with regard to payment of arrears of rent (if any) and rent or mesne profits to the termination of the tenancy, unless this would cause exceptional hardship, and may impose such other conditions as it thinks fit.[169]

Suspended orders are most commonly granted where possession has been sought because the tenant has rent arrears or where it is alleged the tenant has caused nuisance and annoyance to neighbours.[170] Where there are rent arrears, the order will usually be suspended on condition that the tenant pays current rent in future and a regular payment towards the arrears. The court should take into account the tenant's disposable income and level of arrears when assessing what is reasonable for the tenant to pay towards the arrears. If a tenant is in receipt of income support, s/he will usually be ordered to pay not more than 5 per cent of the current single householder rate of income support towards the arrears. At the time this book went to press, £2.20 per week was the most the DSS could deduct from a claimant's benefit to pay in satisfaction of arrears to a landlord.[171]

---

160   RA 1977 s100(1) and (2).
161   RA 1977 s100(5).
162   HA 1985 s85(1) and (2).
163   RA 1977 s106A(1) and (2).
164   RA 1977 s106A(3).
165   HA 1980 s88.
166   Protection from Eviction Act 1977 s4.
167   HA 1988 s9(3).
168   HA 1988 s9(6).
169   RA 1977 s100(3); HA 1985 s85(3); RA 1977 s106A(4); HA 1988 s9(3).
170   RA 1977 Sch 15 Cases 1 and 2; HA 1985 Sch 2 Grounds 1 and 2; HA 1988 Sch 2 Grounds 10, 11 and 14.
171   Social Security (Claims and Payments) Regulations 1987 Sch 9 para 5, as amended.

Warrant of possession

Issue of warrant

If a tenant does not comply with the terms of the suspended order, the landlord can apply for the warrant of possession to be issued. In the public sector, any breach of the order operates to determine the tenancy and the rights, eg to succession, that run with it.[172] Unless the court makes a specific order to the contrary, no leave is required to issue the warrant.[173] Where a possession order is suspended in a 'nuisance' case, it is usual for the court to order that the warrant may not be issued without the leave of the court. Conversely, however, it is rare for such an order to be made in a 'rent arrears' case. Thus, a tenant who has failed to pay current rent and/or regular payments towards arrears as ordered by the court, albeit only for a week or two, may receive a notice that the warrant for possession is about to be executed. In fact where the tenant's circumstances have changed it is possible to return to the court and request that the order be varied or further postponed or suspended,[174] but tenants often do not seek advice in time.

Where the warrant is issued, the tenant can apply for the warrant to be suspended[175] provided that one of the conditions described above applies. A tenant can apply where s/he claims there has been no breach of the terms of the suspended order or where there has been a breach because of a change of circumstance, or because the original order was unrealistic.[176]

Tenants outside the protection of the Rent Act and Housing Acts can apply to suspend the execution of a warrant for possession,[177] but if a suspension is granted, a further application for a suspension will not be successful if the time specified for the suspension has expired.[178] The court has a discretionary power to stay a warrant for possession if it is satisfied that any sum or instalment cannot be paid.[179]

(Remember that it may also be possible to apply to set aside or vary the original possession order – see above.)

---

172 *Thompson v Elmbridge Borough Council* (1987) 19 HLR 526.
173 CCR Ord 26 r17(2).
174 RA 1977 s100(2); HA 1985 s85(2); HA 1988 s9.
175 RA 1977 s100(2); HA 1985 s85(2); HA 1988 s9.
176 *Tower Hamlets London Borough Council v McCarron* (unreported, see September 1988 *Legal Action* 13).
177 *R v Ilkeston County Court ex parte Kruza* (1985) 17 HLR 539.
178 *Moore v Registrar of Lambeth County Court* [1969] 1 WLR 141.
179 County Courts Act 1984 s88.

Grounds for application to suspend or stay the warrant

If a tenant is in arrears with payments which have been ordered by the court, the tenant must be able to show good reason. Examples of good reasons are non-payment of housing benefit to the tenant by a local authority, a sudden reduction in income because of unemployment, that the tenant was not previously represented and the original order was unrealistic in relation to the tenant's disposable income, or non-payment by standing order to the landlord because of a mistake made by the bank.

The court is not likely to be sympathetic if the tenant has failed to make a large number of payments without good reason. In these circumstances a tenant should be advised to pay a lump sum before the hearing. If such a payment is not possible, the tenant should be advised that eviction is likely.

The arrears of rent which are due cannot be reduced or waived by the court (except with the consent of the landlord). If the application is successful the court will further suspend the order and/or reduce the amount of regular payments towards the arrears.

Where the landlord alleges a breach other than non-payment of a financial sum due, eg, further nuisance or annoyance caused to neighbours, if the tenant denies the allegations it is likely that oral evidence will have to be given both by the tenant and landlord and witnesses. The tenant should be prepared for this.

The court has jurisdiction to make more than one order for suspension, but an order having the effect of an indefinite suspension should only be made in very special circumstances.[180]

Procedure

The application for the suspension of the warrant should be made by notice of application (on prescribed form N244 or N245).

The notice of application should state the order requested and the grounds of the application.

The application should be supported by an affidavit which should set out the reasons why the conditions attached to the order have not been complied with. If it is denied that there has been a breach, the manner in which the terms have been complied with should be set out. Copies of relevant documents should be exhibited to the affidavit, eg, letters from the bank, employer or about unpaid housing benefit. The affidavit should seek to persuade the court to exercise its discretionary powers to suspend the warrant.

180 *Vandermolen v Toma* (1981) 9 HLR 91.

Notice

Usually the tenant will be required to give the landlord the minimum of two days' notice of the application, but an *ex parte* application can be made if the court so permits.[181]

Informing bailiffs

The bailiffs should always be informed of the application (or the impending application in an emergency). The warrant will have a different reference number from the court case number and failure to quote this will cause delay at the court office. The bailiffs will usually agree not to execute the warrant until the application has been heard.

Hearing

The hearing will be before a judge in chambers.[182] Where there is a dispute, oral evidence will be taken from both the landlord and the tenant and witnesses where necessary. It has been suggested that if the cause of a tenant's failure to comply with the financial conditions of a suspended order is a delay in receiving housing benefit, a witness summons should be served on a senior official responsible for administering the scheme to attend at the application and explain the cause of the delay.[183] Such a tactic would no doubt be effective not only in obtaining a suspension of the warrant, but in obtaining rapid payment of arrears of housing benefit.

Two factors are always worth stressing where the tenant has not complied with the order: first, the fact that the tenant will lose his or her home unless the application is granted; and, second, the fact that a landlord will often, in practice, be unable to recover the arrears if the tenant is evicted since the judgment for rent arrears will become an ordinary civil debt, which is extremely difficult to enforce. It may, therefore, be in the landlord's interest for execution of the order to be suspended.

The most common issue raised by the landlord is the tenant's unreliability in complying with orders or agreements. It may be stressed that, probably for the first time, the tenant is receiving proper advice and that the order to be made should be carefully pitched so as to be within the tenant's means, unlike previous demands made by the landlord.

---

181   CCR Ord 13 r1(2).
182   CCR Ord 13 r1(4).
183   Nic Madge 'Suspended possession orders' January 1984 *Legal Action* 8.

After eviction

In some cases, the tenant does not seek advice until after s/he has been evicted. Even then it is possible to apply to set aside the possession order and have the tenant reinstated in his or her home.[184]

The evidence required for such an application is identical to that required for an application to set aside before execution of the order. However, the court may be reluctant to set aside if the landlord has relet or sold the property concerned. The affidavit in support should, therefore, provide evidence that the landlord has not relet the property, that it is empty and that s/he still owns it.

Distress for rent

For a more detailed treatment of this topic, see D Forbes 'Beating the bailiff' March 1989 *Legal Action* 13.

Distress for rent

Only a few local authorities use distress for recovery of rent arrears, although housing associations may do so. Private sector landlords of protected or statutory tenants and landlords of the new assured tenants cannot use distress without leave of the court.[185]

Distress involves a certificated bailiff, instructed by the landlord, attending the rented premises and impounding any property there up to the amount of the arrears and the costs of the distress. No warning need be given and no court proceedings taken, so the protection against abuse is minimal. The property is generally left in the dwelling for a period of five to 10 days before removal and sale at auction. The landlord usually hopes to force the tenant to borrow in order to pay the arrears off within that period and thereby save his or her belongings.

Which landlords can use distress?

Landlords have a common law right to distrain for rent. The process involves instructing a bailiff to impound and remove the tenant's property and sell it to reimburse rent arrears.

Housing associations can use distress to recover rent arrears for tenancies that began before 15 January 1989 and which are, therefore, secure tenancies under HA 1985, but may not use the procedure for

---

184   *Governors of Peabody Donation Fund v Hay* (1987) 19 HLR 145; and *London Borough of Tower Hamlets v Abadie* (1990) 22 HLR 264; CCR Ord 37 r8(3).
185   Rent Act (RA) 1977 s147; Housing Act (HA) 1988 s19.

tenancies beginning after 15 January 1989 (assured tenancies under HA 1988) without obtaining leave from the county court.[186]

Private sector landlords of protected or statutory tenants under RA 1977, or of assured tenants under HA 1988, cannot use distress without obtaining leave from the county court.[187]

The court has the same powers to stay, suspend, adjourn or postpone the grant of leave to levy distress as it has under a discretionary ground for possession.[188]

Local authority landlords can use distress without obtaining leave from the county court, whenever the tenancy began. Private sector landlords of tenants who have restricted contracts or whose tenancies are excluded from the protection of RA 1977 or HA 1988 (eg, resident landlords) can use distress without obtaining leave from the court. In practice, very few local authorities use distress, while private sector landlords almost never do so.

Restrictions on distraint for rent

Loss of right to distrain

The landlord loses the right to levy distress in certain circumstances:
- where any court has already given judgment for rent arrears due, the landlord may not distrain for the same rent, but must use county court proceedings;
- tenant leaves the rented property;
- tenant tenders rent, ie, offers the money to the landlord;
- previous distress for the same rent.

Rights of the bailiff

The bailiff's rights are closely circumscribed by law:
- Bailiff may not break in to rented premises.
- Only goods may be distrained, not fixtures or money.
- Only goods on the premises can be distrained unless goods have been fraudulently removed, in which case the bailiff can break in to the premises to which they have been removed and impound them.[189]
- Goods on the premises belonging to third parties can be impounded, but their owner may be able to prevent their removal and sale.
- Certain goods are exempt from distress, namely clothes, beds and bedding worth up to £100, tools of trade worth up to £150, perishable

186   HA 1988 s19.
187   RA 1977 s147; HA 1988 s19.
188   RA 1977 s147; HA 1988 s19; and see page 243.
189   Distress for Rent Act 1737 s3.

items, things actually in use at the time of distraint, and items held for public trade (eg, goods deposited by members of the public for repair).
- Only bailiffs granted a certificate by the county court can distrain and they must produce identification.

Tactics for avoidance of distress

Obtaining an injunction

If the rent demanded is not legally due, there is no right to levy distress and an application can be made to the court for an injunction restraining wrongful distraint and a declaration that no rent is due.

Generally, injunctions and declarations can be obtained only in the High Court (unless ancillary to a damages claim), but may be sought in the county court 'in respect of, or relating to any land or the possession, occupation, use or enjoyment of any land'.[190] This provision, arguably, covers injunctions preventing distress for rent, and it seems worth the risk of issuing in the county court.

An affidavit in support of the application for an injunction will be required. This should deal with the following issues:
- the identity of the landlord and the terms of the tenancy;
- the initial threat to levy distress issued by the landlord;
- the reason why some or all of the money demanded is not due or is not due as rent;
- the steps taken to persuade the landlord that s/he has no right to distrain;
- the landlord's response;
- the likely detriment to the tenant if distress takes place.

The court will grant an interlocutory injunction if it is satisfied that:[191]
- there is a serious question to be tried;
- the balance of convenience is in favour of granting the injunction;
- damages for wrongful distress would be an inadequate remedy;
- there is real likelihood of the distress taking place; and
- grave damage to the plaintiff would result if distress takes place.

Precedents 39 to 41 in part III are examples of a letter before action, particulars of claim and affidavit in support for county court proceedings. In both the High Court and the county court, the notice of application must be served on the defendant at least two clear days before the

---

190   County Courts Act 1984 s22.
191   *American Cyanamid Co. v Ethicon Ltd* [1975] AC 396; *Redland Bricks Ltd v Morris* [1970] AC 652.

hearing.[192] Where there is genuine fear that the landlord will seek to levy distress before the hearing, an *ex parte* application should be made.

Refusing entry to the bailiff
If the tenant and all other occupants of the house ensure that windows and doors are kept shut and locked and that the door is not opened to the bailiff, s/he has no right to break in. However, the bailiff can keep returning as long as rent is owing.

Safeguarding belongings
There are various precautions tenants can take when distress is threatened:
- When the bailiff gains entry, s/he is unlikely to make a thorough search of the dwelling. The tenant may, therefore, hide items of value. This is lawful.
- Cars should not be parked in front of the house nor in the driveway or garage. It seems that the bailiff may distrain items parked on the half of the road nearest the house.
- It is advisable not to bring items of value into the home from elsewhere.
- A fraudulent or clandestine removal of items from the rented premises in order to avoid distress is a criminal offence.[193] However, if a car is driven away in normal use and happens to be parked elsewhere when brought back, the removal is not fraudulent. Similarly, the removal of a television for repair is not fraudulent.
- Where appropriate, ownership of property may be transferred to non-tenants. It will remain liable to being impounded but the owner can prevent its removal or sale.

    Children of any age may own property, but the belongings of spouses are not protected.[194] The property of lodgers and subtenants who pay rent less than quarterly is protected unless a subtenancy was created in breach of the terms of the tenancy.[195] Local authority tenants are not allowed to sublet without the written consent of the landlord, but can have lodgers.[196]
- Property of business partners is not protected nor goods on hire-purchase unless a default notice has been served under the Consumer Credit Act 1974.[197]

---

192   CCR Ord 13 r1; RSC Ord 32 r3.
193   Distress for Rent Act 1737 s3.
194   Law of Distress Amendment Act 1908 s4.
195   Law of Distress Amendment Act 1908 s1.
196   HA 1985 s93.
197   Law of Distress Amendment Act 1908 ss4A(2) and 4(2)(a).

- Lodgers, subtenants and resident family members (other than spouses) are protected and can prevent their goods being removed or sold if they follow a particular procedure.[198]

Procedure to be followed to obtain protection.   After the impounding of, or threat of impounding, goods on the premises, the person who claims ownership of the protected goods must carry out the following procedure:[199]
- prepare an inventory of his or her property on the premises;
- sign the inventory;
- attach the inventory to a notice to the landlord declaring that the tenant has no interest in the property and that it belongs to him or her;
- state what arrears of rent or licence fee are owing to the tenant and what will become due in the future;
- undertake to pay any future rent or licence fee direct to the landlord until the rent arrears of the tenant are cleared.
  It is a criminal offence to make a false declaration.[200]

Preventing sale when distress is unlawful

Where distress has been carried out unlawfully, because exempt items, or protected goods which belong to a family member, have been removed, there are two possible remedies:
a) *Complaint about bailiff's conduct.*   A complaint may be lodged at the county court which granted the bailiff's certificate. S/he will have to reply in writing[201] and the complaint will be heard before the judge. The complainant may attend. A threat to bring a complaint may result in the immediate restoration of property wrongly removed.
b) *Injunction ordering return of goods.*   An injunction may be obtained to prevent the sale of goods wrongly removed and an order for their return. The injunction should be directed at the bailiff and the supporting affidavit should explain the circumstances giving rise to the wrongful distress, give details of the goods removed (including ownership and value), and stress the importance of their return. A copy of the notice of seizure and of any notice and inventory sent to the landlord should be exhibited.

---

198   For details of this, see March 1989 *Legal Action* 14.
199   Law of Distress Amendment Act 1908 s1.
200   Perjury Act 1911 s5.
201   Distress for Rent Rules 1988 r8.

CHAPTER 12

Mortgage Arrears

Summary of enforcement procedures

The remedy for mortgage arrears is for lenders to obtain possession of the mortgaged property and sell it.[1]

The lender must obtain a possession order from the court. Most proceedings are brought in the county court.[2] If possession is obtained, the lender will instruct agents and solicitors to sell the mortgaged property, deduct from the proceeds the sums owed and all the costs incurred and pass the balance, if any, back to the borrower. For a full discussion of this topic, see Luba, Madge and McConnell *Defending Possession Proceedings* 3rd ed., LAG, 1993, pp275–310.

Green form advice and assistance and legal aid

Advisers will be able to negotiate with lenders under the green form scheme. The protection available to borrowers is poor unless the mortgage falls within the Consumer Credit Act 1974 (see page 36), and any agreement reached will almost certainly require repayment of all the arrears within a specified time, or that the borrower sells the property him or herself and moves elsewhere.

Where there is a dispute between the parties as to whether a possession order should be suspended or outright, legal aid should be available to the borrower for legal representation, subject to means. Legal aid staff often do not appreciate that such an argument is a bona fide defence to the claim for outright possession. It may be necessary to stress this point in correspondence.

---

1   Law of Property Act 1925 s101.
2   County Courts Act 1984 s21.

Costs of mortgage possession proceedings

Most mortgage deeds provide that the borrower must pay any costs incurred by the lender in recovering money due under the mortgage. Therefore, the lender does not need an order for costs – the lender merely adds the costs to the money due under the mortgage. The borrower cannot avoid this; s/he may ask the lender's solicitor to have the lender's costs taxed, but this will involve the expense of the taxation fee. It is important, therefore, to remember that any additional steps or hearings will inevitably be charged to the borrower under the mortgage.

Because the chances of defeating a possession claim in its entirety are poor, an order for costs against the lender is unlikely. Thus, the legal aid scheme will probably pay the costs of the borrower. Since the dwelling of the borrower will be preserved in the proceedings, the statutory charge for legal aid will apply.[3]

In practice, if the borrower avoids eviction, s/he will almost always have to pay both parties' costs from the value of his or her home. This should be borne in mind when additional work is required.

Possession proceedings

Before the hearing

In addition to serving proceedings on the borrower, the lender must also arrange service on any spouse who may have rights under the Matrimonial Homes Act 1983.[4]

Disputing arrears

The particulars of claim used by a lender claiming possession must contain information about the arrears, unlike the particulars in a rent claim.[5] The accounting system of lenders is usually far more efficient than that of landlords and the amount of arrears claimed will seldom be in dispute. However, the amount claimed should always be checked.

The lender will generally not claim repayment of the arrears and capital sum in a claim for possession. This is because the lender does not need a judgment to recover the money owed because of the entitlement to sell the mortgaged property. The court can, therefore, make a possession

---

3   Legal Aid Act 1988 s16(6).
4   CCR Ord 6 r1A.
5   CCR Ord 6 r5. Amendments to CCR Ord 6 due to be introduced in 1993 will require mortgagees to set out additional information.

order even if the arrears sum is disputed, provided that it is satisfied that some interest due under the mortgage is at least two months overdue.[6]

Since possession proceedings brought by the lender are almost always held in chambers,[7] the evidence presented by the lender is in the form of an affidavit. This should be provided to the borrower or his or her adviser in good time before the hearing to enable it to be properly considered. If it is not, an adjournment should be sought or the court asked to refuse to admit the affidavit in evidence in the interests of justice.[8]

Disputing a possession order

The main area of dispute will be whether the lender should be granted an outright possession order or a suspended order (see above page 243).

The powers of the court to protect the borrower are limited in most cases. The court must make an outright order for possession unless 'it appears to the court that . . . the mortgagor is likely to be able within a reasonable period to pay any sums due under the mortgage'[9] if the court makes one of the orders listed below.

The options available to the court are:[10]

- to adjourn the proceedings;
- to stay or suspend the execution of the possession order;
- to postpone the date for delivery of possession.

These options are available at any time before execution of the possession order.[11]

'Sums due under the mortgage' are defined as the arrears of interest and capital due under the mortgage at the date of the hearing.[12]

A 'reasonable period' and the degree of likelihood required are not defined and it should therfore be argued that as long a period as possible is 'reasonable'. There are, however, useful dicta. ' . . . one begins with a powerful presumption of fact in favour of the period of the mortgage being the "reasonable period" '.[13] 'In a suitable case the specified period might even be the whole remaining prospective life of the mortgage'.[14] The most important factor is often whether or not the lender's security is

6   Law of Property Act 1925 s103.
7   CCR Ord 49 r1.
8   CCR Ord 20 r9.
9   Administration of Justice Act 1970 s36.
10 Administration of Justice Act 1970 s36.
11 Administration of Justice Act 1970 s36(2).
12 Administration of Justice Act 1973 s8.
13 Per Scarman LJ in *First Middlesbrough Trading and Mortgage Co. Ltd v Cunningham* (1974) 28 P & CR 69 at p75.
14 Per Buckley LJ in *Western Bank Ltd v Schindler* [1977] Ch 1 at p14.

at risk. If the mortgage is small compared to the value of the dwelling, the lender will not be prejudiced by a long period.

Discretionary powers under Consumer Credit Act 1974.   If the mortgage is a loan to an individual for less than £15,000 and from a fringe finance company, it is likely to be a 'regulated agreement' within the meaning of the Consumer Credit Act 1974 (see page 37). A mortgage securing a regulated agreement is specifically enforceable only on an order from the court.[15] The lender must serve a default notice on the borrower and if s/he fails to remedy the default, the lender applies for a possession summons. The borrower may apply to the court for a 'time order' to reschedule the payment of money owed under the regulated agreement.

The discretionary powers of the district judge under the Consumer Credit Act 1974 are much greater than those under the Administration of Justice Acts, as there is no requirement that arrears be paid off within a 'reasonable period'. The court may be able to reduce monthly payments and the rate of interest,[16] but it should be noted that other county court judges have held that the court has no such power. When considering the size and rate of instalments, the court must have regard only to the means of the borrower, not to possible hardship caused to the lender.[17]

Many district judges are unfamiliar with the provisions of the Consumer Credit Act 1974 as they relate to mortgages, so it is necessary to draw their attention to their greater powers of discretion (see Luba, Madge and McConnell *Defending Possession Proceedings* 3rd ed., LAG, 1993, pp289–92).

The borrower could request suspension or postponement of possession on the ground that s/he:

- has a sale agreed, subject to contract;
- has a genuine prospect of employment;
- has a lump sum available;
- will borrow to repay the mortgage; or
- can afford to repay the arrears by instalments.

If the adviser of a borrower has insufficient time to prepare a well-argued case with full information, an adjournment might be sought from the lender or from the court on the grounds that:

- if the proceedings are defended a longer court hearing will be needed;

---

15   Consumer Credit Act 1974 s126.
16   *Cedar Holdings v Jenkins* August 1987 *Legal Action* 19 and cases noted in Luba, Madge and McConnell, *Defending Possession Proceedings*, 3rd edn 1993 at p291.
17   Consumer Credit Act 1974 s129(2).

- the lender will not be prejudiced by an adjournment as interest will continue to accrue; and
- the borrower stands to lose his or her home if an adjournment is refused.

The disadvantage of applying for an adjournment is that it will add to the legal costs which will be added to the mortgage. Courts often expect advisors to be able to find out sufficient information about borrowers' circumstances to represent them, and so requests for adjournment are often refused.

After the hearing

If an outright possession order has been made, the only effective remedy is to apply to have it set aside and a suspended order made instead. The grounds for such an application are identical to those for rent arrears cases (see page 246), and will probably succeed only where grounds for suspension have arisen since the making of the possession order, for example, a relative offers to pay off the arrears.

If a suspended possession order is made, at any time before eviction the borrower may apply to the court for a further suspension or postponement. The procedure is identical to that for rent arrears (see page 246), and grounds for the application might include:

- delay in a proposed sale or receipt of a lump sum;
- request for a longer period for payment of arrears by instalments; or
- request for a reduced level of instalments because of changed circumstances.

After eviction

After eviction it is not possible to apply to suspend execution of the order, but it is still possible to apply to have the order set aside if the borrower was not present at the hearing (see page 248).

Since it may take several months for a sale by the lender to take place, the borrower can still seek to find finance in order to propose repayment of the arrears within a reasonable period. In practice, however, it seems unlikely that a court will set aside an order unless the borrower can repay all the arrears immediately.

If the borrower secures the finance to repay, an application to set aside should be made. The affidavit in support should deal with the following issues:

- why the borrower did not attend the hearing;

- the information necessary to show a defence (ie, that the borrower can pay off the arrears within a reasonable period);
- the borrower's proposals to clear the arrears, including any offer to pay money into court if required;
- other factors which might persuade the court to exercise discretion in the borrower's favour, eg, desperate housing situation, hardship to family, lack of prejudice to lender.

CHAPTER 13

Homelessness

Advisers can play an important role in the assistance of homeless people by negotiating with housing authorities and by challenging decisions by making an application for judicial review. Although some disputes over homelessness are resolved without recourse to the courts, and in some areas a threat to issue proceedings may be effective in persuading a housing authority to change its mind, as housing has become scarcer, authorities have become less likely to alter decisions before proceedings are issued. Tactics will vary according to the housing authority and to the type of homelessness, but the following guidelines may be useful.

Tactics in homelessness cases

There are three fundamental rules:
- applicants should not leave their current accommodation until the housing authority's duties have been clarified;
- whenever a housing authority refuses to house, it must be required to give its reasons in writing, and a challenge to the decision should be considered;
- an immediate written request should be made for the information which the authority has recorded as given it by the applicant in connection with the application.[1]

Dealing with the housing authority

The way in which a housing authority should be approached will depend upon the authority. In more liberal authorities, the appropriate housing officer should be contacted and the case discussed with him or her. If housing is refused the adviser should ask for reasons and make a detailed attendance note of the telephone call. The date, time and name of the

1 Housing Act 1985 s106(5).

officer should be recorded, as well as the content of the conversation. This attendance note may be crucial evidence if legal action becomes necessary.

The telephone call should be followed up with a carefully-worded letter, setting out the applicant's case, with reference to the law. A reply in writing should be requested.

If the reply is negative, the adviser should telephone the legal department: s/he should speak to a solicitor and set out the legal basis of the application. This should be followed up with a letter. This approach will often prove successful if the applicant has a strong case in law.

In other authorities which have a reputation for taking a hard line, attempting to persuade housing officers by speaking to them over the telephone may be a waste of time. In those circumstances the best approach is a letter before action threatening an application for judicial review and requesting information in accordance with s106(5) combined with an immediate application for legal aid.

Publicity

Publicity in the local paper may be effective, but only in selected cases. Publicity may do more harm than good, particularly if the housing authority wants to be seen to be tough, or if the homeless family is from an ethnic minority and may be subjected to attacks.

Legal action

If legal action becomes inevitable, the adviser should maintain the pressure on the housing authority. The legal department should be informed when emergency legal aid is granted, and, when judicial review is sought:

- copies of the notice of application for judicial review and the affidavit in support should be sent to the department even though the application for leave is made *ex parte*; and
- the department should be telephoned or faxed immediately when leave is granted.

Checklist for instructions

1 *Applicant*
   Full name
   Address
   Date of birth/birth certificate/pension book
   Occupation

Place of employment
Income/wages slips
Savings

2 *Any other person reasonably expected to live with the applicant*
Relationship to applicant
All details as in 1 above

3 *Children*
Full names
Addresses
Dates of birth/birth certificates
Schools/colleges

4 *Present accommodation*
Tenure
Name and address of landlord
Size
Rent
Arrears
Date of occupation
Rent book
Court proceedings
Date of leaving

5 *Previous accommodation (if relevant)*
Details as in 4 above

6 *Cause of homelessness*
Court documents, letters etc

7 *Application to housing authority*
When application made
Reference number if on housing waiting list
If refusal, notification received?
Previous applications
Correspondence

8 *Location of belongings*

9 *Medical treatment*
Name and address of GP
Name and address of hospitals with reference numbers
Letter of authority for medical details to be released

10 *Any special personal circumstances*
Eg, alcoholism, violence

When duties arise towards the homeless

Introduction: Housing Act 1985

The duties of housing authorities towards the homeless are contained in the Housing Act (HA) 1985. All references in this chapter are references to that Act. (The 1985 Act consolidated the provisions of the Housing (Homeless Persons) Act 1977, which was accordingly repealed.)

Housing authorities are bound to have regard to the Code of Guidance issued under the Act by the Secretary of State for the Environment in the discharge of their duties to the homeless.[2] The Code is available from HMSO and is printed in volume 4 of the *Encyclopedia of Housing Law and Practice.*

Housing authorities are bound to make reasonable arrangements to receive face-to-face applications and, in urban areas, should have an emergency service during evenings and weekends.[3]

The duties which a housing authority owes to the homeless vary depending on whether the applicant is homeless,[4] threatened with homelessness,[5] in priority need[6] and whether s/he became homeless or threatened with homelessness intentionally[7] and whether s/he has a local connection with the housing authority.[8] These definitions are considered in detail below.

Principal duties of local authorities

The principal duties of housing authorities are as follows:

a) Where the applicant is homeless or threatened with homelessness, but not in priority need, to furnish the applicant with advice and appropriate assistance.[9]

b) Where the applicant is homeless or threatened with homelessness, in priority need, but became homeless or threatened with homelessness intentionally, to furnish the applicant with advice and appropriate assistance[10] and, where s/he is actually homeless, to secure that

---

2   HA 1985 s71(1).
3   *R v London Borough of Camden ex parte Gillan* (1988) 21 HLR 114 and *R v Hackney LBC ex parte Asiliskender* December 1990 *Legal Action* 15.
4   HA 1985 s58(1) and (2).
5   HA 1985 s58(3).
6   HA 1985 s59(1).
7   HA 1985 s60(1) and (2).
8   HA 1985 s61.
9   HA 1985 ss65(4) and 66(3)(a).
10   HA 1985 ss65(3)(b) and 66(3)(b).

temporary accommodation is made available for such a period as it considers will give the applicant a reasonable opportunity of securing accommodation for his or her occupation.[11]

c) Where the applicant is threatened with homelessness, has a priority need, and did not become threatened with homelessness intentionally, to take reasonable steps to secure that accommodation does not cease to become available to the applicant.[12]

d) Where the applicant is homeless, has a priority need and did not become homeless intentionally, to secure that accommodation is made available for the applicant's occupation. This duty is subject to the local connection provisions.[13]

Preliminary duties of local authorities

The preliminary duties of housing authorities are:

a) To make enquiries as to whether the applicant is homeless or threatened with homelessness, and if so to make enquiries as to whether the applicant is in priority need and whether the homelessness or the threatened homelessness was intentional.[14]

b) To notify the applicant of its decision in writing;[15] and

c) To provide temporary accommodation to a homeless or potentially homeless person with an apparent priority need, irrespective of local connection, while it carries out its enquiries to establish if it has a long-term duty.[16]

Definitions

Homelessness

Homeless

A person is homeless if s/he has no accommodation in England, Wales or Scotland. A person is to be treated as having no accommodation for the purposes of the HA 1985 in any of the following circumstances:

a) There is no accommodation which s/he, together with any person who normally resides with him or her as a member of his or her family or in

---

11 HA 1985 s65(3).
12 HA 1985 s66(2).
13 HA 1985 s65(2).
14 HA 1985 s62(1) and (2).
15 HA 1985 s64.
16 HA 1985 s63.

circumstances in which the housing authority considers it reasonable for that person to reside with him or her:[17]
- is entitled to occupy by virtue of an interest in it; or
- is entitled to occupy by virtue of an order of court; or
- has an express or implied licence to occupy; or
- is occupying as a residence by virtue of any enactment or rule of law giving him or her the right to remain in occupation or restricting the right of any person to recover possession of it.

b) S/he has accommodation but:[18]
- cannot secure entry to it; or
- it is probable that occupation of the accommodation will lead to violence from some other person residing in the accommodation, or to threats of violence from some other person residing in the accommodation who is likely to carry out those threats; or
- the accommodation consists of a movable structure, vehicle or vessel, designed or adapted for human habitation and there is no place where s/he is entitled or permitted both to put it and to live in it.

c) S/he is threatened with homelessness when it is likely that s/he will become homeless within 28 days.[19]

Accommodation

Occupation of temporary accommodation does not mean that a person is not homeless.[20]

Accommodation in a women's refuge does not mean that a person is not homeless.[21]

A person living in a night refuge on a night-to-night basis is homeless.[22]

A person may be homeless if s/he is occupying accommodation of a very low standard, for example a very small hut infested with rats and with no main services[23] or a caravan[24] or a beach chalet affected by damp and mould growth.[25]

The applicant may not be homeless even if the accommodation is

17   HA 1985 s58(1) and (2).
18   HA 1985 s58(3).
19   HA 1985 s58(4).
20   *Din v Wandsworth London Borough Council* [1983] 1 AC 657.
21   *R v Ealing London Borough Council ex parte Sidhu* (1982) 80 LGR 534.
22   *R v Waveney District Council ex parte Bowers* [1983] QB 238.
23   *R v South Herefordshire District Council ex parte Miles* (1983) 17 HLR 82.
24   *R v Preseli District Council ex parte Fisher* (1984) 17 HLR 147.
25   *R v Medina Borough Council ex parte Dee* (1992) 24 HLR 562.

overcrowded and inadequate.[26] However, the state of repair of a house and fitness for human habitation should be taken into account.[27]

Accommodation abroad does not count as accommodation for the purposes of s58, which applies only to accommodation in England, Wales or Scotland.[28]

A former licensee with no rights of occupation is homeless.[29]

A service occupier whose licence terminated at the time of termination of his or her contract of employment is homeless.[30]

Rehousing obligations towards asylum seekers have been restricted by an amendment to Pt III of the HA 1985 in the Asylum and Immigration Appeals Act 1993. Section 4 states that if an asylum seeker 'has available for his occupation any accommodation, however temporary . . . nothing in the homelessness legislation shall require the housing authority to secure that accommodation is made available for his occupation'.

Authorities may have regard to immigration status when processing applications.[31] An application for housing under Pt III counts as 'living off public funds' and may adversely affect an applicant's immigration status.

Priority need for accommodation

Priority need

A person has a priority need for accommodation under the Act if:

- s/he has dependent children who are residing with him or her or who might reasonably be expected to reside with him or her;[32]
- s/he is homeless or threatened with homelessness as a result of an emergency such as flood, fire or other disaster (irrespective of whether the person is in any of the other categories of priority need);[33]
- s/he or anyone who resides or might reasonably be expected to reside with him or her is vulnerable as a result of old age, mental illness or handicap or physical disability or other special reason;[34]

26 *R v Hillingdon London Borough Council ex parte Puhlhofer* (1986) AC 484, HL.
27 *R v Borough of Dinefwr ex parte Marshall* (1984) 17 HLR 310.
28 See also *R v Hillingdon Borough Council ex parte Streeting* [1980] 1 WLR 1425.
29 *R v Surrey Heath Borough Council ex parte Li* (1984) 16 HLR 79.
30 *R v Royal Borough of Kensington and Chelsea ex parte Minton* (1988) 20 HLR 648.
31 Code of Guidance paras 4.11 and 4.12 as corrected by *R v Secretary of State for the Environment ex parte London Borough of Tower Hamlets* (1993) *Times* 9 April, CA.
32 HA 1985 s59(1)(b).
33 HA 1985 s59(1)(d).
34 HA 1985 s59(1)(c).

- she is a pregnant woman, or the applicant resides or might reasonably be expected to reside with a pregnant woman.[35]

These definitions are expanded in the Code paras 6.2 to 6.18, and see further, below.

Dependent children

'Dependent children' in s59(1)(b) is usually taken to mean children up to the age of 16, or up to 19 as long as they continue in full-time education.

Custody orders should not be demanded. If the children are dependent, it is a question of fact whether they are living with, or ought reasonably to be expected to live with, the applicant.[36]

The children must be residing with the applicant or must reasonably be expected to reside with him or her, ie the tests are alternative and if the children are in care, or are being looked after by relatives, the applicants will be in priority need.[37] Children do not have a right to apply to a local authority themselves for accommodation under HA 1985 Pt III.[38]

The Children Act 1989 imposes a completely separate duty on social service departments in respect of some young people. Section 20 provides that county and metropolitan boroughs must make accommodation arrangements for children who:
- have no parent or guardian;
- are abandoned;
- have people who have been caring for them who are unable to provide suitable accommodation or care for them;
- are at least 16 and will be at risk if no accommodation is found for them

The duty extends to young persons up to the age of 18, with a discretion to continue to provide accommodation upto the age of 21.

Emergency

The words 'any other disaster' in s59(1)(d) mean a disaster similar to flood or fire. A demolition order is not an emergency.[39]

Vulnerable

'Vulnerable' in s59(1)(c) means vulnerable in relation to housing need and has been defined as 'less able to fend for oneself so that injury or detriment would result when a less vulnerable man would be able to cope without

35   HA 1985 s59(1)(a).
36   *R v London Borough of Ealing ex parte Sidhu* (1982) 80 LGR 534.
37   *Re Islam* [1983] 1 AC 688.
38   *Garlick v Oldham MBC* [1993] 2 All ER 65.
39   *Noble v South Herefordshire District Council* (1983) 17 HLR 80.

harmful effects'. The correct approach is to ask first whether or not there is 'vulnerability', and second whether it arises from those matters set out in the Act, either any one of them, or all of them taken together.[40]

Once prima facie evidence (ie, medical evidence) of vulnerability, such as mental handicap, has been provided to the local authority, it must either accept the evidence or make its own specialist enquiries.[41]

Grand mal epilepsy may render a person vulnerable if the attacks take place with intense regularity.[42]

Rent arrears are an irrelevant consideration which ought not to be taken into account in the context of an enquiry into vulnerability.[43]

Old age is usually treated as commencing on retirement age, but those who are particularly frail or in poor health and approaching retirement age should be treated as qualifying on account of old age.[44]

Housing authorities should draw a distinction between mental illness that is psychotic and mental handicap. 'Mental handicap' is concerned with either subnormality or severe subnormality, although only such subnormality as is relevant to housing.[45]

Those who are blind, deaf or dumb or otherwise substantially disabled, mentally or physically, are vulnerable.

A housing authority should enquire into any 'other special reason' when considering vulnerability. Failure to do so will amount to a misdirection in law.[46] A woman who has been seriously assaulted by her husband/cohabitant may be vulnerable due to 'other special reason'.[47]

Pregnancy

Any period of pregnancy will qualify for the purposes of s59(1)(a).[48]

Intentional homelessness

Intentionally homeless

To prove intentional homelessness under s60, the local authority must be satisfied:[49]

---

40 *R v Waveney District Council ex parte Bowers* [1983] QB 238; *R v London Borough of Lambeth ex parte Carroll* (1988) 20 HLR 142.
41 *R v Bath City Council ex parte Sangermano* (1984) 17 HLR 94.
42 *R v Wandsworth Borough Council ex parte Banbury* (1987) 19 HLR 76.
43 *R v Bath City Council ex parte Sangermano* (1984) 17 HLR 94.
44 Code of Guidance para 6.9.
45 *R v Bath City Council ex parte Sangermano* (1984) 17 HLR 94.
46 *R v Bath City Council ex parte Sangermano* (1984) 17 HLR 94.
47 Code para 6.17.
48 Code para 6.2.
49 HA 1985 s60(1).

a) that the applicant deliberately did something or failed to do something
b) in consequence of which
c) the applicant ceased to occupy accommodation which
d) was available for his or her accommodation, and which
e) it would have been reasonable for him or her to continue to occupy.

Becoming threatened with homelessness intentionally is similarly defined.[50]

An act or omission in good faith on the part of a person unaware of a relevant fact, such as the invalidity of a notice to quit, security of tenure or the availability of financial assistance with rent or mortgage payments, is not to be treated as deliberate for these purposes.[51] An applicant is not entitled to a declaration regarding intentionality prior to becoming homeless (eg, by selling the house).[52]

When considering whether or not it was reasonable for the applicant to remain in occupation of his or her former accommodation, the authority is entitled to have regard to the general circumstances prevailing in relation to housing in its own area.[53]

Section 60 is the most contentious part of the 1985 Act. Section 17 of the 1977 Act, which it supersedes, produced a vast amount of litigation. Each limb of the definition must be satisfied in the application to justify a finding of intentional homelessness. The housing authority must address itself to the correct questions under s60, and in particular whether the accommodation was available for the applicant's occupation and if so whether it was reasonable for the applicant to remain in it.[54] An unchallenged decision of intentional homelessness may be difficult to refute later.[55] The following are very brief guidelines – further details may be found in Hunter and McGrath *Homeless Persons* 4th ed., LAG, 1992.

Deliberate act or omission

The act or omission must be deliberate; an act or omission in good faith where the person was unaware of a relevant fact is not to be treated as deliberate.[56] 'There is a distinction between honest blundering and carelessness on the one hand, where a person can still act in good faith, and

50   HA 1985 s60(2).
51   HA 1985 s60(3).
52   R v London Borough of Hillingdon ex parte Tinn (1988) 20 HLR 305.
53   HA 1985 s60(4).
54   R v Preseli District Council ex parte Fisher (1984) 17 HLR 147.
55   R v Merton London Borough Council ex parte Ruffle (1988) 21 HLR 361.
56   HA 1985 s60(3) and see above.

dishonesty on the other, where there can be no question of the person acting in good faith.[57]

Voluntary departure from tied accommodation or dismissal can constitute an act of intentionality.[58]

A former licensee with no rights of occupation will not usually be intentionally homeless if s/he leaves before a court order is obtained.[59]

Eviction on the grounds of rent arrears, non-payment of mortgage instalments or nuisance can, in some circumstances, justify a finding of intentional homelessness, but there must be a full and proper investigation by the housing authority.[60] Sale of a property because of financial difficulties may, depending upon the facts, also give rise to intentional homelessness.[61]

A possession order does not automatically justify a finding of intentional homelessness and the housing authority must reach its own decision in respect of its duties under the Act.[62]

Choosing to have children cannot justify a finding of intentional homelessness.[63]

A local authority's decision that an applicant was intentionally homeless, because she left accommodation where her boyfriend, who was the father of her child, could not live, was quashed because the local authority had only considered whether she normally lived with him, and not whether it was reasonable for her to live with him.[64]

In consequence

The homelessness must be in consequence of the deliberate act or omission.

The housing authority may go back beyond the immediate cause of homelessness, provided that there is a nexus between the former act of intentionality and the present homelessness.[65]

57 Per Roch J in *R v London Borough of Hammersmith and Fulham ex parte Lusi* (1991) 23 HLR 260.
58 *R v North Devon District Council ex parte Lewis* [1981] 1 WLR 328; *R v Thurrock Borough Council ex parte Williams* (1981) 1 HLR 128.
59 *R v Portsmouth City Council ex parte Knight* (1983) 10 HLR 134 and *R v Hammersmith and Fulham London Borough Council ex parte O'Sullivan* [1991] EGCS 110.
60 *R v Wyre Borough Council ex parte Joyce* (1984) 11 HLR 72; *R v London Borough of Hillingdon ex parte Tinn* (1988) 20 HLR 305; *R v London Borough of Barnet ex parte O'Connor* (1990) 22 HLR 486.
61 *R v Leeds City Council ex parte Adamiec* (1991) 24 HLR 138.
62 *R v Swansea City Council ex parte John* (1982) 9 HLR 56.
63 *R v Eastleigh Borough Council ex parte Beattie (No 1)* (1983) 10 HLR 137.
64 *R v Peterborough City Council ex parte Carr* (1990) 22 HLR 206.
65 *Dyson v Kerrier District Council* [1980] 1 WLR 1205.

The housing authority should not go back to the original cause of homelessness if the chain of causation has been broken.[66]

A housing authority may look back at an initial cause of homelessness unless there has been a break or a period in settled accommodation.[67]

It is not open to an applicant to make repeated applications under the Act without a change of circumstances, but where there are facts which could lead an authority to regard the original intentional homelessness as no longer the operative cause of the homelessness, the authority is required to reconsider the situation.[68]

Ceases to occupy

A failure to take up an offer of housing in which the applicant has never lived cannot qualify as intentional homelessness.[69] An offer of housing may, however, qualify as a sufficient discharge of the authority's duties (see page 279). Failure to take up an offer to renew a tenancy may justify a finding of intentionality.[70]

Accommodation available for occupation

If the applicant leaves accommodation which was available only to the applicant and not to the persons with whom s/he might reasonably be expected by the authority to reside, there cannot be a finding of intentional homelessness.[71] Accommodation will not be available if it is uninhabitable due to vandalism or other cause.[72] An applicant will not be found to be intentionally homeless if his or her home is sold under a separation agreement because s/he is cohabiting.[73]

In *R v Tower Hamlets London Borough Council ex parte Rouf*,[74] a decision that a Bangladeshi man, who had lived in Britain for 15 years, was intentionally homeless because he had left accommodation where he had stayed temporarily in Bangladesh when he had gone to collect his family was quashed. The interviewing officer had failed to consider the two crucial questions involved – was the accommodation still available for his use, and if it was, was it reasonable for him to continue in occupation?

66   *R v Basingstoke and Deane Borough Council ex parte Bassett* (1983) 10 HLR 125.
67   *Din v Wandsworth London Borough Council* [1983] 1 AC 657.
68   *R v South Herefordshire District Council ex parte Miles* (1983) 17 HLR 82.
69   *R v Westminster City Council ex parte Chambers* (1982) 81 LGR 401.
70   *R v Christchurch Borough Council ex parte Conway* (1987) 19 HLR 238.
71   *Re Islam* [1983] 1 AC 688.
72   *City of Gloucester v Miles* (1985) 17 HLR 292.
73   *R v Wimbourne District Council ex parte Curtis* (1985) 18 HLR 79.
74   (1989) 21 HLR 294.

Reasonable to continue to occupy

A battered wife who has deliberately left home should not be expected to return there: she will not normally be deemed intentionally homeless.[75]

A woman might be found intentionally homeless if she refuses to return home where there has been no violence or threats of violence before she left, but the local authority must investigate the circumstances of each case and ought not to insist that every woman who has left the matrimonial home should return there, nor that she should apply to the court for an injunction.[76]

In *R v London Borough of Croydon ex parte Toth*,[77] the applicant was found intentionally homeless despite threats of violence from a man who claimed that he was owed money by her husband. However in *R v Broxbourne Borough Council ex parte Willmoth*,[78] a decision that a woman was not homeless was quashed because the authority had failed to make sufficient enquiries about whether it was reasonable for her to continue to live with her ex-partner from whom she feared violence. In *R v Tynedale District Council ex parte McCabe*[79] a finding that a woman who had left the matrimonial home on account of her husband's violence had 'by abandoning [the] tenancy . . . made [herself] intentionally homeless . . . [and that the] tenancy [was] still available to [her]' was quashed. She could not be intentionally homeless if the tenancy was still available to her. Alternatively if the council accepted that she was homeless because it was not reasonable to occupy the premises, she could not be intentionally homeless. In *R v Northampton Borough Council ex parte Clarkson*,[80] a finding of intentional homelessness where a woman had left accommodation in which her brother was 'pressing his sexual attentions' on her was quashed.

The housing authority cannot rely solely on the provisions of s60(4) but must also investigate other circumstances which have motivated the applicant to leave, such as employment prospects.[81]

It is not reasonable for a lessee to continue to occupy premises where s/he had obtained the lease by a deception which the landlord had discovered. The housing authority should look back at the circumstances prior to the applicant obtaining that accommodation.[82]

---

75   Code para 7.11(b).
76   *R v London Borough of Wandsworth ex parte Nimako-Boateng* (1984) 11 HLR 95.
77   (1984) 18 HLR 493.
78   (1989) 22 HLR 118.
79   (1991) 24 HLLR 384.
80   (1992) 24 HLR 529.
81   *R v Hammersmith and Fulham London Borough Council ex parte Duro-Rama* (1983) 81 LGR 702.
82   *R v Exeter City Council ex parte Glidden and Draper* (1984) 14 HLR 103.

Overcrowding in law (Housing Act 1985 Pt X) may mean that it is not reasonable to continue to occupy accommodation.[83]

It is not reasonable for a family of seven to continue to occupy one room,[84] nor for a family to live in one cabin on a boat with no bath, shower, wc, sink or hot water[85] or for a family of five to live in two small rooms.[86] However, it may be considered reasonable for a family to remain in accommodation in an appalling state of repair.[87]

Good faith

Ignorance of the applicant's legal rights can prevent a finding of intentional homelessness (for example, leaving accommodation on receipt of notice to quit) if the applicant acted in good faith.[88] So can ignorance of other matters, for instance the adequacy of the accommodation available to the applicant.[89] However, an error in law, based on legal advice, will not constitute a 'good faith omission'.[90]

Members of the same household

Where one member of the household could properly be found to be intentionally homeless, the housing authority may have a duty to another member of that household, if that member applies for accommodation and can show that s/he did not acquiesce or collude in the behaviour which caused the intentional homelessness.[91] Even if another member of the household has acquiesced, s/he will not be intentionally homeless if s/he was unaware of a relevant fact.[92] There have, however, been cases where the courts have refused to quash decisions that one spouse acquiesced in the act or omission of the other spouse.[93]

Where parents have been found intentionally homeless, it is not

83   *R v Eastleigh Borough Council ex parte Beattie (No 1)* (1983) 10 HLR 137.
84   *R v Westminster City Council ex parte Ali* (1984) 11 HLR 72.
85   *R v Preseli District Council ex parte Fisher* (1984) 17 HLR 147.
86   *R v London Borough of Tower Hamlets ex parte Ojo* (1991) 23 HLR 488.
87   *R v Gravesham Borough Council ex parte Winchester* (1986) 18 HLR 207.
88   FA 1985 s60(3).
89   *R v London Borough of Wandsworth ex parte Rose* (1984) 11 HLR 107.
90   *R v Eastleigh Borough Council ex parte Beattie (No 2)* (1984) 17 HLR 168.
91   *R v North Devon District Council ex parte Lewis* [1981] 1 WLR 328; *R v Eastleigh Borough Council ex parte Beattie (No 2)* (1984) 17 HLR 168; *R v Ealing London Borough Council ex parte Sidhu* (1982) 80 LGR 534 and *R v Penwith District Council ex parte Trevena* (1984) 17 HLR 526.
92   *R v Mole Valley District Council ex parte Burton* (1988) 20 HLR 479.
93   For example, *R v Swansea City Council ex parte Thomas* (1983) *The Times*, 14 April 1983 (even though the 'acquiescing' partner was in prison at the time); *R v London Borough of Ealing ex parte Salmons* (1990) 23 HLR 272; *R v City of Westminster ex parte Khan* (1991) 23 HLR 230.

possible for children to make an application for housing to a local authority.[94]

Local connection

The local connection provisions of the Act[95] allow one authority to pass to another a housing duty, in the limited circumstances set out below.

A person may have a local connection with an area for one of the following reasons:[96]

- s/he is, or in the past was, normally resident in it and that residence was 'of choice'; or
- s/he is employed in it; or
- family associations; or
- any special circumstance.

Residence is not 'of choice' (for the purposes of the first reason) if it is as a consequence of:

a) service in the armed forces;[97] or
b) detention under an Act of Parliament, eg, in prison or as a compulsory in-patient.[98]

Employment does not count for the purposes of the second reason if it is employment in the armed forces.[99]

An authority can seek to avoid its full housing duty under s65(2) only on account of the local connection provisions: the provisions have no application to any other duty.[100] The provisions will apply only if:[101]

- neither the applicant nor any person who might reasonably be expected to reside with him or her, has a local connection with the area to which application has been made; and
- either the applicant, or a person who might reasonably be expected to reside with him or her, does have a local connection with the area of another authority; and
- neither the applicant, nor any person who might reasonably be expected to reside with him or her, runs the risk of domestic violence in that other authority's area.

94   *Garlick v Oldham MBC* [1993] 2 All ER 65.
95   HA 1985 ss61, 65(2) and 67.
96   HA 1985 s61(1).
97   HA 1985 s61(2)(b).
98   HA 1985 s61(3).
99   HA 1985 s61(2)(a).
100   HA 1985 s67(1).
101   HA 1985 s67(2) and (3).

If there is no local connection with the area of any other housing authority, the obligation remains with the authority to which the application is made,[102] but if the local connection provisions do apply, then the obligation may be passed to the other authority.[103]

The duty to provide accommodation under s68(2) is not a separate duty to that under s67(2). The notified authority will have discharged its duty under s67(2) if on an earlier application by the applicant an offer of accommodation had been unreasonably refused, there being no second incidence of unintentional homelessness.[104]

The provisions apply only if neither the applicant nor those who properly reside with him or her has a local connection with the housing authority. The housing authority cannot apply a 'greater local connection' test.

If there is a dispute between authorities, the interim housing obligation remains with the first authority.[105]

For the purposes of local connection, the risk of domestic violence is the risk of violence from any person with whom, but for the risk of violence, the applicant might reasonably be expected to reside, or from any person with whom the applicant formerly resided, or the risk of threats of violence from any such person who was likely to carry them out.[106] A person may be treated as homeless on account of the risk of domestic violence from a person living in accommodation which she would otherwise have some rights or entitlement to occupy.[107] However, for the purposes of local connection the risk of domestic violence in another part of the country is a risk not only from the person with whom she has hitherto resided, but also from any other person with whom she formerly resided.[108]

A desire on the part of the applicant not to return to an area with which s/he has a local connection does not amount to a special circumstance giving rise to a local connection with a different area.[109]

The exclusion of residence as a result of service in the armed forces refers to the time residence commenced. Holding over after the right to

---

102   R v Hillingdon London Borough Council ex parte Streeting [1980] 1 WLR 1425.
103   HA 1985 s68(2).
104   R v Hammersmith and Fulham London Borough Council ex parte O'Brian (1985)
      17 HLR 471.
105   HA 1985 s68(1).
106   HA 1985 s67(3).
107   HA 1985 s58(3).
108   HA 1985 s67(3).
109   R v London Borough of Islington ex parte Adigun (1986) 20 HLR 600.

occupy married quarters has come to an end does not normally establish a local connection.[110]

A short period of employment or residence will not usually give rise to a local connection.[111]

Local authorities' duties

Duty to make appropriate enquiries

Circumstances in which duty arises

A housing authority will be under a duty to make appropriate enquiries if:[112]

- a person applies to it for accommodation or for assistance in obtaining accommodation; and
- it has reason to believe that s/he may be homeless or threatened with homelessness.

Extent of duty

'Appropriate' enquiries are such enquiries as are necessary:[113]

- to satisfy the local authority as to whether the applicant is homeless or threatened with homelessness; and if the authority is so satisfied
- such further enquiries as may be necessary to satisfy it whether s/he has priority need of accommodation; and
- whether s/he has become homeless or threatened with homelessness intentionally.

Enquiries as to local connection

The authority may make enquiries as to whether or not the applicant has a local connection with the area of another local authority.[114]

Form of enquiries

Enquiries should be made in a sympathetic way.[115] An interpreter should be used if necessary.[116] Enquiries will normally be made into size of

---

110   *R v White Horse District Council ex parte Smith and Hay* (1984) 17 HLR 160.
111   *R v White Horse District Council ex parte Smith and Hay* (1984) 17 HLR 160.
112   HA 1985 s62(1).
113   HA 1985 s62(1) and (2).
114   HA 1985 s66(2).
115   Code para 4.4; *R v West Dorset District Council ex parte Phillips* (1984) 17 HLR 336.
116   *R v Surrey Heath Borough Council ex parte Li* (1984) 16 HLR 79.

household, last accommodation and reasons for leaving it, prospects of return, domestic violence, employment and illness.[117]

Enquiries should cover matters referred to in s59, ie, priority need for accommodation.[118] Medical opinion should be considered since vulnerability may be claimed for medical reasons.[119]

The enquiries need not be 'CID type' enquiries[120] but they must be thorough.[121] An authority acts reasonably if it acts on the material put before it by the applicant.[122] Thus the adviser must ensure that the correct material is presented to the housing authority.

The enquiries must be full and proper enquiries and must be completed *before* the housing authority makes a decision.[123] The burden is on the housing authority to make appropriate enquiries as to whether or not it was reasonable to continue to occupy the accommodation.[124] For an example of a case where a housing authority decision was quashed because of failure to make sufficient enquiries, see *R v Broxbourne Borough Council ex parte Willmoth*.[125] In 'the great majority' of cases these inquiries will not be complete if the homeless person is not interviewed by the authority.[126]

Advisers can speed up these enquiries after having taken instructions by telephoning the housing authority and following up the telephone call with a detailed letter, setting out the applicant's position. A sympathetic adviser will often be able to elicit information from an applicant which might not be forthcoming in the often intimidating surroundings of a housing department. Once instructed, the adviser should try to attend, or arrange for someone else to attend, any further interviews and to take notes. Advisers should also keep written notes of telephone conversations.

If the applicant has left the accommodation against the advice of the housing authority, the authority is still under a duty to make enquiries as to whether or not s/he might have been able to stay on.[127]

Where necessary, the housing authority must look back to enquire how

---

117   Code para 4.7.
118   *R v Ryedale District Council ex parte Smith* (1983) 16 HLR 66.
119   *R v London Borough of Lambeth ex parte Carroll* (1988) 20 HLR 142.
120   *Lally v Royal Borough of Kensington and Chelsea* (1980) *The Times*, 27 March 1980.
121   *R v Dacorum Borough Council ex parte Brown* (1989) 21 HLR 405.
122   *Miller v Wandsworth London Borough Council* (1980) *The Times*, 19 March 1980.
123   *R v Woodspring District Council ex parte Walters* (1984) 16 HLR 73.
124   *R v Reigate and Banstead Borough Council ex parte Paris* (1984) 17 HLR 103.
125   (1989) 22 HLR 118; cf *R v Royal Borough of Kensington and Chelsea ex parte Bayani* (1990) 22 HLR 406.
126   *R v Sevenoaks District Council ex parte Reynolds* (1989) 22 HLR 250.
127   *R v Penwith District Council ex parte Hughes* August 1980 *LAG Bulletin* 187.

it came about that the applicant had ceased to occupy available and reasonable accommodation, even if this means going back several years.[128]

If the authority has not received new information, it is still entitled to reopen its enquiries when the decision has been adverse to the applicant.[129]

Duty to provide temporary accommodation while making enquiries

If the authority has reason to believe that the applicant may be homeless and in priority need, it must secure that accommodation is available for his or her occupation while making its enquiries.[130] The duty extends to the applicant and any person who might reasonably be expected to reside with him or her.[131]

A low standard of belief is all that is necessary to establish the duty, which exists irrespective of any question of a local connection.[132] If the local authority refuses temporary accommodation, the decision should be challenged as quickly as possible.[133]

The authority may require a person housed under this provision to pay such reasonable charges as it may determine for the accommodation,[134] which should be of a reasonable quality although it need not be of quite as high a standard as permanent accommodation.[135]

If, as a result of its enquiries, the housing authority is satisfied that the applicant is homeless, has a priority need, but became homeless intentionally, it has a duty to secure that accommodation is made available for the applicant's occupation for such period as it considers will give the applicant a reasonable opportunity to secure permanent accommodation.[136] There is no definition of or guidance on what is 'a reasonable opportunity'. It has been held that 14 days was wholly inadequate for a couple with one child in the London area: they would need at least three or four months.[137]

---

128 *R v Preseli District Council ex parte Fisher* (1984) 17 HLR 147.
129 *R v Hambleton District Council ex parte Geoghan* [1985] JPL 394.
130 HA 1985 s63(1).
131 HA 1985 s75.
132 HA 1985 s63(2).
133 *R v Rochester City Council ex parte Trotman* (1983) *The Times*, 9 May 1983.
134 HA 1985 s69(2).
135 *R v Exeter City Council ex parte Glidden and Draper* (1984) 14 HLR 103.
136 HA 1985 s65(3).
137 *Lally v Royal Borough of Kensington and Chelsea* (1980) *The Times*, 27 March 1980.

Duty to provide permanent housing

If the authority is satisfied that the applicant is threatened with homelessness, is in priority need, and is not threatened with homelessness intentionally, it has a duty to secure that accommodation does not cease to be available for the applicant,[138] ie, the authority must make arrangements to secure accommodation from when the homelessness actually occurs or must act to prevent the homelessness arising.

If the authority is satisfied that the applicant is homeless, is in priority need and is not intentionally homeless, its duty, subject to the local connection provision, is to secure that accommodation becomes available for the applicant and any person who might reasonably be expected to reside with him or her.[139]

There is no right to be given a permanent home immediately if none is available. The authority may discharge its duty by providing a series of temporary units until a permanent home is found.[140] However, the duty is to provide long-term accommodation even if the original accommodation of the applicant was of a temporary nature.[141]

The authority may discharge its duty by providing accommodation from its own stock, or by securing that the applicant obtains accommodation from some other person, or by giving him or her such advice and assistance as will secure that s/he obtains accommodation from some other person.[142]

The accommodation secured must be suitable for the applicant in terms of house, nature of area and employment prospects, and possibly also the wishes of the applicant if the accommodation offered is in an area distant from his or her local connections, although the accommodation need not be in the authority's own area.[143] 'Suitability' has to be assessed in the light of the personal circumstances of the applicant and his or her household. In *R v London Borough of Brent ex parte Omar*[144] a decision to offer a Somali refugee, who had fled from torture and imprisonment, a basement flat infested with cockroaches in a block where the corridors reeked of urine and which reminded her of prison was quashed.

If the accommodation offered to the applicant is unsuitable, it may be possible to challenge the offer on the grounds either of failure to have regard to the Code of Guidance and to the reasonable needs of the

138   HA 1985 s66(2).
139   HA 1985 s65(2).
140   *R v Bristol Corporation ex parte Hendy* [1974] 1 WLR 498.
141   *R v London Borough of Camden ex parte Wait* (1986) 18 HLR 434.
142   HA 1985 s69(1).
143   *R v Wyre Borough Council ex parte Parr* (1982) 2 HLR 71.
144   (1991) 23 HLR 446.

applicant, or that the accommodation is substandard having regard to housing and public health legislation.[145]

An offer of permanent accommodation should be rejected only after expert advice, since if the housing authority can show that it has discharged its duties by making a single reasonable offer, no further offer will be made.[146] However, the housing authority's duty will be revived by a material change in the applicant's circumstances which makes the accommodation previously offered clearly unsuitable, eg, the birth of another child.[147]

The offer should remain open to the applicant for a reasonable time.[148] The question of suitability of accommodation can be challenged only by judicial review.[149]

Duty to provide advice and appropriate assistance

If the authority is satisfied that the applicant is homeless or threatened with homelessness, but is not in priority need, then its duty is to provide no more than advice and appropriate assistance in order to assist him or her to secure that accommodation becomes available for his or her occupation.[150] A list of housing associations or accommodation agencies may be sufficient to discharge this duty. Local authorities have a duty to ensure that accommodation provided by landlords whose names appear in such lists meets basic standards of safety.[151]

If the authority is satisfied that the applicant is homeless, or threatened with homelessness, and is in priority need, but has become homeless intentionally, it is still under a duty to provide advice and assistance.[152] Further, it is obliged to secure that accommodation is made available for the applicant's occupation for such period as it considers will provide the applicant with a reasonable opportunity to find somewhere for him or herself.[153] This should not be a fixed period for all applicants,

145 *R v Ryedale District Council ex parte Smith* (1983) 16 HLR 66; *R v Exeter City Council ex parte Glidden and Draper* (1984) 14 HLR 103.
146 *R v Westminster City Council ex parte Chambers* (1982) 81 LGR 401.
147 *R v Ealing London Borough Council ex parte McBain* [1985] 1 WLR 1351.
148 *R v London Borough of Wandsworth ex parte Lindsay* (1986) 18 HLR 502.
149 *R v Westminster City Council ex parte Tansey* (1988) 20 HLR 520.
150 HA 1985 ss65(4) and 66(3).
151 *Ephraim v Newham London Borough Council* (1992) *The Times*, 24 January 1992.
152 HA 1985 ss65(3)(b) and 66(3)(b).
153 HA 1985 s65(3)(a).

but a period determined in each case having regard to the applicant's own circumstances and local housing availability.[154]

Duty to protect property of homeless persons

The HA 1985 makes provision for local authorities who have housing duties under the Act to take steps to protect the property of homeless persons.[155] These provisions are of great practical importance to the homeless and should not be ignored.

A duty is owed to any person to whom the authority has become subject to a housing duty.[156]

The duty arises when the authority has reason to believe that there is a danger of loss of, or damage to, personal property, by reason of the person's inability to deal with it, and that no suitable arrangements have been, or are being, made to protect it.[157] This duty does not extend to property used in connection with a business unless the business is conducted at the relevant accommodation.[158] Examples of when this duty would arise are when the person is physically or mentally ill, personally inadequate or unable to afford commercial storage charges.

The duty continues after the authority has ceased to be under the relevant housing duty.[159]

The duty is to take reasonable steps to prevent the loss of, or to prevent or mitigate damage to, such property.[160]

The duty is accompanied by a power to enter, at all reasonable times, any premises which are the usual or last usual place of residence of the person in question, and to deal with any such property in any way which is reasonably necessary.[161] This means that if property has been retained by a landlord, spouse, or cohabitant, the housing authority has power to enter private premises to recover it. The authority is expressly empowered to store the property, or to arrange for its storage.[162]

The duty ends when the authority is of the opinion that there is no

---

154   *Lally v Royal Borough of Kensington and Chelsea* (1980) *The Times*, 27 March 1980.
155   HA 1985 s70.
156   HA 1985 s70(1) and (2).
157   HA 1985 s70(1).
158   *R v Chiltern District Council ex parte Roberts* (1990) 23 HLR 387 – fairground equipment used by travelling showmen.
159   HA 1985 s70(2).
160   HA 1985 s70(1).
161   HA 1985 s70(3)(a) and (b).
162   HA 1985 s70(3)(b).

longer any reason to believe that there is a danger of loss of, or damage to, property by reason of inability to protect or deal with it.[163]

The authority also has the power to protect property in some circumstances even where it does not owe one of the specified housing duties.[164]

Duty to notify applicant of decision

Once enquiries are completed, the housing authority must notify the applicant of its decision, and of the reasons for the decision if the decision is anything other than an acceptance of a full duty to house under ss65(2) and 66(2).[165]

There is an express statutory requirement for the notification to be in writing.[166] The full reasons should be given[167] and the notification should be made as soon as possible. It is good practice for an authority to notify an applicant of its decision within three working days of the completion of enquiries.[168]

The authority cannot defer a decision in the expectation that circumstances may change.[169]

Enforcement

Action for breach of statutory duty

Generally challenges to local authority decisions under HA 1985 Pt III are brought by means of an application for judicial review. However, an action for breach of statutory duty may be brought against the housing authority where the authority has carried out its duties under the Act and reached a decision which entitles the applicant to assistance under the Act but the applicant has been denied that assistance. However, suitability of accommodation may be challenged only by judicial review.[170]

---

163   HA 1985 s70(5).
164   HA 1985 s70(2).
165   HA 1985 s64.
166   HA 1985 s64(5).
167   *City of Gloucester v Miles* (1985) 17 HLR 292.
168   Code para 9.3.
169   *R v Ealing London Borough Council ex parte Sidhu* (1982) 80 LGR 534.
170   See *R v Westminster City Council ex parte Tansey* (1986) 20 HLR 520; *Tower Hamlets London Borough Council v Ali* (1992) *Independent*, 10 April 1992.

A claim for breach of statutory duty may be made in the county court (or High Court if damages claimed are in excess of £25,000).[171]

An attempt should be made to obtain an undertaking from the housing authority to house the applicant pending the hearing of the claim. If no undertaking is obtained, an interlocutory application may be made for a mandatory injunction to direct the housing authority to rehouse the applicant pending a full hearing.[172] The application should be made on notice and supported by an affidavit in support of the application.[173] A minimum of two days' notice is required.[174]

The balance of convenience test for interlocutory injunctions has been held not to apply because an undertaking in damages would be meaningless and a strong prima facie case must accordingly be shown in order to obtain an interlocutory injunction.[175] (See page 186 for procedure in the county court in respect of an application for an interlocutory injunction.)

Judicial review

Circumstances in which an application should be made

Unless an action for breach of statutory duty (above) will lie, enforcement must be by way of an application for judicial review to the High Court.[176] A decision can be impeached only on the principles of public or administrative law, eg, the authority has not acted fairly, or has failed to take something relevant into account or had regard to an irrelevance, has misunderstood or misapplied the law, or has reached a decision which no reasonable authority could have reached.[177] Judicial review should not be used to monitor the actions of local authorities save in exceptional circumstances where local authorities have not behaved in a reasonable or lawful manner.[178]

For further examples of these principles see Hunter and McGrath, *Homeless Persons* 4th ed., LAG, 1992.

If the application is successful, the appropriate order will normally be certiorari, quashing the existing erroneous decision, and remitting the

171   *Thornton v Kirklees Metropolitan Borough Council* [1979] QB 626; *Cocks v Thanet District Council* [1983] 2 AC 286.
172   CCR Ord 13 r6(1).
173   CCR Ord 13 r6(3).
174   CCR Ord 13 r1(2).
175   *De Falco v Crawley Borough Council* [1980] QB 460.
176   Supreme Court Act 1981 s31.
177   *Associated Provincial Picture Houses Ltd v Wednesbury Corporation* [1948] 1 KB 223.
178   *R v Hillingdon London Borough Council ex parte Puhlhofer* [1986] AC 484.

matter back to the authority to approach anew, in the light of the court's decision.[179]

The application should be made as soon as possible and must in any event be made within three months of the authority's decision.[180] If the application is made outside the time limit, the court has a discretion to 'excuse' the delay, but this is a tightly exercised discretion. The court will require sound reasons before it will extend the three-month limit.[181] Delay in obtaining legal aid may be a ground for granting leave out of time.[182]

Procedure

The first hurdle is to obtain legal aid. There can be a tendency on the part of the Legal Aid Board to limit the initial grant of legal aid to obtaining counsel's opinion. This can be a problem where, as in most homelessness cases, there is a need for urgent action. In those circumstances it is sensible to try to persuade the Legal Aid Board to make the initial grant of legal aid limited to making an application for leave to apply for judicial review and, if successful, limited to all stages up to the filing of the respondent's evidence and thereafter obtaining counsel's opinion. It may be argued that making a table application for leave (see note 186) does not involve much more work than obtaining counsel's opinion, and that the best indication of whether a case has a reasonable prospect of success is whether the application for leave is granted or refused.

Leave of the court must be obtained before an application can be made.[183] Leave should be granted if, on the material then available, the court thinks, without going into the matter in depth, that there is an arguable case for granting the relief claimed by the applicant.[184]

An application for leave must be made *ex parte* to a judge by filing in the Crown Office:[185]

a) a notice in prescribed form 86A containing a statement of:
   - the name and description of the applicant;
   - the relief sought and the grounds upon which it is sought;
   - the name and address of the applicant's solicitors;
   - the applicant's address for service; and

---

179 RSC Ord 53 r1.
180 RSC Ord 53 r4.
181 *R v Carter ex parte Lipson* (1984) *The Times*, 1 December 1984.
182 *R v Stratford-on-Avon District Council ex parte Jackson* [1985] 2 WLR 1319.
183 RSC Ord 53 r3(1).
184 *R v Inland Revenue Commissioners ex parte National Federation of Self Employed and Small Businesses Ltd* [1982] AC 617.
185 RSC Ord 53 r3(2).

b) an affidavit which verifies the facts relied on.

Advisers must satisfy themselves that they are fully aware of all the facts to be disclosed, especially if the applicant speaks poor English.[186]

The judge may determine the application for leave without a hearing.[187] If a hearing is required, eg, because the matter is complex even on the papers, or because interlocutory relief is sought, it should be requested in the notice of application.

If an application is refused without a hearing, then a hearing may be sought as if it were an appeal.[188] The application for leave must be renewed within 10 days of being served with a notice of the judge's refusal by lodging, in the Crown Office, notice of intention in form 86B.[189]

A request should be made to the housing authority for it to give an undertaking to house pending the hearing if leave is granted. If the request is refused, an application for an interlocutory injunction should be made at the same time as the application for leave. A hearing should be requested and the housing authority notified of the application and copies of form 86A and the affidavit served on it.[190] A strong prima facie case must be shown in order to obtain an interlocutory injunction;[191] it is not necessary to show that the case is exceptional.[192]

Where leave has been granted, the application is made by originating motion.[193] The notice of motion must be entered for hearing within 14 days after the grant of leave. A copy of the statement in support of the application for leave must be served with the notice of motion.[194] The statement should set out the grounds for challenge in as much detail as possible.

It is important to remember that the supporting affidavit must verify the facts relied on. If there has been delay between notification of decision and the application, this delay should be explained in the affidavit.

---

186   *R v Secretary of State for the Home Department ex parte Mannan* (1984) *The Times*, 29 March 1984.
187   RSC Ord 53 r3 – a 'table application'.
188   RSC Ord 53 r3(4).
189   RSC Ord 53 r3(5).
190   RSC Ord 53 r5(10)(b).
191   *De Falco v Crawley Borough Council* [1980] QB 460; see page 282.
192   *Hammell v Royal Borough of Kensington and Chelsea* (1988) 20 HLR 666.
193   RSC Ord 53 r5(1).
194   RSC Ord 53 r6(1).

Part III

Precedents

Debt emergencies

Precedents for chapter 3: civil and consumer credit debts

1 Letter to creditor requesting a copy of an agreement and information about the sums outstanding

Oneshark Credit Ltd
Gangland Road
Anytown

Dear Madam/Sir

Account No
Sarah Piercy, 15a Anytown Road, Anytown

I enclose a postal order for 50p and I am writing to request a copy of the agreement relating to the above account under which you are now claiming the sum of £200.85 together with the information I am entitled to under section 77/78/79 [see note] of the Consumer Credit Act 1974.

Yours faithfully

Note
Amend to cite the relevant section. A different section of the Act applies according to the kind of credit agreement:

Fixed-sum credit agreement, ie, a loan for a fixed amount from a bank or a credit company. The request should be made under s77.

Running-account credit agreement, ie, bank overdrafts or credit cards where the amount owing can go up as well as down. The request should be made under s78.

Hire agreement. The request should be made under s79.

2   *Application by debtor for a time order*

IN THE ANYTOWN COUNTY COURT   Case No

IN THE MATTER OF THE CONSUMER CREDIT ACT 1974

AND IN THE MATTER OF A REGULATED AGREEMENT DATED
25 AUGUST 1992 AND MADE BETWEEN THE PARTIES HERETO

Between	SARAH PIERCY	Applicant
and	ONESHARK CREDIT LIMITED	Respondents

ORIGINATING APPLICATION

SARAH PIERCY of 15a Anytown Road, Anytown, applies to the court
for an order in the following terms:

That the instalments under the agreement, a copy of which is attached
hereto, shall be reduced to the sum of £40 per month, the first such
payment to be due one month from the date of the court order and that the
term of the agreement be extended for such period necessary to allow the
principal sum and interest to be discharged by these revised instalments.

The grounds on which the applicant claims to be entitled to the order are:

1   The agreement which is attached to the application is a regulated
agreement within the meaning of the Consumer Credit Act 1974, section
8.

2   The agreement was signed by the applicant at the offices of the
respondents at [insert address].

3   The applicant admits that £1,785 is due under the agreement and
that there are arrears of £165 outstanding under the said agreement.

4   That a default notice was served on the applicant by the respondents
on 4th November 1992.

5   That the court has power to make such an order under the provisions
of the Consumer Credit Act 1974, section 129(2)(a).

6   That it is just and reasonable to make such an order having regard to
the means of the applicant which are set out on the attached statement of
income and expenditure.

The name and address of the person upon whom it is intended to serve this
application is:

Oneshark Credit Limited
[address]

The applicant's address for service is 15a Anytown Street, Anytown.

Dated 24 November 1992

Applicant [Signature]

Notes

There is a court fee of £40 payable for an originating application. An application can be made to the court for this fee to be waived. This should be done in writing, explaining why the applicant cannot afford the fee.

The requirements for the information to be included in the originating application are stated in the County Court Rules Ord 49 r4(5). If the agreement itself is not to be attached to the originating application then the date of the agreement and the parties to it with the number of the agreement or sufficient particulars to enable the respondents to identify the agreement must be given. It is essential to include the total balance admitted to be due and the amount of any arrears if known.

The application should be filed in duplicate together with a form of request for the issue of an originating application. Form N203 (form of request for a fixed date summons) can be adapted for this purpose.

3 Affidavit in support of an application for an expedited hearing to obtain a time order

IN THE ANYTOWN COURT   Case No

1. Plaintiff
2. S. Piercy
3. 1st
4. 24 November 1992
5. 24 November 1992

BETWEEN   SARAH PIERCY   Applicant
and   ONESHARK CREDIT LIMITED   Respondents

AFFIDAVIT

I, Sarah Piercy of 15a Anytown Road, Anytown, MAKE OATH AND SAY AS FOLLOWS:

1   I am the applicant in this case and I make this affidavit in support of my application for an expedited hearing of my claim for a time order.

2   I have now produced to me and marked 'SP1' a copy of a conditional sale agreement dated 25 August 1992 between myself and the respondents relating to a Ford Fiesta motor car registration No. F 251 YAX.

3   It can be seen that I purchased the car at the price of £2,000 second-

hand and paid a deposit of £300 receiving the remainder of the sum required on a credit agreement from the respondents. The agreement provides that I should pay the sum of £55 per month over a period of 3 years.

4   I am married with 2 children aged 8 and 11. At the time I signed the agreement, I was working as a school cook earning the sum of £62 per week take home and my husband was working as a station attendant earning the sum of £138 per week take home. I also received £17.45 per week child benefit.

5   I now have produced to me and marked 'SP2' a copy of an income and expenditure statement showing our current income. It can be seen that although my earnings are continuing my husband no longer receives wages but is receiving unemployment benefit. My husband was made redundant from his job at the beginning of October 1992. As a result, my husband's income has dropped from £138 per week to £41.40 per week unemployment benefit.

6   My application for a time order is to reduce the sums payable under the agreement from £55 per month to £40 per month. The income and expenditure sheet attached shows how payment of this sum would allow us to manage our finances and discharge all our essential expenses.

7   When my husband lost his job, he received a redundancy payment of £320 which was used to discharge part of the bills due to Anytown Water plc and to the Anytown Borough Council for our community charge bills. It took 4 weeks for my husband's unemployment benefit to be sorted out during which time we had to survive on my earnings and child benefit. We then received a back payment of unemployment benefit which had to be used to pay the remainder of the community charge bills.

8   As a result of the immediate financial difficulties we faced when my husband was made redundant, we did not manage to pay anything towards the cost of the agreement with the respondents in the months of September and October and on 4 November, the respondents served me with a default notice under the terms of the agreement. I now have this notice produced to me and marked 'SP3'. In addition, the respondents sent me a letter which I now have produced to me and marked 'SP4'. This states clearly that if the arrears on the agreement, then £110, were not brought up to date within 14 days, ther respondents would retrieve the car.

9   I sought advice about the letter and the default notice from the local Citizens Advice Bureau and spoke to the respondents from CAB offices. I asked the respondents to accept the sum of £40 per month instead of £55

per month towards the cost of the credit and to extend the term of the agreement. I spoke to a Mrs Thomas on behalf of the respondents who confirmed that the respondents would take no action to retrieve the car if I wrote in making a request formally to reduce the payments to £40 per month and to extend the term of the agreement and also sent an income and expenditure sheet. Mrs Thomas promised that the respondents would then consider my request. I now have produced to me and marked 'SP5' a copy of the letter that I then wrote.

10   On 22 November, I received a letter from the respondents which I now have produced to me and marked 'SP6'. This states quite clearly that they will not accept a reduced payment nor extend the terms of the agreement and that they have arranged to recover the car in the week commencing Monday 30 November 1992 unless I have paid off the arrears in full by then. When I received this letter from the respondents dated 22 November earlier today, I telephoned the respondents again and said that I would be making an application for a time order. I requested confirmation that the respondents would not recover the car until such time as a court had had an opportunity to consider this application. This request was refused.

11   The car is essential to myself and my family. My mother, who is suffering from cancer and terminally ill, is highly dependent upon me. She lives close to where I work at Anyvillage County Primary School which is 7 miles from Anytown. My children attend the Roman Catholic Primary School in Longtown some 8 miles outside Anytown. Every morning, I need the car to take the children to school and I then drive on to give my mother breakfast. I then go to work to cook the school lunches and after I have finished working at the school, I go back to my mother's and usually cook something for her tea. I then have to drive some 15 miles to the opposite side of Anytown to collect my children from school and take them home. This journey would be impossible without a car. The amount of time available is simply insufficient to get the children to school in one direction and to get to see my mother and to get myself to work in the other direction. The car is therefore essential for my livelihood and without it I could not maintain the contact that my mother needs, could not continue my employment and would have to move my children's school.

12   Unless a time order is made, I will not be able to afford to maintain the car and the respondents will have a right to retrieve it. In the circumstances, and given the fact that the respondents have refused to confirm they will not remove the car in the week commencing 30 November pending the hearing of this application, I submit to the court

that it is appropriate for the hearing of the application for a time order to be expedited. I am therefore applying for a hearing of my application to take place within the next few days.

SWORN BY ME etc.

4   *Particulars of claim seeking an injunction to prevent goods being removed from private premises without a court order*

IN THE ANYTOWN COUNTY COURT   Case No

Between	CLARE ALEXANDER	Plaintiff
and	ONESHARK CREDIT LIMITED	Defendants

PARTICULARS OF CLAIM

1   Under a conditional sale agreement made between the plaintiff and the defendants on 5 June 1992, which is a regulated agreement under the Consumer Credit Act 1974, the defendants provided a Ford Fiesta motor car registration number J 681 BEC to the plaintiff upon the terms set out in that agreement.

2   The plaintiff is in arrears under the terms of the said agreement in the sum of £285.

3   By letter dated 1 December 1992, the defendants informed the plaintiff that persons acting on their behalf would attend her home on 15 December 1992 if she had not cleared the said arrears arising under the said agreement in full and stated that those persons were entitled to enter the garden and garage of her home to remove the said car whether or not she was present and whether or not she gave permission for them to do so.

4   By letter dated 3 December 1992, the plaintiff's advisers, Anytown Citizens Advice Bureau, required the defendants to confirm within a period of 24 hours that no one acting on their behalf would enter the plaintiff's premises and retake the said motor car without a court order.

5   The defendants failed to respond to the request and on 5 December 1992 Angela Smith of the Anytown Citizens Advice Bureau spoke to an unnamed employee of the defendants who confirmed that the defendants considered they had a legal right to enter the premises occupied by the plaintiff by force if necessary in order to retake the said motor car.

6   By a further letter dated 5 December 1992 the plaintiff confirmed to the defendants that they had no permission whatsoever from her to enter her premises for the purposes of retaking the said motor car and stated that unless confirmation was received from the defendants that they

acknowledged that they had no legal right to enter her premises, she would apply for an order from this court forbidding the defendants, their servants or agents from entering the premises.

7   On 8 December 1992, an unnamed servant or agent of the defendants attended the premises of the plaintiff at 12 Anytown Street, Anytown, entered the garden of the plaintiff's home without permission and knocked on the plaintiff's front door. When the plaintiff refused to answer the door, the said servant or agent left the front garden and stood in the highway immediately outside shouting abuse at the plaintiff, stating that he would be returning with the necessary tools to break open the plaintiff's garage and remove the said car and shouting that he wanted his money.

8   In the light of the foregoing, the defendants have indicated an intention to breach their statutory duty under the provisions of section 92 of the Consumer Credit Act 1974. Further, the defendants have indicated an intention to trespass on the premises belonging to the plaintiff.

9   Further the defendants have, by their servant or agent, committed a nuisance by shouting abuse and making threats from the highway.

And the plaintiff claims:

1   An order that the defendants (whether by themselves or by instructing or encouraging any other person) be forbidden from entering the premises at 12 Anytown Street, Anytown, or the garden or garage of those premises except under the authority of a court order.

2   Damages limited to £300 for nuisance and trespass including aggravated and exemplary damages.

3   Costs.

Dated 8 December 1992.

5   Affidavit in support of an application for injunction to restrain entry

IN THE ANYTOWN COUNTY COURT   Case No

1. Plaintiff
2. C Alexander
3. 1st
4. 8 December 1992
5. 8 December 1992

Between	CLARE ALEXANDER	Plaintiff
and	ONESHARK CREDIT LIMITED	Defendants

AFFIDAVIT

I Clare Alexander of 12 Anytown Street, Anytown, MAKE OATH AND SAY AS FOLLOWS:

1   I am the plaintiff in this action.

2   I make this affidavit in support of my application for an injunction against the defendants restraining them from entering my home or the garden or garage of my home in order to recover from me a Ford Fiesta motor car registration No. J 681 BEC which was provided to me under the terms of a regulated agreement under the Consumer Credit Act 1974. I now have produced to me and marked 'CA1' a copy of the agreement.

3   I confirm that I am £285 in arrears in payments under the terms of the agreement. I now have produced to me and marked 'CA2' a statement of my income and expenditure showing the financial difficulties that I am presently in. I have done my best to make payment under the agreement.

4   I now have produced to me and marked 'CA3' a copy of the letter of 1 December 1992 written by the defendants to me which states that they have a right of entry to my home for the purposes of recovering the car including a right of access to my garage and that they would obtain entry by force if necessary even if I was not present.

5   I confirm that on 3 December 1992 I was present when a Mrs Angela Smith from the Anytown Citizens Advice Bureau spoke on the telephone to a person employed by the defendants and requested confirmation within a period of 24 hours that the defendants would not enter my premises for the purposes of retaking the motor car without a court order.

6   I am advised by Mrs Smith and truly believe that the agent of the defendants to whom she spoke refused to comply with her request and indeed confirmed that as far as the defendants were concerned they had a right of entry to my premises and would enter the premises whether or not I was there to retake the car.

7   I now have produced to me and marked 'CA4' a letter dated 3 December 1992 written by Anytown Citizens Advice Bureau to the defendants seeking confirmation that they would not seek to gain entry to the premises without my consent.

8   I was also present on 5 December 1992 when Angela Smith of the Anytown Citizens Advice Bureau again spoke to an unnamed employee of the defendants who again refused to provide the confirmation that we were seeking that they would not gain access to my premises without my

permission. They confirmed that they would gain access without my permission and retake the car.

9   I now have produced to me and marked 'CA5' a copy of the letter I wrote on 5 December 1992 confirming that I would be applying for an injunction unless I received the required confirmation.

10   On 8 December 1992 I can confirm that a person who stated that he was from the defendants attended my premises. He knocked on the door and when I refused to answer it started shouting. He carried on shouting and left my garden. He then stood in the street outside my garden shouting loudly for 10 minutes. I saw him looking around as he was shouting and it was quite clear he was making sure that my neighbours and other persons passing by could hear clearly what he was saying. He was stating that I had his car, that he wanted his money which I owed him, the amount of money which I owed him and stated that he would be returning with a crowbar to prise open my garage to remove the car if I did not pay by the following day.

11   I confirm that I have never at any stage given the defendants permission to enter my garden, my home or my garage.

12   In the light of the above matters, I submit that the court should grant me an injunction against the defendants and their servants and agents preventing them from entering my premises without a court order.

Sworn at Anytown County Court

This 8th day of December 1992

Notes

The following documents should be submitted to the court:
- Two copies of the particulars of claim.
- Request for a fixed-date summons (Form N203).
- Court fee (currently £40).
- Two copies of an application for an injunction.

The application for an injunction should be completed on Form N16A. The wording of the injunction sought will be identical to that stated in the particulars of claim in precedent 4.

In cases of real urgency where it is impossible to achieve service before the creditor is likely to return to recover the goods, an application for an injunction can be made *ex parte*, ie, without giving any notice to the defendant. Such an injunction will usually be granted for a very limited period, eg, 7 days, and an application will then have to be made to renew it at which the defendant will be entitled to attend.

6   Letter to district judge notifying him that goods have wrongly been distrained

Dear Sir/Madam

Oneshark Credit Limited v Piercy
Case No 922516

I act for Mr James Piercy, the husband of the defendant in this case.

On 15 December 1992, a court bailiff acting under a warrant of execution issued by your court attended his premises and removed from the premises two items that belong to him namely: [list of items].

I enclose a copy of the receipt for item 1 in the list showing clearly that it was supplied to Mr Piercy. I enclose a copy of the receipt for item 2 together with a bank statement of Mr Piercy showing that a cheque No. 002518 was written in the sum stated on the receipt on the date stated on the receipt from the bank account of Mr Piercy in his sole name.

In the circumstances, it is clear that these items both belong to Mr Piercy and not to his wife, the defendant.

I should therefore be grateful if these items could be returned since they have been wrongly distrained. I draw your attention to the provisions of section 98 of the County Courts Act 1984 which appear to entitle my client to take action against yourself and/or the bailiff if these items are wrongly sold when they belong to my client and ought to be returned to him.

Yours faithfully

7   Notice of application for a declaration that items are exempt from seizure

IN THE ANYTOWN COUNTY COURT   Case No 922516

| Between | ONESHARK CREDIT LIMITED | Plaintiff |
| and | SARAH PIERCY | Defendant |

NOTICE OF APPLICATION

TAKE NOTICE that the defendant intends to apply to the district judge of this court at the Court House, Anyroad, ANYTOWN on the ____ day of ____ 1992 at ____ o'clock for an order:

That the bailiff should not seize the following items belonging to the defendant as they are exempt from seizure under the provisions of County Courts Act 1984, section 89:

[List of items exempt].

Dated 1 December 1992

Solicitor for the defendant [signature]

8 Application for an expedited hearing of an application to make a garnishee order absolute

The District Judge
Anytown County Court

Dear Madam/Sir

Case No 9205139 Oneshark Credit Limited v Piercy

I act for the Defendant in this case. The plaintiffs have made an application for a garnishee order and an order *nisi* was made on 5 December 1992.

I enclose an affidavit explaining the circumstances in which my client is being placed as a result of the garnishee order *nisi* and the freezing of her bank account with Lloyds Bank.

Please therefore accept this letter as an *ex parte* application for an order under Order 13 rule 4 of the County Court Rules 1981 to abridge the normal notice periods required for the hearing of an application for a garnishee order under Order 30 rule 3 and for a further order that the hearing of the plaintiff's application should take place forthwith or as soon as the court can make arrangements for it to be heard and at whichever court is considered convenient for such a hearing to take place.

Yours faithfully

Precedent for chapter 4: fuel debts

9 Draft letter to be sent to the electricty or gas supplier when a client is paying a debt which is disputed

Dear Madam/Sir

I enclose the sum of £54.00. I do not accept that I am legally responsible for this sum. However, I am paying this sum under duress because you are threatening me with disconnection if I fail to pay. I do not accept that I am legally responsible for this sum or that you are entitled to charge me for it. I am making payment of this sum without prejudice to whether or not I am legally liable to do so and I reserve the right to reclaim this sum for which I am not legally responsible by court action against you.

Yours faithfully

Precedents for chapter 5: arrears of water charges

10   *Notice of application to set aside or suspend judgment*

IN THE WANDARK COUNTY COURT   Case No

Between	WANDARK WATER PLC	Plaintiffs
and	SARAH PIERCY	Defendant

NOTICE OF APPLICATION

TAKE NOTICE that the defendant intends to apply to the district judge of this court at the Court House, Anyroad, Wandark, London SE92 on the ____ day of ____ 1992 at ____ o'clock for an order:

1   That the judgment made on 13 October 1992 in these proceedings be set aside and the defendant be given leave to defend the proceedings.

2   In the alternative, that execution of the judgment be suspended for a period of six months or until further order.

3   In the alternative, that execution of the judgment be suspended upon terms that the defendant pay the sum of £2.15 per week until the judgment debt is satisfied.

And in the event that the order of 13 October is set aside an order for the following directions:

4   That the defendant file a defence within 14 days.

[Add other directions as to discovery etc.]

Dated this 1st day of December 1992.

Solicitor for the defendant [signature]
Address for service:

To the district judge and to the plaintiffs

11 Letter to water company asking for confirmation that no disconnection will take place pending an application to suspend a judgment

1 December 1992

Dear Madam/Sir

Yourselves v S Piercy
94C Darkley Street, Wandark, London SE92
Your reference:

I confirm my telephone conversation with your office earlier today.

An application has today been made to the Wandark County Court to set aside the judgment you have obtained against my client in the above proceedings and I am writing to confirm my request that you agree not to disconnect the supply to these premises pending the hearing of the application.

Unless I receive confirmation by 3 pm this afternoon that no disconnection will take place pending the hearing of the application, then an *ex parte* application will be made to the court for suspension of the judgment pending the hearing and any additional costs incurred will be sought from yourselves in due course.

Yours faithfully

12 Letter to the court asking for judgment to be suspended pending the hearing of an application

1 December 1992

Dear Madam/Sir

Wandark Water plc v Piercy, Case No

I have been consulted by the defendant in this matter.

I enclose:

1 Notice of acting.
2 Notice of application in triplicate.
3 Affidavit in support and a copy for service.

Condition H, paragraph 7.3 of the instrument of appointment of Wandark Water plc as a water company under the Water Industry Act 1991 states it cannot disconnect my client's water supply as long as my client is complying with the terms of any judgment made against her. If the application now being made is successful, my client will not be in breach of such a judgment and the right to disconnect will cease. However, at present and pending the hearing, my client is in breach of the terms of the judgment and the water company will remain entitled to disconnect.

The plaintiffs have refused, after a written request from me and a warning that an *ex parte* application will be made, to guarantee that they will not disconnect pending the application being heard and in those circumstances I would ask that, on an *ex parte* basis, the judgment is suspended pending the hearing of my client's application.

You will see from the terms of the enclosed affidavit that my client is unable to pay the judgment debt at the present time and in those circumstances the court has power under section 71 of the County Courts Act 1984 to suspend the judgment pending the application being heard.

Please therefore treat this letter as an *ex parte* application to suspend the judgment until such time as my client's application has been heard. If you wish me to make this application in person, please contact my office immediately.

Yours faithfully

13   Affidavit in support of an application to set aside or suspend judgment

1. Defendant
2. S Piercy
3. 1st
4. 1 December 1992
5. 1 December 1992

IN THE WANDARK COUNTY COURT   Case No

Between   WANDARK WATER plc   Plaintiffs
and   SARAH PIERCY   Defendant

AFFIDAVIT

I, SARAH PIERCY of 94C Darkley Street, Wandark, London SE92 MAKE OATH and say as follows:

1   I am the joint tenant of 94C Darkley Street, Wandark, London SE92 which I rent from the London Borough of Wandark. My husband, Alan Piercy, is also a joint tenant.

2   I make this affidavit in support of my application to set aside a

judgment made against me on 13 October 1992 by this court or in the altenative to suspend the judgment for a period of six months or in the alternative again to suspend the judgment upon terms that I pay the judgment debt at the rate of £2.15 per week.

3   The judgment made on 13 October 1992 was for the sum of £70.00 which were the water and sewerage charges due for 94C Darkley Street for the period from 1 April 1992 to 30 September 1992.

4   My husband and I moved into 94C Darkley Street and became the tenants on 1 June 1992. Prior to that time we were not the occupiers of the premises and in those circumstances we were not liable for the water rates due for the period from 1 April to 31 May.

5   I therefore submit that the judgment should be set aside on the basis that of the £70.00 that is claimed, £23.33, being the water charges from 1 April to 31 May, are not payable by me. I accept that I am responsible for the balance, ie, £46.67, and the judgment should be entered for this sum.

6   I have occupied 94C Darkley Street from 1 June 1992 to the present time with my three children, aged 11, 8 and 1. From 1 June until 3 September 1992 my husband also lived at this address but on 3 September 1992 he announced that he was leaving me. I have not seen him since though I have had a letter from solicitors acting on his behalf requesting access to the children.

7   My husband is a telephone engineer. I do not know how much he earns but it is a substantial sum. However, I have not received any money by way of maintenance from him since he left and he has given me no indication that he is prepared to pay maintenance. I am advised by solicitors whom I have now consulted that I should be able to obtain some maintenance from him at some stage but that this will take some time to organise.

8   Since 3 September I have been claiming income support for myself and my three children. I receive the sum of £107 per week.

9   I now have produced to me and marked 'SP1' an income and expenditure breakdown showing my income and the day-to-day expenses and other debts for which I am liable. It can be seen that my husband has left me with a substantial number of debts including rent arrears, these arrears for water rates, community charge arrears, three hire-purchase debts, electricity and gas arrears and the debt due on two loans. I relied on his income to be able to make all of these payments and we were not entitled to any benefits prior to his departure.

10   It can be seen from the enclosed income and expenditure sheet that I am in severe financial crises following my husband's departure. I hope to

make an application for a lump-sum payment from my husband to discharge some of these arrears as well as current maintenance but at the present time I am unable to pay the water rates bill which is due from me. It is also jointly due from my husband although the water company has not taken action against him because he had left me by the time the summons was issued.

11   I accept that I am responsible to pay the water charges and I will make every effort to do so when I have the finances available. At the present time I do not have such finances and I therefore submit to the court that it would be appropriate to suspend the judgment in this action for a period of six months to allow me to recover my financial stability and to take action against my husband for the recovery of a lump sum to discharge the debt and other debts that are due.

12   I am advised that under the terms of its instrument of appointment under the Water Industry Act 1991, condition H, paragraph 7, the plaintiff company is not entitled to disconnect my water supply if I have complied with the terms of any judgment issued in these proceedings. If the judgment is suspended for a period of six months, therefore, the water company would not be in a position to disconnect my water supply. I would submit that this is essential in the interests of my three children.

13   If the court is not prepared to suspend the judgment for a period of six months, then I would submit that in the alternative it should make an order that the judgment should be discharged at the rate of £2.15* per week. This is the maximum sum which the water company is entitled to by way of direct deductions from income support under the Social Security (Claims and Payments) Regulations 1989. I would make an application to the Benefits Agency for such payment to be made and if the court had already made an order in those terms, the plaintiff would not be in a position to disconnect as long as it was paid by the direct deductions. If the court saw fit to make an order for £2.15 per week to be payable, I would ask that the first payment should not be payable for a period of two months to enable the Benefits Agency to arrange the direct deductions.

14   However, I am advised that housing costs and fuel charges take priority over water charges for the purposes of direct deductions. Given the extent of my debts to the local authority for rent arrears and to the electricity and gas suppliers for fuel, it is possible that direct deductions for debts due for water and sewerage charges will not be possible from benefit because the maximum deduction that can be made is £6.45* per week. I will be asking that direct deductions are made for these other debts. In those circumstances, I would submit that it would be more

appropriate to suspend the judgment completely for six months to enable me to get back on my feet rather than to make an order for £2.15 per week.

SWORN 1 December 1992
At Anytown County Court, Court House, Anyroad, Wandark,

Before me [solicitor]

Note * 1992/3 rates.

14   Letter from social services to water company

1 December 1992

Wandark Water plc
Water House
Anytown Industrial Estate
Anytown

Dear Madam/Sir

Sarah Piercy, 94C Darkley Street, Wandark, London SE92

Mrs Piercy has made an application to us for assistance with discharging a debt due to you for water charges in respect of 94C Darkley Street. That application is being considered and I am writing to request that disconnection of the supply to 94C Darkley Street should not occur due to the presence of young children in the household.

Yours faithfully

Area Manager
Social Services

15   Model particulars of claim for seeking an injunction against the water company together with notes on procedure

IN THE WANDARK COUNTY COURT   Case No

Between   ARTHUR THOMAS   Plaintiff
and   WANDARK WATER PLC   Defendant

PARTICULARS OF CLAIM

1   The plaintiff is the occupier of premises at 94C Darkley Street, Wandark, London SE92, jointly with Sarah Piercy.

2   By written demand dated 1 February 1993, the plaintiff requested a

supply of water to those premises under the provisions of section 52 of the Water Industry Act 1991.

3   In breach of their duty under section 52, the defendants have failed to supply water to the premises sufficient for domestic purposes on the grounds that they are entitled to impose a condition under the provisions of section 53 of the Water Industry Act 1991 that arrears of water charges in the sum of £44.00 together with disconnection charges of £35.00 shall be paid before connection is made.

4   The plaintiff is not liable for the said water charges and disconnection charges as he was not the occupier of the premises at the time the water charges were due and at the time the disconnection took place.

5   In the circumstances, the defendants are in breach of their statutory duty under section 52 of the Water Industry Act 1991.

And the plaintiff claims:

1   An injunction against the defendants requiring then to provide to the premises at 94C Darkley Street, Wandark, London SE92 a supply of water sufficient for domestic purposes and to maintain the connection between the defendant's water main and the service pipe by which that supply is provided to those premises until there is an interruption of their duty to supply the premises under the provisions of the Water Industry Act 1991.

2   Costs.

Dated 2 February 1993

Solicitor for the plaintiff [signature]

To the district judge and to the defendants

Notes
1   These particulars of claim in duplicate should be provided to the court together with the court fee of £40.00 and a request for a fixed-date summons.

2   As soon as proceedings are issued, an application can be made for an interlocutory injunction in form N16A. The application should be submitted in triplicate and an affidavit in support and a copy of that affidavit should be filed.

3   The terms of the injunction will be identical to those set out in the particulars of claim above.

4   The court in which the proceedings are issued should be the county

court for the district in which the premises are situated. The breach of statutory duty arises in that district and therefore the tort is committed in that area giving jurisdiction to that county court.

5   Note that the county court now has unlimited jurisdiction for actions in tort and s38 of the County Courts Act 1984 now provides that the county court can make any orders that could be made in the High Court, which can include an injunction even where no claim for damages is made. It is therefore not necessary to make any claim for damages. In practice, a claim for damages could be attached to this application, though this draft does not show such a claim.

16   Letter to the court requesting expedited hearing

Dear Madam/Sir

Wandark Water plc v James   Case No

I act for the defendant in these proceedings, Mrs M. L. James.

I enclose:

1   Notice of application to set aside judgment in triplicate.

2   Affidavit in support in duplicate.

Please accept this letter as an application to expedite the hearing.

My client, Mrs James, has no water supply at present. She has two children. Her water supply was disconnected one month ago for failing to pay charges which have been demanded. As can be seen from the enclosed affidavit, she disputes liability for those charges.

As long as the judgment remains in force, the water company is entitled to refuse to reconnect unless she discharges the amount due and disconnection costs. As can also be seen from the enclosed affidavit she does not have sufficient finances to make those payments and is therefore not in a position to have the water supply reconnected.

My client is therefore being seriously prejudiced by the existence of the judgment which the enclosed affidavit shows should never have been obtained. In those circumstances, I should ask that the normal period of time before a hearing should be abridged and that a hearing should be arranged at the earliest opportunity for the application to set aside to be heard.

Yours faithfully

Precedents for chapters 6 and 7: council tax and community charge arrears, and arrears under magistrates' courts orders

17 Complaint to magistrates' court by a person aggrieved by a levy or attempt to levy

COMPLAINT

Magistrates' Courts Act 1980, sections 51 and 52
Magistrates' Courts Rules 1981, rule 4

Anytown Magistrates' Court

Date:

Defendants: Ruthless and Co., Penniless Road, Anytown; and Anytown Borough Council, Civic Offices, Anytown

Matter of complaint

The complainant is aggrieved by a levy carried out by the first defendants on behalf of the second defendants at 15 Anytown Road, Anytown on the 28 the day of July 1992 whereby two items of property belonging to the complainant, which the first defendants had no authority to remove, were removed and are now in the possession of the first defendants, namely one Panasonic 26 inch television and one diamond engagement ring.

The complainant is Alison Smith of 15 Anytown Road, Anytown.

Date of complaint:

18 Particulars of claim seeking an injunction against the bailiff

IN THE ANYTOWN COUNTY COURT   Case No

Between	ARTHUR SMITH	First plaintiff
and	ALISON SMITH	Second plaintiff
and	RUTHLESS AND CO. (A FIRM)	First defendants
and	ANYTOWN BOROUGH COUNCIL	Second defendants

PARTICULARS OF CLAIM

1   The first and second plaintiffs are the joint tenants of a dwelling-house at 15 Anytown Road, Anytown.

2   On 20 April 1992 the second defendants obtained a liability order against the first plaintiff in the Anytown Magistrates' Court for the sum of £180.00 arrears of community charge plus £22.00 costs making a total of £202.00 under the provisions of the Local Government Act 1988 and

the Community Charges (Administration and Enforcement) Regulations 1989.

3   At all material times the first defendants have acted as agents for the second defendants.

4   On 20 June 1992 the first defendants, acting under the authority of the second defendants, attended the dwelling-house at 15 Anytown Road for the purposes of levying distress under regulation 39 of the regulations referred to above.

5   Entry to the dwelling-house was granted by the son of the plaintiffs, Brian Smith (aged 16).

6   The servant or agent of the first defendants, whose name was unknown, who levied distress, stated that the following goods were distrained:

a)   a Matsui fridge-freezer.
b)   a Panasonic 26 inch television.
c)   a diamond engagement ring.

7   The said agent entered details of the goods referred to above on a document purporting to be a walking possession agreement to which he obtained the signature of the said Brian Smith and then left the dwelling-house.

8   The said Brian Smith had no authority to sign any walking possession agreement on behalf of the first plaintiff and the said document is not a valid walking possession agreement.

9   In the light of paragraph 8, since the first defendants left the premises without removing the goods, nor leaving a person in close possession of the goods, nor with a valid walking possession agreement, the first defendants abandoned the distress which had been levied.

10   By letter dated 28 June 1992, the first defendants threatened to return to the dwelling-house to collect the goods and stated that entry to the dwelling-house would be forced unless access was allowed.

11   In the absence of an effective distress having already been levied, the first defendants have no right to force access to the dwelling-house.

12   By a facsimile dated 30 June, the solicitor for the first plaintiff, V. Careful, requested an undertaking from the first defendants that they would not force access to the dwelling-house and that they accepted that they had no legal right to do so. On the same day, he requested a similar undertaking from the solicitors for the second defendants on whose behalf the first defendants were acting. In telephone calls on 1 July 1992, Mr Careful further requested such undertakings from the first defendants and

the second defendants but both refused to give any such undertaking and continued to assert their right to force access to the dwelling-house to remove the said goods.

13   The Panasonic 26 inch television and the diamond engagement ring belong to or are in the legal possession of the second plaintiff and the first plaintiff has no legal claim to possession or ownership of those items.

PARTICULARS

a)   The diamond ring was left to the second plaintiff by her mother upon her death under the terms of her mother's will.

b)   The Panasonic 26 inch television is in the possession of the second plaintiff by virtue of a hire agreement made between herself and Anytown Television Rental Company Limited dated 31 January 1992.

14   The first and second defendants have no right to levy distress against the goods referred to in paragraph 13 and by threatening to return and remove such goods are threatening to interfere with goods belonging to the second plaintiff.

And the first and second plaintiffs both claim:

1   An injunction forbidding the first defendants and/or the second defendants whether by themselves or by instructing or encouraging any other person or otherwise from trespassing against the property at 15 Anytown Road, Anytown by means of forcing entry to the dwelling-house and/or damaging any part of such dwelling-house for the purposes of gaining entry.

And the second plaintiff claims in addition:

2   A declaration that the goods referred to in paragraph 13 above are in her sole ownership and/or possession and are not in the ownership or possession of the first plaintiff.

3   An injunction forbidding the first and second defendants whether by themselves or by instructing or encouraging any other person or otherwise from interfering with the said goods by distraining the goods, removing the goods from the said dwelling-house and/or selling the said goods at auction.

Dated 2 July 1992

19 *Originating application for taxation of bailiff's bill*

IN THE ANYTOWN COUNTY COURT   Case No

IN THE MATTER OF THE COMMUNITY CHARGES
(ADMINISTRATION AND ENFORCEMENT)
REGULATIONS 1989, SCHEDULE 5

Between	ALAN JONES	First plaintiff
and	RUTHLESS AND CO. (A FIRM)	First Defendants
and	ANYTOWN BOROUGH COUNCIL	Second Defendants

ORIGINATING APPLICATION

Order 3, rule 4(1) and Order 38, rule 22

I, Allan Jones, of 25 Anytown Road, Anytown apply to the Court for the taxation of the fees of Ruthless and Co. and I attach a copy of the bill being a demand for payment from Ruthless and Co. of the said fees.

The grounds on which I claim to be entitled to the order are:

1   Ruthless and Co. are bailiffs instructed by Anytown Borough Council under the provisions of regulation 39 of the Community Charges (Administration and Enforcement) Regulations 1989.

2   On 28 April 1992 the second defendants obtained a liability order against me in the Anytown Magistrates' Court for the sum of £180.00 arrears of community charge plus £22.00 costs making a total of £202.00 under the provisions of the Local Government Act 1988 and the Community Charges (Administration and Enforcement) Regulations 1989.

3   On 10 June 1992 the first defendants, acting under the authority of Anytown Borough Council attended my home at 25 Anytown Road for the purposes of levying distress under regulation 39 of the regulations referred to above.

4   By virtue of regulation 39(2) the charges in connection with the distress to which Ruthless and Co. are entitled are set out in Schedule 5 to the 1989 regulations.

5   The sum of £71.30 claimed by Ruthless and Co. as costs on the attached bill are not payable for the following reasons:

  a)   The sum of £7.50 is a sum charged for by them for sending me a letter on 26 May 1992 informing me that if I did not pay the sum due under the liability order they would levy distress. At the time the letter was written, no distress had been levied and they are not entitled to claim for this sum under schedule 5 to the 1989 regulations.

b)   The sum of £3.00 has been charged by Ruthless and Co. for processing a cheque which I sent to them in part payment of the sums due under the liability order, which sum they are not entitled to claim under schedule 5 to the 1989 regulations.

c)   A sum of £5.00 is claimed by Ruthless and Co. for sending me a letter on 3 July 1992 informing me that the said cheque had not been honoured, which sum they are not entitled to under schedule 5 to the 1989 regulations.

d)   The further sum of £55.80 consists of the costs claimed at the rate of £0.45 per day from 5 July 1992 to 6 October 1992. I discharged the full amount due to Ruthless and Co. and to Anytown Borough Council on 5 July 1992 at which time the walking possession agreement which I had signed ceased to have effect under the provisions of regulation 39 of the 1989 regulations. From 5 July 1992 no sums were lawfully due to Anytown Borough Council or to Ruthless and Co. and therefore no walking possession fees were accruing.

The name and address of the persons upon whom it is intended to serve this application are:

Ruthless and Co., Penniless Road, Anytown

The applicant's address for service is 25 Anytown Road, Anytown.

Dated 6 October 1992

[Signed by the applicant]

20 Draft letter to be sent when a client is paying a debt which is disputed

Dear Bailiff

I enclose the sum of £222.00. £202.00 of this sum is the amount due under a liability order including costs and I accept that I am legally responsible to pay it. I do not accept that I am legally responsible for the remaining £20.00. However, I am repaying this sum under duress because I am being threatened with the removal of my goods by way of distress if I do not do so. I do not accept that I am legally responsible for this sum of £20 or that you as bailiff are entitled to charge this £20 fee. I am making payment of this £20 without prejudice to the question whether or not I am legally liable to do so and I reserve the right to reclaim this sum for which I am not legally responsible by court action.

Yours faithfully

21 Particulars of claim to recover disputed sums paid under duress

1   By virtue of a liability order made on 27 June 1992 under the Community Charges (Administration and Enforcement) Regulations 1989 against the plaintiff in proceedings brought by Anytown Borough Council in Anytown Magistrates' Court, the plaintiff was found liable for the sum of £180.00 for the Community Charge in that borough together with the sum of £22 costs totally £202.

2   By a letter dated 20 July 1992, the defendants [the bailiffs] stated that unless the outstanding amount of £202 together with their costs of £20 were paid to them by 27 July 1992, they had no alternative but to attend the dwelling-house of the plaintiff to execute the order by seizing the plaintiff's goods for sale at public auction in order to discharge the debt.

3   The £20 fees claimed by the defendants were claimed by them as fees for the sending of the letter dated 20 July 1992 to the plaintiff prior to levying or attempting to levy the distress. Such fees are not payable under the provisions of schedule 5, paragraph 1 of the Community Charges (Administration and Enforcement) Regulations 1989 and are therefore not due from the plaintiff to the defendant.

4   Under threat of distress for the sum of £20 and the removal and sale of his goods which amounted to duress, the plaintiff paid the sum of £20 costs to the defendants on 28 July 1992.

5   The said sum is recoverable from the defendant by the plaintiff by way of restitution.

And the plaintiff claims the sum of £20.

Housing emergencies

Precedents for chapter 9: harassment and unlawful eviction

22 Particulars of claim for injunction and damages (Note 1)

IN THE ANYWHERE COUNTY COURT   Case No [Note 2]

Between	HARRIET PERKINS	Plaintiff
and	JAMES BROWN	Defendant

PARTICULARS OF CLAIM

1   At all material times the plaintiff has been the protected tenant and the defendant has been the landlord of the premises known as Flat 5, 29 Haringey Square, London N1. The premises consist of one room and a kitchen on the first floor with the shared use of a bathroom and toilet in common with other occupants of the house. [Note 3]

2   The premises are not separately assessed for rating purposes but the house of which they form part has a net annual value for rating purposes of £606. [Note 4]

3   The said tenancy was by written agreement dated 3 July 1986 and is at a rent of £20 per week exclusive of rates, gas and electricity. The said tenancy has not been determined by notice to quit. [Note 5]

4   The said tenancy agreement contains an implied covenant that the defendant would allow the plaintiff quiet enjoyment of her tenancy. [Note 6]

5   By reason of the matters hereinafter set out the defendant is in breach of the said covenant. [Note 7]

PARTICULARS

a) On Wednesday 21 July 1993 the defendant changed the lock of the door to Flat 5, 29 Haringey Square, London N1, thereby preventing the plaintiff from entering her premises.

b) On Wednesday 21 July 1993 the defendant refused to give the plaintiff a key to the said door and informed her that he would not permit her to return to occupy her premises.

c) On Wednesday 21 July 1993 without the permission of the plaintiff, the defendant entered the premises known as Flat 5, 29 Haringey Square, London N1, and removed all the plaintiff's possessions and deposited them in the hall of 29 Haringey Square, causing damage to the plaintiff's television.

6   Further and in the alternative, the defendant has trespassed upon the plaintiff's premises.

7   By reason of the matters aforesaid the plaintiff has suffered loss, damage, distress, anxiety and inconvenience. [Note 8]

PARTICULARS [Note 9]

a) The plaintiff has not had access to her premises since 21 July 1993.

b) On the night of 21 July 1993 the plaintiff was obliged to stay in hotel accommodation overnight.

PARTICULARS OF SPECIAL DAMAGE [Note 10]

a) Hotel accommodation   £15 per night
b) Damage to television pursuant to paragraph 5(iii)   £100

8   The plaintiff claims interest pursuant to section 69 of the County Courts Act 1984 for such periods and at such rates as the court thinks fit.

And the plaintiff claims: [Note 11]

a) An injunction ordering the defendant to re-admit the plaintiff to the premises known as Flat 5, 29 Haringey Square, London N1 forthwith and to supply the plaintiff with a key thereto forthwith and further restraining the defendant by himself, his servants, agents or otherwise from interfering with the plaintiff's quiet enjoyment of the said premises and from trespassing upon the said premises and from removing the plaintiff's possessions from the said premises. [Note 12]

b) Special damages under paragraph 7 above of £115. [Note 13]

c) General, aggravated and/or exemplary damages under paragraph 7 above. [Note 14]

d) Interest pursuant to section 69 of the County Courts Act 1984. [Note 15]

e) Costs. [Note 16]

Dated

Solicitors for the plaintiff who will accept service of all proceedings [signature] [Note 17]

To the chief clerk and to the defendant

Notes

1   The particulars of claim form the basis of the whole action and should be drafted accordingly and not just with a view to obtaining an injunction. The particulars of claim should specify the cause of action, relief or remedy sought and should state the material facts on which the plaintiff relies. The plaintiff will be taken to have admitted the facts in the particulars of claim.

2   Fill in the name of the appropriate county court. Leave the case number blank – this will be entered by the court. If there is more than one plaintiff or defendant the names should be set out on different lines and the parties identified as first plaintiff, second plaintiff etc. It is acceptable to identify a defendant by one name, eg, Hill (Male), if that is all that is known.

3   The first paragraph must describe the status of the parties to the action and their relationship to each other. This example is straightforward but where the plaintiff's status is more complex it can be defined as 'residential occupier' and a second paragraph can be added to explain the status in detail. The exact premises should be identified fully including the flat number and the location of the room(s).

4   It is essential to identify the premises and net annual value of the land for rating if an injunction only is sought.[1]

5   If there is no written agreement, then state how the agreement was made. Never admit a valid notice to quit unless you are sure it is valid and do not include matters which the plaintiff wishes to dispute.

6   Paragraphs 4, 5 and 6 specify the causes of action. If there is more than one cause of action state them all.

7   The particulars should set out the actual events (in chronological order) which constitute the cause of action alleged.

8   In general, the list of damages should be as wide as possible in order not to limit the judge at the trial. However, each claim must be valid. A physical injury can be added if appropriate.

9   The particulars should clearly specify damage and suffering to which the plaintiff has been subjected. If there is evidence on which exemplary

1   CCR Ord 6 r4.

and/or aggravated damages can be claimed it should be emphasised in these particulars.

10   Each item of special damage and cost should be listed.

11   The claim should contain all the elements of the relief or remedy the occupier is seeking from the court.

12   The exact form of the injunction wanted should be set out and should be the same as the draft order.

13   Enter the total sum of special damage claimed.

14   Aggravated and exemplary damages should be expressly pleaded.[2]

15   Interest cannot be claimed unless specifically pleaded.[3]

16   A claim for costs should always be included because even if the plaintiff is legally aided, the statutory charge will attach to any damages awarded.

17   The particulars of claim must be signed by the plaintiff if acting in person or by the solicitor if on the court record and must state the plaintiff's address for service.[4]

23   Application for injunction (general form) [note 1]

IN THE ANYWHERE COUNTY COURT   Case No

| Between | HARRIET PERKINS | Plaintiff |
| and | JAMES BROWN | Defendant |

By application in pending proceedings

The plaintiff applies to the court for an injunction order in the following terms:

That the defendant be forbidden whether by himself or by instructing or encouraging any other person from [note 2] interfering with the plaintiff's quiet enjoyment of premises known as Flat 5, 29 Haringey Square, London N1 and from trespassing upon the said premises and from removing the plaintiff's possessions from the said premises; And that the defendant do readmit the plaintiff to the said premises forthwith and do supply the plaintiff with a key to the said premises forthwith;

2   *Millington v Duffy* (1984) 17 HLR 232.
3   CCR Ord 6 r1A; *Ward v Chief Constable of Avon and Somerset* (1985) *The Times*, 17 July 1985.
4   CCR Ord 6 r18.

And that the defendant do pay the costs of and incidental to this application in any event. [Note 3]

The grounds of this application are set out in the sworn statement of Harriet Perkins.

This sworn statement is served with this application.

This application is to be served upon James Brown, of 45 Motown Towers, Detroit Lane, Wandark, London SE26.

This application is filed by ____ solicitors for the plaintiff whose address for service is ____ .

Signed [Note 4]   Dated

This section to be completed by the court [Note 5]

To

of

This application will be heard by the (district) judge

at ____ on ____ the ____ day of ____ 199_ at ____ o'clock.

If you do not attend at the time shown the court may make and injunction order in your absence.

If you do not understand anything in this application you should go to a solicitor, legal advice centre or a Citizens Advice Bureau.

Notes

1   Prescribed Form N16A.

2   Here set out the relief required. If more than one form of relief is required make it clear if it is in the alternative.

3   Always request the costs of the interlocutory application. If the plaintiff is legally aided and damages are awarded at the substantive hearing, the statutory charge will apply.

4   The application should be signed by solicitors if they are acting for the plaintiff.

5   The court officer will fill in the date and time when the application will be heard.

24 *Affidavit in support of application for injunction* [Note 1]

IN THE ANYWHERE COUNTY COURT   Case No [Note 2]

Between   HARRIET PERKINS   Plaintiff
and   JAMES BROWN   Defendant

AFFIDAVIT IN SUPPORT OF PLAINTIFF'S APPLICATION FOR INJUNCTION [Note 3]

I, HARRIET PERKINS of Flat 5, 29 Haringey Square, London N1, writer, MAKE OATH and say as follows: [Note 4]

1   I am the plaintiff in this case and I make this affidavit in support of my application for an interlocutory injunction. Save where it otherwise appears, I make this affidavit from my own knowledge. [Note 5]

2   I have been living at the above address since 4 July 1986. I was granted a weekly tenancy of the flat at a rent of £20 per week exclusive of rates, gas and electricity. The accommodation consists of one room and a kitchen on the first floor with shared use of a bathroom and toilet in common with other occupants of the house. [Note 6] There is now produced and shown to me marked 'HP1' a true copy of the tenancy agreement dated 3 July 1986. [Note 7]

3   I had no trouble with the defendant until about a year ago when he told me that he wanted to increase the rent to £30 per week. I took advice about this, and told the landlord that I was not prepared to pay the increased rent unless it was registered by the rent officer. Since I refused to pay the increased rent, the defendant has become more and more abusive towards me when I have paid my rent and on one occasion in March 1988 he said to me in a threatening manner, 'If you won't pay me more rent you will have to go'. [Note 8]

4   On Tuesday 20 July 1993 the defendant came to collect my rent in the normal way. He asked me once again if I would pay the £30 per week and I refused. He then became very angry and threw my rent book at me and said, 'I have had enough of you. You will have to leave'. I told him that I had no intention of leaving and he went off down the stairs in a rage shouting abuse and reiterating that I would have to leave.

5   I was very frightened by the landlord's behaviour and the next day, Wednesday 21 July, I telephoned a solicitor to make an appointment. Unfortunately she was unable to see me until the next day.

6   On Wednesday 21 July I arrived home at the usual time of about 6pm. On entering the front door of 29 Haringey Square I saw that all my belongings were in the hall. I went upstairs to my flat and discovered that I was unable to gain entry as the lock had been changed.

7   I then went to the flat of a neighbour Janice Young who told me that she had seen the landlord carrying my belongings down the stairs at about 2pm.

8   I telephoned the defendant at his home, and asked him to give me a key to the door to my flat. He told me on the telephone that he had changed the lock and that he would not give me a key to my flat, and that he would not permit me to live there any longer. He told me that I must leave that night and take my belongings with me. The defendant was extremely aggressive towards me on the telephone and I was very frightened by his behaviour.

9   As I had nowhere to stay on the night of 21 July I had to stay at the Sunrise Hotel. There is now produced and shown to me marked 'HP2' a true copy of the receipt from the hotel.

10   I cannot afford to continue to stay in a hotel and I do not have anywhere else to stay. In the circumstances I asked this Honourable Court to make an Order to enable me to re-enter my flat immediately. [Note 9]

SWORN this ____day of ____1993
At ____

Before me ____
Solicitor [signature] [Note 10]

IN THE ANYWHERE COUNTY COURT   Case No

Between	HARRIET PERKINS	Plaintiff
and	JAMES BROWN	Defendant

EXHIBIT HP1 [Note 11]

This is the exhibit marked 'HP1' referred to in the affidavit of HARRIET PERKINS of Flat 5, 29 Haringey Square, London N1.

SWORN this ____ day of ____ 1993
Before me ____
Solicitor [signature]

Notes

1   A well-drafted affidavit is crucial in an application for an interlocutory injunction and it may well be the only document which the judge will read at this stage. The main affidavit is almost always that of the plaintiff but witnesses may also file affidavits if appropriate. Deponents of affidavits should be reminded that they may be cross-examined on the contents of their affidavits and that false or exaggerated claims will merely prejudice the plaintiff's application.

2   See note 2 to precedent 22.

3   There is no correct title but it is good practice for the title to show the identity of the deponent and the purpose of the affidavit. Every affidavit must be endorsed with a note showing on whose behalf it is filed.

4   This is the standard introduction to an affidavit and should always be included. If the person does not intend to swear an affidavit, the words, 'Do solemnly sincerely and truly declare and affirm' should be substituted for 'Make oath'. The word 'affirmation' should be substituted for 'affidavit' throughout.

5   The first paragraph should establish the relationship of the deponent to the action and the purpose of the affidavit.

6   Where the deponent is the occupier, the second paragraph should set out the details of occupation with an explanation of how the occupier came to take up occupation if appropriate.

7   Copies of the agreement, rent book or any other document substantiating the status of the plaintiff should be exhibited to the affidavit. The number of the exhibit includes the initials of the person making the affidavit and its number. There is a new number sequence for each exhibit and this sequence should be followed where more than one affidavit is filed.

8   The body of the affidavit should set out, in a sequence of logical statements in numbered paragraphs, the facts relied on in support of the application for an interlocutory injunction. The affidavit should be clear and unrepetitive and should substantiate and elaborate upon the particulars of claim. The contents of the affidavit should persuade the judge that it is appropriate to grant an interlocutory injunction, which is not automatic. Interlocutory relief is in the discretion of the court and the onus is on the applicant to show that the injunction is necessary. It should state which of the facts are within the deponent's knowledge and which

are based on information or belief. The sources and grounds of the information or belief should be stated.[5]

9   The final paragraph of the affidavit should set out the relief that the plaintiff is seeking.

10   The affidavit will be signed before a solicitor or court officer authorised to witness affidavits. These details should be entered on copies of the affidavit before they are served on the defendant.

11   The exhibit must be attached to, and identified by, a certificate signed by the person before whom the affidavit is sworn.

25   Injunction order [Note 1]

IN THE ANYWHERE COUNTY COURT   Case No

Between	HARRIET PERKINS	Plaintiff
and	JAMES BROWN	Defendant

If you do not obey this order you will be guilty of contempt of court and you may be sent to prison [Note 2]

On the ____ of ____ 199_ the court considered an application for an injunction.

The court ordered that James Brown is forbidden whether by himself or by instructing or encouraging any other person from [Note 3] interfering with the plaintiff's quiet enjoyment of premises known as Flat 5, 29 Haringey Square, London N1 and from trespassing upon the said premises and from removing the plaintiff's possessions from the said premises.

This order shall remain in force until further order.

And it is ordered that James Brown shall readmit the plaintiff to the said premises forthwith and shall supply the plaintiff with a key to the said premises forthwith.

It is further ordered that the costs of the plaintiff's application shall be reserved until trial of this action.

If you do not understand anything in this order you should go to a solicitor, legal advice centre or a Citizens Advice Bureau.

Notes

1   A draft of the injunction is required except where the case is one of urgency.[6] This form is based on prescribed form N16 (interim injunction).

5   CCR Ord 20 r10(5).
6   CCR Ord 13 r6(6).

2   It is essential that the injunction is endorsed with a penal notice so that an application for committal for contempt can be made if necessary.[7]

3   The terms of the draft injunction should be the same as set out in the particulars of claim and in the notice of application.

Precedents for chapter 10: disrepair

26   Particulars of claim for injunction and damages (note 1)

IN THE ANYWHERE COUNTY COURT   Case No [Note 2]

Between   SARAH PIERCY   Plaintiff
and   THE LONDON BOROUGH OF WANDARK   Defendant

PARTICULARS OF CLAIM

1   The plaintiff is and was at all material times the sole tenant of premises known as 94C Darkley Street, Wandark, London SE92. The defendant authority is and was at all material times the landlord of the premises. [Note 3]

2   The premises are situated on the top floor of a converted terraced property and consist of two bedrooms, living-room, kitchen and bathroom and are self-contained.

3   The said tenancy is a weekly tenancy and commenced by written agreement on 30 June 1988. The current rent is £30 per week exclusive of water rates, gas or electricity. [Note 4]

4   By reason of the matters set out in paragraphs 1, 2 and 3 above, the tenancy is one to which the implied covenant to repair contained in section 11 of the Landlord and Tenant Act 1985 applies. [Note 5]

5   By reason of the matters hereinafter set out, the defendant authority is in breach of its obligations under the Landlord and Tenant Act 1985. [Note 6]

PARTICULARS

a) Since the commencement of the tenancy, the roof over the rear bedroom has leaked so that rain has penetrated into the room causing dampness and damage to furnishings and possessions. The plaintiff has had to keep buckets in place when it rains but often the floor becomes wet. On Tuesday 20 July 1993 the water penetration was so

---

7   CCR Ord 29 r1(3); see page 190.

great that it caused the ceiling plaster to fall in on the bed of the plaintiff's son, who is aged 11.

b) Since the commencement of the tenancy the window frames to all the rooms have been ill-fitting, causing draughts.

6 The defendant authority has had notice of these defects. [Note 7]

PARTICULARS

a) By numerous oral complaints by the plaintiff to Mr David Walker who is an officer of the defendant authority and as estate manager in the neighbourhood office has responsibility for the plaintiff's premises. These complaints have been made since the commencement of the tenancy by telephone and in person.

b) By reason of a letter to the defendant authority dated 2 June 1992 from Wandark Housing Resources Centre.

c) By reason of an inspection made by Mr John Castle, an officer of the defendant authority on 14 September 1992.

d) By reason of a telephone call from the plaintiff's solicitors to the said Mr Walker on 20 July 1993 and a letter to the defendant authority from the plaintiff's solicitors on the same date.

7 By reason of the breach aforesaid the plaintiff has suffered loss and damage. [Note 8]

PARTICULARS

a) The rear bedroom has been damp and unpleasant and unsafe to sleep in. The decorations have been ruined. On occasions the plaintiff's 11-year-old son has had to sleep with the plaintiff because the child's bedroom was too wet to sleep in. On 20 July 1993 ceiling plaster and water fell on the child's bed and floor of the room at 2am while the child was asleep. The room is now uninhabitable. [Note 9]

b) All the rooms have been draughty and cold except in the height of summer. Consequently it has been difficult to heat the flat properly and both the plaintiff and her son have suffered from colds and coughs.

PARTICULARS OF SPECIAL DAMAGE [Note 10]

The following items have been damaged by rainfall in the bedroom:

a)	Child's bed	£50.00
b)	Wardrobe	£40.00
c)	Bedding	£30.00
d)	Carpet	£100.00
	Total	£220.00

The plaintiff has had to pay increased heating costs of £240.

8   The plaintiff claims interest pursuant to section 69 of the County Courts Act 1984 for such periods and at such rates as the court thinks fit.

And the plaintiff claims: [Note 11]

a) An injunction ordering the defendant authority to carry out the following works forthwith: [Note 12]
1) Repair of the roof of the said premises so that water does not penetrate into the bedroom.
2) Reinstatement of the ceiling of the said bedroom.
3) Redecoration of the walls and ceiling of the said bedroom.
4) Repair of all the window frames to fit properly.

b) Special damages of £460 under paragraph 7. [Note 13]

c) General damages. [Note 14]

d) Interest pursuant to section 69 of the County Courts Act 1984. [Note 15]

e) Costs. [Note 16]

Dated

Solicitors for the plaintiff [signature]
who will accept service for all proceedings. [Note 16]

To the chief clerk and to the defendant and its solicitors

Notes

1–3   See notes 1–3 to precedent 22.

4   The LTA 1985 s11 applies only to tenancies granted after 24 October 1961, so it is essential to include the date of commencement of the tenancy. Details of the rent will be relevant when damages are assessed and must, therefore, also be included.

5   The repairing covenant can be set out in greater detail if necessary.

6   Paragraph 5 specifies the cause of action. If there is more than one cause of action, state them all. Particularise all the breaches in logical order, not just those which it is sought to remedy by way of an interim injunction. Make sure that the items particularised come within the ambit of the breach of covenant or tort which has been pleaded.

7   It is essential to plead particulars of notice for breach of contract. It is not necessary in tort. Keep the particulars of notice in the same order as the items of disrepair pleaded in the previous paragraph.

8–16   See notes to precedent 22.

27 Notice of application for injunction

IN THE ANYWHERE COUNTY COURT   Case No

Between   SARAH PIERCY   Plaintiff
and   THE LONDON BOROUGH OF WANDARK Defendant

By application in pending proceedings

The plaintiff applies to the court for an injunction order in the following terms:

> That the defendant do within 28 days of service of this order carry out the following works of repair to premises known as 94C Darkley Street, Wandark, London SE92, namely:
>
> a) replacement of all missing slates to the roof of the premises so as to prevent further water penetration; and
> b) reinstatement of the ceiling to the rear bedroom in the premises;
>
> And that the defendant do pay the costs of and incidental to this application in any event.

The grounds of this application are set out in the sworn statement of Sarah Piercy.

This sworn statement is served with this application.

This application is to be served upon the London Borough of Wandark, Town Hall, Water Lane, Wandark, London SE92.

This application is filed by ____ solicitors for the plaintiff.
Signed   Dated

This section to be completed by the court

To
of

This application will be heard by the (district) judge
at ____ on ____ the ____ day of ____ 199– at ____ o'clock.

If you do not attend at the time shown the court may make an injunction order in your absence.

If you do not understand anything in this application you should go to a solicitor, legal advice centre or a Citizens Advice Bureau.

Note
The notes to precedent 23 apply equally here.

28 Affidavit in support of application for injunction

IN THE ANYWHERE COUNTY COURT   Case No

Between   SARAH PIERCY   Plaintiff
and   THE LONDON BOROUGH OF WANDARK Defendant

AFFIDAVIT OF THE PLAINTIFF

I, SARAH PIERCY, of 94C Darkley Street, Wandark, London SE92, nurse, MAKE OATH and say as follows:

1 I am the plaintiff in this action and I make this affidavit in support of my application for a mandatory injunction to issue to the defendant authority to carry out repairs to my premises. Except where it otherwise appears, I make this affidavit from my own knowledge.

2 I have the sole tenancy of 94C Darkley Street, Wandark, London SE92 where I live with my son Russell whose date of birth is 10 July 1982. My landlord is Wandark London Borough Council and my tenancy commenced on 30 June 1988. I recall that I signed a tenancy agreement at the Housing Department in Honeypot Lane but I do not have a copy of the agreement and do not remember being given one. My current rent is £30 per week. My rent payments are up to date. There is now produced and shown to me marked 'SP1' a true copy of my rent card.

3 My accommodation is a self-contained flat on the top floor of a three-storey terraced property. It comprises two bedrooms, living-room, kitchen and bathroom and was newly converted when my tenancy commenced in June 1988. Prior to taking up this tenancy I had been living with my son in one room in a damp basement.

4 Although my son and I moved into our accommodation at the end of June, it soon became clear that the accommodation was cold and draughty because of ill-fitting windows. More importantly, however, I also realised that the roof was defective and was allowing rainwater to penetrate into the bedroom where my son slept. I had noticed a small damp patch on the ceiling when I had inspected the accommodation and had been told by the council officer (whose name I do not know) that it would dry out. When it had rained a few times, I realised the damp patch was growing.

5 I complained about the windows and the leaking roof on a number of occasions by telephoning and in person, usually to Mr David Walker, who is the estate manager responsible for my property. To begin with I was told that the builders who did the conversion had to be contacted.

6 The damp patch gradually grew, and after a year or so water began to

leak through the ceiling. I had to put buckets underneath the leaks, but gradually the leaking could not be contained in buckets and the water would spill on to the floor and furnishings. When it was raining or I knew it was likely to rain my son would share my bed with me. However, it was not possible to live like this all the time both because my sleep is disrupted when I share a bed with him and also because I need my privacy. I could not change the rooms round because my son's room is too small for my bedroom furniture. Neither my son nor I could sleep in the living-room as there is not sufficient space for a bed and I do not have a sofa.

7   I continued to make complaints to the neighbourhood office. In June 1992 I sought advice from the Wandark Housing Resources Centre because the ceiling in my son's bedroom was beginning to bulge and I was afraid that it might fall in. An adviser at the Centre wrote a letter to the defendant authority about the leaking roof and there is now produced and shown to me marked 'SP2' a true copy of that letter. After that, a surveyor, Mr John Castle, came to inspect my accommodation on 14 September 1992 and I showed him the ceiling in my son's bedroom. Mr Castle did not make any commitment to me about repairs but I saw him taking notes and he went out into the back garden and appeared to be looking at the roof. I was hopeful that after a professional person had seen the problem the roof would soon be mended.

8   However, no action was taken and my son and I continued to live in the way I have described, collecting water in buckets and sharing a bed when necessary. During the winter of 1992–3 I was so worried about the roof that Russell and I shared a bed most of the time, particularly when it had been snowing or raining.

9   As the weather got better, I decided it was safe to let Russell go back into his room. However, in the early hours of the morning of Tuesday 20 July 1993 there was a very heavy storm. I had not realised that it was likely to rain as it had been a beautiful clear evening. I awoke to hear a cry from Russell. I rushed into his bedroom and found that part of the ceiling had collapsed and water was pouring on to the floor and on to his bed. There were pieces of plaster all over the room, including at the end of Russell's bed, although he himself was not hurt. However, he was extremely frightened and shocked by the incident. I got very little sleep that night as I had to clear up the mess in Russell's room, and reassure him that he was safe.

10   At 9am on the morning of Tuesday 20 July I telephoned the neighbourhood office. I spoke to Mr David Walker who told me 'not to be hysterical' but assured me that someone would be round to mend the roof before 4pm. I took the day off work in order to ensure that the

builders would have access but no one came. By 3.30pm no one had arrived and I telephoned the environmental health service but was told that no one there could help me because I was a council tenant. At 4pm I telephoned the Wandark Housing Resources Centre who arranged an emergency appointment for me to see a local solicitor at 4.30pm.

11   When I saw the solicitor she made a telephone call to Mr David Walker, and also to Mr Lloyd-George, who I understand is a solicitor in the local authority's legal department. My solicitor told me that both officers had assured her that repairs would be carried out the following morning. She followed up these telephone calls by sending a letter to the legal department which, although typed and delivered on 20 July, would not have been received by an officer in the legal department until the office opened the following day. There is now produced and shown to me marked 'SP3' a true copy of that letter. I stayed at home all day on Wednesday 21 July but no one came to the house.

12   My solicitor arranged for a surveyor to inspect my premises. A Mr B Nidder came round to my house at 6pm on Wednesday 21 July and carried out a thorough inspection both internally and externally. He also took photographs. I respectfully refer the court to Mr Nidder's affidavit sworn on 22 July 1993 to which are exhibited his report and the photographs.

13   At present, my son and I are sleeping in one bed which we cannot do indefinitely. However, I am even more concerned about a hole in the ceiling of my son's bedroom through which I can see the sky. If it rains again before repairs are carried out, the room will be flooded and the rest of the ceiling will collapse.

14   In the circumstances, I ask this Honourable Court to grant a mandatory injunction ordering the Wandark London Borough Council to repair the roof to my premises so that water does not penetrate into the rear bedroom, to reinstate the ceiling and to redecorate the ceiling and walls.

SWORN this _____ day of _____ 1993
At

Before me
Solicitor/Commissioner for Oaths [signature]

Note

The notes to precedent 24 also apply here, except that the second paragraph should set out details of the tenancy including the commencement date; name of landlord; rent; and names of those who occupy the premises. A description of the premises should also be included in this paragraph, or in the following paragraph as in this example.

Exhibits must be attached to and identified by a certificate signed by the person before whom the affidavit is sworn.

29   *Draft order for interlocutory injunction*

IN THE ANYWHERE COUNTY COURT   Case No

Between   SARAH PIERCY   Plaintiff
and   THE LONDON BOROUGH OF WANDARK   Defendant

If you do not obey this order you will be guilty of contempt of court and you may be sent to prison

On the ____ of ____ 199– the court considered an application for an injunction.

The court ordered that the London Borough of Wandark shall within 28 days of service of this order carry out the following works of repair to premises known as 94C Darkley Street, Wandark, London SE92, namely:
a) replacement of all missing slates to the roof of the premises so as to prevent further water penetration; and
b) reinstatement of the ceiling to the rear bedroom in the premises;

It is further ordered that the costs of the plaintiff's application shall be reserved until trial of this action.

If you do not understand anything in this order you should go to a solicitor, legal advice centre or a Citizens Advice Bureau.

Note
The notes to precedent 25 also apply here.

Precedents for chapter 11: possession proceedings

30 *Notice of seeking possession*

NOTICE OF SEEKING POSSESSION

Housing Act 1985, section 83

This notice is the first step towards requiring you to give up possession of your dwelling. You should read it very carefully.

1 To Sarah Piercy

* *If you need advice about this notice, and what you should do about it, take it as quickly as possible to a Citizens Advice Bureau, a housing aid centre, or a law centre, or to a solicitor. You may be able to receive legal aid but this will depend on your personal circumstances.*

---

2 The London Borough of Wandark intends to apply to the court for an order requiring you to give up possession of:

94C Darkley Street, Wandark, London SE92

* *If you are a secure tenant under the Housing Act 1985, you can only be required to leave your dwelling if your landlord obtains an order for possession from the court. The order must be based on one of the grounds which are set out in the 1985 Act (see paragraphs 3 and 4 below).*
* *If you are willing to give up possession without a court order, you should notify the person who signed this notice as soon as possible and say when you would leave.*

---

3 Possession will be sought on Ground 1 of Schedule 2 to the Housing Act 1985, which reads:

'Rent lawfully due from the tenant has not been paid or an obligation of the tenancy has been broken or not performed.'

* *Whatever grounds for possession are set out in paragraph 3 of this notice, the court may allow any other grounds to be added at a later stage. If this is done, you will be told about it so you can argue at the hearing in court about the new ground, as well as the grounds set out in paragraph 3, if you want to.*

---

4   Particulars of each ground are as follows:–

You have rent arrears outstanding of £550.52 as at 22 November 1993.

* *Before the court will grant an order on any of the grounds 1 to 8 or 12 to 16, it must be satisfied that it is reasonable to require you to leave. This means that, if one of these grounds is set out in paragraph 3 of this notice, you will be able to argue at the hearing in court that it is not reasonable that you should have to leave, even if you accept that the ground applies.*

* *Before the court grants an order for possession on any of the grounds 9 to 16, it must be satisfied that there will be suitable alternative accommodation for you when you have to leave. This means that the court will have to decide that, in its opinion, there will be other accommodation which is reasonably suitable for the needs of you and your family, taking into particular account various factors such as the nearness of your place of work, and the sort of housing that other people with similar needs are offered. Your new home will have to be let to you on another secure tenancy or a private tenancy under the Rent Act of a kind that will have similar security.* **There is no requirement for suitable alternative accommodation where grounds 1 to 8 apply.**

* *If your landlord is not a local authority, and the local authority gives a certificate that it will provide you with suitable accommodation, the court has to accept the certificate.*

* *One of the requirements of ground 10A is that your landlord must have approval for the redevelopment scheme from the Secretary of State (or, in the case of a housing association landlord, the Housing Corporation). The landlord must have consulted all secure tenants affected by the proposed redevelopment scheme.*

---

5   The court proceedings will not be begun until after 9 January 1994

* *Court proceedings cannot be begun until after this date, which cannot be earlier than the date when your tenancy or licence could have been brought to an end. This means that if you have a weekly or fortnightly tenancy, there should be at least four weeks between the date this notice is given and the date in this paragraph.*

* *After this date, court proceedings may be begun at once or at any time during the following 12 months. Once the 12 months are up this notice will lapse and a new notice must be served before possession can be sought.*

[signature]

On behalf of: The London Borough of Wandark
Town Hall, Anyroad, Wandark, London SE92
Telephone number: 081-811 1138
Date: 22 November 1993

31   *Particulars of claim for possession and rent arrears*

IN THE ANYWHERE COUNTY COURT   Case No

Between   THE LONDON BOROUGH OF WANDARK   Plaintiffs
and   SARAH PIERCY   Defendant

PARTICULARS OF CLAIM

1   The defendant is the tenant of the dwellinghouse known as 94C
Darkley Street, Wandark, London SE92 which was let by the plaintiffs to
the defendant at the weekly rent of £20, since increased to £32. The said
tenancy is a secure tenancy as defined by section 85 of the Housing Act
1985.

2   The plaintiffs seek possession of the said premises on ground 1 of
Schedule 2 to the Housing Act 1985 on the grounds that rent lawfully due
from the defendant has not been paid.

3   The reasons for taking this action are that the defendant has failed to
pay her rent on the dates due despite numerous requests from the plaintiffs
and their authorised agents.

4   On 22 November 1993 the plaintiffs served a notice of seeking
possession of the said premises on the defendant which stated that court
proceedings would not be begun until after 9 January 1994.

5   The said rent is £806.52 in arrear.

6   The net anual value of the said premises for rating is £152.

And the plaintiffs claim:
a) Possession of the said dwellinghouse.
b) Arrears of rent of £806.52 as at 16 January 1994.
c) Further rent at £32 per week from 16 January 1994 until the date of
the hearing.
d) Costs.

Dated

Solicitors for the plaintiffs [signature]
Address for service

To the chief clerk and to the defendant

32   *Request for further and better particulars of claim*

IN THE ANYWHERE COUNTY COURT   Case No

Between   THE LONDON BOROUGH OF WANDARK   Plaintiffs
and   SARAH PIERCY   Defendant

REQUEST FOR FURTHER AND BETTER PARTICULARS OF THE PARTICULARS OF CLAIM

1   Of 'The defendant is the tenant of the dwellinghouse known as 94C Darkley Street, Wandark, London SE92, which was let by the plaintiffs to the defendant at the weekly rent of £20, since increased to £32'.

REQUEST

1) Specify the date the tenancy commenced and whether the tenancy was oral or in writing. If in writing, provide a copy of the tenancy agreement.
2) Specify:
   a) the rent and rates at the commencement of the tenancy;
   b) the dates on which it is alleged that increases of rent and/or rates took effect and the amount of rent and rates following such increases;
3) Provide copies of any alleged notices of increase of rent served on the defendant and specify the date upon which they are alleged to have been served and in what manner they were allegedly served.

2   Of 'The reasons for taking this action are that the defendant has failed to pay her rent on the dates due, despite numerous requests from the plaintiffs and their authorised agents'.

REQUEST

1) Specify the allegedly numerous requests from the plaintiffs and their authorised agents, in each case stating whether the request was oral or in writing and the identity of the agent by whom the alleged request was made.

3   Of 'On 22 November 1993 the plaintiffs served a notice of seeking possession of the said premises on the defendant'.

REQUEST

1) Specify the manner of alleged service of the alleged notice of seeking possession and, if served personally, by whom it was served.
2) Provide a copy of the Notice of Seeking Possession allegedly served on the defendant.

4   Of 'The said rent is £806.52 in arrear'.

REQUEST

1) For each week from when the alleged arrears first arose to date, provide a breakdown of the weekly rent, water rates and heating charges due, each payment received from the Defendant or on the Defendant's behalf and each credit made to the rent account in respect of housing benefit showing the dates when such rent, water rates and heating charges were due and such payments and/or credits were made.

Dated

Solicitors for the defendant [signature]
Address for service

To the chief clerk and to the plaintiffs

33 Notice of application for further and better particulars of claim and discovery

IN THE ANYWHERE COUNTY COURT   Case No

Between   THE LONDON BOROUGH OF WANDARK   Plaintiffs
and   SARAH PIERCY   Defendant

NOTICE OF APPLICATION

TAKE NOTICE that the defendant intends to apply to the district judge of this court at the Court House, Anyroad, Wandark, London SE92, on _____ the _____ day of _____ 199– at _____ o'clock for an order:

1   That the plaintiffs do within 14 days file and serve the further and better particulars of the particulars of claim contained in the request for further and better particulars filed on behalf of the defendant dated 10 February 1989 and that in default thereof the particulars of claim be struck out and the plaintiffs' claim be dismissed.

2   That the plaintiffs provide a list of documents to the defendant within 14 days listing the documents in their possession, custody or control relating to the matters in question in this action including:

a) copies of all notices of increase in rent and notices of seeking possession alleged to have been served on the defendant;
b) copies of all applications for housing benefit made by the defendant, calculations of housing benefit entitlement and notices of entitlement issued to the defendant and by the Treasurer's Department to the Housing Department;
c) copies of all rent records;

d) copies of certificates received from the Department of Social Security relating to housing benefit;

e) copies of all correspondence with the defendant regarding the alleged arrears of rent;

f) copies of all other documentation in the possession, custody or power of the plaintiffs relating to rent and housing benefit,

and that in default thereof the particulars of claim be struck out and the plaintiffs' claim dismissed.

3 That the plaintiffs allow the defendant to inspect the documents referred to in clause 2 above within 21 days.

4 That the costs of this application be paid by the defendant in any event.

Dated

Solicitors for the defendant [signature]
Address for service

To the chief clerk and to the plaintiffs

34 Defence to particulars of claim for possession

IN THE ANYWHERE COUNTY COURT   Case No

Between   THE LONDON BOROUGH OF WANDARK   Plaintiffs
and   SARAH PIERCY   Defendant

DEFENCE

1 Paragraph 1 of the particulars of claim is admitted save that it is not admitted that the current rent has been validly increased to £32 per week.

2 Paragraph 3 of the particulars of claim is denied.

3 No admission is made as to the service or validity of any alleged notice of seeking possession as alleged in paragraph 4.

4 Paragraph 5 of the particulars of claim is denied.

5 Paragraph 6 of the particulars of claim is admitted.

6 It is denied that the plaintiffs are entitled to possession under ground 1 of Schedule 2 to the Housing Act 1985 or at all.

7 Further, or in the alternative, the defendant claims the protection of the Housing Act 1985 and denies that it is reasonable for an order for possession to be made.

Dated

Solicitors for the defendant [signature]
Address for service

To the chief clerk and to the plaintiffs

35 Notice of application to suspend warrant of possession
[*Note 1*]

IN THE ANYWHERE COUNTY COURT   Case No

Between   **JAMES BROWN**   Plaintiff
and   **SARAH PIERCY**   Defendant

NOTICE OF APPLICATION
TO SUSPEND WARRANT OF POSSESSION

The defendant wishes to apply for an order in the following terms:

1) That the warrant for possession number 000000 issued within these proceedings on 17 August 1993 be suspended.

2) That there be no order for costs save for legal aid taxation of the defendant's costs. [Note 2]

The grounds of this application are that the defendant has been unable to comply with the terms of the order dated 26 February 1993 because she was made redundant in May 1993.

Dated

Solicitors for the defendant [signature]
Address for service

This section to be completed by the court

To the plaintiff
TAKE NOTICE that this application will be heard by the judge at ____ on ____ at ____ o'clock.

IF YOU DO NOT ATTEND THE COURT WILL MAKE SUCH ORDER AS IT THINKS FIT

Notes

1   The notes to precedent 23 apply equally here, except in relation to costs (see note 2 below).

2   In this instance it would not be appropriate to apply for costs against the plaintiff. However, if there had been no breach, or if the plaintiff had

ignored letters from the defendant or his or her advisers it might be appropriate to make a claim for costs.

36   Affidavit in support of application to suspend warrant of possession [Note 1]

IN THE ANYWHERE COUNTY COURT   Case No [Note 2]

Between	JAMES BROWN	Plaintiff
and	SARAH PIERCY	Defendant

AFFIDAVIT OF SARAH PIERCY [Note 3]

I, SARAH PIERCY of Flat D, 2 Tufnell Street, London NW45, cook, MAKE OATH and say as follows: [Note 4]

1   I am the defendant in this case and I make this affidavit in support of my application for the warrant of possession issued on 17 August 1993 to be suspended. Except where it otherwise appears, I make this affidavit from my own knowledge. [Note 5]

2   I have a statutory tenancy of premises known as Flat D, 2 Tufnell Street, London NW45. The plaintiff is the landlord of the premises. I am the sole tenant of the premises and I live there with my two children Paul and Carol Piercy aged 10 and 6 respectively. The tenancy commenced in April 1985. The present rent is £20 per week. [Note 6]

3   Although the tenancy is in my sole name, until 1990 I occupied the premises with George Piercy who is the father of my two children. We are not and never have been married although I took Mr Piercy's name. In 1990 the relationship broke down and on 24 December 1990 Mr Piercy left the flat and I have not seen him since that time. [Note 7]

4   At the time Mr Piercy left I was employed by the Tufnell Education Authority as a cleaner at St Mary's School, May Town Avenue, London NW45. Until that time, I had never been in arrears with rent. However, although I was working, I found it very difficult to pay all the outgoings on the flat as well as feeding and clothing myself and the children, and unfortunately I fell into arrears with my rent payments.

5   In January 1993 the plaintiff issued a summons for possession against me on the ground that I had not paid rent lawfully due to him. The case was heard on 26 February 1993 and at that time the arrears of rent were £600. An order for possession was made against me but it was suspended on the condition that I pay the full current rent each week and in addition I was ordered to pay another £5 per week in satisfaction of the arrears of

rent. I was not represented in court on that day as I thought I would have to pay to see a solicitor which I could not afford. I was worried about paying £5 per week extra but I thought that if I did not agree I would be evicted.

6   I did manage, with some difficulty, to keep up the payments for the first four weeks but at the end of March I was told that I would be made redundant from my job at the end of May. I was not entitled to any redundancy pay because I had not been in the job long enough. There is now produced and shown to me marked 'SP1' a true copy of the letter from the Tufnell Education Authority confirming these matters. [Note 8]

7   I was unable to find other employment straight away and from 1 June 1993 to 30 July 1993 I was in receipt of income support for myself and two children. I once again found myself in severe financial difficulties and unable to pay the whole of the extra payment for arrears of rent, although I did pay my current rent each week. I have been advised that I should have applied to the court to have the order of 26 February 1993 varied when I became unemployed but I did not know this.

8   I have now found a new job and I am employed as cook by John Jones and Co at their headquarters in Oxford Road, London SE6. I am paid £120 per week gross and I receive £76 per week net. There is now produced and shown to me marked 'SP2' a true copy of my payslip for the week ending 14 August 1993.

9   I apologise to the court for the fact that I did not comply with the terms of the order made on 26 February 1993 but I found it impossible because of my change in circumstances. I feel that I am now able to pay the current rent of £20 and £5 per week towards the arrears and in the premises I ask the court to suspend the warrant for possession which was issued on 17 August 1993 within these proceedings. [Note 9]

SWORN this ____ day of ____ 1993
At ____

Before me ____
Solicitor/Commissioner for Oaths [signature] [Note 10]

Notes

1   A well-drafted affidavit is crucial in an application to suspend the warrant for possession. If the application fails, the tenant will be evicted. The suspension of the warrant is a discretionary remedy, and the affidavit should be persuasive although not exaggerated. The tenant should be reminded that s/he may be cross-examined on the contents of the affidavit.

2 The case number will be that already shown on the previous pleadings in the case. It must be quoted and if it is not the court may refuse to allow the affidavit to be filed.

3-5 See notes 2-4 to precedent 24.

6 The address of the premises, the status of the deponent and the current rent should be included.

7 The body of the affidavit should set out, in a sequence of logical statements in numbered paragraphs, the facts relied on in support of the application. The affidavit should be clear and unrepetitive and should make clear the reasons why there has been a breach of the terms attached to the suspended order. Remember that the judge hearing the application may well have imposed the terms, and the reasons for non-compliance should be as convincing as possible. The affidavit should state which of the facts are within the deponent's knowledge and which are based on information or belief. The sources and grounds of the information or belief should be stated.[8]

8 The copy of any correspondence or other documentation substantiating claims made by the defendant should be exhibited to the affidavit. The number of an exhibit includes the initials of the person making the affidavit and its number. There is a new number in sequence for each exhibit and this sequence should be followed where more than one affidavit is filed. The originals of the exhibits should be available at court when the application is heard. Exhibits should be attached to, and identified by, a certificate signed by the person before whom the affidavit is sworn.

9-10 See notes to precedent 24.

Precedents for chapter 13: homelessness

37 Notice of application for leave to apply for judicial review [Note 1]

IN THE HIGH COURT OF JUSTICE

Applicant Ref. No. JD/10267/Piercy [Note 2]	Notice of APPLICATION for leave to apply for judicial review (Ord 53 r3)	Crown Office Ref. No. [Note 3]

---

8 CCR Ord 20 r10(5).

This form must be read together with notes for guidance obtainable from the Crown Office. [Note 4]

To the Master of the Crown Office, Royal Courts of Justice, Strand, London WC2A 2LL

Name, address and description of applicant [Note 5]	Sarah Piercy 18 Essex Walk Wandark London SE92

Judgment, order, decision or other proceeding in respect of which relief is sought [Note 6]	Decision of Wandark Borough Council Dated 15 July 1992 that the applicant is homeless intentionally within the meaning of the Housing Act 1985

RELIEF SOUGHT [Note 7]

1   An order of certiorari to quash the decision of the Wandark Borough Council, dated 15 July 1992, that the applicant has become homeless intentionally within the meaning of the Housing Act 1985.

2   An order of mandamus requiring the Wandark Borough Council to determine according to law the applicant's application for accommodation or for assistance in securing accommodation within the Housing Act 1985.

3   A mandatory injunction requiring the Wandark Borough Council to provide the applicant with temporary accommodation pending the full hearing of this application.

Name and address of applicant's solicitors or, if no solicitors acting, the address for service of the applicant. [Note 8]

[Name, address and telephone number of solicitor]

GROUNDS ON WHICH RELIEF IS SOUGHT [Note 9]

1   The applicant is a single parent with two children aged 10 and 11 who live with her by reason whereof she is in priority need of accommodation within the meaning of the Housing Act 1985. The applicant's marriage was dissolved on 19 February 1992.

2   The applicant is a homeless person within the meaning of the said Act by reason of the matters set out below.

3   Until 1989, the applicant and her children lived with the applicant's then husband at 20 Essex Walk, Wandark, which was accommodation let to the applicant and her ex-husband by the respondent authority.

4   In 1989, the applicant's ex-husband decided that the family should go to live in Australia. The applicant was told by her ex-husband that the family could stay with his aunt in Sydney and that he would be able to find permanent employment so that the family would be able to apply to stay permanently.

5   In October 1989, the applicant and her ex-husband and children flew to Australia. They surrendered their council tenancy in the belief that they would be able to remain in Australia on a permanent basis. In the event they were not permitted to remain in Australia and after nine months, ie, in July 1990 they were deported back to England.

6   On their return to England, the applicant, her ex-husband and the children went to stay with the applicant's sister-in-law at 47 The Ridings, Chichester. Unfortunately, the marriage, which had been in difficulties prior to going to Australia, deteriorated, and in September 1990 the applicant left her ex-husband and went with the children to stay with friends, Mr and Ms T Smith at 18 Essex Walk, Wandark.

7   At the beginning of October 1990 the applicant issued a petition for divorce and on 2 January 1991 she was granted a decree nisi, together with custody, care and control of the two children.

8   In December 1990 the applicant applied to the respondent authority for housing under the Housing Act 1985 but the application was rejected on the ground that she had become homeless intentionally by surrendering her tenancy at 20 Essex Walk, in October 1989, in order to go to Australia.

9   On 19 February 1991, the applicant's marriage was dissolved.

10   In early June 1991, the friends with whom the applicant was staying decided to quit their accommodation and on 7 June 1991 they notified the local authority accordingly. On the same day they gave notice to the applicant to leave her accommodation within 14 days.

11   On 8 June 1991, the applicant again applied to the respondent authority for housing under the Housing Act 1985.

12   By a letter dated 15 July 1991, the respondent authority informed the applicant that she was homeless intentionally within the meaning of section 17 of the Housing Act 1985 because 'you voluntarily vacated secure accommodation at 20 Essex Walk, Wandark, on 24 October 1989'.

13   The said decision is wrong in law for the following reasons:

a) The cause of homelessness was the departure from the applicant's sister-in-law's house at 47 The Ridings, Chichester.

b) The reason for the said departure was the breakdown of the marriage and, accordingly, there was no continuous chain of unbroken causation between the departure for Australia and the application to the respondent authority.

14   The respondent authority has failed to have regard, or proper regard, to the accommodation at 47 The Ridings and has consequently failed to consider whether it was reasonable for the applicant to remain in occupation of it.

Dated

Solicitors for the applicant [signature]

Notes

1   The notice of application must be made in the prescribed form 86A.[9]

2   Enter the solicitors' own reference here.

3   Leave blank – the Crown Office will enter the court reference number, which must be quoted at all times.

4   The notes for guidance are extremely helpful for the inexperienced adviser. They will be sent if requested by a telephone call to the Crown Office (071-405 7641).

5   A description is not necessary as any applicant will be an individual. Make sure the full name and address are entered.

6   Make sure the date of the decision is included and the name of the housing authority which made it.

7   If more than one form of relief is sought, each form must be claimed here. It must be made clear whether the second form of relief is alternative to or additional to any other form of relief claimed. If damages are sought they should be claimed here.

9   *Supreme Court Practice 1993* appendix A vol 2 Pt 2 para 84.

8   Make sure the correct address is entered. It is advisable to include a reference and telephone number so that court officials have this information immediately available.

9   If there has been any delay in seeking relief, the reason should be included in the grounds. The grounds should set out in logical order the basis of the application. Extreme care should be taken not to include irrelevant details but it should be remembered that these grounds will be relied on in the substantive application. The grounds should be detailed enough to enable the judge to grant leave without a hearing.

38   *Affidavit in support of application for judicial review*

App: S Piercy 1st: 22.3.93 [Note 1]

IN THE HIGH COURT OF JUSTICE   No of matter [Note 3]
QUEEN'S BENCH DIVISION [Note 2]

R
v.
WANDARK BOROUGH COUNCIL
EX PARTE PIERCY

AFFIDAVIT OF SARAH PIERCY [Note 4]

I, SARAH PIERCY, of 18 Essex Walk, Wandark, London SE92, unemployed, [Note 5] MAKE OATH and say as follows: [Note 6]

1   I am the applicant in this matter and I make this affidavit in support of my application for judicial review of the decision of Wandark Council dated 15 July 1992 that I am homeless intentionally within the meaning of the Housing Act 1985. [Note 7] Save where it otherwise appears, I make this affidavit from my own knowledge. [Note 8]

2   The factual background to the homelessness of myself and my two children is set out in the notice of application. Until October 1989, my then husband and I had a joint tenancy of accommodation at 20 Essex Walk, Wandark, which was let to us by Wandark Borough Council. [Note 9]

3   I married my ex-husband in 1979. He drank heavily throughout the marriage and we separated for six weeks in 1987 because I could no longer tolerate his behaviour. There was subsequently a reconciliation because we were both concerned about the effect a divorce would have on the children. My ex-husband promised that he would change and give up his drinking and, indeed, he kept to this promise for some time.

4   My ex-husband was an electrician and he had been dissatisfied with his employment for several years. In 1989, he decided that we should all go to live in Australia where he felt he would find a better job and we would be able to make a new start. I was worried about the move, and in particular about leaving my friends and family. At one time, it was suggested that my ex-husband should go ahead alone but I was anxious that if he did so, this might precipitate the breakdown of our marriage.

5   My ex-husband told me that he had contacted the Australian high commission and had been told that we would be permitted to stay with his aunt and that if he found a job we could apply to stay on a permanent basis. He led me to believe that he would have no difficulty in finding employment.

6   In October 1989 the family flew to Australia. We gave up our council tenancy although our permission to remain in Australia was limited to six months. We did this because we believed that it was a permanent move, and in any event we thought it wrong to keep a home in this country when it was our plain intention to settle in Australia. When we were in Australia, our marriage improved and it appeared that we had indeed overcome our difficulties and that there was a stable future ahead of us. Unfortunately, the employment situation was unpredictable and although my ex-husband found a job initially, it was only on a temporary basis and he was unable to find secure employment. Because of this, we were not, in the event, permitted to remain in Australia on a permanent basis and in July 1990 we had to return to this country.

7   When we came back, we had nowhere to live because we had given up our tenancy. We did not apply to the council for housing at this stage because we felt we ought to try to find somewhere ourselves. However, we found it impossible with children to find private rented accommodation and we went to stay with my sister-in-law at 47 The Ridings, Chichester. My sister-in-law lived with her husband and two children and had a three-bedroomed house. This meant that my ex-husband and I and the children all had to share one bedroom. The situation rapidly became intolerable. My ex-husband was very depressed on his return and started to drink heavily and was violent towards me which was a familiar pattern of behaviour. I was too frightened to remain living with him and it rapidly became apparent to me that the marriage had irretrievably broken down.

8   I moved out with the two children in September 1990 and went to stay with friends, Mr and Ms T Smith at 18 Essex Walk, Wandark. Despite one or two meetings with my ex-husband, there was no doubt that the marriage was finished and at the beginning of October 1990 I filed a petition for divorce on the ground of my husband's unreasonable behaviour.

9   My ex-husband did not defend the proceedings and on 2 January 1991 I was granted a decree nisi and custody, care and control of the two children.

10   Although I was made very welcome by Mr and Ms Smith, it was understood right from the beginning that the accommodation they had offered me was only of a temporary nature and that I must find myself somewhere to live. In December 1990 I applied to the Housing Department for help but I was told that I had given up my tenancy at 20 Essex Walk voluntarily and that by doing this I had made myself homeless and that Wandark Council therefore had no obligation to assist me in any way. I have since been advised and verily believe that on the face of it the decision of the council was wrong in law but I did not know at the time that I could challenge the decision.

11   On 19 February 1991 my marriage was dissolved by decree absolute.

12   By this time, Mr and Ms Smith had told me that they intended to quit their accommodation because Ms Smith, who was a civil servant, had been transferred to another part of the country and the whole family intended to move. On 7 June 1991, they notified Wandark Council of their intention to quit within 28 days, and on the same day they gave me notice to leave their accommodation within 14 days. They wished me to leave in order that they might have some time in which to pack up and make arrangements to move.

13   When I received the notice, I was extremely upset as I had nowhere to live with the children. I went to see a solicitor who advised me that I did have a right to housing under the Housing Act and that I should once again apply to the council. I did this and my application was once again refused. There is now produced and shown to me marked 'SP1' a letter dated 15 July 1991 from Wandark Council in which it states that I am not eligible for permanent rehousing because I 'voluntarily vacated secure accommodation at 20 Essex Way, Wandark on 24 October 1989'. [Note 10]

14   It is my respectful submission that it is not open to the council to find that I became homeless intentionally when I left 20 Essex Walk because that is not the cause of my homelessness. The reason that I am now homeless is because of the breakdown of my marriage and accordingly there is no continuous chain of unbroken causation between my departure for Australia and my application to the local authority. I respectfully submit that the respondent authority has failed to consider the true reason for my homelessness, ie, the breakdown of my marriage, and that accordingly it has improperly determined my application.

15   My present position is that I have nowhere to stay after tomorrow when I must leave my present temporary accommodation. I therefore seek the leave of this honourable court to proceed with this application for judicial review of the respondent authority's decision, in order that the said decision may be quashed and the respondent authority ordered properly to determine my application under the Housing Act 1985 and further I ask that pending the hearing of my application, the respondent authority be ordered to secure accommodation for myself and my two children.

SWORN by the above-named SARAH PIERCY

At ____
This ____ day of ____ 1993
Before me ____
Solicitor/Commissioner for oaths [signature] [Note 11]

IN THE HIGH COURT OF JUSTICE
QUEEN'S BENCH DIVISION

R

v

WANDARK BOROUGH COUNCIL

EX PARTE PIERCY

This is the exhibit marked 'SP1' referred to in the affidavit of SARAH PIERCY sworn this ____ day of ____ 1993
Before me ____
Solicitor/Commissioner for oaths [signature]

Notes

1   The affidavit must be endorsed with a note showing on whose behalf it is filed, initials and surname of deponent, number of affidavit in relation to deponent, and date when sworn. An affidavit which is not so endorsed may not be filed or used without leave of the Court.[10]

2   The name of the court and the title of the case must be included in the affidavit.[11]

3   The court reference number will be entered by the Crown Office.

4   There is no correct formal title. The title shown here is the simplest but it may be expanded as appropriate, eg, 'Affidavit of Sarah Piercy in support of her application for judicial review'.

10   RSC Ord 41 r9(5); *Practice Direction (Evidence: Documents)* [1983] 1 WLR 992.
11   RSC Ord 41 r1(1).

5   The affidavit must be expressed in the first person and must state the place of residence of the deponent and his/her occupation or, if s/he has none, his/her description.[12]

6   If the deponent does not wish to take an oath, eg, because s/he has no religion or his or her religion prohibits oath taking, then s/he may affirm. The words following the address should be 'do solemnly and sincerely and truly declare and affirm as follows'. The document should be referred to as an affirmation (and not affidavit) throughout.

7   The opening paragraph should explain the nature of the affidavit.

8   An affidavit may contain only such facts as the deponent is able of his or her own knowledge to prove.[13] However, an affidavit sworn for the purpose of being used in interlocutory proceedings may contain statements of information or belief with the sources and grounds thereof.[14] The affidavit must set out and verify all facts relied on. In particular all the grounds set out in a statement must be included and verified in the affidavit. All material facts, including those which are to the detriment of the applicant, must be included in the affidavit. If leave is obtained on false statements or a suppression of material facts in the affidavit, the court may refuse an order on this ground alone.[15]

9   Dates and numbers must be expressed in figures not words.[16]

10   Exhibits: any document to be used in conjunction with an affidavit must be exhibited, and not annexed to the affidavit.[17] An exhibit must be identified by a certificate of the person before whom the affidavit is sworn.[18] Copies of letters should be exhibited in bundles rather than individually and they should be arranged in sequence with the earliest at the top. Any exhibit containing a number of pages must be numbered consecutively at the centre bottom of each page.[19]

11   The affidavit must be signed by the deponent and the jurat must be completed and signed by the person before whom it is sworn.[20] The full address of the place where the affidavit was sworn must be included. An affidavit must never end on one page with the jurat following overleaf.

---

12   RSC Ord 53 r1(4).
13   RSC Ord 41 r5(1).
14   RSC Ord 41 r5(2).
15   *R v Kensington Income Tax Commissioners ex parte Polignac* [1917] 1 KB 509.
16   RSC Ord 41 r1(7).
17   RSC Ord 41 r11(1).
18   RSC Ord 41 r11(2).
19   *Practice Direction (Evidence: Documents)* [1983] 1 WLR 992.
20   RSC Ord 41 r1(8).

39   Letter before action to stop distress for rent

Rent Recovery Officer
Wandark Borough Council   25 November 1988

Dear Madam/Sir,

Sarah Piercy: 94C Darkley Street, Wandark, London SE92

I have been consulted by Sarah Piercy who is your tenant at the above address.

She has shown me your letter to her which she received three days ago and her rent book. In your letter you demanded payment of £550.52 and stated that if this sum were not paid in full within 14 days you would instruct the Council's bailiff to levy distress against her goods.

My client contacted you to try to make arrangements to repay by instalments but was informed that at least £300 must be paid within the 14-day period to avoid distress by the bailiff.

My client's rent book shows a debit adjustment on the 1st November 1988 of £385. When she enquired about this she was informed that this was an adjustment for overpaid housing benefit. I also understand that at the beginning of her existing tenancy you made a direct debit entry for £145, being alleged arrears from her previous tenancy.

I would inform you that you are not entitled to recover allegedly overpaid housing benefit in your capacity as landlord. The Housing Benefit (General) Regulations 1987 lay down the procedure for recovery, which has not been followed. Furthermore, you are not entitled to recover arrears from a previous tenancy as rent under this tenancy.

After deduction from the alleged arrears of £385 which you are not entitled to demand as overpaid housing benefit and £145 as alleged arrears from her previous tenancy, my client is, in fact, in credit with her rent. It follows that you are not entitled to instruct the bailiff to levy distress.

I would therefore advise you that unless I receive written confirmation from you that you will not instruct the bailiff to distrain by 12 noon tomorrow, or a fax or telephone undertaking from a solicitor to the Council to that effect I am instructed to apply to the Court for an injunction restraining you from levying distress.

Yours faithfully,

V Careful

cc Solicitor to the Council

40 *Particulars of claim for injunction to prevent distress*

IN THE ANYWHERE COUNTY COURT   Case No

Between   SARAH PIERCY   Plaintiff
and   THE LONDON BOROUGH OF WANDARK   Defendants

PARTICULARS OF CLAIM

1 The Plaintiff is the tenant and the Defendants are landlords of a dwellinghouse known as 94C Darkley Street, Wandark, London SE92, which is let to the Plaintiff under a weekly tenancy, which is a secure tenancy within the meaning of section 185 of the Housing Act 1985.

2 The net annual value for rating purposes of the said dwellinghouse is £152.

3 By letter of the 18th November 1988, the Defendants demanded the sum of £550.52 for arrears of rent under the said tenancy from the Plaintiff and informed the Plaintiff that they intended to instruct a bailiff to levy distress for the said sum unless it was paid within 14 days.

4 The Plaintiff is not in arrears of rent in the sum of £550.52 or at all.

5 By letter of the 25th November 1988 the solicitor for the Plaintiff invited the Defendants to confirm that they would not instruct a bailiff to distrain for alleged rent arrears.

6 The Defendants have refused to confirm that they do not intend to instruct a bailiff to recover the said sum of £550.52 and have stated that they intend to proceed to instruct the bailiff to recover that sum.

7 By reason of paragraph 4 above, the Defendants have no lawful authority to instruct a bailiff to recover any sums from the Plaintiff by distress or any other means.

AND THE PLAINTIFF CLAIMS:-

(i) An injunction restraining the Defendants by their bailiffs from levying distress against the goods of the Plaintiff;
(ii) A declaration that no rent is owed by the Plaintiff to the Defendant under the said tenancy;
(iii) Costs.

Dated this   day of   1989

Solicitors for the Plaintiff
[*signature*]

Address for Service

To the Registrar and to the Defendants

41   Affidavit in support of application for injunction to prevent distress

1 Plaintiff
2 S Piercy
3 1st
4 26th November 1988

IN THE ANYWHERE COUNTY COURT   Case No

Between   SARAH PIERCY   Plaintiff
and   THE LONDON BOROUGH OF WANDARK   Defendants

AFFIDAVIT

I, SARAH PIERCY of 94C Darkley Street, Wandark, London SE92, Assistant Cook, MAKE OATH and say as follows:-

1   I am the weekly tenant of 94C Darkley Street, Wandark, London SE92. The Defendants are my landlords and are a local authority. By virtue of section 14 of the Rent Act 1977 my tenancy is not a protected tenancy.

2   I now have produced to me and marked "SP1", a letter sent to me by the Defendants dated the 18th November 1988, which I recieved a day or two later. In it they demand payment of £550.52 and warn that if this sum is not paid within 14 days they will instruct a bailiff to levy distress against my goods.

3   I contacted the Defendants as soon as I got the letter. I offered to pay the sums claimed by instalments of £5 per week, although I did not know how the figures were calculated. I assumed the Defendants must be right. I spoke to a Mr Williams in the rent recovery section. He said I must pay £300 immediately or they would proceed with the distress and I could pay the balance at £5 per week.

4   I could not possibly raise £300 so I sought advice.

5   I now have produced to me and marked "SP2" a copy of my Rent

Book for 1988/89. This shows a debit adjustment of £385 on the 1st November 1988. When this entry was made I asked the cashier what it was for and was informed that I had been overpaid housing benefit and this was the amount overpaid which the Defendants had to recover.

6   When my tenancy started in January 1988, the Defendants put a debit entry of £145 on my first rent book and my rent account which was arrears they say I owed on my previous property at 24 Windmill Street, Wandark. This sum has been included in my rent arrears ever since and I believe it to be still included in the figure of £550.52 given by the Defenants in their letter.

7   I am advised that overpaid housing benefit is not recoverable as rent but only under the Housing Benefit (General) Regulations 1987. No written notification of a determination that housing benefit has been overpaid as required under those regulations has ever been provided to me.

8   I am advised that arrears of rent from a previous tenancy do not constitute rent for the existing tenancy and cannot be recovered by distress.

9   After deduction of the £385 that the Council has wrongly treated as recoverable rent because of housing benefit it says I have been overpaid, and a further £145 which it has wrongly treated as recoverable rent, which is money due under a previous tenancy from the alleged arrears figure of £550.52, this leaves me with a rent credit of £29.70 rather than with rent arrears.

10   In the circumstances I would submit that the Defendants have no right to levy distress for rent against me.

11   I now have produced to me and marked "SP3" a copy of a letter written by my Solicitor to the Defendants on the 25th November 1988 advising them to withdraw their threat to use distraint against me.

12   I am informed by my solicitor, Mr V Careful, and I believe that he spoke to a solicitor in the Council's Legal Department on the afternoon of the 26th November. Mr Careful informs me and I believe that the solicitor concerned, Ms K Jones, said that the Council had never had any problems recovering overpaid housing benefit and former tenants' arrears in this way before and saw no need to change its practice now. She said the Council would oppose any application for an injunction which she saw as groundless.

13   I am a single parent with three children aged 11, 8 and 1 year. I am advised that the bailiff could remove my gas cooker, fridge, television,

radio, clock, baby's buggy, table, chairs, settee, carpets and many other items the family are using all the time, which are essential to our well-being, as well as the only valuable item I have, which is a vase which was left to me when my mother died and which is very important to me as the only memento I have of my mother.

14   In the circumstances I would ask the court to grant me an injunction restraining the Defendants from levying execution against my goods and a declaration that I owe them no rent.

SWORN this   day of   1989
At

Before me [*signature*]
Solicitor

APPENDIX 1

Useful addresses

Director General of Electricity Supply, Office of Electricity Regulation, Hagley House, Hagley Road, Birmingham B16 8QG.

Director General of Gas Supply, Office of Gas Supply, Second Floor, South Side, 105 Victoria Street, London SW1 6QT. Telephone 071–828 0898.

Office of Water Services, Centre City Tower, 7 Hill Street, Birmingham B5 4UA. Telephone 021–625 1300.

APPENDIX 2

Checklist of factors which the court will probably take into account in deciding the issue of joint liability for community charge

Relevant factors to be taken into account when deciding whether there are one or two households where the parties are married and living in the same house seem likely to include:

- whether they eat separately or together;
- whether they store and cook food separately or together;
- the arrangements for payment of housing costs;
- the sleeping arrangements;
- the other living arrangements, eg, use of sitting-room; whether they claim benefit jointly or separately (the rules concerning eligibility for income support are worded similarly but not identically to those for joint liability for the community charge).[1]

Relevant factors to be taken into account in deciding whether a party who is temporarily absent may still be considered part of the household seem likely to include:

- the parties' intentions regarding the future, ie, whether separation is intended to be permanent;
- the length of absence;
- the permanence of alternative living arrangements;
- the existence of judicial separation or divorce proceedings.

Relevant facts to be taken into account in deciding whether parties are living together as husband and wife seem likely to include:

- the proportion of time they spend living in the same home;
- whether one party has another home;
- the length of the relationship and its stability;
- the financial arrangements between the parties;
- the existence of any sexual relationship;
- the existence of any children of the relationship;
- whether the woman has adopted the man's name;
- the extent to which the parties present themselves as a couple.

1   Social Security Act 1986 s20(11).

Index

Injunction *cont*
  distress for rent, tactics for avoidance
    of, 250–251
  electricity supply, preventing
    disconnection of, 88, 93
  gas supply, preventing disconnection
    of, 88, 93
  harassment and unlawful eviction. *See*
    Harassment and unlawful eviction
  magistrates' court order, arrears under,
    156
  water supply,
    action to prevent disconnection,
      111, 112
    entitlement to disconnect, removal
      of, 112
Interpleader proceedings
  court bailiff having levied execution,
    61

Judgment
  civil court, creditors seeking to
    enforce, 19–20
  water charges, relating to,
    application to court to suspend
      terms of, 107–108
    application to set aside, 111
Judicial review
  homelessness, application relating to,
    282–284
Jurisdiction
  administration order, relating to,
    18–19

Land
  trespass to, 179–180
Landlord
  distress for rent, use of, 248–249
Legal aid
  mortgage arrears, procedures relating
    to, 253
  possession proceedings, 237, 239
Legal charge
  exempt agreement secured by, 37
Legal remedies
  administration order. *See*
    Administration order
  availability of, 14
  bankruptcy. *See* Bankruptcy
  disrepair, relating to. *See* Disrepair

Legal remedies *cont*
  harassment and unlawful eviction. *See*
    Harassment and unlawful eviction
  single debt emergency, 6–7
  usefulness of, 30–34
  voluntary arrangement. *See* Voluntary
    arrangement
Liability order
  council tax and community charge
    arrears. *See* Council tax and
    community charge arrears
Local authority
  disrepair,
    emergency procedures, 194–196
    role relating to, 194
  harassment and unlawful eviction,
    powers relating to, 172–176
  homelessness, duties relating to. *See*
    Homelessness

Magistrates' court
  administration order, application for,
    bailiff due to levy distress, 154
    distress levied but goods not yet
      removed, 156
    goods removed but not yet sold,
      157
  arrears under orders of, precedents,
    306–311
  bailiff,
    collection of arrears by,
      civil proceedings, 146
      criminal proceedings, 145–146
      generally, 145
      matrimonial proceedings, 146
    due to levy distress,
      administration order, application
        for, 154
      applying for time to pay,
        152–154
      bankruptcy order, application for,
        154
      generally, 152
      interim order pending voluntary
        arrangement, 154
      warrant of distress, making
        representations against issue of,
        154
    refusing entry to, 155